Complicated Grief

How can complicated grief be defined? How does it differ from normal patterns of grief and grieving? Who among the bereaved is particularly at risk? Can clinical intervention reduce complications?

Complicated Grief provides a balanced, up-to-date, state-of-the-art account of the scientific foundations surrounding the topic of complicated grief. In this book, Margaret Stroebe, Henk Schut, and Jan van den Bout address the basic questions about the concept, manifestations, and phenomena associated with complicated grief. They bring together researchers from different disciplines, providing a broad range of cultural and societal perspectives, to enable the reader to access the scientific knowledge base regarding complicated grief, on both theoretical and empirical levels.

The book is divided into four main sections:

- an exploration of the nature of complicated grief;
- diagnostic categorizations;
- contemporary research on complicated grief;
- treatment of complicated grief.

Illuminating the foundations and new innovations in research, *Complicated Grief* will be essential reading for professionals working with bereavement such as clinical psychologists, health psychologists, psychiatrists, and researchers, as well as graduate students of psychology and psychiatry.

Margaret Stroebe is Professor at the Department of Clinical and Health Psychology, Utrecht University, and the Department of Clinical Psychology and Experimental Psychopathology, University of Groningen, The Netherlands.

Henk Schut is Associate Professor at the Department of Clinical and Health Psychology, Utrecht University, The Netherlands.

Jan van den Bout is Professor of Clinical Psychology at Utrecht University, The Netherlands.

Complicated Grief

Scientific foundations for
health care professionals

**Edited by
Margaret Stroebe,
Henk Schut and
Jan van den Bout**

LONDON AND NEW YORK

First published 2013
by Routledge
27 Church Road, Hove, East Sussex BN3 2FA

Simultaneously published in the USA and Canada
by Routledge
711 Third Avenue, New York NY 10017

Routledge is an imprint of the Taylor & Francis Group, an informa business

British Library Cataloguing in Publication Data
A catalogue record for this book is available from the British Library

Library of Congress Cataloging in Publication Data
Complicated grief : scientific foundations for health care professionals / Margaret Stroebe, Henk Schut and Jan van den Bout (eds). – 1st ed.
p. cm.
ISBN 978-0-415-60393-5
1. Grief. 2. Grief therapy. 3. Loss (Psychology) I. Stroebe, Margaret S. II. Schut, Henk Prof. III. Van den Bout, Jan.
BF575.G7C66 2012
155.9'37–dc23
2012003796

ISBN: 978-0-415-60393-5 (hbk)
ISBN: 978-0-415-62505-0 (pbk)
ISBN: 978-0-203-10511-5 (ebk)

Typeset in Times by Prepress Projects Ltd, Perth, UK

Printed and bound by CPI Group (UK) Ltd, Croydon, CR0 4YY

For Colin Murray Parkes

Contents

Illustrations

Figures

Tables

Contributors

Paul A. Boelen is Professor of Clinical Psychology at Utrecht University, cognitive–behavioral psychotherapist at the Ambulatorium – the outpatient mental health care clinic of Utrecht University – and Head of Post-Master Education for Health Care Psychologists in the Utrecht region. He has published over 50 peer-reviewed articles, mostly about assessment and cognitive–behavioral theory and treatment of prolonged grief disorder in children and adults.

Kathrin Boerner is Senior Research Scientist at the Research Institute on Aging of Jewish Home Lifecare, New York, and an Associate Professor in the Brookdale Department of Geriatrics & Palliative Medicine at Mount Sinai School of Medicine. Her training is in developmental psychology with particular expertise in adult development and aging. Her research, primarily supported by the National Institutes of Health, focuses on adaptation to major life changes related to chronic illness, end of life, and bereavement. She has made major contributions to the literature on coping with serious illness and bereavement for over a decade.

George A. Bonanno is Professor of Clinical Psychology and Director of the Loss, Trauma, and Emotion Lab in the Department of Counseling and Clinical Psychology at Teachers College, Columbia University. His research and scholarly interests center on the question of how human beings cope with loss, trauma, and other forms of extreme adversity, with an emphasis on resilience and the salutary role of personality, positive emotion, and emotion regulatory processes. His research has been funded by the National Institutes of Health and the National Science Foundation. He co-edited the book *Emotion: Current Issues and Future Directions* (Guilford).

Jan van den Bout is Professor of Clinical Psychology at Utrecht University, The Netherlands. His main research interest is about emotional problems after loss and psychotrauma. Being a licensed psychotherapist and cognitive therapist, he was for many years President of the European Association for Behavioural and Cognitive Therapies (EABCT). In the aftermath of the Chernobyl disaster, he carried out humanitarian and research projects in Russia, Byelorussia, and Ukraine.

Laurie A. Burke is a clinical psychology PhD candidate at the University of Memphis, where she is a bereavement researcher, studying loss and grief. She is also interested in how individuals uniquely bond with primary attachment figures, forming deep relationships that are compromised and mourned as a result of loss. Her recent publications are based on her study of complicated grief, and the role that social support and spirituality play in helping or hindering loss accommodation for individuals traumatized by loss. Additionally, she investigates predictors of complicated grief: what makes some grievers vulnerable to greater levels of severity in bereavement distress. Her recent projects include an ongoing, thorough examination of the African American grief experience, violent death bereavement, bereavement in end-of-life care, complicated grief risk factors, and measuring and developing an intervention for *complicated spiritual grief:* a spiritual crisis following loss.

Rachel Cooper is Senior Lecturer in Philosophy at Lancaster University, UK. Her publications include *Classifying Madness: A Philosophical Examination of the Diagnostic and Statistical Manual of Mental Disorders* (Springer) and *Psychiatry and Philosophy of Science* (Acumen). She is currently working on the concept of disorder and on the philosophical foundations of classification in psychiatry.

Atle Dyregrov is a clinical and research psychologist and the director of the Center for Crisis Psychology in Bergen, Norway. Dr. Dyregrov is the author of numerous publications, journal articles, and more than 15 books. He has conducted research on various subjects relating to bereavement, trauma, and disaster. He is one of the founding members of the European Society for Traumatic Stress Studies and the Children and War Foundation.

Kari Dyregrov is a researcher at the Center for Crisis Psychology, Bergen, Norway, and a senior researcher at the Norwegian Institute of Public Health. She is conducting research in the field of grief, traumatic bereavement, suicide, and organization of psychosocial assistance in the community. She is the first author of several publications. She initiated the Norwegian Association for Suicide Survivors, for which she received the Farberow Award in 2007.

Francesca Del Gaudio is a Research Assistant in the Department of Psychiatry and Behavioral Sciences at Memorial Sloan-Kettering Cancer Center.

Ann-Marie Jelena Golden is a cognitive scientist and a health psychologist working at the Medical Research Council (MRC) Cognition and Brain Sciences Unit (CBU) in Cambridge, UK. Her main applied clinical/research interests are in the area of grief/loss, depression, anxiety, and trauma. Dr. Golden works with children, adults, and the elderly who have experienced emotional and cognitive difficulties related to complicated grief, anxiety, depression, trauma, and stress that may or may not be related to physical problems. She is specifically interested in the interplay between cognitions and emotions in common mood and anxiety disorders, looking at emotion regulation, resilience, and intrusive and avoidant tendencies, as well as autobiographical and working memory. Dr. Golden's professional development has benefited from a broad base of skills related to compassionate focused therapy for disorders associated with shame and guilt; mindfulness-based interventions; meaning-breaking, meaning-making; and grief therapy as narrative reconstruction. She is also a co-founder of the Cambridge Mindfulness Centre (UK). Dr. Golden recently relocated to Canada (Toronto, Ontario) and has started working with Professor Stephen Fleming and Dr. Leslie Balmer. She also collaborates with the Mindfulness Clinic and Princess Margaret Hospital in Toronto.

Marcel A. van den Hout is Professor of Clinical Psychology and Experimental Psychopathology at Utrecht University. He is a practicing clinical psychologist, teaches mainly about emotion and its disorders, and has published many papers, mainly on the understanding and treatment of anxiety disorders.

Jennifer Jacobs is Research Officer at the University of Western Sydney and has co-authored publications on pediatrics, mental health, and public health. Current research interests include early childhood prevention of mental health problems and other difficulties.

David W. Kissane is the Jimmie C. Holland Chair, Attending Psychiatrist and Chairman of the Department of Psychiatry and Behavioral Sciences at Memorial Sloan-Kettering Cancer Center. He is also Professor of Psychiatry at the Weill Medical College of Cornell University.

Rolf J. Kleber is Professor of Psychotraumatology, Utrecht University, and Head of the Research Foundation Arq, The Netherlands. Professor Kleber has conducted and supervised research projects on the psychotherapy outcome of posttraumatic stress disorder, work-related trauma, late sequelae of war stress, psychosocial consequences of disasters, and cross-cultural aspects of health. He is also a consultant in the fields of mental health care after serious life events and cross-cultural psychology.

Yuelin Li is an Associate Attending Psychometrician and Statistician in the Department of Psychiatry and Behavioral Sciences at Memorial Sloan-Kettering Cancer Center and Associate Professor of Psychology in Psychiatry at the Weill Medical College of Cornell University.

Jeffrey C. L. Looi is Associate Professor and Deputy Head of the Academic Unit of Psychological Medicine, Australian National University Medical School, Canberra, Australia. He is an academic neuropsychiatrist active in clinical practice, research, and teaching. He was a Fulbright Scholar at UCLA Medical School and is a Visiting Researcher at the Karolinska Institute, Stockholm. He has been a co-author of more than 150 publications in neuropsychiatry and cognitive neuroscience.

Anthony Mancini is Assistant Professor in the Department of Psychology at Pace University, Pleasantville Campus, New York. His research focuses on the different patterns of adjustment people display after an acutely stressful event, such as the death of a loved one, war, and traumatic injury, and the factors that predict those patterns. His work also explores the clinical implications of research findings on grief and posttraumatic disorder. His work is supported by grants from the National Institutes of Health. He is the author of over 30 articles and book chapters.

Mario Mikulincer is Professor and Dean of the School of Psychology at the Interdisciplinary Center (IDC), Herzliya, Israel. His main research interests are attachment theory, terror management theory, personality processes in interpersonal relationships, coping with stress, and grief-related processes. He has published numerous books and over 300 journal articles and book chapters, serves as a member of the editorial boards of various journals, and is the editor of the *Journal of Social and Personal Relationships*. He received the EMET Prize in Psychology and a Distinguished Mid-Career Award from the International Association for Relationship Research.

Michelle Moulds is Associate Professor, Clinical Psychologist, and ARC Australian Research Fellow in the School of Psychology at the University of New South Wales, Sydney. Her research comprises experimental and clinical studies that examine the interplay of cognitive processes and memory in clinical disorders, with a focus on depression. She is a widely published author.

Robert A. Neimeyer is Professor of Psychology, University of Memphis, where he also maintains an active clinical practice. Neimeyer is an extensively published author, his works including *Techniques of Grief Therapy: Creative Practices for Counseling the Bereaved* and *Grief and Bereavement in Contemporary Society: Bridging Research and Practice*, and serves as editor of the journal *Death Studies*. Dr. Neimeyer is a frequent workshop presenter, and is currently working to advance a more adequate theory of grieving as a meaning-making process. Dr. Neimeyer served as President of the Association for Death Education and Counseling and Chair of the International Work Group for Death, Dying, & Bereavement. In recognition of his scholarly contributions, he has been granted the Eminent Faculty Award by the University of Memphis, and made a Fellow of the American Psychological Association.

Mary-Frances O'Connor is a clinical psychologist and Assistant Professor in the Department of Psychology at the University of Arizona. Her research has included the neuroimaging of bereaved persons, and the immune and endocrine aspects of their emotional functioning. She recently completed data collection for an NIA-funded K01 award, applying these methods to older widows between 65 and 80 years of age. She has published her work in many scholarly journals including *Death Studies*.

John Ogrodniczuk is Associate Professor and Director of the Psychotherapy Program in the Department of Psychiatry, University of British Columbia. John has written and published many articles. He serves as Associate Editor for

Psychotherapy Research and is on the editorial board for three other journals including *Journal of Personality Disorders*.

William E. Piper is Professor Emeritus in Psychiatry at the University of British Columbia. His research interests include process and outcome investigations of both individual and group psychotherapies. He has published approximately 200 articles and book chapters as well as six books.

Holly G. Prigerson is Director of the Center for Psycho-oncology & Palliative Care Research at the Dana-Farber Cancer Institute, and Associate Professor of Psychiatry at Harvard Medical School. She has published many peer-reviewed articles on the topic of bereavement. She is an advisor to the DSM-5. The research that she and her group has conducted has provided the evidence base for the inclusion of Prolonged Grief Disorder in DSM-5 and ICD-11.

Therese A. Rando is a clinical psychologist and the Clinical Director of The Institute for the Study and Treatment of Loss (ISTL) in Warwick, Rhode Island, USA. The ISTL provides mental health services through psychotherapy, training, supervision, and consultation, and specializes in: loss and grief; traumatic stress; and the psychosocial care of persons with chronic, life-threatening, or terminal illness, and their loved ones. Since 1970, Dr. Rando has consulted, conducted research, provided therapy, written, and lectured internationally in areas related to loss, grief, illness, dying, and trauma. Current professional foci include treatment of complicated mourning, self-help after sudden and traumatic death, loss of a child, the interface between posttraumatic stress and grief, anticipatory mourning, and specialized intervention techniques in the treatment of traumatic bereavement. A recipient of numerous professional awards and a national media resource expert in dying, death, loss, and trauma for the American Psychological Association, Dr. Rando has over 80 published works pertaining to the clinical aspects of thanatology. Among them, she is the author of the forthcoming *Coping with the Sudden Death of Your Loved One: Self-Help for Traumatic Bereavement*. Among her existing published works are *Treatment of Complicated Mourning*; *Grief, Dying, and Death: Clinical Interventions for Caregivers*; and *How To Go On Living When Someone You Love Dies*. Dr. Rando also serves on the editorial boards of *Death Studies* and *Omega*. For more specifics on Dr. Rando or The ISTL, visit www.thereserando. com.

Beverley Raphael is Professor of Population Mental Health and Disasters at the University of Western Sydney, and Professor of Psychological and Addiction Medicine at the Australian National University. She is an internationally recognized expert in the field of bereavement, trauma, and disasters, and has published extensively in these fields.

Paul C. Rosenblatt is Emeritus Professor of Family Social Science at the University of Minnesota. His current projects include a study of knowing and not knowing in intimate relationships, work on alternative ways to conceptualize grief, and an analysis of how African American novelists depict the impact of racism on African American families. He has published several books on grief and bereavement.

Edward (Ted) Rynearson is Clinical Professor of Psychiatry at the University of Washington and Medical Director of the Separation and Loss Service at the Mason Medical Center in Seattle. He has written a wide range of articles and book chapters on traumatic grief after violent dying and is the author of *Retelling Violent Death* and *Violent Death: Resilience and Intervention beyond the Crisis*.

Henk Schut is Associate Professor of Clinical and Health Psychology at Utrecht University, The Netherlands. His research interests cover processes of coping with loss and the efficacy of bereavement care and grief therapy. Dr. Schut also works as a trainer for professionals (e.g., medical specialists, funeral directors) in dealing with bereaved people and he supervises postacademic clinical psychologists in their research projects. He is coauthor of a number of scientific and professional articles and books on grief, bereavement, and death.

Phillip R. Shaver is Distinguished Professor of Psychology at the University of California, Davis, USA. His main research interests are attachment theory, human motivation and emotion, close relationships, personality development, and the effects of meditation on behavior and the brain. He has published numerous books, journal articles, and book chapters and serves as a member of the editorial boards of various journals. He is a fellow of both the American Psychological Association and the Association for Psychological Science, received a Distinguished Career Award from the International Association for Relationship Research, and was President of that organization.

Margaret Stroebe is Professor at the Department of Clinical Psychology, Utrecht University, and Department of Clinical Psychology and Experimental Psychopathology, University of Groningen, The Netherlands. Her research interests cover theoretical approaches to grief and grieving, interactive patterns of coping, and the efficacy of bereavement intervention. With Henk Schut she developed the Dual Process Model of Coping with Bereavement. She is widely published.

Birgit Wagner is a cognitive–behavioral therapist and working as a researcher at the Department of Psychosomatic Medicine, University of Leipzig, with a focus on posttraumatic stress disorder and complicated grief. She has published numerous articles on grief-related issues such as bereavement interventions. Current research includes Internet-based interventions after loss and trauma in intercultural settings.

Jerome Wakefield is University Professor, Professor of Social Work, and Professor of the Conceptual Foundations of Psychiatry, and Affiliate Faculty in Bioethics and in the Center for Ancient Studies, at New York University. He holds doctorates in clinical social work and in philosophy, both from the

University of California at Berkeley, and writes on issues at the intersection of philosophy and the mental health professions. His recent work has focused on the concept of mental disorder and the validity of psychiatric diagnostic criteria in distinguishing disorder from normal forms of suffering. He is currently completing a two-volume study of Freud's case history of Little Hans and its significance in the history of psychoanalysis, to be published by Routledge.

Edward Watkins is Professor of Experimental and Applied Clinical Psychology, University of Exeter. He is a research clinical psychologist and co-founder and director of the Mood Disorders Centre and the Sir Henry Wellcome Building for Mood Disorders Research. His research is focused on understanding key cognition–emotion processes in depression, in particular negative repetitive thought (rumination) and its underlying mechanisms, through experimental research, and then translating these insights into more efficacious psychological interventions such as rumination-focused cognitive–behavioral therapy. His research has been supported by the Medical Research Council, Wellcome Trust, and NARSAD. He has published many articles.

Talia I. Zaider is an Assistant Attending Clinical Psychologist in the Department of Psychiatry and Behavioral Sciences at Memorial Sloan-Kettering Cancer Center and Professor of Psychiatry at the Weill Medical College of Cornell University.

Part I
Introduction

1 Introduction

Outline of goals and scope of the book

Margaret Stroebe, Henk Schut, and
Jan van den Bout

A basic motive in compiling this volume has been to try to gain understanding of complicated grief, at a time in history when this seems particularly pertinent. In general terms, complicated grief (CG) can be understood as something like a "derailing" of the normal, usually painful process of adapting to the loss of a significant person. However, it will become evident to readers of the current volume that different definitions and criteria have been adopted to try to describe the concept more precisely, for both scientific and clinical purposes. To provide some basis for comparison: our earlier definition of CG has been along the lines of

> a clinically-significant deviation from the (cultural) norm (i.e., that could be expected to pertain, according to the extremity of the particular bereavement event) in either (a) the time course or intensity of specific or general symptoms of grief and/or (b) the level of impairment in social, occupational, or other important areas of functioning. (Stroebe, Hansson, Schut, & Stroebe, 2008, p. 7)

However, such an apparently detailed characterization has shortcomings (e.g., it does not explicitly specify different types of complications that have been suggested, such as absent, delayed, or chronic grief). Further difficulties in operationalizing and applying such a definition will become apparent through the pages of this book.

In our view, CG is perhaps the most important contemporary topic of concern both for the scientific community of bereavement researchers and for health care professionals supporting bereaved people. This is reflected in a huge expansion of research, which has resulted in broader and deeper understanding of CG in recent decades: Earlier assumptions have been put to empirical test, new research domains have been added, innovative techniques have been applied, novel theoretical perspectives have been introduced, and significant developments in intervention programming have been realized. Different academic and clinical disciplines have been involved in this endeavor. Many of these contributions have bearing on – or are a direct consequence of – the consideration whether complicated/prolonged grief should be included as a category of mental disorder in the next edition of the *Diagnostic and Statistical Manual of Mental Disorders* (DSM-5) of the American Psychiatric Association. Currently, developments point in the direction of the inclusion of such a category in the near future.

Notwithstanding such advancements, there is often still lack of clarity or integration, and there are differences of opinion with respect to fundamental issues surrounding CG – ones that go beyond the problems of definition, raised earlier. Furthermore, although the body of knowledge on CG has increased considerably in the past few decades, there are still many limitations in understanding and in empirical investigation. Many fundamental questions remain unanswered. Many theoretical claims still need to be put to empirical test. Empirical research has improved significantly over the last decade but it still has not always been rigorous. Along similar lines, intervention efficacy studies have sometimes lacked adequate methodology (e.g., control groups, preferably attention-placebo control groups, and long-term follow-up measurements). Such gaps in knowledge and shortcomings in investigation need to be identified and directions for future empirical study inventoried.

In our view, it seems appropriate at this point in time to take stock, to compile and assess the contribution of the scientific knowledge base regarding CG, on not only theoretical and conceptual but also empirical levels. Balanced inclusion of a variety of different perspectives and approaches within one volume is timely, to enable review of these diverse contributions, and to relate this research base, where possible, to contemporary societal and practice issues, and to provide critical appraisal of ongoing research and societal developments relating to the topic of CG. Thus, the objective for this volume is to provide a balanced, up-to-date, state-of-the-art account of the scientific foundations surrounding CG. Key questions will be addressed by our authors, such as: How is CG distinct from normal grief, or from other psychiatric disorders? Should it be included in DSM? How can CG best be measured/assessed? Is there an *absent grief* subtype of CG? How efficacious is professional intervention? Can we prevent CG, or at least identify those at most risk? Have we established determinants of CG, or pinpointed underlying mechanisms? What are the implications of CG for health, well-being, and daily functioning?

We hope this review will be of relevance to the bereavement research community, health care professionals, and policy makers. However, it is important to emphasize that the volume is not designed as a sourcebook for practitioners seeking practical tips or concrete guidelines for intervention with bereaved persons. Rather, it is intended – insofar as can be done in a single volume – to provide an overview of contemporary research on CG in relationship to practice, identifying developments in the field, discussing current controversial issues, encouraging debate about them, proposing research, and – again where possible – deriving implications for treatment and implementation agendas for the future. In line with this, the aim of the book is to approach the topic from diverse perspectives, allowing authors the freedom to elaborate on their own scientific standpoint, to respect different types of scholarship rather than to strive for consensus. Nevertheless, the editors try in the final chapter to assess the contribution of the volume as a whole to scientific knowledge about complicated grief.

The volume is divided into six parts. After outlining the scope of the volume in the remaining part of this chapter, the focus in Part II (Chapters 2–6) is on different conceptualizations of CG. Here the phenomena and manifestations associated with CG are explored. These chapters provide a variety of disciplinary perspectives. In Chapter 2, Rachel Cooper reviews diverse philosophical approaches that can potentially help us address key questions relating to complicated grief, examining how common philosophical accounts of disorder can elucidate the concept of CG. First: What is disorder? Fundamental points are raised: Might we think of normal grief as being a mental injury analogous to physical injury? Second, philosophical work on the role of classification in science is drawn on to discuss the question whether CG should be considered a distinct disorder, or a variant of another condition (ones that are already in the DSM system). At the outset, with this contribution, awareness is gained of the complexity of the issues we are dealing with. In Chapter 3, written by Paul Rosenblatt, the perspective shifts to consideration of CG in different cultures from those Western ones where CG has mostly been investigated. This raises fundamental problems: Deviant grieving may not be seen as a "complication" in the same way as Western cultures view it, or the loss experiences and concerns may be very different from ours, ones that do not fit the language of a DSM category, for example. Rosenblatt emphasizes that CG and research on CG are grounded in a particular culture and we should be cautious about applying this in other cultures. His perspective brings to light basic questions on a societal level: What, for example, is the place of psychological treatment in the face of economic, political, or environmental disasters? In Chapter 4, Theresa Rando elucidates the concept of CG among adults from the standpoint of her clinical practice, illustrating how a clinical perspective on CG can clarify scientific understanding. She considers CG as a distinct diagnostic entity as well as a clinical phenomenon, addressing some controversial and/or problematic issues, and arguing the need to consider CG from both these angles. Consideration is given to different forms and functions of CG. She suggests her own operationalization of CG, based on a conceptual model, which she puts forth for further discussion and research. In Chapter 5, by Kathrin Boerner, Anthony Mancini, and George Bonanno, CG is regarded in the context of normal grief, thus looking more from the perspective of the opposite side of the coin. Focus is on the complex distinction between *uncomplicated* and *complicated* grief. What distinguishes these phenomena, how prevalent are they, and what underlies the formation of the different response patterns to loss of a loved one? Drawing on their extensive research examining the course of grief over time, these authors relate the patterns to different trajectories of grief and grieving and describe predictors for complicated or uncomplicated grief patterns. Importantly, they attest to the resilience of the majority of bereaved people. Finally in this section, attention turns to the nature of CG in a specific subgroup of bereaved individuals. Within the scope of this book, valuable though examination of specific kinds of bereavement is for our understanding of CG, we have been able to select only two special cases. Here we focus on CG among children (in a later section we include consideration of CG following violent death). With few exceptions, there has been little research on CG among children so far. One of the exceptions has been the work of Atle and Kari Dyregrov, who contribute Chapter 6. In what ways and to what extent does CG in children parallel or differ from that among adults? This chapter covers several important topics, each being related specifically to children's grief: the phenomenology of CG; its distinctiveness from normal grief; assessment and treatment of CG; and risk factors. The authors stress the importance of enhancing knowledge about the phenomenology, assessment, and treatment of problems among children.

In Part III (Chapters 7–12), categorization of CG as a mental health condition is the central underlying theme. This brings the discussion regarding DSM inclusion, which was mentioned earlier, center-stage. Chapters in this section provide a variety of viewpoints. In the first of these (Chapter 7), Paul Boelen and Holly Prigerson present arguments in favor of CG becoming a new psychiatric condition, based on their extensive research. They review studies that in their view support the case that CG (or, in their terms, also prolonged grief disorder, abbreviated to PGD) meets the definition of a mental/psychiatric disorder and that it should therefore be included in the DSM system. They go on to describe the criteria that they have derived from their empirical and conceptual work for PGD/CG. Given this, they explain why they consider it timely to include PGD/CG in the DSM system; they outline the consensus criteria, detail the available empirical evidence, and indicate how they think CG should be conceptualized and assessed. By contrast, in the following chapter (Chapter 8), by Jerome Wakefield, critical issues to do with CG's entry in the DSM system are brought forward, so that the reader is able to assess both the pros and cons of this (potential) major development. Wakefield examines six arguments put forward by advocates of the proposal in support of CG's conceptual validity. He argues that, despite the enormous effort to research CG over the past decades, close inspection of these aspects reveals deficiencies that lead him to conclude that the majority of persons who would be diagnosed under the CG proposal are suffering from lengthy but normal grief. Next (Chapter 9), and again with DSM inclusion in mind, Jan van den Bout and Rolf Kleber draw on the experience gained from the related area of posttraumatic stress disorder (PTSD) to consider what consequences could ensue should CG be included as a diagnostic category in DSM-5. PTSD was already included in DSM-III in 1980, so there has been time to assess the scientific, clinical, and societal consequences. These researchers identify some positive aspects (e.g., the furtherance of research on a wide range of traumatic experiences, and development and testing of new models on origins and maintenance). They also pinpoint matters for concern (e.g., controversy about diagnostic criteria, clinical utility, and accuracy of prevalences) that could apply in the case of CG too. Whereas Chapter 9 focuses on lessons learned from PTSD for a diagnostic category of CG, in Chapter 10, by Beverley Raphael, Jennifer Jacobs, and Jeff Looi, the interest is in placing CG in the context of other disorders. Again, traumatic experiences and PTSD provide a useful domain for discussion of this, in the final chapter in this section. Manifestations and phenomena following the stressors of trauma and loss through bereavement are described, as well as overlapping versus distinct symptomatology (and associated additional complications). Issues of comorbidity and possible etiologies of PTSD and CG are discussed. Finally, assessment and management strategies for CG with trauma syndromes as comorbidity are outlined.

Part IV (Chapters 11–15) covers contemporary empirical research on risk factors, processes, and mechanisms associated with CG. First, who among bereaved persons are most vulnerable to CG; can we identify empirically supported factors that predict susceptibility to CG? In Chapter 11, Laurie Burke and Robert Neimeyer have taken on the daunting task of reviewing the extensive body of scientific research on risk factors, sifting the literature to find those studies that are the most informative with respect to CG. They cover intra- and interpersonal as well as situational features that increase an individual's vulnerability. As far as possible given the current state of knowledge, they link these risk factors to the full range of responses to bereavement, and point to factors that merit further scientific and clinical investigation. Subsequent chapters in this section cover a range of perspectives that help understand cognitive and emotional functioning in persons with CG. Two chapters focus on specific processes. First, Edward Watkins and Michelle Moulds explore the role of rumination and of repetitive thought in CG (Chapter 12). Given that rumination has to do with repeatedly dwelling on personal concerns and feelings, it stands to reason that it may be related to chronic grief. Does it in fact contribute to the development or maintenance of CG? Does it have constructive or unconstructive consequences? These questions are explored in this chapter, on the basis of extant evidence, considering recent theoretical and empirical approaches to rumination and exploring their relevance for understanding CG and its treatment. They provide an integrative model that helps to guide both research and clinical practice. Second, Ann-Marie Golden focuses on autobiographical memory (Chapter 13), that is, memories specifically concerned with the recollection of previously experienced personal events, which – importantly – contribute to a person's sense of self. In the context of CG, one key feature of autobiographical memory is *overgenerality* (the tendency to recollect in terms of regularities across multiple experiences rather than specific events), being linked as it is with psychopathology. The phenomenon of overgeneral memory bias in relationship to CG is described, research is reviewed, and methodologies and limitations are suggested. Future research lines are laid out specifically for CG investigation, to further detail the psychological mechanisms involved; the clinical relevance of this research line is considered. On a different level, the next chapter in this section (Chapter 14), by Mario Mikulincer and Phillip Shaver, examines the relationship between attachment patterns and CG, following the attachment theory perspective. This theory has had and still has enormous influence in the bereavement field. The authors summarize this approach and present their own psychodynamic model of the activation and functioning of the attachment behavioral system, using it to conceptualize two types of CG: chronic grief and prolonged absence of grieving. They review relevant research findings linking anxious attachment to chronic and avoidant attachment to absent grief. They delineate implications of their perspective for diagnosis, case formulation, and therapy of bereaved clients with CG. Shifting directions again, the section closes with a chapter on physiological mechanisms and the neurobiology of CG by Mary-Frances O'Connor (Chapter 15). This represents a new area of research into CG. The chapter reviews current studies of these mechanisms, including functional magnetic resonance imaging (fMRI) studies of bereavement, genetic analysis, and endocrine data. The evidence is placed in the context of literature on the physiology of the stress response, the biological attachment system, and theories of physiological co-regulation. The benefits of using physiological and neurological variables in bereavement research, as part of a multi-method approach, are described and it is shown how this line of investigation has potential to increase understanding of CG.

Part V (Chapters 16–20) spans a variety of topics relating to the treatment of complicated grief. The first few chapters present a number of intervention principles, paradigms, and procedures, to enable the reader to understand different types of professional help that may be available and appropriate, and to learn the extent to which these programs have been tested for their efficacy. In the first of these (Chapter 16) the authors, Paul Boelen, Jan van den Bout, and Marcel van den Hout, describe a new theoretically based treatment program for CG, based on the cognitive–behavioral approach (CBT). They review theoretical underpinnings and the effectiveness of treatment based on CBT. They then describe their own theoretical approach applying CBT to PGD/CG. They explain how this framework may be useful not only for generating hypotheses about causes and processes but for designing effective interventions for PGD/CG. They go on to describe their treatment program for PGD/CG based on this approach, and to review research testing the effectiveness of CBT interventions for PGD/CG. Chapter 17, by Birgit Wagner, introduces a different contemporary perspective to the treatment of CG, namely, that which is Internet-based; most Internet-based approaches are also based on a cognitive–behavioral framework. She gives an overview of computerized and Internet-based interventions for (complicated) grief, describing the different treatment approaches that are currently available, ranging from those that provide some level of therapist support to online bereavement self-help groups. She describes procedures used in Internet intervention programs and identifies key components of the therapist-supported interventions. She discusses the effectiveness of these programs for CG and elaborates on the advantages and disadvantages of Internet-based therapeutic interventions. In the next two chapters in this section we turn from individual to group perspectives in relationship to treatment. As David Kissane, Talia Zaider, Yuelin Li, and Francesca Del Gaudio argue in Chapter 18, bereavement is not an event that affects an individual alone, but one that typically occurs in the family context. Thus, they explore the possibility that family therapy initiated already during the palliative care phase might prevent the development of CG. They place their work within the literature on family intervention in bereavement care and go on to describe their family therapy program. As they explain, this program targets those deemed at risk; it identifies types of families that are likely to do poorly. They present preliminary results regarding the effectiveness of this ongoing research. A different group perspective is adopted by William Piper and John Ogrodniczuk in Chapter 19. In today's cost-conscious environment, group therapies could be considered an increasingly attractive treatment modality. The authors have conducted extensive short-term therapy groups for clients with CG. They highlight two models on which they base their therapy, namely interpretive and supportive therapy, detailing the different objectives of these and comparing them with other therapies in the field. They give details of the technical manuals produced to guide therapists and illustrate how these may be used. The various trials that these investigators have so far conducted to try to establish the effectiveness of these therapy programs are outlined and compared with those of other treatments. Finally in this section, in Chapter 20, Edward Rynearson, Henk Schut, and Margaret Stroebe focus on the second of the two special types of bereavement included in this volume, one which would also seem particularly associated with CG (and thus especially relevant for treatment): bereavement following violent causes of death. They first examine the concept of violent death. Then they review studies on the prevalence and distinctive features of CG following violent death. They describe remaining challenges (e.g., who precisely should be included in the CG category among those bereaved following a violent death?). Models of assessment are featured, and an overview of the limited research on intervention efficacy for CG is provided.

In the last section of the book, Part VI (Chapter 21), the editors review the contributions to this volume, and they assess the state of scientific knowledge and the implications for research and practice. They discuss key issues and try to provide well-balanced conclusions, based on the considerations raised and the evidence provided by the authors.

Reference

Stroebe, M. S., Hansson, R. O., Schut, H., & Stroebe, W. (2008). *Handbook of bereavement research and practice: Advances in theory and intervention*. Washington, DC: American Psychological Association.

Part II

The nature of complicated grief

Conceptual approaches

2 Complicated grief

Philosophical perspectives

Rachel Cooper

This chapter examines how work in the philosophy of medicine, philosophy of science, and moral philosophy can help elucidate the concept of complicated grief. The chapter addresses two key questions.

First, what is disorder? I examine various accounts from the philosophy of medicine, ranging from the purely descriptive account proposed by Boorse (1975, 1976, 1977, 1997), who argues that disorders are biological dysfunctions, through to accounts that claim that disorder is a value-laden concept and that disorders are necessarily bad. In each case, I examine implications for the concept of complicated grief. On some accounts, normal grief might itself be considered a disorder, and so at points considering whether complicated grief is a disorder becomes entwined with considering whether normal grief is a disorder. Thus, in the first part of this chapter, I consider the following issues: Does complicated grief involve a biological dysfunction? Is grief a bad thing, or a necessary part of the good human life? Can normal grief and complicated grief be clearly distinguished? Might we think of normal grief as being a "mental injury" analogous to physical injury?

Second, I will examine how work in the philosophy of science might contribute to debates over whether complicated grief should be considered a distinct disorder, or whether it should be considered a mere variant of some other condition, for example major depressive disorder (MDD), posttraumatic stress disorder, or adjustment disorder. Here I will set out philosophical work on the role of classification in science, and show how it can contribute to determining the conditions under which we should conclude that complicated grief is a distinct kind of disorder.

What is a disorder? Is complicated grief a disorder?

Philosophers have written little that explicitly addresses the issue of whether complicated grief should be considered a disorder. However, there is a large body of work on the concept of disorder that can be directly applied to this issue. In the philosophy of medicine, accounts of disease, disorder, or illness (in the literature the terms tend to be used interchangeably) can be split into two main camps. On the one hand, there are descriptivists, who claim that whether a condition is a disorder is purely a matter of biological fact. On the other hand, there are normativist positions, which claim that whether a condition is a disorder depends, at least in part, on whether it is a bad thing.

The best-known descriptivist account has been proposed by Boorse (1975, 1976, 1977, 1997). In a range of publications, Boorse has proposed that a condition is a disorder if and only if it is a biological dysfunction. His basic idea is that the bodies and minds of human beings can be thought of as consisting of numerous subsystems, such as organs, mental modules, and more diffuse systems, such as the system made up of blood vessels. Each subsystem has a particular natural function, which is whatever it normally does that contributes to the organism's overall goals of reproduction and survival. For example, the function of the eye is to enable sight, and the function of the heart is to pump blood round the body. When we are healthy each of our subsystems fulfills its function. However, when we suffer from a disorder one or more subsystems fail to function at a level that is average for comparable organisms (i.e., the subsystem functions at a level significantly below that which we might expect given our age and sex).

Boorse's account is attractive insofar as it accounts for a number of commonplace intuitions. On Boorse's account, whether there is a disorder depends simply on natural biological facts, and medics will thus be best qualified to determine whether a condition is a disorder.

Despite its attractions, however, Boorse's account faces problems and has been heavily criticized. The biggest difficulty for a Boorse-style account is that many people have a strong intuition that disorders must necessarily be bad. As he proposes a purely descriptive account Boorse cannot accommodate this intuition. For Boorse, whether a condition is a disorder comes down to a purely biological question; if there a biological dysfunction there is a disorder and whether the condition is a bad thing is irrelevant. Tensions over this point came to a head in discussions about homosexuality (Bayer, 1981). During the 1970s the question of whether homosexuality is pathological was heavily debated. On Boorse's account the question hinges on whether homosexuality involves some biological dysfunction. The possibility of kin-selection effects and other atypical selection mechanisms mean that answering this question is far from straightforward. In any case it seemed to many that questions about the biological significance of homosexuality missed the genuine issue. To many, the key question in addressing whether homosexuality is pathological is whether homosexuality is harmful; insofar as homosexuality is not a bad thing it cannot be a disorder, and questions about biological functioning seem irrelevant.

Following these debates, Wakefield proposed his highly influential account of disorder (Wakefield, 1992a, 1992b, 1993, 1999; Chapter 8 in this volume). Wakefield's account sets out to accommodate the intuition that a condition can be a disorder only if it is bad. On his account, disorders are *harmful* dysfunctions, where whether a condition is harmful is to be determined by current social norms. For Wakefield, whether or not homosexuality is a dysfunction, insofar as it is not harmful, it will not be a disorder. Wakefield's account has been hugely influential. Key figures involved in the construction of the DSM (the classification of mental disorders produced by the American Psychiatric Association) have written of their admiration for his account, and indeed suggest that explicitly adopting Wakefield's account might helpfully guide future revisions to the classification system (Spitzer, 1999).[1]

For Boorse, if one wants to know whether complicated grief is a disorder one should ask whether it is a biological dysfunction. For Wakefield, in order to be a disorder, complicated grief would need to both involve some evolutionary dysfunction and also be harmful.

Boorse has not written about grief, but Wakefield considers normal grief and complicated grief in a number of his writings. Writing together with Horwitz in *The Loss of Sadness: How Psychiatry Transformed Normal Sorrow into Depressive Disorder* (Horwitz & Wakefield, 2007), Wakefield argues at length that forms of normal sadness, amongst which he includes normal grief, must be distinguished from depression. Using his account of disorder, he suggests that, although both normal sadness and depression may be harmful, normal sadness involves no biological dysfunction, and should thus not be classed as a disorder, whereas true depression does involve dysfunction and thus counts as a disorder. Why do Horwitz and Wakefield think that normal sadness is normal functioning? Because they think that there is an evolutionary explanation for those feelings of sadness that arise in appropriate circumstances. Normal feelings of sadness can be identified thus:

> they emerge because of specific kinds of environmental triggers, especially loss; they are roughly proportionate in intensity to the provoking loss; and they end when the loss situation ends or gradually cease as natural coping mechanisms allow an individual to adjust to the new circumstances and return to psychological and social equilibrium. (Horwitz & Wakefield, 2007, p. 16)

Horwitz and Wakefield thus think that normal grief does not count as a disorder because it involves no evolutionary dysfunction. If Wakefield's claims about functioning are correct, then a Boorsean would have to agree with him on this matter.

Horwitz and Wakefield also write, briefly, about complicated grief. Here they do think it reasonable to think that there is some evolutionary dysfunction, and thus they are happy to accept that complicated grief counts as a disorder. They write:

> When grief involves extreme immobilisation, pronounced psychotic ideation, or severe symptoms that persist despite the passage of time and changing circumstances, then it can be presumed that an individual's reaction to the death of an intimate has caused a breakdown in his or her psychological functioning . . . such pathological states constitute Complicated Grief. (Horwitz & Wakefield, 2007, p. 33)

Following Wakefield, can we simply conclude that normal grief involves no dysfunction and thus is not a disorder, whereas complicated grief does involve some evolutionary dysfunction and thus is a disorder? Unfortunately not. This is what the accounts of Boorse and Wakefield imply, but there are reasons why many doubt that their accounts of the concept of disorder are correct. The key concern is whether it is indeed the case that all disorders have to be biological dysfunctions. The discipline of evolutionary psychopathology suggests that this may not be so; there may be some mental disorders that confer an evolutionary advantage and are thus not dysfunctions (Wilson, 1993). Psychopathy or generalized anxiety disorder, for example, may have an evolutionary explanation (Akiskal, 1998; Mealey, 1995). Of course, all evolutionary-based accounts of psychopathology are controversial. However, it at least makes sense to think that some disorders may have an evolutionary explanation, and this is sufficient to show that it cannot be part of our concept of disorder that there has to be an evolutionary dysfunction. Wakefield's account implies that by definition all disorders would have to be evolutionary dysfunctions, but *evolutionarily adaptive disorder* is not an oxymoron.

Given the criticisms of Wakefield's account, some accounts of disorder have been developed that completely separate the question of whether a condition is a disorder from the question of whether there is an evolutionary dysfunction. A range of such accounts are on offer. Some claim that individuals are healthy if they have bodies and minds that will enable them to live good lives (at least if environmental and social conditions are favorable). To a first approximation, this is the view of Megone (1998, 2000), Nordenfelt (1995), and Richman (2004), although these philosophers differ in the details of their accounts and on how they characterize the good life. Other philosophers agree that disorders are necessarily bad states, but think that additional criteria must also be met before a condition can be considered a disorder. Reznek (1987, pp. 163–164) proposes that a disorder is an abnormal bodily or mental condition which requires medical intervention and which harms standard members of the species in standard conditions. He takes it that we decide what we will count as abnormal ("abnormal" functions as a call to action stating that we consider dealing with the harmful condition to be a priority), and that "medical interventions" can be defined enumeratively, using a list of possible pharmacological and surgical interventions (p. 94). Along similar lines, I have argued that by "disease" we mean a condition that it is a bad thing to have, that is such that we consider the afflicted person to be unlucky, and that can potentially be appropriately medically or psychologically treated (Cooper, 2002, 2005).

All these accounts hold that a condition can be a disorder only if it is a bad thing. On such accounts a key question in determining whether complicated grief (or normal grief) is a disorder is whether it is bad. At first glance, grief in all its varieties looks to be a bad thing. The grieving person feels unhappy and finds everyday tasks difficult. However, we should pause before concluding that we would be better off without grief. Grieving for a loved one involves not simply negative affect, but also activities such as remembering the good times one has had. Paul Rosenblatt (1996) points out that "A bereaved parent may remember a child's laughter, the tender feelings of holding a sleeping infant, or a child's creative mischief. Thus recurrent grief is not like recurrent illness. It can be a link with the best of life" (p. 55). Not only may grief involve mixed feelings, there are good reasons to think that grieving for a loved one is essentially tied up with having loved him or her in the first place. The President's Council on Bioethics (2003) considers the possibility of medicating away grief and asks us to consider the following thought experiment (pp. 254–255). Suppose on your death nobody mourned. How would you feel if on your death your family and friends simply popped some pills and forgot about you? Would you consider this a good thing? Most people do not want their family and friends to simply move on. Those who are ungrieved in death were unloved in life.

How is it that a capacity to love might be tied up with a capacity to grieve? According to many accounts, to have an emotion at one point in time commits one to other emotions in other circumstances (Helm, 2001). Thus, if I love my son then this commits me to feel various other emotions in various circumstances. If my son does well I will be pleased. If he is in danger I will be concerned. And if he dies I will grieve. On such a picture, grieving for a dead loved one is rationally connected with having loved him or her in the first place. We might want to qualify this idea somewhat, as the death of a very old and ill person might, all things considered, be a good thing, and here grief may be less apt. Plausibly, loving someone will commit me to grieving for his or her death only if the death is regrettable. Nonetheless there will be a conceptual link between love and grief. Note that the link between grief and love here is supposed to be a rational connection, rather than being, say, a side-effect of our evolutionary heritage (for the idea that grief must be a side-effect of our evolved ability to form attachments see Frances, 2010). The idea is that loving someone commits any rational being, whether that being has the evolved vulnerabilities of humans or not, to feel grief in appropriate contexts. On this picture grief is not some unfortunate side-effect but is essentially tied to our capacity to love.

Following on from such thoughts, Radden and Solomon both argue that the conceptual link between love and grief is such that grief is a moral emotion (Radden, 2009, p. 102; Solomon, 2007, p. 75). Grief on the regrettable death of a loved one is not only expected, or rationally appropriate, it is *morally required*. In appropriate circumstances, a virtuous person will feel grief, and one who does not grieve is condemned as callous (assuming that some pathology is not preventing grief).

I suggest that the idea that there is a conceptual link between loving someone and grieving when he or she dies is on the right tracks but we need to be careful when thinking about exactly what is implied. In the normal case I will love someone when they are alive and then some time later, when they die, grieve for them. However, suppose that something happens that prevents me from grieving: I die before the loved one, or come to suffer from severe dementia, or take medication that flattens my emotional responses. As all these things happen after the time when I loved, my love cannot be affected by these later happenings; we should not countenance the possibility of backwards causation here. Thus we should not say that if we love someone this implies that we *must* later grieve at their death, but rather that if we love someone this implies that we will be vulnerable to feeling grief later (if we are still in a state that makes grief possible when they die). On such a picture, if I entered into relationships knowing that in the event of bereavement I would use drugs to take away feelings of normal grief, this would be problematic, as, insofar as it removed the risk involved in loving, it would alter the nature of love. (In the same sort of way, rock climbing with ropes is a different type of activity from free climbing.)

Suppose we accept that exposing ourselves to the risk of grief is an essential part of loving someone. Following such reasoning we might see normal grief as an essential risk in a good human life. Still, only grief that is proportionate to the loss is conceptually tied to love. On such a picture we can imagine two types of problematic case. First, there is the person who grieves too little. Such a person either is suffering from a pathological condition – absent grief, or repressed grief, or whatever – or has some character flaw, such as callousness, and never truly loved in the first place. Second, there is the person who grieves too much or too severely. Such a person suffers from complicated grief.

Can we conclude that normal grief is a part of the flourishing human life and thus normal, whereas complicated grief is grief that is disproportionate and thus pathological? Unfortunately, matters are not quite so clear-cut, as problems emerge in determining whether grief is proportionate. How long should a person grieve? When I imagine my death, it seems to me both fitting and right that my partner would feel sad for about 6 months. However, on reflection it can be no accident that this seems right to me! As an inhabitant of a twenty-first-century European country this is what I have come to expect. However, we know that in some cultures the period expected for mourning is comparatively short, whereas in others a truly dedicated partner is expected to mourn for much longer (Stroebe, Gergen, Gergen, & Stroebe, 1996). Given that our expectations about normal grieving are clearly culturally shaped, and given that determining how long one should grieve on some basis other than societal norms will be deeply problematic, distinguishing between normal grief and grief that is too intense or lasts for too long will be difficult. Normative accounts of disorder tell us that grief is not a disorder so long as it plays a proper part in enabling us to lead flourishing lives, but it is unclear how we might decide how much grief a flourishing human should feel. At bottom the question depends on decisions about the sorts of individuals we want to be and the sorts of societies we want to live in – and these are hard issues indeed. To make things yet harder, not only is determining the nature of the good life intrinsically difficult, complications arise when we reflect on the fact that our ideas about the good life are plausibly shaped by the economic and political structure in which we live. Contemporary Western culture idealizes people who are independent, happy, and reliable, and it is surely no accident that these characteristics are also those that enable an individual to be economically productive in an advanced capitalist society. Persons whose grief is "dis-ordered" are a liability in our society, and this will create additional pressures to medicalize the symptoms of unusually intense or long-lasting grief (Walter, 2006). Very severe and long-lasting grief is plausibly a bad thing, but drawing the line between the normal and the pathological is problematic.

So far we have considered accounts of disorder that specify criteria that must be met for a condition to count as a disorder. Boorse thinks that disorders are biological dysfunctions, Wakefield that disorders are harmful dysfunctions, and the other philosophers we considered hold that disorders must be harmful (and maybe meet some other criteria too). If we adopt one of these accounts then the way to find out whether complicated grief (or normal grief) is a disorder is to see if it meets the necessary and sufficient conditions. Following such reasoning, we have considered whether complicated grief, or normal grief, might be an evolutionary dysfunction, and whether these conditions are harmful or necessary components of a good human life.

Apart from the philosophical accounts of the concept of disorder that we have considered, there are also definitions that lie outside the philosophical traditions but that have been influential and much discussed. Most importantly, the DSM has included a definition of mental disorder since the publication of the DSM-III in 1980:

> each of the mental disorders is conceptualized as a clinically significant behavioural or psychological syndrome or pattern that occurs in an individual and that is typically associated with either a painful symptom (distress) or impairment in one or more areas of functioning (disability). In addition there is an inference that there is a behavioural, psychological, or biological dysfunction, and that the disturbance is not only in the relationship between the individual and society. (APA, 1980, p. 6)

In the DSM-III, uncomplicated grief is distinguished from depression by fiat. The diagnostic criteria for depression instruct clinicians that uncomplicated grief "is not considered a mental disorder even when associated with the full depressive syndrome" (APA, 1980, p. 213). Instead those individuals who manifest what may be a "full depressive syndrome" in the context of bereavement are to be given a V-code (i.e., a non-disorder code) (APA, 1980, p. 333). The DSM-III does, however, allow that bereavement may be "complicated by the development of a Major Depression," which may be diagnosed in bereaved persons who display very severe problems. By the DSM-IV, the reasoning behind excluding grief is made explicit and the definition of mental disorder has been revised to include a criterion specifying that the "syndrome or pattern must not be merely an expectable and culturally sanctioned response to a particular event, for example, the death of a loved one" (APA, 1994, p. xxi). Proposals for the DSM-5 currently suggest that the grief exclusion clause will be removed from the criteria for MDD. Proponents of this change reason that there is little to distinguish cases of depression that are caused by bereavement and those that are caused by other stressors (Kendler, 2010; Kendler, Myers, & Zisook, 2008). Advocates have also lobbied for the inclusion of a new category of complicated grief, and current proposals for the DSM-5 suggest that criteria for bereavement related disorder will be included in an appendix for further study.

In the philosophical literature, Wilkinson (2000) considers the DSM-IV definition of disorder and how it might apply to grief. He is especially critical of the DSM-IV's claim that an "expected and culturally sanctioned response to external events" should not be considered a disorder. Wilkinson notes that, in physical medicine, injuries are generally "expected responses to external events" and yet also are considered as disorders. Following Engel (1961), Wilkinson asks us to compare grief to a burn, which is an expected response to burning in the same sort of way that grief is an expected response to the loss of a loved one. Engel and Wilkinson both suggest that we might conceive of grief as being a psychic injury. (Alternatively, Wilkinson suggests that if we are convinced that normal grief is not a disorder then some approach other than the DSM way of defining disorder will be needed.) The concept of "psychic injury" has been little explored, and could usefully be considered further.

Finally, two philosophical accounts should be mentioned that both resist the notion that whether a condition is a disorder should be determined by asking whether some necessary and sufficient conditions obtain. Lilienfeld and Marino (1995) suggest that it is not possible to find an adequate definition of "mental disorder" because mental disorder is a Roschian concept (Rosch, 1978). A Roschian concept is one where no definition of the concept can be provided, but where we decide whether a particular case belongs to a category on the basis of its overall similarity to prototypical cases. In the case of "mental disorder," prototypical examples are schizophrenia and psychotic depression. Other conditions are classified as "mental disorders" if they seem similar enough to these prototypical mental disorders. On this account if we want to know whether complicated grief should be considered a disorder we should ask whether it is similar enough to conditions like psychotic depression and schizophrenia. On such an account, complicated grief would plausibly pass the test, and could fairly be considered a disorder.

In *What Is Mental Disorder?* Bolton (2008) suggests that if we want to know when psychiatric treatment is justifiable then setting out by asking whether the condition is a disorder may not be the most useful approach to take. In his view, attempts to define the concept of mental disorder have failed. However, Bolton believes that psychiatry can justifiably continue to operate even in the absence of a satisfactory account of mental disorder. Bolton seeks to place the distressed patient at the heart of his account. The patients come for help, and mental health professionals seek to help them in a way that is recognizably medical, as opposed to, say, economic or educational. Determining when such interventions are appropriate depends on diverse factors, such as whether the problem is most effectively dealt with by medical or other means, and also ethical and political decisions regarding the sort of lives we wish to lead. Thus, on Bolton's view, the key questions will be whether complicated grief can be helpfully treated by health care professionals, and whether we think such treatments ethically justifiable. If Bolton is right, philosophical debates about the nature of mental disorder will turn out to be merely a distraction.

At this point one might be tempted to conclude that as philosophers cannot agree amongst themselves there is little to be learnt from them. However, I suggest that some useful pointers can be taken from the philosophical literature. We have seen that accounts of disorder are contested, but on all available accounts complicated grief is likely to count as a disorder. Although what counts as normal mourning varies from culture to culture, insofar as the symptoms of complicated grief go far beyond those of normal grief in intensity and duration there are good grounds to think that some evolutionary dysfunction might be involved. Furthermore, such a syndrome is plausibly not conducive to living a flourishing life. The symptoms of complicated grief are relevantly similar to those of conditions that are generally accepted to be disorders. Bolton, who is skeptical of the usefulness of the term *mental disorder*, will also probably accept that complicated grief can justifiably be treated by health care professionals. We have come across only one potential reason to hesitate before concluding that complicated grief is a disorder: The distinction between grief that is considered appropriate and that which is excessive is not clear-cut but is culturally shaped. Though this is a worry, I suggest that we are on safe ground if we hold that we can at least be certain that very severe symptoms cannot be conducive to a leading a good life, and can rightly be considered pathological.

The case of normal grief is more problematic. Those who hold that disorders must involve evolutionary dysfunctions may doubt whether there is any dysfunction here. Those with normative accounts of disorder may consider normal grief to be an essential component of a good human life. Insofar as love and grief are conceptually connected, reducing our capacity to experience normal grief would reduce our ability to love. On the other hand, Wilkinson has suggested that we might think of normal grief as a "psychic injury" analogous to a burn, and this idea might be fruitfully explored further.

Is complicated grief a distinct disorder?

In much of the literature arguing that complicated grief is a valid disorder the questions of whether complicated grief is a disorder and the question of whether it is a distinct condition from other conditions are run together. I suggest that these questions are best kept distinct. We can distinguish two sorts of question:

1 Is condition X genuinely a disorder – as opposed to some type of non-disorder condition, for example a vice, or a normal variation, or a good variation? For example, we might ask whether normal grief is pathological or a necessary component of a flourishing human life.
2 Is condition X genuinely a different kind of condition from condition Y? For example, we might ask whether complicated grief is distinct from MDD or posttraumatic stress disorder (PTSD).

The distinction between these two sorts of question can be made clearer by considering an analogy. Suppose we set out to classify weeds, and define *weeds* as unwanted plants. We will face many difficult questions. Are daisies weeds? What about blackberries? A classification that sets out to list all and only weeds will become mired in controversy. However, in parallel with these questions there will be other types of question that might prove easier to address: Are blackberries really a distinct species from raspberries, for example? How should hybrid berries be classified? In the same sort of way that the question of whether a blackberry is a weed is distinct from the question of whether blackberries are of a different species to raspberries, so too the question of whether complicated grief is a disorder is a different question from whether complicated grief is distinct from other conditions (MDD, PTSD, or whatever it might be).

How might we determine whether a condition should be considered distinct from other conditions? In their classic paper, Robins and Guze (1970) suggest that a condition can be considered distinct if it is shown to differ from other conditions in terms of phenomenology, etiology and correlates, outcome, clinical course, and response to treatment. Following such reasoning, those who argue that complicated grief is best considered to be distinct from other conditions have sought to locate differences in these validators (Lichtenthal, Cruess, & Prigerson, 2004; Prigerson, Vanderwerker, & Maciejewski, 2008). Taking a somewhat different approach, Boelen and van den Bout (2005) use factor analysis to suggest that complicated grief, depression, and anxiety are distinct syndromes. Meanwhile, Stroebe and Schut (2005–2006) use a conceptual approach to argue that trauma and grief are overlapping but distinct (insofar as some peaceful deaths will not be traumatic, and some traumas do not result in death).

What might the philosophical literature contribute to such debates? I suggest that an account of classification proposed by Dupré (1981, 1993) may help us think about the relevant issues. Dupré puts forward an account that he calls promiscuous realism. The key idea is that the world is a messy and complex place, and that depending on our interests we may usefully classify in diverse ways. Dupré asks us to imagine a multidimensional quality space in which the entities in some domain have been plotted (he considers biological organisms, but his ideas can be generalized). In such a space, entities that are similar will be found close together, whereas those that are very different will be found far apart. In the space it will be possible to find various clusters of entities that are highly similar to each other. We can expect the patterns of similarities to be highly complex; there will be clusters within clusters, groups of entities that cluster in certain dimensions, but not others, and so on. Thinking in terms of such a space, Dupré notes that there will be very many clusters that we might choose to pick out. Depending on our interests we might focus on certain dimensions, or focus in at greater or lesser degrees of resolution.

Dupré's picture is compatible with the reasoning employed in debates whether complicated grief is a distinct condition. Suppose one wants to argue that complicated grief should be considered a distinct condition. How should one reason? On Dupré's picture the important task is to demonstrate that cases of complicated grief differ from the other condition in some important respect: phenomenology, treatment response, or whatever it might be. Such reasoning is indeed that adopted by those who wish to argue that complicated grief is a distinct condition. On the other hand, suppose one wants to argue that complicated grief should be classified alongside some other condition. Then the task is to show that complicated grief and the other condition are alike in some important respect.

The key insight provided by Dupré's account is that in general it is possible to produce multiple useful but incompatible classifications of some domain. The classification one will develop depends on the properties in which one is interested. Dupré (2001) discusses classification in biology. He notes that species can be defined in different ways, for example by relations of ancestry or by current characteristics. Different ways of classifying focus on different properties and are most useful in different biological subdisciplines. Evolutionary theorists will find it most useful to classify by patterns of ancestry; ecologists will find it more useful to classify on the basis of current characteristics. In such a situation, Dupré suggests that a thousand flowers should be allowed to bloom and that different subdisciplines should be permitted to classify as they find most useful.

On Dupré's picture, empirical data are of course relevant to decisions about how complicated grief should be classified, but, once all the empirical data are in, deciding whether complicated grief should be classified with other conditions or apart may be a matter for choice. It may turn out that both those who consider complicated grief to be a mere variant of some other disorder and those who consider it to be importantly distinct have fair points to make, and that proponents of the different positions merely concentrate on different features of the conditions. If this turned out to be the case, on Dupré's picture it would be permissible to employ different classifications for different purposes. For example, those interested in developing treatments might classify in one way, whereas those exploring the factors that make particular individuals vulnerable to developing the disorder might classify in another. There may be no one answer to the question of whether complicated grief should be considered a distinct disorder or a mere variant.

Conclusion

In this chapter I have explored how philosophical work might contribute to elucidating the concept of complicated grief. In the first section, I set out common philosophical accounts of disorder. Although accounts of disorder are contested, current prominent accounts suggest that complicated grief should be considered a disorder. In the second section, I considered whether complicated grief should be considered a distinct condition or merely a variant of some other condition. I suggested that insights taken from Dupré's work on promiscuous realism suggest that multiple answers to this question might be justified. The world is a complex and messy place and multiple conflicting classifications might prove useful for different purposes. For some purposes it may be helpful to consider complicated grief alongside other conditions; for others it might best be considered separately.

Acknowledgments

I am grateful to Alison Stone and the editors of this volume, who read and commented on an earlier draft of this chapter.

Note

1   Despite this endorsement of Wakefield's account, there are good reasons for thinking that the DSM has not actually employed an evolutionary account of dysfunction. As Bolton (2008, pp. 139–151) points out, Wakefield's account is of limited practical use, as in most cases of mental disorder whether or not there is an evolutionary dysfunction remains unclear.

References

Akiskal, H. (1998). Toward a definition of generalised anxiety disorder as an anxious temperament type. *Acta Psychiatrica Scandinavica Suppl, 393*, 66–73.

APA (American Psychiatric Association). (1980). *Diagnostic and statistical manual of mental disorders* (3rd edn.). Washington, DC: American Psychiatric Association.

APA. (1994). *Diagnostic and statistical manual of mental disorders* (4th edn.). Washington, DC: American Psychiatric Association.

Bayer, R. (1981). *Homosexuality and American psychiatry*. New York: Basic Books.

Boelen, P., & van den Bout, J. (2005). Complicated grief, depression, and anxiety as distinct postloss syndromes: A confirmatory factor analysis study. *American Journal of Psychiatry, 162*, 2175–2177.

Bolton, D. (2008). *What is mental disorder?* Oxford: Oxford University Press.

Boorse, C. (1975). On the distinction between disease and illness. *Philosophy and Public Affairs, 5*, 49–68.

Boorse, C. (1976). What a theory of mental health should be. *Journal for the Theory of Social Behaviour, 6*, 61–84.

Boorse, C. (1977). Health as a theoretical concept. *Philosophy of Science, 44*, 542–573.

Boorse, C. (1997). A rebuttal on health. In Hunter, J., & Almeder, R. (Eds.) *What is disease?* (pp. 1–134). Totowa, NJ: Humana Press.

Cooper, R. (2002). Disease. *Studies in History and Philosophy of Biological and Biomedical Science, 33*, 263–282.

Cooper, R. (2005). *Classifying madness: A philosophical examination of the Diagnostic and Statistical Manual of Mental Disorders*. Springer: Dordrecht.

Dupré, J. (1981). Natural kinds and biological taxa. *Philosophical Review, 90*, 66–90.

Dupré, J. (1993). *The disorder of things*. Cambridge, MA: Harvard University Press.

Dupré, J. (2001). In defence of classification. *Studies in History and Philosophy of Biological and Biomedical Sciences, 32*, 203–219.

Engel, G. (1961). Is grief a disease? A challenge for medical research. *Psychosomatic Medicine, 23*, 18–22.

Frances, A. (2010, August 15). Good grief. *New York Times*.

Helm, B. (2001). *Emotional reason*. Cambridge: Cambridge University Press.

Horwitz, A., & Wakefield, J. (2007). *The loss of sadness: How psychiatry transformed normal sadness into depressive disorder*. Oxford: Oxford University Press.

Kendler, K. (2010). *Notes on the proposed the deletion of the grief exclusion criterion from the criteria for Major Depression*. Retrieved November 26, 2010, from http://www.dsm5.org/about/Documents/grief%20exclusion_Kendler.pdf.

Kendler, K., Myers, J., & Zisook, S. (2008). Does bereavement-related major depression differ from major depression associated with other stressful life events? *American Journal of Psychiatry, 165*, 1449–1455.

Lichtenthal, W., Cruess, D., & Prigerson, H. (2004). A case for establishing complicated grief as a distinct mental disorder in DSM-V. *Clinical Psychology Review, 24*, 637–662.

Lilienfeld, S., & Marino, L. (1995). Mental disorder as a Roschian concept: A critique of Wakefield's "Harmful Dysfunction" analysis. *Journal of Abnormal Psychology, 104*, 411–420.

Mealey, L. (1995). The sociobiology of sociopathy: An integrated evolutionary model. Reprinted in Baron-Cohen, S. (Ed.) (1997) *The maladapted mind* (pp. 133–189). Hove: Psychology Press.

Megone, C. (1998). Aristotle's function argument and the concept of mental illness. *Philosophy, Psychiatry and Psychology, 5*, 187–201.

Megone, C. (2000). Mental illness, human function and values. *Philosophy, Psychiatry and Psychology, 7*, 45–65.

Nordenfelt, L. (1995) *On the nature of health: An action-theoretic approach* (2nd edn.). Dordrecht: Kluwer.

President's Council on Bioethics. (2003) *Beyond therapy: Biotechnology and the pursuit of happiness*. Washington, DC: President's Council on Bioethics.

Prigerson, H., Vanderwerker, L., & Maciejewski, P. (2008). A case for inclusion of prolonged grief disorder in DSM-V. *Grief Matters, Autumn*, 23–32.

Radden, J. (2009). *Moody minds distempered: Essays on melancholy and depression*. Oxford: Oxford University Press.

Reznek, L. (1987). *The nature of disease*. London: Routledge and Kegan Paul.

Richman, K. (2004). *Ethics and the metaphysics of medicine*. Cambridge, MA: MIT Press.

Robins, E., & Guze, S. B. (1970). Establishment of diagnostic validity in psychiatric illness: Its application to schizophrenia. *American Journal of Psychiatry, 126*, 983–987.

Rosch, E. (1978). Principles of categorization. In Rosch, E., & Lloyd, B. (Eds.), *Cognition and categorization* (pp. 27–48.) Hillsdale, NJ: Lawrence Erlbaum Associates.

Rosenblatt, P. (1996) Grief that does not end. In Klass, D., Silverman, P., & Nickman, S. (Eds.), *Continuing bonds: New understandings of grief* (pp. 45–59). Philadelphia: Taylor & Francis.

Solomon, R. (2007). *True to our feelings*. Oxford: Oxford University Press.

Spitzer, R. (1999). Harmful dysfunction and the D.S.M. definition of mental disorder. *Journal of Abnormal Psychology, 108*, 430–432.

Stroebe, M. & Schut, H. (2005–2006). Complicated grief: A conceptual analysis of the field. *Omega, 52*, 53–70.

Stroebe, M., Gergen, M., Gergen, K., & Stroebe, W. (1996). Broken hearts or broken bonds? In Klass D., Silverman P., & Nickman S. (Eds.), *Continuing bonds: New understandings of grief* (pp. 31–44). Philadelphia: Taylor & Francis.

Wakefield, J. (1992a.). The concept of mental disorder: On the boundary between biological facts and social value. *American Psychologist, 47*, 373–388.

Wakefield, J. (1992b.). Disorder as harmful dysfunction: A conceptual critique of D. S. M.-III-R's definition of mental disorder. *Psychological Review, 99*, 232–247.

Wakefield, J. (1993). Limits of operationalization: A critique of Spitzer and Endicott's (1978) proposed operational criteria for mental disorder. *Journal of Abnormal Psychology, 102*, 160–172.

Wakefield, J. (1999). Evolutionary versus prototype analyses of the concept of disorder. *Journal of Abnormal Psychology, 108*, 374–399.

Walter, T. (2006). What is complicated grief? A social constructionist answer. *Omega: The Journal of Death and Dying, 52*, 71–79.

Wilkinson, S. (2000). Is "normal grief" a mental disorder? *Philosophical Quarterly, 50,* 289–304.

Wilson, D. (1993). Evolutionary epidemiology: Darwinian theory in the service of medicine and psychiatry. Reprinted in Baron-Cohen, S. (Ed.) (1997) *The maladapted mind* (pp. 39–56). Hove: Psychology Press.

3 The concept of complicated grief

Lessons from other cultures

Paul C. Rosenblatt

Psychiatric diagnostic categories and psychiatric standards for what is normal and healthy and what is not are saturated with the standards of Western culture (Caplan, 1985; Charmaz & Milligan, 2006; Fabrega, 1987). Psychiatry created its standards, perspectives, and vocabulary out of the language, ideas, values, and social forms of Western culture. Psychiatry focuses on emotions, beliefs, intentions, impulses, and actions that have no objective reality independent of culture (Fabrega, 1987).

Using the standards, perspectives, and vocabulary of one culture in order to make sense of the emotions, beliefs, intentions, impulses, and actions of people in other cultures is risky. Can we respectfully evaluate the healthiness and appropriateness of what people think, feel, say, and do without understanding what is healthy and appropriate in their own culture?

Grief scholars are not in full agreement about what constitutes complicated grief (Stroebe & Schut, 2005–2006). However, I believe the analysis offered here applies equally well to all conceptualizations of complicated grief as involving grief that goes on too long and too intensely or that is absent or very muted.

Typically writings about complicated grief do not say explicitly that what they say about complicated grief applies to people in all cultures. However, it seems to me that this standard pattern of psychological writing in which statements are not made about qualifications or limitations with regard to culture implies that the analysis offered applies universally. It may well be true that there are aspects of human psychology that are invariant across cultures, but with regard to emotions and concepts of normality versus pathology in expressing emotions there are reasons to think that a psychological language that makes it seem that all humans are the same can be misleading. There seems to me to be a claim of applicability to all humans inherent in writings that say "complicated grief is such-and-such and comes with these symptoms," when those writings offer no sense that there are limits coming from the culture and language of the people who were and were not studied. The perspective in this chapter is that the concept of complicated grief and research on complicated grief are grounded in a particular culture, and so we should be cautious about applying the work on complicated grief to people of other cultures. Also, to the extent that we all live in pluralistic societies, the caution would include a sense that, with regard to the people in our own society, the concept and clinical implications of complicated grief may apply only to some.

In some cultures the symptoms of complicated grief are not problematic

Wikan (1988) reported that in Cairo, Egypt, a bereaved mother whose grieving went on for years, with palpable suffering, muted depression, withdrawal, inactivity, and self-absorption, was seen as sane and making cultural sense. The parents of Israeli soldiers who died while serving in the military may grieve for decades, and in Israel that grief is honored and understandable (Malkinson & Bar-Tur, 2000). Charmaz and Milligan (2006) claimed that historically in the United States and Europe what is now seen as a problem, grief that is too intense over a very long time, was at one time seen as normal. Similarly, Stearns (1994) wrote that there was a time when middle-class people in the United States saw intense ongoing grief as more or less inevitable and laudable. Possibly the normality of what Charmaz and Milligan (2006) and Stearns (1994) wrote about was the normality of mourning, rather than of grief, if one can distinguish between the rituals of loss (mourning) and emotional expressions that are not part of rituals (grief). However, if they were writing mainly about grief, it is only in recent times that strong and enduring grief has been seen as a problem by middle-class people in the United States and Europe.

Cross-cultural variation in ideas about deviant grieving

There are indigenous notions of deviant grieving in many cultures. Sometimes the standards of other cultures resemble the standards implied in the diagnosis of complicated grief. For example, the Toraja of Indonesia are concerned about any bereaved person who does not adequately express feelings of grief (Hollan, 1992; Wellenkamp, 1988). The Ifaluk of Micronesia worry about any newly bereaved person who does not quickly get back to ordinary daily life after a good cry (Lutz, 1985). However, in some cultures, the standards for grief are at odds with the idea of complicated grief. The Balinese, for example, worry about a grieving person who does not present a happy and smooth outer appearance at all times following a loss (Wikan, 1990). In a number of cultures people might most commonly be concerned about a deviant grieving that might offend the spirit of the deceased or fail to help the spirit of the deceased appropriately.

In many cultures, people can be said to try to police or stop the deviant grieving of a person in their community. In Bali, grieving people who do not seem happy are cheered up by friends and relatives, teased, and told they should be happy (Wikan, 1990). From culture to culture the reasons for others to pressure a person who is grieving deviantly differ. In Bali, the pressure comes because people fear that a person who is overtly grieving is vulnerable to sorcery (Wikan, 1990). In another example of community reactions to deviant grieving, Maschio (1992) wrote about a widow on the island of New Britain who fought to continue her grieving for her husband when those who had the role of ending her public display of grieving tried to quiet her. She wanted to continue avoiding pork and wearing soot marks on her face and a loin cloth of her dead husband around her neck, but her resistance to ending her public display of grieving provoked anger in others, and she was scolded.

But then the concept of "deviance" is problematic. The concept of "deviance" presumes a clear set of standards for grieving. Yet in many societies there are multiple standards; for example, in Tana Toraja, Indonesia, Christian beliefs and standards of grieving coexist with indigenous beliefs and standards (Adams, 1993). In fact, a pattern of contradiction between earlier ways of grieving and more recent ones brought by outsiders is common around the world. Among the consequences of the multiplicity of standards is that there are many people in the world who know that however they grieve they will be judged deviant by the standards of some in their social environment. Consider the Maisin people of Papua New Guinea, living with the conflict between more recently adopted Christian standards for grieving and standards that antedate the Christian standards (Barker, 1985). By older standards, mourning for years after the death is proper (Barker, 1985), but by the newer, Christian standards, those activities may be inappropriate. One might look at the older pattern and say that it is in some sense more basically human; for example, it fits evidence that normal grief can be long term, even lifelong (Klass, Silverman, & Nickman, 1996). However, the traditional pattern, according to Barker, was not only about grief but about competition among widows, the relationships among kin groups, beliefs about regeneration following a loss, and other matters that are unrelated to continuing grief as described in the Klass, Silverman, and Nickman book. However, the oddity of the Maisin by Western standards still reinforces the idea that, in pluralistic societies where there are multiple and diverse standards by which to evaluate grieving, there are reasons to question labeling some pattern of grieving deviant and of concern.

Other problematic assumptions underlying the concept of complicated grief

From a cross-cultural perspective, there are a number of assumptions that I suspect are commonly made in writings about complicated grief that are worth making explicit. One that has already been discussed is the assumption that grief that goes on too long and too intensely is a problem in need of treatment. What other assumptions are there that may underlie the concept of complicated grief?

Assumption that someone's grief arises from a discrete, time-limited loss

It seems to me that one assumption about complicated grief, when there is a judgment that grief has gone on too long, is that there is a discrete point in time at which the loss can be said to occur. That point of time serves as the marker from which the duration of grieving can be measured, and duration matters in what I have seen of DSM-5 draft texts about grief. However, from a cross-cultural perspective, thinking in terms of grief arising at a discrete point in time is challenged by the experiences of people for whom a specific loss goes on continuously, occurs again and again, or is part of an ongoing series of losses. There are, for example, a number of North American native cultures that have experienced severe historical traumas, including near-genocide, mass sexual abuse, and the destruction of culture and the social and physical environment, and these losses have been spread over many years and continue (Brave Heart & DeBruyn, 1998; Tafoya & Del Vecchio, 2005). A diagnosis of complicated grief and treatment of complicated grief may well be usefully carried out without assessing that appropriateness of grief duration, but to the extent that grief duration is a factor in assessment, there could be situations in which, by the standards of some culture, it is a mistake to assume grief can be assessed, based on a discrete starting point.

Assumption that grieving in all cultures is rather the same

As was said above, the language of much that is written about complicated grief could be understood to imply that grieving in all cultures is more or less the same. If that is assumed, is it a reasonable assumption to make? There is considerable evidence that people deal with and talk about losses quite differently from one culture to another (Charmaz & Milligan, 2006; Currer, 2001; Rosenblatt, 2001; Wierzbicka, 2003).

Wierzbicka (2003) challenged the universality of grief, beginning with the observation that in her native Polish there is no term for *grief*. From her perspective, the English language gives a privileged position to grief, but it is a mistake to claim universality for grief on the basis of that. For her, the interesting question was not something like: When is grief too prolonged? It was: "Why should English have singled out the experience that it calls *grief* from the great ocean of human emotions as a subject of special attention and given it a distinct name?" (p. 582). Tracing the history of the English term *grief*, which used to mean other things than sorrow and pain over a death, she came to the idea that the English term *grief* developed as a culturally based idea that grief should be short term and should not interfere too much with one's pursuit of happiness (p. 584). This is in contrast to her native Poland, where she felt that there is a widespread belief that it is good and appropriate to mourn for a lifetime (Polish has a word for *mourning*) for great loss (p. 588). Implied in this is a sense she offered that, in English, "grief" disrupts normal life, but in some societies normal life is to feel sorrow and great pain, to mark that something terrible has happened (e.g., p. 592). So from her perspective not only does culture shape, limit, influence, define, and give meaning to grief, it also creates it or does not create it as a human emotion following loss. That I as an observer of Polish people who have experienced a loss may think I observe grief seems to me, if I understand Wierzbicka correctly, not to be relevant, since it is not what I observe but what they feel and how they put words to it that matters. That there is a word in Polish for *mourning* does not mean that a person who thinks and feels in Polish does not grieve, because I assume that Wierzbicka draws the standard distinction between *grief* as a matter of feeling and *mourning* as a culturally called for way of behaving after a loss. So Poles may mourn in ways that could look to an observer from a culture in which "grief" is part of the vocabulary as though they were grieving, but what they are doing and feeling may be rather different from grief.

Related to this, Klass (1999) indicated that there are a number of cultures in which people's concerns following a death seem to be about separating from and being protected from the deceased. Klass then argued that cultures differ in the meta-interpretative schemes that are engaged when a death occurs, and paying attention to those schemes we will find that there is not a single grief or mourning scheme that is dominant in all cultures.

Moreover, implied in the notion of complicated grief is the notion of something like recovery from grief. *Recovery* is a concept in Western culture; but in other cultures there may be no sense of recovery from grief and no sense that something like recovery is normal or desirable (Rosenblatt, 2008). From this perspective, is it a mistake to claim that "recovery" in bereavement is or should be a universal process? And then is it a mistake to impose the concept on people whose cultural background leads them to other values and processes than recovery from grief after a loss? And if complicated grief treatment with people from diverse cultures must be carried out with a diversity of desired outcomes, and not just "recovery" as a desired outcome, how are those diverse outcomes to be defined and assessed?

Assumption that the individual is what needs healing

Looking at prolonged or intense grief as a psychological problem may lead to ignoring or discounting what grieving people would say about their economic, political, or environmental challenges. Imagine that a Guatemalan widow whose husband has been assassinated by the military because he spoke out against injustices continues years after his death to show symptoms of complicated grief; and imagine that she says that her pain is in large part about the economic, political, and environmental system that oppresses poor Guatemalans. If we take her words seriously, she may not appreciate efforts to help her to move to a state in which her grief is less intense and dominates her life less. For her, the grief may be about ongoing injustices, and to lessen or turn away from the grieving may be a betrayal of important values. In cases like hers, focusing only on a psychological problem and not on the context and stated realities and desires of those we are trying to help might not be welcomed or respectful.

Cultural critique of the concept of complicated grief

The foregoing suggests a cultural critique of the concept of complicated grief, and along with it the concept of diagnostic categories, the psychologizing of problems that reflect problems in political and other larger systems, and the disenfranchisement of indigenous ways of understanding and dealing with loss. If we want to understand and help people from various cultures in ways that are most respectful and helpful, we need to examine the fit between their grieving and what is appropriate in their culture (Shapiro, 1996). If we know what the person's culture expects, reinforces, models, and offers as meaning we will understand not only what is appropriate but also reasons why it is appropriate; for example, what a death such as the one for which the person is grieving means in that person's culture and what various ways of expressing emotion mean.

Arguably there are ways in which, by applying standards of a culture that is not that of the client or not the only one of the client, diagnosis and treatment can be harmful. Some critics of contemporary mental health diagnosis and treatment that is not culturally attuned have raised the question of whether there is policing linked to the concept of complicated grief and treatment for it (Foote & Frank, 1999; Walter, 1999, 2005). The critics who assert that policing goes on in the area of bereavement have written that one reason for such policing may be that bereavement that goes on too long or too intensely is not what employers want. They also raised questions about the possibility that focus on the bereaved individual takes the focus of potential critics away from larger processes that may be responsible for a loss. For example, treating the widow of a U.S. soldier killed in Iraq in terms of complicated grief may take the focus away from the circumstances in U.S. politics that led to and maintained military involvement in Iraq. Inherent in this line of criticism is the idea that when diagnosis and treatment "police" the cultural and situational contexts of the person's grieving are ignored (Foote & Frank, 1999) and, to the extent that the policing is effective, the person accepts being defined in that way. Of course, from a culturally attuned perspective, one would also want to respect the realities of clinicians who provide good faith help to the bereaved. However, we must keep in mind the Foucauldian perspective, that therapy polices, in trying to understand the larger contextual forces that may push psychological treatment in some directions more than others.

A related line of criticism regarding possible cultural and situational insensitivity in mental health work can be found in Gone's (2008) remarks about "cultural proselytizing." Gone, writing about mental health work with American Indians, argued that there can be a kind of cultural imperialism in saying mental health language should be adopted by others. He asserted that promoting mental health discourse in work with American Indians could be seen as serving to silence critics of what the culture from which that discourse comes has done to American Indians. Related to that, Adelson (2008) pointed out how using a mental health language about psychological stress undermines, smothers, and diminishes discourse about the inequities and oppressions that led to the psychological stress. It becomes a mental health problem, not a problem of historical and current injustice. From that perspective, imposing a mental health view on people in cultures that arguably have been oppressed in some way by a dominant Western culture might be seen as a step toward silencing client critiques of that oppression. As Charmaz and Milligan (2006) asserted, ongoing, intense grief over injustices often provides strong motivation to people who are involved in protests and political action that aim to end political violence and injustices. We are legitimately in the business of helping people to deal with great psychological pain, but should not be in the business of suppressing efforts to change oppressive situations. So the clinician will have to be sensitive to issues of oppression while helping people with what seems to be complicated grief when that grief can be seen as stemming from oppressive situations.

Clients from many different cultures

In pluralistic societies (most countries on the planet), it is risky and seen by some as culturally disrespectful and unhelpful to impose the standards of one culture on people from other cultures. However, that is what seems to be going on if one takes the standards one culture has for emotional expression and pathologizes what people do who are from cultures with different standards. Fabrega (1987) made that point with regard to illness, and, to the extent that making complicated grief a DSM category makes complicated grief an illness, one can join Fabrega in raising questions about the appropriateness of applying one culture's standards to people from other cultures. Psychiatric diagnosis imposes a set of cultural meanings, and so psychiatric diagnosis across cultures always raises questions of validity (Good & DelVechio Good, 1986; Stroebe, Gergen, Gergen, & Stroebe, 1996; Watters, 2010). How can we be sure we are not reifying the diagnosing culture's ways of understanding, making them universally real when we know only that in their culture of origin they have reality standing? Claims of universal biological or psychological processes may be made to support the universalistic application of psychiatric diagnoses, but those claims can also be understood as culturally based. It is risky to use theories grounded primarily in a single culture as a basis for prescriptive assertions from and claims by experts rooted in that culture that there is sure, universal knowledge about what is normal and good bereavement and what is a problem in need of help (Small & Hockey, 2001).

One might argue that the complicated grief framework is well supported by evidence, but the evidence and its interpretation are culturally saturated. As someone who has tried to carry out research in a number of cultures, I believe that there is no psychological research method that is not saturated with the assumptions, ways of thinking, beliefs, and values of a specific culture. From that perspective it can be argued that there is not validity in an objective sense for cross-cultural applicability of research findings, just a claim of validity. For example, the primary way of assessing complicated grief involves a questionnaire, not a culturally sensitive interview. That the questionnaire can be translated into the languages of other cultures and produce similar results does not mean the questions have validity across cultures and does not mean the questions are attuned at all to cultural realities in these other cultures. In fact, the very act of translating the questions is fraught with cultural complexities. In areas of emotion and psychology, things do not translate well. There is not a standard cross-cultural way for experiencing feelings or putting feelings into words (Kirmayer, 2005). So it is difficult to know what people's answers to translated questionnaires mean to them. Writing as though there are human universals in experience, expression, thought, feeling, and communication is a rhetorical form and a statement of belief, but ignoring other realities does not make them go away. Possibly any psychological research on humans must rest on assumptions that can be questioned from some perspectives, and projects assessing grief with paper and pencil measures certainly make such assumptions (e.g., Small, 2001). If there is a cultural component to reading and answering questions and writing questions and interpreting answers, I have not seen research on complicated grief that accounts for those cultural processes. If it is assumed that the answers to questions are true and can be interpreted without problems, that, I think, is a mistake.

Everyone I know who works to help grieving people seems to me to be well intentioned, but there can be dark sides to efforts to curtail mourning. Redmond (2008), for example, wrote about the pressure from the Australian Ministry of Health on indigenous Australians to abandon or shorten their mourning periods, with the explicit goal of making them more ready for work in the mainstream economy. So the message may be that "we care about your pain," but it also is that "we want you to be available to work and to be off the dole." Related to this, Pratt (1994) showed how intolerant businesses in the United States are of grieving, giving an average of 3 days of bereavement leave to grieving employees. Pratt argued that such intolerance of grieving does not reflect culture so much as it shapes and drives it. From the perspective of the work of Redmond and Pratt, the form of complicated grief treatment that reflects these larger economic issues would seem to be treatment of grief that goes on too long and too intensely.

As a number of social critics who write about grief have pointed out, there has been a movement in the United States, and other societies where Western medicine has a strong influence, toward constructing grief as a disease instead of an emotion (Averill & Nunley, 1988; Charmaz & Milligan, 2006; Foote & Frank, 1999; Walter, 2005), and that pushes grief into the domain of the medical model. Among the many critics of the medical model, the model that makes distress and social difficulties into illnesses to be treated, are critics who see the model as a tool of social control, as defining people's reactions to injustice as illness, as defining sane reactions to insane situations as insane, as imposing one culture's realities on people whose cultures give them quite different realities, and as silencing people who protest against government and corporate harm-doing by labeling them as needing therapy. From that perspective we must be very careful not to become part of the problem in using a medical model of individual distress.

People in one culture can be changed by people from another culture, especially if the people in the latter culture have economic and political power. Consider the power in the mental health area of U.S. and European-based drug companies and the U.S. and European medical establishment, a power that comes with dominance in research funding and publication, considerable power in medical school and postgraduate medical education, and power to shape public policy. That power affects the research that is published and becomes a knowledge base for people of all cultures, affects what is taught to medical students in all cultures, and affects the power of U.S. and European drug companies to market their products worldwide. So there are many people around the world who now seem to accept the U.S. medical model of how people express a wide range of distress (Watters, 2010). The changes are both in expert opinion and practice and in how ordinary people in the culture think, feel, and act (Watters, 2010). Efforts to change a culture can work, and we can see that in the history of changing cultural standards and practices in the United States for grief (Stearns, 1994). The medical model for dealing with bereavement, like the medical model for other forms of distress, has become central to the ways that many people around the world think about grief and how they make meanings and channel their concerns. Thus, these people may define personal grief that goes on too long or too intensely as a problem in need of treatment, and thus they may accept a diagnosis of complicated grief and the treatment that follows such a diagnosis. That does not mean the medical model is universally valid or that the concept of complicated grief has meaning in all cultures. However, it does mean that, within certain cultural contexts, complicated grief can be said to be real. From that perspective, an important task in research on complicated grief is to be able to distinguish people for whom a complicated grief diagnosis is meaningful and respectful from people for whom such a diagnosis is inappropriate.

Therapeutic treatment for bereavement has an important and valuable place for people whose cultural perspectives make such treatment meaningful and desirable. However, for clinicians who want to work with bereaved people, the argument in this chapter is that a checklist of symptoms and the definitiveness of a universal categorization of some forms of grieving as normal and others as complicated and in need of therapy must be used with caution. There must be a genuine openness to the realities, perspectives, cultures, social situations, and understandings of each person. Two people with the same checklist score may well be in need of very different attention because of the realities, meanings, and so on in which their responses are embedded. Clinical work must then rely on the hallowed clinical traditions of listening and understanding. The clinician must learn and work with the realities of the client, because it is the client's realities, not the therapist's realities, that are key to understanding what is going on and providing help.

Cultural formulation

DSM-IV included what has been labeled as "cultural formulation" (American Psychiatric Association, 1994), which includes the injunction to attend to culture. For example, there is this in the section on anxiety disorders:

> Culturally prescribed ritual behavior is not in itself indicative of Obsessive–Compulsive Disorder unless it exceeds cultural norms, occurs at times and places judged inappropriate by others of the same culture, and interferes with social role functioning . . . Mourning may lead to an intensification of ritual behavior that may appear to be an obsession to a clinician who is not familiar with the cultural context. (American Psychiatric Association, 1994, p. 420)

The passages like that in DSM-IV do not say how to assess a person's cultural background, how a "norm" is to be assessed, whether the concept of "norm" makes sense for all clients, and what to do clinically once the cultural background is known. Moreover the DSM-IV cultural formulation gives mixed messages about what to do with cultural information. For example, there is this caution about being too attuned to culture in a discussion of major depressive episodes: "It is . . . imperative that the clinician not routinely dismiss a symptom merely because it is viewed as the 'norm' for a culture" (p. 324). Also, the cultural material in DSM-IV that enjoins sensitivity to culture is typically a few sentences surrounded by many paragraphs written as though culture were irrelevant and there were an unambiguous and clearly known truth regarding the disorder that would apply in all cultures. For example, following a statement that points out that the norms for duration of bereavement vary across cultures the next sentence is "The diagnosis of Major Depressive Disorder is generally not given unless the symptoms are still present 2 months after the loss" (p. 684), with no sense of how the previous sentence might relate to this one. Appendix I (pp. 843–844) of DSM-IV offers a brief outline of what to assess culturally, but I do not see in it enough help to assess well or to translate what is learned into clinical decisions and actions. In fact the cultural formulation was added rather late in the creation of DSM-IV and without much work at integrating it into the rest of the volume (Mezzich, 2008).

Since the publication of DSM-IV in 1994, there has been a great deal of development in mental health specialties (including those working with bereavement) of a literature base, workshops, and training programs to produce greater cultural sensitivity. However, arguably there is still a tension in mental health fields between the idea that diagnosis and treatment must be tailored to culture and the idea that the same diagnostic and treatment research and language apply to everyone.

I imagine that the editors of DSM-5 will go further than those for DSM-IV in acknowledging the situational and cultural relativity of the DSM diagnostic classification system. First steps have been taken to develop the field beyond the mere injunction to be culturally sensitive, for example a guide to cultural formulation assessments (e.g., Rohlof, 2008). The dual-process model (Stroebe & Schut, 1998) is one way to account flexibly for cultural differences in grieving. However, based on my own admittedly unrepresentative and subjective experience, the DSM cultural formulation cautions are yet to become a universal and well-integrated part of practice and scholarship. I hope that this chapter and this volume will help us to move toward the day when the leading edge of scholarship and clinical practice on complicated grief will provide rich examples of how to work with the complexities of people's cultural situations. One must also expect that efforts to move toward greater cultural sensitivity will have a rational and deliberative quality but will also involve struggle. As one example of such struggle, DSM-5 apparently will remove the bereavement exclusion from the section on major depressive disorders, and a number of reputable grief scholars have written in opposition to that removal (Balk, Noppe, Sandler, & Werth, 2011) on grounds that could be understood to say that removal of the bereavement exclusion is harmful for all people. One can see in the clash of views differences in ideas of what is culturally sensitive, and one can also see an area in which there will be contentious debate. However, we should not shy away from such debate. Ideally it is in such debate that we learn from each other, ideas are clarified, and in the end the people we serve benefit.

References

Adams, K. M. (1993). The discourse of souls in Tana Toraja (Indonesia): Indigenous notions and Christian conceptions. *Ethnology, 32*, 55–68.

Adelson, N. (2008). Discourses of stress, social inequities and the everyday worlds of First Nations women in a remote northern Canadian community. *Ethos, 36*, 316–333.

American Psychiatric Association. (1994). *Diagnostic and statistical manual of mental disorders* (4th edn.). Washington, DC: American Psychiatric Association.

Averill, J. R., & Nunley, E. P. (1988). Grief as an emotion and as a disease: A social-constructionist perspective. *Journal of Social Issues, 44*(3), 79–95.

Balk, D. E., Noppe, I., Sandler, I., & Werth, J., Jr. (2011). Removing the exclusionary criterion about depression in cases of bereavement: Executive summary of a report to the ADEC board of directors. *ADEC Forum, 37*(2), 24–26.

Barker, J. (1985). Missionaries and mourning: Continuity and change in the death ceremonies of a Melanesian people. *Studies in Third World Cultures, 25*, 263–294.

Brave Heart, M. Y. H., & DeBruyn, L. M. (1998). The American Indian holocaust: Healing historical unresolved grief. *American Indian and Alaska Native Mental Health Research, 8*(2), 60–82.

Caplan, P. J. (1985). *They say you're crazy: How the world's most powerful psychiatrists decide who's normal*. Reading, MA: Addison-Wesley.

Charmaz, K., & Milligan, M. J. (2006). Grief. In Stets, J. E., & Turner, J. H. (Eds.), *Handbook of the sociology of emotion* (pp. 516–543). New York: Springer.

Currer, C. (2001). Is grief an illness? Issues of theory in relation to cultural diversity and the grieving process. In Hockey, J., Katz J., & Small, N. (Eds.), *Grief, mourning and death ritual* (pp. 49–60). Philadelphia: Open University Press.

Fabrega, H., Jr. (1987). Psychiatric diagnosis: A cultural perspective. *Journal of Nervous and Mental Disease, 175*, 383–394.

Foote, C. E., & Frank, A. W. (1999). Foucault and therapy: The disciplining of grief. In Chambon, A. S., Irving, A., & Epstein, L. (Eds.), *Reading Foucault for social work* (pp. 157–176). New York: Columbia University Press.

Gone, J. P. (2008). Introduction: Mental health discourse as western cultural proselytization. *Ethos, 36*, 310–315.

Good, B. J., & DelVechio Good, M.-J. (1986). Cultural context of diagnosis and therapy: A view from medical anthropology. In Miranda, M. R., & Kitano, H. H. L. (Eds.), *Mental health research and practice in minority communities: Development of culturally sensitive training programs* (pp. 1–27). Washington DC: U.S. Dept. of Health and Human Services, Pub. No. (ADM) 86-1466.

Hollan, D. W. (1992). Emotion, work and value of emotional equanimity among the Toraja. *Ethnology, 31*, 45–56.

Kirmayer, L. (2005). Culture, context and experience in psychiatric diagnosis. *Psychopathology, 34*, 192–196.

Klass, D. (1999). Developing a cross-cultural model of grief: The state of the field. *Omega, 39*, 153–178.

Klass, D., Silverman, P. R., & Nickman, S. L. (Eds.). (1996). *Continuing bonds: New understandings of grief*. Washington, DC: Taylor & Francis.

Lutz, C. (1985). Depression and the translation of emotional worlds. In Kleinman, A., & Good, B. (Eds.), *Culture and depression* (pp. 63–100). Berkeley: University of California Press.

Malkinson, R., & Bar-Tur, L. (2000). The agony of grief: Parents' grieving of Israeli soldiers. *Journal of Personal and Interpersonal Loss, 5*, 247–261.

Maschio, T. (1992). To remember the faces of the dead: Mourning and the full sadness of memory in southwestern New Britain. *Ethos, 20*, 387–420.

Mezzich, J. E. (2008). Cultural formulation: Development and critical review. In Mezzich, J. E., & Caracci, G. (Eds.), *Cultural formulation: A reader for psychiatric diagnosis* (pp. 87–92). Lanham, MD: Jason Aronson.

Pratt, L. (1994). Business temporal norms and bereavement behavior. In Fulton, R., & Bendiksen, R. (Eds.), *Death and identity* (3rd edn., pp. 263–287). Philadelphia: Charles Press.

Redmond, A. (2008). Time wounds: Death, grieving and grievance in the Northern Kimberly. In Glaskin, K., Tonkinson, M., Musharbash, Y., & Burbank, V. (Eds.), *Mortality, mourning and mortuary practices in indigenous Australia* (pp. 69–86). Burlington, VT: Ashgate.

Rohlof, H. (2008). The cultural interview in the Netherlands: The cultural formulation in your pocket. In Mezzich, J. E., & Caracci, G. (Eds.), *Cultural formulation: A reader for psychiatric diagnosis* (pp. 203–213). Lanham, MD: Jason Aronson.

Rosenblatt, P. C. (2001). A social constructionist perspective on cultural differences in grief. In Stroebe, M. S., Hansson, R. O., Stroebe, W., & Schut, H. (Eds.), *Handbook of bereavement research: Consequences, coping, and care* (pp. 285–300). Washington, DC: American Psychological Association Press.

Rosenblatt, P. C. (2008). Recovery following bereavement: Metaphor, phenomenology, and culture. *Death Studies, 32*, 6–16.

Shapiro, E. (1996). Family bereavement and cultural diversity: A social developmental perspective. *Family Process, 35*, 313–332.

Small, N. (2001). Theories of grief: A critical review. In Hockey, J., Katz, J., & Small, N. (Eds.), *Grief, mourning and death ritual* (pp. 19–48). Philadelphia: Open University Press.

Small, N., & Hockey, J. (2001). Discourse into practice: The production of bereavement care. In Hockey, J., Katz, J., & Small, N. (Eds.), *Grief, mourning and death ritual* (pp. 97–124). Philadelphia: Open University Press.

Stearns, P. N. (1994). *American cool: Constructing a twentieth century emotional style.* New York: New York University Press.

Stroebe, M., Gergen, M., Gergen, K., & Stroebe, W. (1996). Broken hearts or broken bonds? In Klass, D., Silverman, P. R., & Nickman, S. L. (Eds.), *Continuing bonds: New understandings of grief* (pp. 31–44). Washington, DC: Taylor & Francis.

Stroebe, M., & Schut, H. (1998). Culture and grief. *Bereavement Care, 17*(1), 7–11.

Stroebe, M., & Schut, H. (2005–2006). Complicated grief: A conceptual analysis of the field. *Omega, 52*, 53–70.

Tafoya, N., & Del Vecchio, A. (2005). Back to the future: An examination of the Native American holocaust experience. In McGoldrick, M., Giordano, J., & Garcia-Preto, N. (Eds.), *Ethnicity and family therapy* (3rd edn., pp. 55–63). New York: Guilford.

Walter, T. (1999). *On bereavement: The culture of grief.* Philadelphia: Open University Press.

Walter, T. (2005). What is complicated grief? A social constructionist perspective. *Omega, 52*, 71–79.

Watters, E. (2010). *Crazy like us: The globalization of the American psyche*. New York: Free Press.

Wellenkamp, J. C. (1988). Notions of grief and catharsis among the Toraja. *American Ethnologist, 15*, 486–500.

Wierzbicka, A. (2003). Emotion and culture: Arguing with Martha Nussbaum. *Ethos, 31*, 577–600.

Wikan, U. (1988). Bereavement and loss in two Muslim communities: Egypt and Bali compared. *Social Science and Medicine, 27*, 451–460.

Wikan, U. (1990). *Managing turbulent hearts: A Balinese formula for living*. Chicago: University of Chicago Press.

4   On achieving clarity regarding complicated grief

Lessons from clinical practice

Therese A. Rando

Without trying to be humorous, *complicated grief is quite complicated*. Its causes, forms, risk factors, comorbid conditions, associated elements, and treatment requirements can differ markedly among individuals.

The purpose of this chapter is to elucidate complicated grief in adults through lessons imparted from clinical practice. Focusing upon complicated grief as both a *distinct diagnostic entity* as well as a *clinical phenomenon*, it is apparent that some confusion and lack of clarity exists. After addressing several controversial issues and the diversity of its forms, it is suggested that the field move toward operationalizing a definition of complicated grief and establishing a generic comprehensive conceptual model for it.

Before proceeding, a small but important clarification is necessary. Elsewhere, I argue strongly for the benefits of distinguishing *grief* from *mourning* and identify problems resulting when this is not done (Rando, 1993, 2012). Although I wholeheartedly maintain these assertions regarding the importance of discriminating between these two terms, out of respect for this volume's editors and for easier communication within this particular book, I have temporarily adopted its terminology. Consequently, for this chapter, I use *grief* to mean the reactions one has to loss and *grieve* to refer to what one does over time to cope with it and its consequences.

Where are we now regarding complicated grief?

Historically, professional understanding of complicated grief has suffered from a lack of consensus regarding definition, different theoretical conceptualizations, obscurity of criteria differentiating normal from complicated grief, and confusion regarding issues of comorbidity (Stroebe et al., 2000). Further, imprecise terminology, methodologically deficient studies, and missing operationalizations held sway. Yet, despite these handicaps, there is still much that can be said about complicated grief today.

In the last few decades, there has been a significant increase in research and clinical investigation into complicated grief. A great amount of attention to it swirls around the debate over including a complicated grief disorder in the next edition of the *Diagnostic and Statistical Manual of Mental Disorders* (5th edn.;

DSM-5; American Psychiatric Association, forthcoming; currently due in 2013) and, if so, what the diagnostic criteria should be. Two major proposals have been offered by Horowitz and associates (Horowitz et al., 1997) and Prigerson and colleagues (Prigerson et al., 1999).

The latter group has amassed the most empirical support for its proposed disorder, now termed *prolonged grief disorder* (PGD). As described by Prigerson, Vanderwerker, and Maciejewski (2008), those with PGD are essentially stuck in a state of chronic mourning characterized by significant separation distress marked by intense yearning for the deceased and ruminative or intrusive thoughts about the loss. Other associated symptoms may include difficulty accepting the death, anger or bitterness over it, and personal traumatization and diminishment because of it. In its wake, there is dysfunction in one or more important areas of life, trouble trusting others, and difficulty moving on with life, which is perceived to be empty and meaningless now and in the future.

Although there is impressive research documenting the usefulness of PGD (see Prigerson et al., 2008, for a review), arguments for it are not without their share of criticism (e.g., Hogan, Worden, & Schmidt, 2004; Rubin, Malkinson, & Witztum, 2008; Stroebe et al., 2000). It takes only a cursory review of the literature or a superficial discussion with certain clinicians to see clearly that great passion and extremely spirited debate are often generated by its proposed inclusion. I contend that much of this comes from a lack of clarity about both PGD and complicated grief.

Complicated grief as a distinct diagnostic entity

Reviewing the professional literature and listening to the self-reports of practitioners, it appears that the vast majority of clinicians in the United States, and many others elsewhere, would heartily endorse a diagnostic category for complicated grief. There have been many public calls for development of such a distinction (e.g., Hartz, 1986; Horowitz, Bonanno, & Holen, 1993; Jacobs, 1993; Prigerson & Jacobs, 2001; Rando, 1993), as well as countless private ones. Nevertheless, concerns have been raised as to potential negative ramifications of such a category (e.g., Rubin, Malkinson, & Witztum, 2008; Stroebe et al., 2000).

Despite some measure of agreement regarding the need for a DSM category for complicated grief, there is significantly less consensus regarding what specifically should compose it. Arguably, the main controversy within contemporary grief literature arises around PGD, given that it is the predominant set of diagnostic criteria proposed. It is also here where some significant mischaracterization occurs.

Regarding PGD as a diagnostic entity for complicated grief

Despite desires for a complicated grief disorder diagnosis, many are reluctant to embrace PGD. They perceive the syndrome to be valid as far as it goes in describing a select group of mourners with attachment-related issues, but view it as being too restrictive to be as useful as needed for a complicated grief disorder category.

They see it as unsuitable for encompassing the myriad ways they know complicated grief is manifested. In other words, they believe the syndrome accurately pertains, but only for a subset of complicated grievers.

In the fray of the debate over the appropriateness of PGD for inclusion into the DSM, it appears two errors are made repeatedly. First, there is misinterpretation of what PGD actually represents. Second, there is overfocus upon it to the detriment of fully appreciating the complexity of complicated grief and developing a comprehensive conceptual model for it.

The fallacy of PGD as "equivalent" to complicated grief

In examining empirical and clinical literature regarding PGD, one more often than not finds a grave mistake: There is an equation of PGD with complicated mourning. Yet *equate* means *make equal* and the reality is that complicated grief is *more* than just PGD, thus not equivalent to it. This *great equation myth*, as I term it, is not only inaccurate, but harmful. It is harmful because some people assume that PGD is the sole way a mourner exhibits complicated grief. Should he or she manifest something different, it may not be recognized as the complication in bereavement that it, in fact, signals. Appropriate intervention may not take place and inaccurate pathologization can occur. Rejection of this myth is the basis for many people's inability to accept PGD.

The fact is that the developers of PGD have put it forth as just one form of complicated grief disorder. These originators have explicitly specified that "focus . . . on PGD is *not* [italics added] intended to imply that this disorder is the *only* [italics added], or even the *primary* [italics added], complication that may follow from bereavement" (Prigerson et al., 2008, p. 173). However, far too many professionals have mistaken PGD as equal to complicated grief as opposed to being one representation of it.

Even experienced researchers and clinicians have equated the two. For example, in a 2009 special article for *World Psychiatry*, "Grief and Bereavement: What Psychiatrists Need to Know," the respected researchers Zisook and Shear write about complicated grief as "the current designation for a syndrome of prolonged and intense grief . . . [in which] bereaved individuals . . . find themselves in a repetitive loop of intense yearning and longing" (Zisook & Shear, 2009, pp. 67–69). Here and in the rest of the article, it is clear the authors are referring to PGD. They make statements about complicated grief, yet describe PGD specifically. And they do this even though they include in that same article a discussion of grief-related major depressions, with such depressions identified as a complication of bereavement. In other words, although Zisook and Shear equate complicated grief with PGD, they actually disprove that very point once they discuss grief-related major depression, since that indicates *ipso facto* that complicated grief has other forms as well. PGD simply cannot be equivalent to complicated grief since there is obviously more to complicated grief than just PGD.

Zisook and Shear are by no means the only ones to make this equation and to fail to mention that there are other forms besides it. A brief survey of empirical studies addressing PGD reveals that this happens fairly often. The findings of such researchers are not being questioned here. The sole issue is their not distancing themselves from the great equation. Researchers and writers who permit PGD to represent all of complicated grief – as opposed to just a single form of it – are perpetuating an untruth and doing a disservice. Simple phrases such as "PGD is one form of complicated grief" or "As one example of complicated grief, we examined PGD" would clearly convey that complicated grief can be manifested in other ways. This could go a long way in defusing the source of much conflict regarding PGD.

The bottom line is that we must accurately appreciate what PGD is and what it is not. What it is is a distilled set of grief symptoms that reliably and accurately predict enduring distress and dysfunction (H. Prigerson, personal communication, February 4, 2011). It is just *one* of a number of forms of complicated grief, not the only one. (Others will be discussed below.) It is also an excellent example of what today's research can reveal. However, it does *not* represent all of complicated grief, and cannot legitimately be equated to it. The plain truth – recognized by the proposers of PGD but not necessarily by those who have supported them – is that plenty of people with complicated grief do not have PGD. To only look at complicated grief in that one fashion is to eliminate a huge proportion of those with complications in their bereavement. The subtype must not be mistaken for the overarching category.

Complicated grief as a clinical phenomenon

We can learn much about complicated grief from clinical practice, which helps illustrate that it is more complex than could be encompassed by just one presentation (e.g., PGD). Below, I discuss what clinical practice reveals about its forms and functions, after first addressing a controversial issue.

What about discrepancies between clinical observation and empirical investigation?

In several areas, discrepancies have been identified between what has been reported in the clinical literature about complicated grief and what has been demonstrated empirically (e.g., Bonanno, Boerner, & Wortman, 2008). This seems particularly relevant regarding treatment efficacy, the existence of certain syndromes, and the predictive validity of various risk factors. In each domain, clinical observation has sometimes come to conclusions that have not been supported empirically (at least not yet). What does this mean? Should we cast aside clinical observations made repeatedly through the years by solid clinicians because it conflicts with or is unsupported by empirical studies? Yet, is it not true that many clinicians had been operating according to some "myths" we now know empirically to be untrue (see Wortman & Silver, 2001)?

In this age of emphasis on empiricism, we ought not dismiss what clinical practice has taught, but must not accept it uncritically either. For the benefit of the bereaved, we must strive to find ways to integrate the best of both ways of knowing. To do so, it helps to understand why such differences exist. I would suggest that one explanation stems from the sometimes discrepant foci of clinicians and researchers. These not only give each group different viewpoints, but can yield apparently differing conclusions. (Although I speak of differences here, it is with awareness that some are both clinician and researcher, as well as that both groups share a common goal to understand and assist in bereavement.)

Let us look at treatment efficacy as an example. In general, clinicians writing about their observations of complicated grief contend with individuals who are self-referred, seen relatively late in bereavement, and present for tertiary prevention intervention – all of which factors are associated with more effective treatment outcome (Schut & Stroebe, 2005). Further, this population is often seen in individual treatment over a period of time. Clinicians have seen treatment work with this population they serve, and have written about complicated grief from that perspective.

In contrast, bereavement researchers typically deal with another group, which includes not only the aforementioned grievers clinicians typically see, but others as well. I submit that these others, outside the subset seen by clinicians, are the source for most of the discrepancies. As reported in a meta-analysis of bereavement outcome studies by Neimeyer and Currier (2009), these other grievers were not self-referred (they were solicited or outreached); were not specifically indicated for therapy (they were not complicated grievers, but merely people who had suffered loss or were at risk for problems); and received interventions often quite different from those delivered by clinicians, which transpired in relatively time-limited formats, after a variety of recruitments (i.e., aggressive outreach and media and community advertising were included), and within group sessions lacking a therapy focus.

It is not surprising that researchers' conclusions vary at times from their clinical colleagues, given that they have essentially been dealing with two different areas of focus within the same population; clinicians tend in general to deal with a subset of the grief spectrum (i.e., those with complications), whereas researchers in general deal with the entire spectrum (i.e., those with and without complications). This is why research is specifically mandated with complicated grievers, in order to see whether the clinical observations derived from work with them are empirically supported.

Three other factors might explain some of the inconsistencies sometimes found between clinical practice and research findings: equating measures of distress with complicated grief, failure to get beyond merely looking at symptoms to evaluate underlying grief processes, and overgeneralization of clinicians' beliefs.

Amount of distress does not always portend complications in grief processes. Although there certainly is a correlation between distress and complicated grief, one can be in great pain on some measures – especially after the loss of a healthy, close, and warm relationship – but still move on to grieve healthily. Currently, we tend to measure symptoms of distress, but not underlying grief processes. Thus, in the exemplary Changing Lives of Older Couples Study, Carr (2008) found increased yearning and anxiety after the death of a spouse who had been confi-dante and helpmate. She felt this challenged the longstanding clinical observa-tion that those losing spouses after conflicted marriages had more complications. However, this could well be an artifact of looking at symptoms only and not grief processes as well. In other words, it is only natural that there would be more distress when losing a close and warm relationship as opposed to losing a strained one. The more relevant issue is whether that actually translated into complicated grief processes because of it.

To my knowledge, Carr inferred complicated grief by the symptoms that were present, and not by any measurement of the griever's engagement in grieving processes per se. I would contend that one can be enormously distressed by the loss of a spouse yet, because of not having the conflictual issues a person with a strained marriage would have, could move forward to grieve without complica-tions. This is because grieving is not just about having symptomatic reactions, but about what one does to cope with and adapt to the loss that stimulated those reactions, as well as managing those reactions themselves.

Unfortunately, this was unable to be empirically tested because we currently lack sufficient ability to measure grief processes per se – in fact, as observed below, we have not even agreed upon what they might be – and only have measures of symptoms. This speaks to the need for our field to take steps to operationalize grieving, develop instruments to assess it, and not rely so heavily on assessment of symptoms exclusively. Further, it underscores the necessity to better differenti-ate conceptually between acute grief reactions to loss and processes undertaken to cope with and adapt to that loss (see Rando, 1993, 2012). Too often they are confounded.

Finally, we sometimes see discrepancies because some people have mischar-acterized clinicians' assumptions. They overlook clinicians' focus on the idiosyn-cratic situation of the griever, and mistakenly portray them as holding absolute and universal expectations (e.g., "Everyone has to express great emotion"), which, of course, is easily disproved and taken as clinical error. In fact, wise clinicians do not maintain such universal views. Rather, the issue is: Are particular grievers, with their own idiosyncratic factors operating, expressing whatever there is they need to express, how they need to express it, and when? Their perspective flows from meeting the needs of the griever, not from a universal expectation that eve-ryone has to express great emotion. Those criticizing clinical wisdom often fail to appreciate this, overstate what many clinicians believe, and then claim to debunk "myths" that many do not hold.

Four forms of complicated grief

In clinical practice, we find that complicated grief manifests in a variety of forms. This coincides with the conclusion that "complicated grief is not a single syndrome" (Stroebe, Hansson, Schut, & Stroebe, 2008, p. 6) and echoes the diversity of clini-cal presentations found in the literature (for reviews, see Bowlby, 1980; Jacobs, 1993; Middleton, Raphael, Martinek, & Misso, 1993; Parkes & Weiss, 1983;

Rando, 1993; Raphael, 1983). Synthesizing the literature regarding outcomes of loss, Rando (1993) identified four different types of presentation for complicated grief: symptoms, syndromes, diagnosable mental or physical disorders, and death.

Recognizing that not all adversity subsequent to a death stems directly from it, and to avoid false positives, Rando (2003) specified two criteria for presentations to be indicative of complicated grief: They must have developed or significantly worsened since the death in question, and must be associated with some compromise, distortion, or failure of some normal grief process(es). When one or both criteria are absent, the manifestations cannot be construed as a type of complicated grief (e.g., they may be comorbid with but independent of it, such as depression from unrelated problems).

Complicated grief symptoms

> John's wife died of breast cancer at 33. It took John 8 years, one divorce, and two therapists before he realized that he was furious at his God for taking his wife and at himself for being unable to protect her. In the interim, John had complicated grief that manifested through extreme death anxiety and a pattern of overreaction to experiences entailing separation and loss.

In this form of complicated grief, the mourner experiences some psychological, behavioral, social, or physical symptoms of distress, disability, dysfunction, pathology, or loss of freedom. Although inadequate in terms of number, intensity, duration, or type to meet criteria for any of the other three forms of complicated grief, these symptoms accompany a compromise, distortion, or failure in one or more of the normal processes of grief. For a list of symptoms constituting clinical indicators of complicated grief, see Rando (1993). To my knowledge, complicated grief symptoms as a form of complicated grief per se have not been subjected to empirical study yet.

Complicated grief syndromes

> Jacqueline's estranged husband and three friends were on a fishing trip when their boat capsized. No bodies were found. After a period of shock, she commenced 9 years of "floating" through life, feeling disconnected, chronically bewildered and confused, going from job to job and relationship to relationship, anxious and always awaiting another loss to befall her.

Complicated grief symptoms can coalesce into any of eight complicated grief syndromes. Seven of them are identified in the clinical literature: absent grief

(Deutsch, 1937; Bowlby, 1980); delayed grief (e.g., Raphael, 1983); inhibited grief (e.g., Raphael, 1983); distorted grief (of the extremely angry and guilty types; Raphael, 1983); conflicted grief (Parkes & Weiss, 1983); unanticipated grief (Parkes & Weiss, 1983); and chronic grief (Bowlby, 1980; Parkes & Weiss, 1983). The eighth syndrome is PGD, which has been empirically derived as cited above and is described as a type of chronic grief.

Empirical investigation of PGD has been mentioned earlier. Only some of the other syndromes have been researched, and even then minimally. The literature "indicates that minimal or absent grief reactions are very prevalent, whereas delayed grief reactions are quite rare" (Bonanno et al., 2008, p. 290). According to Stroebe et al. (2008), "chronic (or prolonged) grief has been generally well accepted as a pathological category, whereas delayed, inhibited, and absent grief remain the subject of much debate" (p. 8). Despite this, chronic and absent grief have been well explained by the dual process model of coping with bereavement (DPM; Stroebe & Schut, 2010). To the extent that the unanticipated grief syndrome is associated with traumatic bereavement, there has been more research (for reviews, see Armour, 2006; Pearlman, Wortman, Feuer, Farber, & Rando, in press).

Diagnosable mental or physical disorder

At 25 years old, Carl came to therapy at the suggestion of family concerned by his increasing sadness. He had dropped out of a stellar sophomore year in college, following the death of his girlfriend. Afterwards, he held a series of low-level, dead-end jobs before moving back with his parents. Now, Carl meets diagnostic criteria for a major depressive disorder.

Without warning, Gisele's husband informed her he had been having an affair. Furious because she did not "understand," he drove straight into a tree, killing himself instantly. Gisele grieved little and demonstrated few changes in behavior. Eleven months later, she was referred for psychotherapy by a physician alarmed by her development of severe colitis.

Investigations into morbidity after loss consistently show that bereavement can cause much suffering, associated with severe consequences to health and well-being (Stroebe, Schut, & Stroebe, 2007). It has been axiomatic in the field since the classic Institute of Medicine Study that bereaved individuals are at increased risk for physical and mental illness (Osterweis, Solomon, & Green, 1984). Recent long-term studies corroborate this (e.g., Jones, Bartrop, Forcier, & Penny, 2010).

In terms of complicated grief specifically, research into PGD (and forerunners) found it associated with heightened risk of both mental and physical impairments

(Prigerson et al., 2008). When complicated grief is examined in terms of mental health, there have been remarkably consistent findings that it can result in psychiatric disorders, particularly along the depressive and anxiety spectrums (e.g., Middleton et al., 1993; Raphael, Minkov, & Dobson, 2001; Stroebe, Schut, & Stroebe, 2007).

Death

Giorgio's father impulsively killed himself when it was discovered he had embezzled his client's money to cover gambling debts. At 34, Giorgio immediately moved back to his hometown with his own family to care for his bereaved mother. Wracked with shame and rage, he began to drink. Fifteen years later, Giorgio died in an alcohol-related one-car crash.

Complicated grief can be manifested in death that is consciously chosen (i.e., suicide). This coincides with research identifying it as a risk factor for completed suicide (Luoma & Pearson, 2002) and suicidality (Latham & Prigerson, 2004). Further, death resulting from complicated grief-related behavior can be subintended or unintended (Rando, 1993), stemming from the griever's behavior (e.g., car crash from drunk driving, as illustrated above, or neglect of health care).

Two functions of complicated grief

Clinical practice suggests two functions served by complicated grief: avoidance and connection (Rando, 1993). Given the variability among grievers and their situations, these may be the only elements consistent across all types of complicated grief.

> In all forms of complicated [grief], the mourner attempts to do two things: (a) deny, repress, or avoid aspects of the loss, its pain, and the full realization of its implications for the mourner and (b) hold on to and avoid relinquishing the lost loved one. These attempts, or some variation thereof, are what underlie and cause complications in the . . . processes of [grief]. (Rando, 1993, p. 149)

There is much in the literature corroborating this. Numerous researchers have documented the critical role of avoidance in complicated grief, including Parkes (1987), who identified it as being evident in all kinds of "atypical" grief he encountered, as well as numerous others who pinpoint avoidance as a central feature associated with complicated grief (e.g., Boelen & van den Bout, 2010; Shear, 2010; Stroebe, Boelen, et al., 2007).

The griever's holding on to the deceased (also known as maintaining continuing bonds) has been the focus of much discussion and research (e.g., Boelen, Stroebe, Schut, & Zijerveld, 2006; Field & Filanosky, 2010; Rubin, 1999). There

have been enough findings confirming associations with complicated grief to justify further investigations to identify under which conditions continuing bonds is
adaptive and under which conditions it is not.

Next steps

Current knowledge regarding complicated grief suggests two next steps to clarify
it and further its development: operationalizing its definition and developing a
comprehensive conceptual model for it.

An operationalized definition

A very surprising fact about complicated grief is how many definitions of it are
remarkably non-specific. A well-regarded definition illustrates this below, presented with one for "grief," upon which it rests:

> Grief is the term applied to the primarily emotional (affective) reaction to the
> loss of a loved one through death . . . it also incorporates diverse psychologi-
> cal . . . and physical . . . manifestations. (Stroebe et al., 2008, p. 5)

> Complicated grief . . . [is] a clinically significant deviation from the (cultural)
> norm . . . in either (a) the time course or intensity of specific or general symp-
> toms of grief and/or (b) the level of impairment in social, occupational, or
> other important areas of functioning. (p. 7)

Both definitions describe, but do not operationalize. It is clear that complicated
grief constitutes a derailing of normal grief, but exactly what is being derailed is
unclear. First and foremost, this leaves the field of grief relatively confused about
the overly abstract object of our attention. Without explicitly delineated ways
hypothesized to actualize its functioning and delineate its processes, how can we
as a field accurately communicate, describe, compare, contrast, treat, and research
grieving that is complicated? How do we know what it entails or if we are referring to the same thing? It seems unscientific to be defining the phenomenon in
such vague and nebulous terms. Complicated grief begs to be concretized not only
so we can ensure we are all talking about the same situation, but so it can be put
to empirical investigation. Understanding of complicated grief and, ultimately,
assistance to the bereaved are fundamentally best served by an accurate definition
identifying its hypothesized underlying processes in testable terms.

There are other reasons to move toward operationalizing complicated grief.
Missing an operationalized delineation of what is hypothesized as necessary to
grieve healthily, clinicians lack a framework for specifically what to promote and/
or intervene in to transform complicated into uncomplicated grief. Researchers
lack definitive elements to investigate.

Furthermore, abstract definitions mean clinicians operate without clear-cut
criteria against which to evaluate a person's grieving status. This knowledge of
where a person is relative to hypothesized processes underlying healthy grieving

is one of three basic areas to consider to appreciate any griever's responses properly. The others are the 43 sets of factors influencing grief reactions (psychological, social, and physical; Rando, 2012) and current levels of functioning. Such multidimensional determinants are in line with Middleton et al.'s (1993) assessment that "Grief is being viewed increasingly as a complex and evolving process, requiring the use of a multidimensional model" (p. 60) and support their prognostication: "It seems unlikely that pathological grief will become a unitary concept. Instead, future research will likely adopt a multidimensional framework" (ibid.).

Precisely because reactions are so relative, multiply determined, and idiosyncratic, complicated grief cannot be determined merely by presence or absence of specific symptoms alone. We know that symptoms indicate complicated grief only when we take them into account given the situation of *this* person, dealing with *this* loss, at *this* time, under *these* circumstances, and then evaluate them in light of where that person is in relation to hypothesized processes of healthy grieving. A particular symptom present in concert with healthy grieving is not necessarily indicative of complicated grief, but the same one in the absence of healthy grieving could be. The clinical question should be: Is the griever, given the context of his or her own unique grief situation, doing what is necessary to grieve healthily?

Obviously, to answer this question it is necessary to operationalize what is hypothesized as required to grieve healthily. There have been notable attempts to do this, including Stroebe and Schut's (1999) DPM, Worden's (2009) four tasks, and Rando's (1993, 2012) six "R" processes. These last are: Recognize the loss; React to the separation; Recollect and re-experience the deceased and the relationship; Relinquish the old attachments to the deceased and the old assumptive world; Readjust to move adaptively into the new world without forgetting the old; and Reinvest. They are employed here to exemplify how a complicated grief definition potentially could be operationalized: *Complicated grief is present whenever, considering the idiosyncratic situation of the griever and his or her current functioning, there is some compromise, distortion, or failure of one or more of the six "R" processes of grieving.*

Such a definition permits consideration of the multidimensional elements in the griever's idiosyncratic situation, plus evaluation of that person in relation to a standard set of hypothesized operationalized grief processes that can be recognized, measured, and manipulated.

A comprehensive conceptual model

A subsequent step in developing complicated grief is to construct a generic comprehensive conceptual model for it. Rubin, Malkinson, and Witztum (2008) have argued that the multidimensional complexity of complicated grief demands recognition of an array of responses, not the restricted set associated with PGD. Further, any model must be robust enough to encompass the varieties of complicated grief presentations. Despite insufficient empirical backing at this point, there is simply too much clinical history and support to dismiss non-PGD forms of complicated grief (e.g., delayed or inhibited), which "make considerable theoretical and clinical sense . . . and would seem to merit inclusion [within a spectrum of complicated grief]" (Stroebe & Schut, 2005–2006, p. 66).

It appears that a generic comprehensive conceptual model of complicated grief should account for eight elements: its idiosyncratic nature; explanatory theories; the coping driving it; integral issues and current functioning associated with it; its functions; its forms; and hypothesized operationalized processes. Although it would be premature to consider proposing other DSM diagnoses of complicated grief to expand its scope beyond PGD, it is not premature to start discussing models incorporating such elements. They could serve as springboards for research that ultimately would bring such diagnoses into existence. Along the way, they could aid thanatologists in appreciating relationships between all types of bereavement complications, their etiologies, and their presentations, while providing researchers with specific variables to investigate.

I believe that numerous advantages would accrue from such a model. Primarily, it would avoid the reductionism that has obfuscated the complexity of complicated grief. Multiple influencing factors would be considered (e.g., attachment style, culture, death characteristics); bereavements with and without trauma could be incorporated; complicated grief displaying as mental and/or physical disorders would be contained; subclinical manifestations would not be overlooked; diverse theoretical conceptualizations could offer explanations (e.g., psychoanalytic, attachment, trauma/stress, constructivist); and associated integral issues would be included (e.g., relationship with the deceased, meaning making, resource deficiencies). Importantly, it would recognize different routes to the common pathway of grieving process complications. So, for example, complicated grief signaled by inability to adapt could be due to any number of things (not solely attachment problems per PGD), such as personal traumatization secondary to the death circumstances, social disenfranchisement, excessive guilt, dynamics of child loss, or failure to make meaning, among other possibilities. Such crucial stimulants of complicated grief would be given their due and could be targeted for treatment and research.

Conclusion

To achieve currently needed clarity on complicated grief, it appears necessary to appreciate it as both a distinct diagnostic category and a clinical phenomenon; grasp the realities of PGD; understand complicated grief's forms and functions; operationalize its definition; and develop a comprehensive conceptual model for it. Elements of such a model that might provide more lucidity are put forth here for discussion and research. Others are invited to do similarly. Hopefully, such actions stimulate meaningful discourse and research in the field and add to the understanding and treatment of the richly complex experience of complicated grief.

Bibliography

American Psychiatric Association. (forthcoming). *Diagnostic and statistical manual of mental disorders* (5th edn.). Washington, DC: Author.

Armour, M. (2006). Violent death: Understanding the context of traumatic and stigmatized grief. *Journal of Human Behavior in the Social Environment, 14*, 53–90.

Boelen, P., & van den Bout, J. (2010). Anxious and depressive avoidance and symptoms of prolonged grief, depression, and post-traumatic stress disorder. *Psychologica Belgica, 50*, 49–67.

Boelen, P., Stroebe, M., Schut, H., & Zijerveld, A. (2006). Continuing bonds and grief: A prospective analysis. *Death Studies, 30*, 767–776.

Bonanno, G., Boerner, K., & Wortman, C. (2008). Trajectories of grieving. In Stroebe, M., Hansson, R., Schut, H., & Stroebe, W. (Eds.), *Handbook of bereavement research and practice: Advances in theory and intervention* (pp. 287–307). Washington, DC: American Psychological Association.

Bowlby, J. (1980). *Attachment and loss: Vol. 3. Loss: Sadness and depression.* New York: Basic Books.

Carr, D. (2008). Factors that influence late-life bereavement: Considering data from the Changing Lives of Older Couples Study. In Stroebe, M., Hansson, R., Schut, H., & Stroebe, W. (Eds.), *Handbook of bereavement research: Advances in theory and intervention* (pp. 417–440). Washington, DC: American Psychological Association.

Deutsch, H. (1937). Absence of grief. *Psychoanalytic Quarterly, 6*, 12–22.

Field, N., & Filanosky, C. (2010). Continuing bonds, risk factors for complicated grief, and adjustment to bereavement. *Death Studies, 34*, 1–29.

Hartz, G. (1986). Adult grief and its interface with mood disorder: Proposal of a new diagnosis of complicated bereavement. *Comprehensive Psychiatry, 27*, 60–64.

Hogan, N., Worden, J., & Schmidt, L. (2004). An empirical study of the proposed complicated grief disorder criteria. *Omega, 48*, 263–277.

Horowitz, M., Bonanno, G., & Holen, A. (1993). Pathological grief: Diagnosis and explanation. *Psychosomatic Medicine, 55*, 260–273.

Horowitz, M., Siegel, B., Holen, A., Bonanno, G., Milbrath, C., & Stinson, C. (1997). Diagnostic criteria for complicated grief disorder. *American Journal of Psychiatry, 154*, 904–910.

Jacobs, S. (1993). *Pathologic grief: Maladaptation to loss.* Washington, DC: American Psychiatric Press.

Jones, M., Bartrop, R., Forcier, L., & Penny, R. (2010). The long-term impact of bereavement upon spouse health: A 10-year follow-up. *Acta Neuropsychiatrica, 22*, 212–217.

Latham, A., & Prigerson, H. (2004). Suicidality and bereavement: Complicated grief as psychiatric disorder presenting greatest risk for suicidality. *Suicide and Life-Threatening Behavior, 34*, 350–362.

Luoma, J., & Pearson, J. (2002). Suicide and marital status in the United States, 1991–1996: Is widowhood a risk factor? *American Journal of Public Health, 92*, 1518–1522.

Middleton, W., Raphael, B., Martinek, N., & Misso, V. (1993). Pathological grief reactions. In Stroebe, M., Stroebe, W., & Hansson, R. (Eds.), *Handbook of bereavement: Theory, research, and intervention* (pp. 44–61). New York: Cambridge University Press.

Neimeyer, R., & Currier, J. (2009). Grief therapy: Evidence of efficacy and emerging directions. *Current Directions in Psychological Science, 18*, 352–356.

Osterweis, M., Solomon, F., & Green, M. (Eds.). (1984). *Bereavement: Reactions, consequences, and care.* Washington, DC: National Academy Press.

Parkes, C. (1987). *Bereavement: Studies of grief in adult life* (2nd edn.). Madison, CT: International Universities Press.

Parkes, C., & Weiss, R. (1983). *Recovery from bereavement*. New York: Basic Books.

Pearlman, L., Wortman, C., Feuer, C., Farber, C., & Rando, T. (in press). *Treating traumatic bereavement: Intervening with survivors of sudden death*. New York: Guilford Press.

Prigerson, H., & Jacobs, S. (2001). Traumatic grief as a distinct disorder: A rationale, consensus criteria, and a preliminary empirical test. In Stroebe, M., Hansson, R., Stroebe, W., & Schut, H. (Eds.), *Handbook of bereavement research: Consequences, coping, and care* (pp. 613–645). Washington, DC: American Psychological Association.

Prigerson, H., Shear, M., Jacobs, S., Reynolds, C., Maciejewski, P., Davidson, J., et al. (1999). Consensus criteria for traumatic grief: A preliminary empirical test. *British Journal of Psychiatry, 174*, 67–73.

Prigerson, H., Vanderwerker, L., & Maciejewski, P. (2008). A case for inclusion of prolonged grief disorder in DSM-V. In Stroebe, M., Hansson, R., Schut, H., & Stroebe, W. (Eds.), *Handbook of bereavement research and practice: Advances in theory and intervention* (pp. 165–186). Washington, DC: American Psychological Association.

Rando, T. (1993). *Treatment of complicated mourning*. Champaign, IL: Research Press.

Rando, T. (2003). Public tragedy and complicated mourning. In Lattanzi-Licht, M., & Doka, K. (Eds.), *Living with grief: Coping with public tragedy* (pp. 263–274). Washington, DC: Hospice Foundation of America.

Rando, T. (2012). *Coping with the sudden death of your loved one: Self-help for traumatic bereavement*. Indianapolis, IN: Dog Ear Publishing.

Raphael, B. (1983). *The anatomy of bereavement*. New York: Basic Books.

Raphael, B., Minkov, C., & Dobson, M. (2001). Psychotherapeutic and pharmacological intervention for bereaved persons. In Stroebe, M., Hansson, R., Stroebe, W., & Schut, H. (Eds.), *Handbook of bereavement research: Consequences, coping, and care* (pp. 587–612). Washington, DC: American Psychological Association.

Rubin, S. (1999). The two-track model of bereavement: Overview, retrospect and prospect. *Death Studies, 23*, 681–714.

Rubin, S., Malkinson, R., & Witztum, E. (2008). Clinical aspects of a DSM complicated grief diagnosis: Challenges, dilemmas, and opportunities. In Stroebe, M., Hansson, R., Schut, H., & Stroebe, W. (Eds.), *Handbook of bereavement research and practice: Advances in theory and intervention* (pp. 187–206). Washington, DC: American Psychological Association.

Schut, M., & Stroebe, M. (2005). Interventions to enhance adaptation to bereavement. *Journal of Palliative Medicine, 8*, S140–S147.

Shear, M. (2010). Exploring the role of experiential avoidance from the perspective of attachment theory and the dual process model. *Omega, 61*, 357–369.

Stroebe, M., Boelen, P., van den Hout, M., Stroebe, W., Salemink, E., & van den Bout, J. (2007). Ruminative coping as avoidance: A reinterpretation of its function in adjustment to bereavement. *European Archives of Psychiatry and Clinical Neuroscience, 257*, 462–472.

Stroebe, M., Hansson, R., Schut, H., & Stroebe, W. (2008). Bereavement research: Contemporary perspectives. In Stroebe, M., Hansson, R., Schut, H., & Stroebe, W. (Eds.), *Handbook of bereavement research and practice: Advances in theory and intervention* (pp. 3–25). Washington, DC: American Psychological Association.

Stroebe, M., & Schut, H. (1999). The dual process model of coping with bereavement: Rationale and description. *Death Studies, 23*, 1–28.

Stroebe, M., & Schut, H. (2005–2006). Complicated grief: A conceptual analysis of the field. *Omega, 52*, 53–70.

Stroebe, M., & Schut, H. (2010). The dual process model of coping with bereavement: A decade on. *Omega, 61*, 273–289.

Stroebe, M., Schut, H., & Stroebe, W. (2007). Health outcomes of bereavement. *The Lancet, 370*, 1960–1973.

Stroebe, M., van Son, M., Stroebe, W., Kleber, R., Schut, H., & van den Bout, J. (2000). On the classification and diagnosis of pathological grief. *Clinical Psychology Review, 20*, 57–75.

Worden, J. (2009). *Grief counseling and grief therapy* (4th edn.). New York: Springer.

Wortman, C., & Silver, R. (2001). The myths of coping with loss revisited. In Stroebe, M., Hansson, R., Stroebe, W., & Schut, H. (Eds.), *Handbook of bereavement research: Consequences, coping, and care* (pp. 405–429). Washington, DC: American Psychological Association.

Zisook, S., & Shear, K. (2009) Grief and bereavement: What psychiatrists need to know. *World Psychiatry, 8*, 67–74.

5 On the nature and prevalence of uncomplicated and complicated patterns of grief

Kathrin Boerner, Anthony D. Mancini, and George Bonanno

Complicated grief has been variously defined, but most theorists understand it as a form of grief characterized by persistent, intense longing and yearning for the deceased (separation distress), intrusive thoughts or images, emotional numbness, anger or guilt related to the loss, a sense of emptiness, and reactivity in response to cues (e.g., Horowitz et al., 1997; Prigerson, 2004; Shear, Frank, Houck, & Reynolds, 2005). At the same time, persons with complicated grief often avoid people and places they associate with the loss, because of the intense distress those reminders evoke. Thus, complicated grief tends to involve a vacillation between an anxious preoccupation with and an avoidance of memories of the deceased. In addition, complicated grievers commonly have difficulty redefining themselves (Mancini & Bonanno, 2006), and often experience difficulties forming satisfying new relationships or engaging in potentially rewarding activities.

To understand complicated grief, it is first necessary to be familiar with the distinction between complicated and uncomplicated forms of grief. Although there are at this point some defined criteria for what constitutes complicated grief, such definitions are largely lacking for grief patterns that are normative and do not warrant a complicated grief diagnosis. Only one pattern has traditionally been considered as normal grief (a period of distress followed by recovery). Variations from this response pattern, such as consistent minimal distress following bereavement, were suspected to be pathological in nature (i.e., inhibited or absent grief) and most likely to result in another version of pathological grief: delayed grief.

These traditional ways of thinking about grief were heavily influenced by clinical observation and a very limited empirical database. Our understanding of grief has increased tremendously following large-scale studies with prospective longitudinal data that include data from before the death to years after the loss, allowing the full range of possible grief patterns to emerge. The purpose of this chapter is to delineate different pathways of grieving that to date have been well established empirically, as well as describing how these pathways have revolutionized our understanding of different types of grief response.

Historical background

The earliest taxonomies of individual differences in grief reaction were based primarily on clinical observation or on data sets based on psychiatric samples. Not surprisingly, the earliest models of bereavement outcome focused primarily on the distinction between normal and abnormal or pathological forms of grieving. Using these models, bereavement scholars pondered the question of what constitutes a normal grief course. In addition, they focused attention on the possible role played by avoidant or defensive processes in delaying the onset of grief.

One of the earliest comparative descriptions of normal and pathological forms of grieving came from Parkes's (1965) ground-breaking study of bereaved psychiatric patients. Parkes distinguished three types of pathological grief reaction: chronic grief, inhibited grief, and delayed grief. Bowlby (1980) later echoed this taxonomy to propose disordered forms of mourning that could be arrayed along a single conceptual dimension. Anchoring one end of the continuum was *chronic mourning*. At the other end, Bowlby placed the *prolonged absence of conscious grieving* (p. 138). He maintained that those showing an absence of conscious grieving "may appear to be coping splendidly" (p. 153) but are often tense and short-tempered, with tears just below the surface. Bowlby believed that physical symptoms (e.g., headaches and heart palpitations) were also common in this group, and that, sooner or later, many of those who consciously avoid grieving become depressed, often in response to a subsequent, more minor loss.

Based on the evidence available at the time, Raphael (1983) also proposed a number of "morbid or *pathological* patterns of grief" (p. 59). These included chronic, unresolved grief reactions as well as the *absence of grief* in which "the grieving affects or mourning process may be totally absent, partially suppressed, or inhibited" (p. 60). Like Bowlby, she noted that some bereaved people seem to cope remarkably well, and often carry on "as if nothing had happened." Although she acknowledged that such responses "may be seen as evidence of strength and coping by many" (p. 205), she too argued that in most cases they were actually markers of psychopathology.

In 1984, the Institute of Medicine released a report summarizing the state-of-the-art knowledge about bereavement. The report concluded that the death of a loved one produced a "near universal occurrence of intense emotional distress . . . with features similar in nature and intensity to those of clinical depression" (Osterweis, Solomon, & Green, 1984, p. 18). The report also concluded that "absent grief" was a "pathological" form of mourning that "represents some form of personality pathology" and that "persons who show no evidence of having begun grieving" should receive "professional help" (p. 65). Several years later, Middleton, Moylan, Raphael, Burnett, and Martinek (1993) surveyed an international sample of researchers, theorists, and clinicians working in the field of bereavement. A compelling majority of these experts endorsed the idea that "absent grief" was a pathological grief reaction that usually stemmed from denial or inhibition of the normal grief reaction. This response was almost always viewed as maladaptive in the long run.

But is this really the case? When people experience relatively mild or short-lived grief reactions, should this be considered atypical or pathological? Wortman and Silver (1989) noted that there was no convincing empirical evidence to support this assertion. More recently, Bonanno and colleagues (e.g., Bonanno, 2004,

2005) have argued that many bereaved people show a clear resilience in the face of loss. At the other end of the spectrum, it might also be questioned whether psychopathology observed during bereavement should always be interpreted as an abnormal grief reaction. Might not at least some of the chronic dysfunction be attributed to an enduring emotional disturbance that pre-dates the loss? In the following sections, we review the evidence regarding the prevalence of different patterns of grief, with a particular focus on evidence for the experience of intense distress following the death of a loved one, as well as for delayed grief and chronicity in poor adjustment to bereavement.

Grief trajectories

Among people who have faced the loss of a loved one, is it true that distress is commonly experienced? Will distress or depression emerge at a later date among those who fail to exhibit distress in the first several weeks or months following the loss? We identified several studies that provide information bearing on these questions. Most of these studies focused on the loss of a spouse (Boerner, Wortman, & Bonanno, 2005; Bonanno & Field, 2001; Bonanno, Keltner, Holen, & Horowitz, 1995; Bonanno, Moskowitz, Papa, & Folkman, 2005; Bonanno et al., 2002; Lund et al., 1985–1986; Vachon et al., 1982; Zisook & Shuchter, 1986), with several of these examining response to loss following a time of caregiving for a chronically ill loved one (Aneshensel, Botticello, & Yamamoto-Mitani, 2004; Bonanno et al., 2005; Chentsova-Dutton et al., 2002; Li, 2005; Schulz, Mandelson, & Haley, 2003; Zhang, Mitchell, Bambauer, Jones, & Prigerson, 2008). A few studies examined reactions to the death of a child (Bonanno et al., 2005; Wijngaards-de Meij et al., 2008; Wortman & Silver, 1993). These studies assessed depression or other forms of distress in the early months following the death, and then again anywhere from 13 to 60 months after the loss. The construct of depression/distress was operationalized differently in the different studies. For example, some studies utilized the Symptom Checklist-90 (SCL-90) depression subscale and/or Diagnostic and Statistical Manual of Mental Disorders (DSM)-based Structured Clinical Interview (SCID; e.g., Bonanno et al., 2005); other studies such as the Changing Lives of Older Couples Study (CLOC) used the Center for Epidemiologic Studies Depression Scale (CES-D; e.g., Bonanno et al., 2002). For each study, the investigators determined a cut-off score to classify respondents as high or low in distress or depression.

The longitudinal studies identified here provide evidence regarding the prevalence of different patterns of grief. The pattern that was traditionally considered to be "normal" grief (moving from high distress to low distress over time) was found among 41% of participants in a study on loss of a child from sudden infant death syndrome (SIDS; Wortman & Silver, 1987), and anywhere between 9% and 41% in studies on conjugal loss (see Wortman & Boerner, 2011, for a review). Furthermore, in these studies, evidence for "minimal" or "absent" grief (scoring low in distress consistently over time) was found for 26% in the SIDS study, and for anywhere between 41% and 78% in the studies on loss of a spouse (Wortman

& Boerner, 2011). Taken together, these studies provided evidence that different patterns of grief can typically be found in response to different types of losses (e.g., death of a spouse or child); that what was traditionally viewed as a "normal" pattern of grief is never experienced by a majority, in some cases even only by a minority; and that the absence of intense distress is not at all an uncommon phenomenon. However, none of these studies had a prospective design spanning from the time before the loss to the time after. Thus, the ability to capture trajectories of distress was rather limited.

This limitation was overcome in more recent prospective studies. In the CLOC study on conjugal loss, which assessed older adults 3 years before and up to 18 months after the loss (Bonanno et al., 2002; Bonanno, Wortman, & Nesse, 2004), nearly half of the participants (46%) experienced low levels of distress consistently over time and were labeled "resilient." Only 11% showed so-called "common" grief. Another trajectory in this study referred to as "depressed–improved" reflected elevated distress before the loss and improvement after the loss (10%). A similar pattern of reduced distress levels following the loss was detected in prospective studies that included both pre- and post-loss data on caregivers of dementia patients (Aneshensel et al., 2004; Schulz et al., 2003; Zhang et al., 2008), as well as on caregiver samples that included a variety of illnesses (Li, 2005). In two of these studies (Aneshensel et al., 2004; Zhang et al., 2008), only about 17% showed a pattern of distress reflecting "common" grief following the death. Moreover, Aneshensel and colleagues observed a pattern of stable but low distress (64%) and absent distress (11%) in a majority of their participants, and Zhang and colleagues found persistently absent depression in about half of their sample.

Taken together, in all studies, less than half of the sample showed what traditionally was considered normal grief. In the methodologically more advanced prospective studies described above, such a reaction was even shown by only a small minority of respondents. In fact, in the CLOC study on conjugal loss (Bonanno et al., 2002), the relatively small proportion of those who showed the pattern of moving from high distress to low distress over time was almost equal to those who showed a depressed–improved pattern of being more distressed before the loss, followed by improvement after the loss. Most importantly, however, the available evidence shows that "minimal" grief is very common. The number of respondents failing to show elevated distress or depression at the initial or final time point was sizable, ranging from one quarter of the sample to more than three quarters of the sample. In fact, in the available prospective studies that included data from before and after the death, the resilient trajectory consistently emerged for at least half of the sample. Similarly, a comparison of non-bereaved and bereaved individuals (who lost either a child or a spouse; Bonanno et al., 2005) showed that, in terms of distress levels, slightly more than half of the bereaved did not significantly differ from the matched sample of non-bereaved individuals when assessed at 4 and 18 months post loss.

It should be noted that labels such as "minimal" grief mean not an absence of distress after the loss, but rather that, despite brief spikes in distress (Bonanno et al., 2005) or a short period of daily variability in well-being (Bisconti, Bergeman,

& Boker, 2006), people with these patterns had generally managed to function at or near their normal levels (Bonanno, 2005). The prevalence of the "minimal" grief reaction alone calls into question the assumption that failure to show distress following a loss is pathological. In fact, it suggests that understanding why so many people do not exhibit significant distress following a loss should become an important research priority.

Evidence for delayed grief

Does the failure to display overt grief and sadness predispose a person to a "delayed" grief reaction or later health problems? The data from the longitudinal studies we identified fail to support this view. In two studies, there were no respondents showing a delayed grief reaction (Bonanno & Field, 2001; Zisook & Shuchter, 1986). In the remaining studies, the percentage of respondents showing delayed grief ranged from 0.02% to 5% (Wortman & Boerner, 2011, for a review), indicating that if delayed grief does occur it is exceedingly rare. Nor do physical symptoms appear to emerge among those who fail to experience distress soon after the loss. Both the Boerner et al. (2005) and Bonanno and Field (2001) studies are convincing on this point, because conjugally bereaved individuals were assessed over a 4- and 5-year period, respectively, using multiple outcome measures. Similar findings emerged in a study by Middleton and colleagues. Based on cluster analyses of several bereaved samples, the authors concluded that there was no evidence for delayed grief (Middleton, Burnett, Raphael, & Martinek, 1996). Nonetheless, in the previously described survey conducted by Middleton et al. (1993), a substantial majority of researchers and clinicians (76.6%) indicated that delayed grief does occur.

Evidence for chronicity

Empirical evidence suggests that, whereas most bereaved individuals do not seem to experience intense distress for extended periods of time, a significant minority of people develop long-term difficulties. In each of the longitudinal bereavement studies mentioned previously, for example, a pattern of persistent distress or "chronic grief" emerged. This pattern of chronic grief was found among 30% of participants who lost a child from SIDS (Wortman & Silver, 1987), and anywhere between 8% and 26% of the conjugally bereaved (Wortman & Boerner, 2011, for a detailed review). Recent caregiving studies have found similar percentages for the chronic grief trajectory among bereaved caregivers (ranging from 8% to 17%; e.g., Aneshensel et al., 2004; Zhang et al., 2008).

In our prospective work on conjugal loss (Bonanno et al., 2002), the availability of pre-loss data made it possible to further distinguish two types of chronic distress. Although chronically elevated depressive symptoms during bereavement were evidenced by 23% of the sample, these participants formed two distinct trajectories. One trajectory, constituting 16% of the sample, suggested an unambiguous chronic grief reaction. These participants manifested low levels of depression prior to the loss but then showed elevated depression at 6 and 18 months of bereavement. A second smaller group, constituting 8% of the sample, had markedly elevated depression prior to bereavement and then showed only a slight increase and remained depressed during bereavement. Both groups had higher levels of grief-specific symptoms (e.g., yearning) measured at 6 and 18 months of bereavement than all other participants, and did not differ from each other in their level of grief symptoms. However, as we discuss below, additional data suggested that one of these trajectories represented a relatively pure chronic grief reaction whereas the other pattern was more representative of a pre-existing chronic depression.

Most classic grief theorists (e.g., Jacobs, 1993) discuss the notion of chronic grief but fail to indicate how long it typically lasts and whether it abates at some point. To address this issue, we conducted a follow-up analysis investigating whether the chronic grievers and the chronically depressed would remain distressed up to 48 months post loss (Boerner et al., 2005). Overall, the chronic grief group experienced an intense and prolonged period of distress but, by the 48–month time point, the grief of this group did resolve. In contrast, the chronically depressed group clearly demonstrated long-term problems, with little indication of improvement between 18 and 48 months. This group not only showed the poorest adjustment 4 years after the loss but also struggled the most with questions about meaning. These differential findings for the chronic grief and depression group underscore the need to further refine the criteria used to identify those who are at risk for long-term problems.

Are these grief trajectories veridical, or are they merely arbitrary distinctions? More recently, Mancini, Bonanno, and Clark (2011) examined grief trajectories using latent growth mixture modeling. This approach allows bereavement trajectory patterns to emerge in a non-arbitrary and purely empirical manner, addressing critical limitations of prior approaches. The authors used a panel data set of over 16,000 German citizens followed for over 20 years that included pre-loss measures of functioning. This analysis revealed a four-trajectory solution that mirrored the prototypical outcome trajectories to a surprising degree. What emerged were resilient (58.7%), chronic post-loss distress (21.3%), chronic pre- and post-loss distress (14.6%), and improved (5.4%) trajectories. These analyses offered important confirmatory support for the trajectory patterns described earlier, indicating that there are complicated and uncomplicated (or resilient) patterns of response following a loss.

Predictors of grief trajectories

A variety of contextual, situational, and person-centered factors can potentially contribute to whether a person displays a complicated or uncomplicated grief trajectory (Bonanno, 2004; Mancini & Bonanno, 2009). However, because relatively few studies have identified trajectories of bereavement and even fewer have used pre-loss data, our understanding of these factors is still somewhat limited. Nevertheless, extant research has identified factors that are associated with each of the trajectory patterns discussed earlier. Next we discuss these predictors.

Resilience

There is consistent evidence across studies that resilient individuals are generally unlikely to have a history of prior mental health problems or to show any other signs of dysfunction in their lives (e.g., Bonanno, Boerner, & Wortman, 2008; Wortman & Boerner, 2011, for a review). For example, an examination of pre-bereavement measures in the CLOC study (Bonanno et al., 2002) showed that, prior to the spouse's death, this group did not have conflicted or low-quality marital relations with the spouse, nor were they ambivalent about or excessively dependent on the spouse. They also did not evidence extreme scores on any of the personality measures included in the study such as extraversion or emotional stability. Rather, participants in the resilient group scored higher than other participants on several pre-loss measures suggestive of resilience-promoting factors that would better prepare them for coping with the impeding loss. For example, they reported relatively high levels of instrumental support, and scored higher than other participants on questionnaire measures of belief in a just world and acceptance of death. Overall, it seemed that participants in the resilient group were able to cope with their loss in a very positive way (Bonanno et al., 2004). They were better able than other participants to gain comfort from talking about or thinking about the spouse. For example, they were more likely than other bereaved people to report that thinking about and talking about their deceased spouse made them feel happy or at peace. They had low scores on avoidance/distraction, suggesting that their lack of distress is indicative of good adjustment rather than defensive denial. They also reported the fewest regrets about their behavior with the spouse, or about things they may have done or failed to do when he or she was still alive. Finally, participants in the resilient group were less likely to try to make sense of or find meaning in the spouse's death. Thus, they did not engage in any type of ruminative thought about the loss.

Improvement during bereavement

By definition, and in contrast to the stable low depression and resilient groups, the improved participants were highly depressed prior to the loss. However, it is not necessarily clear that this reflects a history of prior mental health problems. Rather, evidence from different studies suggests that behind the scenes of a depressed–improved trajectory one is likely to find serious illness and a demanding caregiving situation. As mentioned above, this trajectory has been found to be the most dominant pattern in caregiving and bereavement studies (e.g., Schulz et al., 2003). Similarly, Bonanno and colleagues (Bonanno et al., 2002) found that virtually all the participants in the depressed–improved group had been contending with a seriously ill spouse at the time of the pre-bereavement interviews. This was an elderly sample and illness among the spouses was not uncommon. However, no other group was so clearly characterized by spousal illness as the improved group.

Given the demands and burden of providing care to a seriously ill person, it is unsurprising that this group also showed a relatively unfavorable profile on other pre-bereavement measures of the CLOC study. They had the poorest-quality marriages of all participants, making the least positive and most negative evaluations of their spouse and marriage, and scoring higher on a measure of ambivalence toward the spouse in the pre-bereavement interviews. They also scored high on measures of emotional instability (neuroticism), introspection, and perceived personal injustice. However, despite this conspicuously unfavorable pre-bereavement profile, the improved group dropped to relatively low levels of depression and reported relatively low levels of grief symptoms during bereavement. Like the resilient group, the improved participants were also relatively less likely to search for meaning in the loss. Given the difficulties they had experienced prior to the death of their spouse, it is tempting to assume that people could improve this much only by relying heavily on denial or distraction during bereavement. Yet, again like the resilient group, the improved participants had relatively low scores on a set of questionnaire items that tapped the use of avoidance or distraction (Bonanno et al., 2004). Although the improved participants reported thinking and talking about the loss less frequently than the resilient group, and reported the lowest levels of comfort from memories of the spouse, it is noteworthy that they exhibited marked increases in the ability to find comfort from thinking or talking about the spouse (the only group of participants in the CLOC study to do so). By 18 months of bereavement they had increased so much in this regard that they were no longer distinct from the resilient group on this variable. Finally, and of particular note, those in the improved group were fully aware of the remarkable progress they had made. This group scored higher than any other group on a scale designed to measure the perception of pride in coping ability. The improved group was also more likely than other participants in the CLOC study to report becoming more confident and becoming a stronger person as a result of dealing with the loss of their spouse.

Chronic grief and distress

Both response patterns, chronic grief and depression, were characterized by high levels of distress during bereavement, but only the latter pattern also involved high distress prior to the loss. To further elucidate the nature of these patterns, Bonanno et al. (2002) identified their pre-loss predictors. Chronic grievers were likely to have had healthy spouses, to rate their marriage positively, and to show high levels of pre-loss dependency on the spouse (e.g., stating that no one could take the spouse's place). The chronically depressed group was less positive about their marriage than chronic grievers, but equally dependent on their spouse. Further analyses examined the context and processing of the loss at 6 and 18 months post loss (Bonanno et al., 2004). Results indicated that chronic grief stems from an enduring struggle with cognitive and emotional distress related to the loss, whereas chronic depression results more from enduring emotional difficulties that are exacerbated by the loss. For example, at 6 months post loss, chronic grievers were more likely to report current yearning and emotional pangs, and they reported thinking and talking about the deceased more often than did chronically depressed individuals.

Together, these findings suggest that during bereavement the chronic grief group was struggling primarily with the loss of a beloved and vital spouse on whom they were also dependent. In addition, because the spouses for this group were typically healthy in the years prior to their death, this struggle was most likely exacerbated by a lack of anticipation or psychological preparation for the loss. In contrast, the pre-bereavement characteristics of people showing a chronic depression trajectory suggested that whatever negative reactions they might have had to the spouse's death were layered upon an already considerable number of ongoing psychological difficulties.

Although the distinction between chronic grief and depression has greatly informed the ways in which we think about high distress patterns in response to loss, we would also like to highlight some of the work that has furthered our understanding of long-term adjustment difficulties in a more general way. For example, a trajectory of chronic distress has also been found in the population of bereaved caregivers. As described above, although for many caregivers symptoms of depression and grief decline rapidly after the death and return to near normal levels within a year of the death (e.g., Schulz et al., 2003), a sizable minority continues to experience high levels of stress and psychiatric problems after death. High levels of caregiving burden, feeling exhausted and overloaded, and lack of support have consistently been found to be associated with negative bereavement outcomes (Gross, 2007; Hebert, Dang, & Schulz, 2006). In addition, a study with dementia caregivers found that among the caregivers with clinical levels of complicated grief were not only those who were in difficult caregiving situations (e.g., caring for a more cognitively impaired patient), but also some who reported very positive features of the caregiving experience (Schulz, Boerner, Shear, Zhang, & Gitlin, 2006). This intriguing finding suggests first of all that positive and negative aspects of caregiving can coexist, and that there may be some positive caregiving experiences that can also put a person at risk for subsequent difficulties. This may be the result of two related factors: Losing their loved one deprives these individuals of a meaningful and important role; and a positive view of caregiving may be a reflection of a very close relationship between caregiver and the person they cared for that might have been the center of the caregiver's life (Boerner, Schulz, & Horowitz, 2004).

As noted above, another aspect that is likely to contribute to the described patterns of grief is preparedness for the death. For example, in the CLOC study, those with a trajectory of chronic grief tended to have healthy spouses and were probably rather unprepared for their spouse's death. However, even in the context of illness and caregiving, it seems clear that, despite providing high-intensity care, often for years, many bereaved caregivers perceive themselves as unprepared for the death. There is also evidence that those who do feel unprepared typically report more depressive, anxiety, and complicated grief symptoms (Hebert et al., 2006). However, we need to gain a better understanding of what it means to be prepared. Based on a series of focus groups with caregivers, Hebert and colleagues proposed that preparedness has emotional (e.g., being at peace with prospect of death), pragmatic (e.g., having funeral arrangements planned), and informational (e.g., medical aspects of end of life) components (Hebert, Schulz,

Copeland, & Arnold, 2009). This study also showed that, for example, a person could feel prepared with respect to the informational and pragmatic components, but yet feel entirely unprepared emotionally. Overall, this work suggests that even the relatively certain prospect of death does not necessarily translate into being prepared for what lies ahead, and that this may be an important area for professionals to address in their encounters with caregivers, before and after the loss.

Finally, not only circumstances around the death but also cause of death are generally considered as important predictors of bereavement outcomes. Specifically, complications in grieving are more likely if the death was sudden and violent (Kaltman & Bonanno, 2003; Mancini, Prati, & Black, 2011; Murphy, Johnson, Chung, & Beaton, 2003). Adjustment difficulties are more likely in response to the death of a child, particularly if the death occurred under sudden or violent circumstances. Rather, experiencing intense distress is considered as normative. In fact, comparing the different studies with data on grief trajectories described above, the highest percentage of respondents showing a pattern of consistently high levels of distress following the loss came from the study on the death of a child from SIDS (Wortman & Silver, 1987). Another important consideration is the striking difference among the studies on conjugal loss in the percentage of respondents evidencing chronic grief (ranging from 8% to 26%). This may be related to differences in the age of the respondents, and hence the untimeliness of the loss in some of these studies (e.g., Vachon et al., 1982; loss of a spouse in mid- rather than late life).

Concluding thoughts

Research has clearly demonstrated that the pattern of "normal grief" is not nearly as common as was long assumed, and that variations from this response pattern, such as consistent minimal distress following the death of a loved one, not only are rather common but can also constitute a very adaptive response to loss. Moreover, research studies have shown that under certain circumstances, for example when death occurs after a long period of illness and caregiving, distress levels may be heightened during the time leading up to the death, and then subsequently decline.

A better understanding of the prevalence and variety of grief patterns is critical for health care professionals because it allows them to meet bereaved individuals with realistic expectations and an empirically grounded understanding of what represents complicated versus uncomplicated patterns of grief. As a result, the health care professional is less likely to impose an expectation of how one should grieve. Such expectations may undermine a person's coping and result in unnecessary distress (Wortman & Boerner, 2011).

At the same time, it is important for health care professionals to be aware that complicated grief reactions do occur in a significant minority of bereaved individuals, and to know the symptoms of complicated grief, as well as characteristics or circumstances (e.g., having a history of prior mental health problems, or experiencing extremely high levels of caregiving burden) that may increase the likelihood of a complicated grief reaction. Health care professionals may be in a position to help address some of these issues during the time prior to death (e.g., help find additional support to reduce burden when caregiving needs begin to become overwhelming), or they may have a key role in connecting bereaved individuals who seem more severely distressed to the appropriate support source, by making a referral to a clinician who can diagnose complicated grief and provide or recommend a specific intervention strategy geared toward the individual's needs.

References

Aneshensel, C. S., Botticello, A. L., & Yamamoto-Mitani, N. (2004). When caregiving ends: The course of depressive symptoms after bereavement. *Journal of Health and Social Behavior, 45*, 422–440.

Bisconti, T. L., Bergeman, C. S., & Boker, S. M. (2006). Social support as a predictor of variability: An examination of the adjustment trajectories of recent widows. *Psychology and Aging, 21*, 590–599.

Boerner, K., Schulz, R., & Horowitz, A. (2004). Positive aspects of caregiving and adaptation to bereavement. *Psychology and Aging, 19*, 668–675.

Boerner, K., Wortman, C. B., & Bonanno, G. A. (2005). Resilient or at risk? A four-year study of older adults who initially showed high or low distress following conjugal loss. *Journal of Gerontology: Psychological Science, 60B*, P67–P73.

Bonanno, G. A. (2004). Loss, trauma, and human resilience: Have we underestimated the human capacity to thrive after extremely aversive events. *American Psychologist, 59*, 20–28.

Bonanno, G. A. (2005). Resilience in the face of potential trauma. *Current Directions in Psychological Science, 14*, 135–138.

Bonanno, G. A., Boerner, K., & Wortman, C. B. (2008). Trajectories of grieving. In Stroebe, M., Hansson, R., Schut, H., & Stroebe, W. (Eds.), *Handbook of bereavement research and practice: 21st century perspectives* (pp. 287–307). Washington, DC: American Psychological Association Press.

Bonanno, G. A., & Field, N. P. (2001). Evaluating the delayed grief hypothesis across 5 years of bereavement. *American Behavioral Scientist, 44*, 798–816.

Bonanno, G. A., Keltner, D., Holen, A., & Horowitz, M. J. (1995). When avoiding unpleasant emotion might not be such a bad thing: Verbal-autonomic response dissociation and midlife conjugal bereavement. *Journal of Personality and Social Psychology, 46*, 975–985.

Bonanno, G. A., Moskowitz, J. T., Papa, A., & Folkman, S. (2005). Resilience to loss in bereaved spouses, bereaved parents, and bereaved gay men. *Journal of Personality and Social Psychology, 88*, 827–843.

Bonanno, G. A., Wortman, C. B., Lehman, D. R., Tweed, R. G., Haring, M., Sonnega, J., et al. (2002). Resilience to loss and chronic grief: A prospective study from pre-loss to 18 months post-loss. *Journal of Personality and Social Psychology, 83*, 1150–1164.

Bonanno, G. A., Wortman, C. B., & Nesse, R. M. (2004). Prospective patterns of resilience and maladjustment during widowhood. *Psychology and Aging, 19*, 260–271.

Bowlby, J. (1980). *Attachment and loss, vol. 3: Loss: Sadness and depression*. New York: Basic Books.

Chentsova-Dutton, Y., Shuchter, S., Hutchin, S., Strause, L., Burns, K., Dunn, L., et al. (2002). Depression and grief reactions in hospice caregivers: From pre-death to 1 year afterwards. *Journal of Affective Disorders, 69*, 53–60.

Gross, J. (2007, November 19). Study finds higher outlays for caregivers of older relatives. *New York Times*, p. A18.

Hebert, R. S., Dang, Q., & Schulz, R. (2006). Preparedness for the death of a loved one and mental health in bereaved caregivers of patients with dementia: Findings from the REACH study. *Journal of Palliative Medicine, 9*, 683–693.

Hebert, R. S., Schulz, R., Copeland, V. C., & Arnold, R. M. (2009). Preparing family caregivers for death and bereavement: Insights from caregivers of terminally ill patients. *Journal of Pain Symptom Management, 37*, 3–12.

Horowitz, M. J., Siegel, B., Holen, A., Bonanno, G. A., Milbrath, C., & Stinson, C. H. (1997) Diagnostic criteria for complicated grief disorder. *American Journal of Psychiatry, 154*, 904–910.

Jacobs, S. (1993). *Pathological grief: Maladaptation to loss*. Washington, DC: American Psychiatric Press.

Kaltman, S., & Bonanno, G. A. (2003). Trauma and bereavement: Examining the impact of sudden and violent death. *Journal of Anxiety Disorders, 17*, 131–147.

Li, L. W. (2005). From caregiving to bereavement: Trajectories of depressive symptoms among wife and daughter caregivers. *Journal of Gerontology, 60B*, P190–P198.

Lund, D. A., Dimond, M. F., Caserta, M. S., Johnson, R. J., Poulton, J. L., & Connelly, J. R. (1985–1986). Identifying elderly with coping difficulties after two years of bereavement. *Omega, 16*, 213–224.

Mancini, A. D., & Bonanno, G. A. (2006). Resilience in the face of potential trauma: Clinical practices and illustrations. *Journal of Clinical Psychology: In Session, 62*, 971–985.

Mancini, A. D., & Bonanno, G. A. (2009). Predictors and parameters of resilience to loss: Toward an individual differences model. *Journal of Personality, 77*, 1805–1832.

Mancini, A. D., Bonanno, G. A., & Clark, A (2011). Stepping off the hedonic treadmill: Individual differences in response to major life events. *Journal of Individual Differences, 32*, 144–152.

Mancini, A. D., Prati, G., & Black, S. (2011). Self-worth mediates the effects of violent loss on PTSD symptoms. *Journal of Traumatic Stress, 24*, 116–120.

Middleton, W., Burnett, P., Raphael, B., & Martinek, N. (1996). The bereavement response: A cluster analysis. *British Journal of Psychiatry, 169*, 167–171.

Middleton, W., Moylan, A., Raphael, B., Burnett, P., & Martinek, N. (1993). An international perspective on bereavement related concepts. *Australian & New Zealand Journal of Psychiatry, 27*, 457–463.

Murphy, S. A., Johnson, L. C., Chung, I., & Beaton, R. D. (2003). The prevalence of PTSD following the violent death of a child and predictors of change 5 years later. *Journal of Traumatic Stress, 16*, 17–25.

Osterweis, M., Solomon, F., & Green, F. (Eds.) (1984). *Bereavement: Reactions, consequences, and care*. Washington, DC: National Academy Press.

Parkes, C. M. (1965). Bereavement and mental illness. *British Journal of Medical Psychology, 38*, 1–26.

Prigerson, H. (2004). Complicated grief: When the path of adjustment leads to a dead-end. *Bereavement Care, 23*, 38–40.

Raphael, B. (1983). *The anatomy of bereavement*. New York: Basic Books.

Schulz, R., Boerner, K., Shear, K., Zhang, S., & Gitlin, L. N. (2006). Predictors of complicated grief among dementia caregivers: A prospective study of bereavement. *American Journal of Geriatric Psychiatry, 14*, 650–658.

Schulz, R., Mendelson, A. B., & Haley, W. E. (2003). End-of-life care and the effects of bereavement on family caregivers of persons with dementia. *New England Journal of Medicine, 349*, 1936–1942.

Shear, K., Frank, E., Houck, P. R., & Reynolds, C. F. III. (2005). Treatment of complicated grief: A randomized controlled trial. *Journal of the American Medical Association, 293*, 2601–2608.

Vachon, M. L. S., Rogers, J., Lyall, W. A., Lancee, W. J., Sheldon, A. R., & Freeman, S. J. J. (1982). Predictors and correlates of adaptation to conjugal bereavement. *American Journal of Psychiatry, 139*, 998–1002.

Wijngaards-de Meij, L., Stroebe, M., Schut, H., Stroebe, W., van den Bout, J., van der Heijden, P. G., & Dijkstra, I. (2008). Parents grieving the loss of their child: Interdependence in coping. *British Journal of Clinical Psychology, 47*, 31–42.

Wortman, C. B., & Boerner, K. (2011). Reactions to the death of a loved one: Myths of coping versus scientific evidence. In Friedman, H. S. (Ed.), *Oxford handbook of health psychology* (pp. 441–479). New York: Oxford University Press.

Wortman, C. B., & Silver, R. C. (1987). Coping with irrevocable loss. In VandenBos, G. R., & Bryant, B. K. (Eds.), *Cataclysms, crises, and catastrophes: Psychology in action* (pp. 189–235). Washington, DC: American Psychological Association.

Wortman, C. B., & Silver, R. C. (1989). The myths? of coping with loss. *Journal of Consulting and Clinical Psychology, 57*, 349–357.

Wortman, C. B., & Silver, R. C. (1993). Reconsidering assumptions about coping with loss: An overview of current research. In Filipp, S. H., Montada, L., & Lerner, M. (Eds.), *Life crises and experiences of loss in adulthood* (pp. 341–365). Hillsdale, NJ: Erlbaum.

Zhang, B., Mitchell, S. L., Bambauer, K. Z., Jones, R., & Prigerson, H. G. (2008). Depressive symptom trajectories and associated risks among bereaved Alzheimer disease caregivers. *American Journal of Geriatric Psychiatry, 16*, 145–155.

Zisook, S., & Shuchter, S. R. (1986). The first four years of widowhood. *Psychiatric Annals, 16*, 288–294.

6 Complicated grief in children[1]

Atle Dyregrov and Kari Dyregrov

Introduction

A new grief disorder has been suggested for inclusion in the fifth edition of the *Diagnostic and Statistical Manual for Mental Disorders* (DSM-5; see Prigerson et al., 2009). However, children are not mentioned in the proposal. It is important that our understanding and intervention efforts reflect the uniqueness of children's grief and that an adult diagnosis is not inappropriately used for children. In this chapter we will first describe the consequences of and risk/protective factors associated with childhood bereavement. Then we will discuss what constitutes complicated grief in children, including why the proposed diagnosis of prolonged grief disorder is inadequate for capturing the variety of complicated grief reactions in children. Finally, we present what is known about intervention following bereavement in childhood and discuss some important issues in this regard.

Consequences of childhood bereavement

It is estimated that around 4% of children in Western countries experience the death of a parent before they reach the age of 18 (Pearlman, Schwalbe, & Cloitre, 2010). In addition, many young people experience the death of siblings, close friends, and other loved ones. The death of a parent or child in a family will usually result in a profound crisis in children and adolescents (Luecken, 2008; Tremblay & Israel, 1998), increasing the occurrence of mental health problems (Cerel, Fristad, Verducci, Weller, & Weller, 2006; Dowdney, 2000; Dyregrov & Dyregrov, 2005; Pfeffer, Karus, Siegel, & Jiang, 2000; Silverman & Worden, 1993), decline in school performance, social withdrawal and behavioral problems (Dowdney et al., 1999; Dyregrov, 2009; Luecken, 2008), and somatic complaints (Silverman & Worden, 1992). A minority (approximately 20%) evidence more severe problems (Dowdney, 2000; Worden & Silverman, 1996). A large Swedish register study showed increased mortality following parental death, especially when death was due to unnatural causes (Rostila & Saarela, 2011).

In addition to mental health problems, early parental loss has been associated with physical health problems throughout life, in both epidemiological and correlational studies (for a review see Luecken, 2008). The loss of a sibling results in rates of problems equivalent to the loss of a parent (Worden, Davies, & McCown,

1999). Higher and more persistent rates of internalizing problems have been found among bereaved girls than among boys (Schmiege, Khoo, Sandler, Ayers & Wolchik, 2006; Worden & Silverman, 1996). The bulk of the research implies an increased risk of depression in adulthood (Coffino, 2009; Jacobs & Bovasso, 2009).

Risk and protective factors

Although this is not based on a thorough review of all child bereavement studies, we have extracted some important risk and protective factors found in numerous studies. A variety of factors can increase or decrease the risk of a child developing problems in the aftermath of a loss. Usually risk and protective factors mirror each other: A good family climate will be protective whereas a negative family climate is associated with risks.

To the extent that a death leads to massive changes in the child's daily environment – if the economic situation demands that the family move, resulting in the loss of contact with friends, having to change school, and so on – the possibility of negative mental health changes increases (Coffino, 2009). Parents can find themselves with increased responsibilities and tasks, and possible financial difficulties, and thus have less time to spend with children. This may also make them less emotionally available. Altogether, this may result in decreased parental capacity. Substantial variance in children's psychopathology could be explained by subsequent life disruption and parental unavailability.

Good parental or primary caregiver capacity that succeeds in providing warmth and discipline has been shown to be protective for bereaved children (Haine, Wolchik, Sandler, Millsap, & Ayers, 2006; Lin, Sandler, Ayers, Wolchik, & Luecken, 2004) and conversely poor-quality parenting and lack of support at home are risk factors for a poor psychological outcome (Luecken, 2008; Tremblay & Israel, 1998). Children's (traumatic) grief levels have been found to be strongly related to the emotional reactions of the caregiver at the time of death and the degree of sadness in the home when retrospectively assessed 21 months after the death (Brown et al., 2008). Saldinger, Porterfield, and Cain (2004) have shown how mothers show greater child-centeredness than fathers and have also documented severe breakdown in parental attunement due to their preoccupation with a dying spouse. Caregivers in bereaved families following a sudden parental loss (suicide, accident, and sudden natural death) show increased rates of depression, anxiety, posttraumatic stress disorder (PTSD), suicidal ideation, and functional impairment compared with matched non-bereaved control families (Melhem, Walker, Moritz, & Brent, 2008). This may place children at further jeopardy.

Losing a mother results in more problems than losing a father (Brent, Melhem, Donahue, & Walker, 2009), including higher child mortality risk (Rostila & Saarela, 2011). In families that lose a mother the burden of changes often falls most heavily on daughters, who often assume more responsibility for household tasks and care of siblings (Worden, 1996). Female gender is associated with increased vulnerability (Schmiege et al., 2006). Riches and Dawson (2000), in an excellent qualitative study, have explored how a widower's early remarriage can complicate the bereaved daughter's grief resolution, leaving her with a sense of betrayal and reduced opportunities for conversational remembering among family and friends. This may prolong a daughter's grief. Gender differences may change as societal roles and expectations change.

If one follows a temporal organization of risk factors, pre-loss exposure to death is a risk factor for later mental health problems (Worden, 1996), as is new stressors in the post-loss environment (Hagan, Luecken, Sandler, & Tein, 2010). Less is known about the risk factors associated with the death itself. There is some indication that violent deaths result in more problems than non-violent causes (Brent et al., 2009; Dyregrov, Nordanger, & Dyregrov, 2003; Worden, 1996), that children who witness physical distress in their dying parents struggle more than those who do not (Saldinger, Cain, & Porterfield, 2003), that stronger grief reactions are related to the caregiver's emotional reactions at the time of death, and that children who themselves experience life-threat during the event in which a parent dies experience stronger grief reactions than others (Brown et al., 2008). From research on parental capacity and warmth (Lin et al., 2004), and on sadness in the home (Brown et al., 2008), there is reason to believe that the immediate post-loss emotional climate as well as the family's communication and fact-sharing propensity (Saler & Skolnick, 1992) are important for functioning over time.

Small children are totally dependent on adults for adequate information about the loss and about the normality of their own reactions. Without being able to talk freely with the surviving parent and others, risk of forming misinterpretations increases (see Tremblay & Israel, 1998, for a review). In adults, catastrophic misinterpretations of grief reactions have been found to be associated with increased levels of prolonged grief (Boelen, van den Bout, & van den Hout, 2010). Clinical experience suggests that children form more misinterpretations than adults, as they lack life experience and direct access to information about what happened, and studies are needed to address this.

Normal and complicated grief in children

There is as yet no clear definition of what is normal and complicated grief in children. The division is more difficult than for adults because children are undergoing development of important brain areas involved in emotion and cognition as well as gaining rapid and new life experience (Gunnar & Quevedo, 2007). The development of these brain areas forms the basis for regulating emotions and understanding the loss and its long-term consequences. If, added to this, one considers the influence of parental reactions and different family practice regarding communication of facts, feelings, thoughts, and so on, the separation of complicated grief from normal grief becomes difficult. In addition, grief may manifest itself in different ways in children from in adults, and its manifestations will vary across cultures.

Although no clear definition of healthy grieving exists, the focus usually is on the individual's ability to accept the reality of the death, cope with the emotional ramifications, and adjust to the changes in one's life. In addition, progressing through normal developmental stages, resuming one's life and being able to remain functional in school or other domains of life are usually taken into account (Dyregrov, 2009; Goodman et al., 2004; Worden, 1996). Although stage models of progression through grief have largely been abandoned, healthy grieving is often conceptualized as fulfilling certain tasks (Worden, 1996). However, many studies originate in the United States and the focus on adaptability and return to function found in this society may be less suited for understanding grief in children in different cultural and historical contexts. What then constitutes complicated grief in children?

A new diagnosis: made for adults

As mentioned at the beginning of this chapter, a new grief disorder has been suggested for inclusion in the DSM-5 (Prigerson et al., 2009). Presently it is grouped under adjustment disorders and is termed bereavement related disorder (http://www.dsm5.org/ProposedRevision/Pages/proposedrevision.aspx?rid=367). Besides having lost a significant other, it involves persistent yearning, preoccupation with the lost person, different distress reactions, and social/identity disruption. The diagnosis should not be made until at least 12 months after the death and the disturbance should cause clinically significant impairment in social, occupational, or other important areas of functioning.

There are several problems in adopting this disorder for children. It includes only one type of grief: where grief continues unabated. Clinically we do not see this type as frequently among children as among adults on account of children's lack of tolerance of emotions. Another problem with the adult proposal is the heavy emphasis on functional impairment. This is more difficult to assess among children, especially pre-school children. Within the trauma field this has led to the development of an alternative set of scoring criteria for PTSD at pre-school age (Scheeringa, 2008). A parallel development can be expected if a grief diagnosis is adopted for children. The duration criterion of 12 months is also troublesome for children. Waiting 12 months until diagnosis may be very unfortunate as it will leave plenty of time for maladaptive parental strategies to solidify problems or for misunderstandings or misperceptions to be more ingrained in children's thoughts and behavior. Our own clinical experience, in line with others' (Dowdney et al., 1999), suggests that 12 months is too long to wait before intervening. If children have problems that seriously affect their functioning and relationships, or the loss results in maladaptive family dynamics, mental health support should be instigated earlier.

Bowlby's concept of pathological mourning

A good starting point for describing complicated grief in children is John Bowlby's original work. Bowlby (1963) impressively depicted several types of complicated grief that echoes what we meet in clinical practice. He used not the term *complicated grief*, but the term *pathological mourning*. He used *mourning* not so much to denote cultural practices and expressions of grief, as is common today, but more like the term *grief* is used nowadays: defining emotional, physiological, cognitive, and behavioral reactions to the death of someone significant (Stroebe, Hansson, Stroebe, & Schut, 2002). Bowlby described the following subtypes of pathological mourning: (a) persistent and unconscious yearning to recover the lost object; (b) intense and persistent anger and reproach expressed towards various objects, including the self; (c) absorption in caring for someone else who has also been bereaved, amounting to compulsion; and (d) denial that the object is permanently lost – absence of grief (here the death is not acknowledged, but there is some awareness of it). Bowlby did not see these types as mutually exclusive, and proposed that they could be found in combinations with anxiety, depression, and hysterical and psychopathic behavior. He linked healthy mourning to the restoration of function, whereas in pathological mourning the bereaved person remained preoccupied with the lost person in thought and action. He stressed that open expression of yearning for the lost object, accompanied by sadness and crying, and anger and reproach at the object for its desertion, were necessary conditions for healthy mourning. In our opinion, although his description of children's complicated grief is very acute, his description lacks the type in which children struggle with posttraumatic problems following their loss, and he also underemphasizes the problems that ensue in children as a result of the family climate or adults' inadequate handling of the death or its consequences. Bowlby's types reflect the lack of recognition of trauma at that time. Although basing the categorization on adults, Worden (1996) listed similar types of complicated grief to those of Bowlby, adding a masked type: reactions that resemble physical or other psychiatric disorders that the bereaved do not associate with the death.

Traumatic experiences and loss

Traumatic aspects related to witnessing the death, finding the body, or having fantasies about what happened can lead to complicated grief reactions. They are prominent enough to be recognized as a distinct type, although the reactions that ensue can also be subsumed under posttraumatic stress reactions or PTSD. Grief and trauma often become intertwined. However, from reading the literature published in recent years, it seems that the focus in childhood grief has become centered on traumatic grief (see Goodman et al., 2004). Coming from the trauma field, Cohen and colleagues (Cohen, Goodman, Brown, & Mannarino, 2004) formed the construct of "childhood traumatic grief" (CTG) to conceptualize debilitating grief reactions in children and adolescents. This is grief following a loss that the child experiences as traumatic, when he or she evinces significant PTSD symptoms that prevent the child's grief processing. CTG also keeps the child from approaching happy memories (Cohen, Mannarino, & Staron, 2006). Trauma processing takes precedence over grief processing. Though the trauma focus may have taken some of the attention away from other forms of complicated grief, this focus has made us much more aware of the interaction of trauma and grief following many deaths. The similarity in PTSD symptoms and cortisol levels found among children who have experienced loss events and children who have experienced traumatic events (e.g., abuse, witnessing violence) (Taylor, Weems, Costa, & Carrión, 2009) also underscores the importance of understanding the interaction of trauma and loss.

In the following subsections we outline a few important aspects that are specific to children and that may complicate their reactions following a loss.

Poor informational climate and loss

Family dynamics may aggravate complicated grief reactions in children or make them more likely to develop. Intensified reactions may result when facts are not communicated, information is kept from the child, or the emotional climate is restricted or parents are unresponsive to their child's needs (Lin et al., 2004). This is an under-studied area, probably because it resides in the complex interactional processes between the child and his or her environment. We believe it may be fruitful to enhance the focus on these dynamics because children with such living conditions become especially vulnerable. For this group of children, trauma-specific grief therapy would not suffice and a family-oriented approach is recommended to stimulate more open and direct communication about the death and its consequences.

Lack of emotional tolerance and loss

Research on grieving adults has not found evidence of delayed grief (Bonanno & Field, 2001). In clinical work with children we see that lack of emotional tolerance of the loss is evident and children try to regulate grief in tolerable doses and use more avoidance and postponement than adults. It is known that frequent use of an explicit strategy to regulate emotions can quickly render the initiation of the strategy more implicit (automatic) over time (Gyurak, Gross, & Etkin, 2011). Tremblay and Israel (1998) mention that children's lack of fluency in identifying and describing feeling states may also lead to more somatic expression of distress. Saldinger and colleagues (2004) speculate that grieving children who score below the norm for measures of anxiety and depression struggle to ward off feelings, in order not to feel overwhelmed by them. Delayed or repressed reactions may be so frequent in children that they can be seen as normal reactions, reflecting children's lack of emotional regulation capability. However, normal lack of emotional responsiveness as a way to approach grief in tolerable doses is different from almost total blockage of grief reactions. This form of overregulation will usually be associated with functional decline if it continues over time. Clinically, some children will deny any emotions tied to the lost person and may start avoiding conversations about or memories of the deceased, often becoming dysfunctional in some area, such as at school. Empirical work needs to be undertaken to clarify when this way of modulating emotions become dysfunctional and represents a type of complicated grief, and when it serves as a coping method associated with a good long-term outcome.

Measuring grief

Several questionnaires are presently available to measure grief in children.

1   The Hogan Sibling Inventory of Grief (Hogan, 1990) has 46 items, half of
    which measure positive growth. A recent version has been shortened to 20
    items (Hogan et al., in review).
2   The Extended Grief Inventory developed by Layne, Savjak, Saltzman, and
    Pynoos (2001) is currently being improved and renamed as the UCLA Grief
    Reactions Scale (Layne, Kaplow, & Pynoos, 2011). This measures three
    dimensions: traumatic grief; positive connection to the deceased; and com-
    plicated grief reactions.
3   The Traumatic Grief Inventory for Children (Dyregrov et al., 2001) is built on
    an early version of an adult scale, the Inventory of Traumatic Grief (Prigerson
    et al., 1995).

An inspection of the two most used scales – the Hogan scale and the UCLA
scale – indicates little overlap. Perhaps a better strategy for scale development
would be to agree first on various subtypes of complicated grief and then develop
items that can map these dimensions.

Interventions for grief in children

The two meta-analytic studies of bereavement interventions for children have
looked not specifically at complicated grief, but at grief interventions generally.
They arrive at somewhat different conclusions. Currier, Holland, and Neimeyer
(2007) included 13 controlled studies and reported a small, non-significant, effect
size of 0.14. They concluded that the interventions do not generate the positive
outcomes found for other professional psychotherapeutic interventions, with the
exception of some studies that intervened in a time-sensitive manner for those
with a genuine need for intervention. They advocated early screening and focusing interventions on high-risk groups such as those showing signs of "childhood
traumatic grief." Rosner, Kruse, and Hagl (2010) included a total of 27 treatment
studies, and conducted two meta-analyses: one on controlled studies ($n = 15$) and
one on uncontrolled studies ($n = 12$). The effect size was 0.35 and 0.49, respectively, and the authors concluded that the results favor was for bereaved children.
They reported that for uncontrolled studies larger effects were found with a longer
time interval between bereavement and intervention. Most studies have been
conducted using group treatments. There is some indication that individual and
group treatment may yield similar results (Salloum & Overstreet, 2008). Although
there are a variety of bereavement groups available for bereaved children, few
have been scrutinized for their effect on health. Although Currier and colleagues
(2007) assumed that participants with manifest symptoms and functional impairment would benefit more from treatment, they found that controlled studies
showed only a trend in this direction, whereas uncontrolled studies confirmed

their assumptions. However, for the two studies that had identified children with complicated grief, the weighted average effect size was 0.68. Inclusion of different studies and a slightly different statistical procedure in the two meta-analyses may explain the different results.

In general it seems that interventions that target those who struggle with symptoms – tertiary interventions – show most potential. A high level of symptoms is not synonymous with a complicated grief reaction, as symptoms include various conditions (depression, behavioral problems, anxiety, etc.), but it does indicate that those evincing most problems in various areas benefit most from the interventions studied.

Recently, interventions have been inspired by advances within cognitive–behavioral therapy (CBT) for trauma and loss in adults, and trauma-focused grief therapy in manualized forms has developed for children. These manuals have proven efficient (Cohen et al., 2006; Shear, 2009). Data indicate that a trauma-focused grief intervention can benefit children regardless of the manner in which a parent died (McClatchey, Vonk, & Palardy, 2009). Generally, grief interventions appear to be most successful when treatment is designed to attend to both trauma and grief symptoms (Cohen, Mannarino, & Knudsen, 2004; Cohen et al., 2006; Layne et al., 2008), and there are some data showing that, once trauma symptoms have been resolved, grief symptoms may respond to brief interventions (Cohen et al., 2006). However, although focus on the trauma aspects of the loss is important, other forms of grief complications receive less attention and clinicians may be less equipped to handle them, for lack of appropriate intervention strategies. A child who is avoiding reminders at all costs will need to be helped differently from a child who is crying all the time, yearning for the lost one.

Resource limitations and research on intervention to date justify a conservative approach targeting service provision for those who show emotional or behavioral problems. Still, a more proactive approach may be warranted as it is in the early period following loss that adults make important decisions regarding sharing information with their children, including them in rituals, and return to kindergarten and school. Based on their data from suddenly bereaved adolescents, Brent and colleagues (2009) suggest a window of opportunity in which to prevent or attenuate further depressive episodes in youth shortly after a parent's death. Inclusion in funeral and memorial services serves the child's grieving process better than non-attendance (Silverman & Worden, 1992; Weller, Weller, Fristad, Cain, & Bowes, 1988). However, from clinical experience we would emphasize the importance of preparing children for these services and providing proper adult support, as well as follow-up subsequent to the service (Dyregrov, 2008).

Strengthening parental capacity

From the research literature it seems of almost greater importance to secure continued parental capacity following a partner or child loss than to secure help for children directly. As more than half of surviving parents (with children between 2 and 16 years old) evidence reactions indicating a probable psychiatric disorder following a partner loss (Dowdney et al., 1999), or the loss of a child (Dyregrov et al., 2003), securing early help and providing support to adult caretakers should be a priority. Upholding or restoring parental capacity when struggling in the aftermath of a partner or child loss may well produce results better than general programs targeting children directly. Identifying depression, complicated grief, and PTSD in caregivers by using screening measures may be an advisable strategy.

The importance of what has been termed "positive parenting," consisting of caregiver warmth and consistent discipline (Haine et al., 2006), has been identified as an important protective resource for children through Sandler and colleagues' program (Sandler et al., 2008). Saldinger and colleagues (2004) also found that child-centered parenting was associated with fewer symptoms and more positive perceptions of the living parent by the child. Sandler and colleagues' guided preventive intervention, termed the Family Bereavement Program, which is theoretically based and is the most rigorously evaluated program to date, has targeted the putative mediators of parental demoralization, negative life events, parental warmth, and stable positive events in the family. Recently Sandler and his group (Sandler et al., 2010) documented the long-term effects of their program in a randomized controlled trial. Although the program was effective regarding intrusive grief scores (intrusive thoughts about the loved one), it was less successful in reducing present grief (e.g., still crying when thinking about the loved one). They concluded that the program reduced problematic grief responses of parentally bereaved youths over a 6-year period. However, the results of their intervention must be regarded as modest and there seems to be room for improvement in the model, maybe incorporating more strategies taken from trauma-focused programs. Their program is not targeting children identified with complicated grief, but it may have the potential to prevent the development of such problems.

Tremblay and Israel (1998) mention that it may be conceivable that one can foster too much preoccupation with grief feelings, something that can undermine the child's attempts to regain a positive focus on his or her experience. Parents often bring children who do not talk, usually boys, to our clinical attention, or they put pressure on them to talk. This happens regardless of any functional loss in the young person. The parental expectation and pressure for overt grief from children may place an extra burden on them (Silverman & Worden, 1993). Thus, although an open communication climate seems to be important in families, there is a delicate balance for caregivers and helpers not to put too much pressure on children to talk about the death.

Although the meta-analytic studies do not indicate the need for intervention for all, there should be a good possibility of preventing the complicated grief resulting from inadequate parental/family handling of the death. Given the sparse research on early family intervention we should be cautious about withholding early help to the family, as early intervention may enhance parents' efforts to cope with what has happened and thereby also be a resource for their children (Dyregrov, 2001; Dyregrov, 2002).

Elements in therapeutic help for children

From the studies adapting trauma-focused grief strategies it seems evident that therapeutic work with bereaved children manifesting complicated grief involves psychoeducation about normal grief and trauma reactions; building a narrative of the events experienced; challenging misperceptions and misunderstanding about the event or their own reactions (cognitive restructuring); targeting eventual traumatic aspects of their loss, including handling traumatic reminders; attention to aspects of grief, including longing, guilt, and others' reactions; support from others; broadening their coping skills (including ability to regulate emotions); meaning making; and continuing of the relationship to the deceased.

Written disclosure interventions following trauma, in which individuals express thoughts and emotions, have been associated with improved health in adults (Pennebaker, 1997), and recently cognitive–behavioral writing therapy using a structured form of writing has proven effective for various types of trauma in children (van der Oord, Lucassen, van Emmerik, & Emmelkamp, 2010). However, writing interventions have not shown the same promise following loss experiences. Recently, more directed written exposure, especially focusing on benefit finding, has proven more efficacious (Lichtenthal & Cruess, 2010). The research on the use of such interventions with children and adolescents has only just begun. A manualized written disclosure protocol for children who have experienced disasters (Yule et al., 2005) is currently being tested out in several countries and preliminary research indicates that it can be beneficial for bereaved children (Kalantari, Yule, Dyregrov, Neshatdoost, & Ahmadi, 2012).

Conclusion

Being a child leads to unique challenges following a loss. It would be unfortunate if the area of grief in children were not to establish its own knowledge base. An insensitive extrapolation from adult complicated grief to explain complicated grief in children, using a diagnosis established for adults, could possibly lead to an unfortunate focus on one type of complicated grief in children. Children in development have immature systems for emotional and cognitive regulation. They are dependent on adults, who themselves may be grieving with limited capacity and availability to support and provide the information that children need to cope. Future studies must ensure that we better define different subtypes and dynamics of complicated grief in children, develop appropriate measures to identify them, and put in place appropriate intervention approaches to provide specific help for various manifestations of complicated grief.

Note

1   This project was funded by the Egmont Foundation.

References

Boelen, P. A., van den Bout, J., & van den Hout, M. A. (2010). A prospective examination of catastrophic misinterpretations and experiential avoidance in emotional distress following loss. *Journal of Nervous and Mental Disease, 198*, 252–257.

Bonanno, G. A., & Field, N. P. (2001). Examining the delayed grief hypothesis across 5 years of bereavement. *American Behavioral Scientist, 44*, 798–816.

Bowlby, J. (1963). Pathological mourning and childhood mourning. *Journal of American Psychoanalytic Association, 11*, 500–541.

Brent, D., Melhem, N., Donohoe, M. B., & Walker, M. (2009). The incidence and course of depression in bereaved youth 21 months after the loss of a parent to suicide, accident, or sudden natural death. *American Journal of Psychiatry, 166*, 786–794.

Brown, E. J., Amaya-Jackson, L., Cohen, J., Handel, S., de Bocanegra, H. T., Zatta, E., et al. (2008). Childhood traumatic grief: A multi-site empirical examination of the construct and its correlates. *Death Studies, 32*, 899–923.

Cerel, J., Fristad, M. A., Verducci, J., Weller, R. A., & Weller, E. B. (2006). Childhood bereavement: Psychopathology in the 2 years postparental death. *Journal of the American Academy of Child and Adolescent Psychiatry, 45*, 681–690.

Coffino, B. (2009). The role of childhood parent figure loss in the etiology of adult depression: Findings from a prospective longitudinal study. *Attachment & Human Development, 11*, 445–470.

Cohen, J., Goodman, R. F., Brown, E. J., &Mannarino, A. (2004). Treatment of childhood traumatic grief: Contributing to a newly emerging condition in the wake of community trauma. *Harvard Review of Psychiatry, 12*, 213–216.

Cohen, J. A., Mannarino, A. P., & Knudsen, K. (2004). Treating childhood traumatic grief: A pilot study. *Journal of American Academy of Child and Adolescent Psychiatry, 43*, 1225–1233.

Cohen, J. A., Mannarino, A. P., & Staron, V. R. (2006). A pilot study of modified cognitive–behavioral therapy for childhood traumatic grief (CBT-CTG). *Journal of American Academy of Child and Adolescent Psychiatry, 45*, 1465–1473.

Currier, J. M., Holland, J. M., & Neimeyer, R. A. (2007). The effectiveness of bereavement interventions with children: A meta-analytic review of controlled outcome research. *Journal of Clinical Child and Adolescent Psychology, 36*, 253–259.

Dowdney, L. (2000). Childhood bereavement following parental death. *Journal of Psychology and Psychiatry, 41*, 819–830.

Dowdney, L., Wilson, R., Maughan, B., Allerton, M., Schofield, P., & Skuse, D. (1999). Psychological disturbance and service provision in parentally bereaved children: Prospective case–control study. *British Medical Journal, 319*, 354–357.

Dyregrov, A. (2001). Early intervention: A family perspective. *Advances in Mind–Body Medicine, 17*, 9–17.

Dyregrov, A. (2008). *Grief in children: A handbook for adults* (2nd edn.). London: Jessica Kingsley.

Dyregrov, A., Yule, W., Smith, P., Perrin, S., Gjestad, R., & Prigerson, H. (2001). *Traumatic Grief Inventory for Children (TGIC)*. Bergen, Norway: Children and War Foundation.

Dyregrov, K. (2002). Assistance from local authorities versus survivors' needs for support after suicide. *Death Studies, 26*, 647–669.

Dyregrov, K. (2009). The important role of the school following suicide: New research about the help and support wishes of the young bereaved. *Omega: Journal of Death and Dying, 59*, 147–161.

Dyregrov, K., & Dyregrov, A. (2005). Siblings after suicide: "The forgotten bereaved." *Suicide and Life Threatening Behaviour, 35*, 714–724.

Dyregrov, K., Nordanger, D., & Dyregrov, A. (2003). Predictors of psychosocial distress after suicide, SIDS and accidents. *Death Studies, 27*, 143–165.

Goodman, R. F., Cohen, J., Epstein, E., Kliethermes, M., Layne, C., Macy, R. D., et al. (2004). *Childhood traumatic grief education materials.* Childhood Traumatic Grief Task Force Education Materials Subcommittee, National Childhood Traumatic Stress Network. Retrieved September 5, 2010, from nctsnet.org/nctsn_assets/pdfs/reports/childhood_traumatic_grief.pdf.

Gunnar, M., & Quevedo, K. (2007). The neurobiology of stress and development. *Annual Review of Psychology, 58*, 145–173.

Gyurak, A., Gross, J. J., & Etkin, A. (2011). Explicit and implicit emotion regulation: A dual-process framework. *Cognition & Emotion, 25*, 400–412.

Hagan, M. J., Luecken, L. J., Sandler, I. N., & Tein, J.-Y. (2010). Prospective effects of post-bereavement negative events on cortisol activity in parentally bereaved youth. *Developmental Psychobiology, 52*, 394–400.

Haine, R. A., Wolchik, S. A., Sandler, I. N., Millsap, R. E., & Ayers, T. S. (2006). Positive parenting as a protective resource for parentally bereaved children. *Death Studies, 30*, 1–28.

Hogan, N. (1990). Hogan Sibling Inventory of Bereavement. In Touliatos, J., Perlmutter, B., & Straus, M. (Eds.), *Handbook of family measurement techniques* (p. 524). Newbury Park, CA: Sage.

Hogan, N. S., Schmidt, L. A., Camp, N., Barrera, M., Compas, B. E., Davies, B., et al. (in review). Development and testing of the Hogan Inventory of Bereavement for Children and Adolescents. *Omega: Journal of Death and Dying*.

Jacobs, J. R., & Bovasso, G. B. (2009). Re-examining the long-term effects of experiencing parental death in childhood on adult psychopathology. *Journal of Nervous and Mental Disease, 197*, 24–27.

Kalantari, M., Yule, W., Dyregrov, A., Neshatdoost, H., & Ahmadi, S. J. (2012). Efficacy of writing for recovery on traumatic grief symptoms of Afghan refugee bereaved adolescents. *Omega: Journal of Death and Dying, 65*, 139–150.

Layne, C. M., Kaplow, J., & Pynoos, R. S. (2011). *UCLA Grief Reactions Scale.* Unpublished psychological test, University of California, Los Angeles.

Layne, C. M., Saltzman, W. R., Poppleton, L., Burlingame, G. M., Pasalić, A., Duraković, E., et al. (2008). Effectiveness of a school-based group psychotherapy program for war-exposed adolescents: a randomized controlled trial. *Journal of the American Academy of Child and Adolescent Psychiatry, 47*, 1048–1062.

Layne, C. M., Savjak, N., Saltzman, W. R., & Pynoos, R. S. (2001). *Extended Grief Inventory.* Unpublished psychological test, University of California, Los Angeles.

Lichtenthal, W. G., & Cruess, D. G. (2010). Effects of directed written disclosure on grief and distress symptoms among bereaved individuals. *Death Studies, 34*, 475–499.

Lin, K. K., Sandler, I. N., Ayers, T. S., Wolchik, S. A., & Luecken, L. L. (2004). Resilience in parentally bereaved children and adolescents seeking preventive services. *Journal of Clinical Child and Adolescent Psychology, 33*, 673–683.

Luecken, L. J. (2008). Long-term consequences of parental death in childhood: Psychological and physiological manifestations. In Stroebe, M. S., Hansson, R. O., Schut, H., & Stroebe, W. (Eds.), *Handbook of bereavement research and practice* (pp. 397–416). Washington, DC: American Psychological Association.

McClatchey, I, S., Vonk, M. E., & Palardy, G. (2009). Efficacy of a camp-based intervention for childhood traumatic grief. *Research on Social Work Practice, 19*, 19–30.

Melhem, N., Walker, M., Moritz, G., & Brent, D. A. (2008). Antecedents and sequelae of sudden parental death in offspring and surviving caregivers. *Archives of Pediatric Adolescent Medicine, 162*, 403–410.

van der Oord, S., Lucassen, S., van Emmerik, A. A. P., & Emmelkamp, P. M. G. (2010). Treatment of post-traumatic stress disorder in children using cognitive behavioural writing therapy. *Clinical Psychology and Psychotherapy, 17*, 240–249.

Pearlman, M. Y., Schwalbe, K. D., & Cloitre, M. (2010). *Grief in childhood: Fundamentals of treatment in clinical practice*. Washington, DC: American Psychological Association.

Pennebaker, J. W. (1997). *Opening up: The healing power of expressing emotions* (rev. edn.). New York: Guilford Press.

Pfeffer, C., Karus, D., Siegel, K., & Jiang, H. (2000). Child survivors of parental death from cancer or suicide: Depressive and behavioral outcomes. *Psycho-oncology, 9*, 1–10.

Prigerson, H. G., Horowitz, M. J., Jacobs, S. C., Parkes, C. M., Aslan, M., Goodkin, K., et al. (2009). Prolonged grief disorder: Psychometric validation of criteria proposed for DSM-V and ICD-11. *PLoS Medicine*, *6*(8), e1000121. doi:10.1371/journal.pmed.1000121

Prigerson, H. G., Maciejewski, P. K., Reynolds, C. F., Bierhals, A. J., Newsom, J. T., Fasiczka, A., et al. (1995). Inventory of Complicated Grief: A scale to measure maladaptive symptoms of loss. *Psychiatry Research, 59*, 65–79.

Riches, G., & Dawson, P. (2000). Daughters' dilemmas: Grief resolution in girls whose widowed fathers remarry early. *Journal of Family Therapy, 22*, 360–374.

Rosner, R., Kruse, J., & Hagl, M. (2010). A meta-analysis of interventions for bereaved children and adolescents. *Death Studies, 34*, 99–136.

Rostila, M., & Saarela, J. M. (2011). Time does not heal all wounds: Mortality following the death of a parent. *Journal of Marriage and Family, 73*, 236–249.

Saler, L., & Skolnick, N. (1992). Childhood parental death and depression in adulthood: Roles of surviving parent and family environment. *American Journal of Orthopsychiatry, 62*, 504–516.

Saldinger, A., Cain, A., & Porterfield, K. (2003). Managing traumatic stress in children anticipating parental death. *Psychiatry, 66*, 168–181.

Saldinger, A., Porterfield, K., & Cain, A. C. (2004). Meeting the needs of parentally bereaved children for child-centered parenting. *Psychiatry, 67*, 331–352.

Salloum, A., & Overstreet, S. (2008). Evaluation of individual and group grief and trauma interventions for children post disaster. *Journal of Clinical Child & Adolescent Psychology, 37*, 495–507.

Sandler, I. N., Ma, Y., Tein, J., Ayers, T. S., Wolchik, S., Kennedy, C., & Millsap, R. (2010). Long-term effects of the family bereavement program on multiple indicators of grief in parentally bereaved children and adolescents. *Journal of Consulting and Clinical Psychology, 78*, 131–143.

Sandler, I. N., Wolchik, S. A., Ayers, T. S., Tein, J-Y., Coxe, S., & Chow, W. (2008). Linking theory and intervention to promote resilience in parentally bereaved children. In Stroebe, M. S., Hansson, R. O., Schut, H., & Stroebe, W. (Eds.), *Handbook of bereavement research and practice* (pp. 531–550). Washington, DC: American Psychological Association.

Scheeringa, M. S. (2008). Developmental considerations for diagnosing PTSD and acute stress disorder in preschool and school-age children. *American Journal of Psychiatry, 165*, 1237–1239.

Schmiege, S. J., Khoo, S. T., Sandler, I. N., Ayers, T. S., & Wolchik, S. A. (2006). Symptoms of internalizing and external problems: Modelling recovery curves after the death of a parent. *American Journal of Preventive Medicine, 31*, 152–160.

Shear, M. K. (2009). Grief and depression: Treatment decisions for bereaved children and adults. *American Journal of Psychiatry, 166*, 746–748.

Silverman, P. R., & Worden, J. W. (1992). Children's reactions to the death of a parent in the early months after the death. *American Journal of Orthopsychiatry, 62*, 93–104.

Silverman, P. R., & Worden, J. W. (1993). Determinants of adjustment to bereavement in younger widows and widowers. In Stroebe, M., Stroebe, W., & Hansson, R. (Eds.), *Handbook of bereavement: Theory, research, and intervention* (pp. 208–226). New York: Cambridge University Press.

Stroebe, M. S., Hansson, R. O., Stroebe, W., & Schut, H. (2002). *Handbook of bereavement research: Consequences, coping, and care.* Washington, DC: American Psychological Association.

Taylor, L. K., Weems, C. F., Costa, N. M., & Carrión, V. G. (2009). Loss and the experience of emotional distress in childhood. *Journal of Loss and Trauma, 14*, 1–16.

Tremblay, G. C., & Israel, A. C. (1998). Children's adjustment to parental death. *Clinical Psychology: Science and Practice, 5*, 424–438.

Weller, E. B., Weller, R. A., Fristad, M. A., Cain, S. E., & Bowes, J. M. (1988). Should children attend their parent's funeral? *Journal of the American Academy of Child and Adolescent Psychiatry, 27*, 559–562.

Worden, J. W. (1996). *Children and grief.* New York: Guilford Press.

Worden, J. W., Davies, B., & McCown, D. (1999). Comparing parent loss with sibling loss. *Death Studies, 23*, 1–15.

Worden, J. W., & Silverman, P. R. (1996). Parental death and the adjustment of school-age children. *Omega: Journal of Death and Dying, 33*, 91–102.

Yule, W., Dyregrov, A., Neuner, F., Pennebaker, J., Raundalen, M., & van Emmerik, A. (2005). *Writing for recovery: A manual for structured writing after disaster and war.* Bergen: Children and War Foundation.

Part III

Diagnostic categorization

Scientific, clinical, and societal implications

7 Prolonged grief disorder as a new diagnostic category in DSM-5

Paul A. Boelen and Holly G. Prigerson

Introduction

A minority of bereaved individuals develops persistent, disabling, and distressing symptoms of grief. As yet, there is no category for a bereavement related disorder in the most frequently used classification system, the *Diagnostic and Statistical Manual for Mental Disorders* (DSM). Since the mid-1990s, researchers and clinicians have increasingly pled for the inclusion of a syndrome of grief – by turns referred to as pathological, complicated, and, more recently, prolonged grief disorder – in the DSM system. Horowitz and colleagues proposed criteria for "pathological grief" in 1993 (Horowitz, Bonanno, & Holen, 1993) and refined criteria for "complicated grief disorder" in 1997 (Horowitz et al., 1997). Comparable to posttraumatic stress disorder (PTSD), this condition was conceptualized as consisting of intrusive symptoms and signs of avoidance and failure to adapt. In that same period, two influential studies were published by Prigerson and colleagues. In one of these studies, Prigerson, Frank et al. (1995) differentiated symptoms of complicated grief from bereavement-related depression and found complicated grief to be associated with health impairments over and above depression. In the other study, the Inventory of Complicated Grief (ICG) was introduced as a 19-item measure of complicated grief, together with data supporting the scale's psychometric properties (Prigerson, Maciejewski, et al., 1995).

The Prigerson, Frank et al. (1995) study was the first to provide evidence that complicated grief is a distinct and disabling condition. From 1995 onwards, several studies – some of which are cited below – have replicated this finding. The second study provided researchers with a tool to study the validity and correlates of complicated grief and is now the most commonly used and well-validated measure of complicated grief. These initial studies culminated in publication of "consensus criteria" for complicated grief in the late 1990s (Prigerson, Shear, et al., 1999). According to these criteria, complicated grief encompassed symptoms of separation distress (e.g., yearning) and traumatic distress (symptoms representing a sense of being traumatized by the loss) present to the point of functional impairment for at least 2 months. Somewhat later, the time criterion was extended to 6 months and symptoms of traumatic distress were no longer distinguished from symptoms of separation distress because these symptoms were found to load on a single dimension (Prigerson & Jacobs, 2001).

Since the publication of the DSM-IV-TR (APA, 2000) and these early studies, dozens of studies have been published supporting the diagnostic validity of complicated grief (CG), or prolonged grief disorder (PGD), as it is now termed – henceforth abbreviated as PGD/CG. In this chapter, we will elucidate that PGD/CG meets the definition of a mental/psychiatric disorder and, as such, should be included in the DSM system. In addition, proposed standardized criteria for PGD/CG will be described.

Can PGD/CG be defined as a formal disorder?

Robins and Guze (1970) described five taxonomic principles for establishing the validity of a disorder. They proposed that diagnostic validity could be incrementally improved by increasingly precise clinical description, delineation of syndromes from other disorders, and empirical studies on underlying psychobiological mechanisms. This publication guided refinement of the definition of mental disorder in later editions of the DSM and research on psychometric properties of existing and new syndromes. Stein et al. (2010) recently proposed a revised set of criteria for the definition of a mental/psychiatric disorder for DSM-5, building on this earlier work. In this section, we will argue that PGD/CG meets these criteria (for similar reviews see Prigerson & Jacobs, 2001; Prigerson et al., 2009; Shear et al., 2011).

A behavioral or psychological syndrome or pattern that occurs in an individual

People suffering from PGD/CG are essentially stuck in a state of chronic grief – grief being defined as a state of wanting what you cannot have, a sense of craving for the deceased that does not abate with time (Prigerson & Maciejewski, 2008). Their inability to accept the separation and reluctance to make adaptations to life cause a continued desire to be close to their loved ones, and protest and pain whenever they confront the impossibility of fulfilling this desire. These responses are maintained and exacerbated by confusion about self-identity, a sense of foreshortened future, and a sense that life is empty and meaningless without the lost person. Although these reactions may occur in uncomplicated grief, in PGD/CG these reactions are persistently distressing and disabling beyond the first few months post loss. Thus, PGD/CG constitutes a clearly identifiable and recognizable cluster of symptoms that can be reliably assessed using the ICG (Prigerson, Maciejewski, et al., 1995) or its updated version the PG-13 (Prigerson et al., 2009). As described below, the syndrome can be distinguished from normal/uncomplicated grief and depression and anxiety.

Consequences of the syndrome are clinically significant distress or disability

There is evidence from concurrent and prospective longitudinal studies that elevated levels and clinical caseness of PGD/CG are associated with sleep disturbances, suicidal ideation, increased substance misuse, reduced quality of life, and other physical and mental health impairments (Prigerson et al., 2009; Shear et al., 2011). Critically, many studies have shown that these associations emerge even when controlling for the shared variance between PGD/CG and concomitant depression and anxiety (e.g., Bonanno et al., 2007; Prigerson et al., 2009). Thus, PGD/CG symptoms have proven to have *incremental validity*. That is, many bereaved people suffering from emotional problems would be missed if clinicians relied only on conditions currently found in the DSM. Findings of linkages of PGD/CG symptoms with distress and disability are robust across subgroups of bereaved people divided by age, gender, mode of death, kinship to the deceased, and cultural background (Prigerson & Jacobs, 2001).

The syndrome is not merely an expectable response to common stressors

Several studies have estimated prevalence rates of PGD/CG in different samples (e.g., Fujisawa et al., 2010; Kersting, Brähler, Glaesmer, & Wagner, 2011; Morina, Von Lersner, & Prigerson, 2011). Although different criteria were used to identify PGD/CG cases, in all these studies, prevalence rates were below 25% indicating that meeting criteria for PGD/CG "caseness" is not the norm. In a series of studies Bonanno and colleagues examined trajectories of grief symptoms over time (e.g., Bonanno et al., 2002; Chapter 5 of this volume). These studies also indicated that only a minority of mourners ($\leq 25\%$ dependent on the sample under investigation) displayed a pattern of persistent intense grief. In fact, across studies, more than half of the people displayed a pattern of consistently low levels of distress, suggesting that resilience and not chronic grief is the expectable response to bereavement.

Some authors have argued that a categorical distinction between PGD/CG and normal/uncomplicated grief – evidence that PGD/CG symptoms are *phenomenologically* distinct from those of normal grief – should be established before PGD/CG can become an official disorder (Hogan, Worden, & Schmidt, 2004). However, these concepts are better described as two extremes of a single dimension of grief severity. A recent taxometric investigation confirmed this (Holland, Neimeyer, Boelen, & Prigerson, 2009).

This is not to say that PGD/CG and normal/uncomplicated grief overlap completely. Studies by Boelen and van den Bout (2008), Boelen and colleagues (2003), and Prigerson, Maciejewski, and colleagues (1995) showed that scores on the ICG were more strongly associated with quality of life impairments than were scores on the Texas Revised Inventory of Grief (TRIG; Faschingbauer, Zisook, & DeVaul, 1987), a measure tapping relatively benign grief reactions (e.g., crying). These findings suggest that persistently high levels of PG/CG symptoms, but not necessarily other grief symptoms, represent a maladaptive bereavement reaction.

The syndrome reflects an underlying psychobiological dysfunction

There is evidence that PGD/CG meets this criterion. Reynolds et al. (1999) found that depressive symptoms but not grief symptoms declined in bereaved people taking nortriptyline, suggesting that different biological dysfunctions underlie both conditions. Bonanno et al. (2007) found that, in mourners interviewed about their loss, PGD/CG severity was associated with *reduced* heart rate and PTSD severity with *increased* heart rate, a finding also pointing to a specific physiological response. O'Connor et al. (2008; also Chapter 15 in this volume) conducted an intriguing functional magnetic resonance imaging (fMRI) study in which they found that women with PGD/CG, but not those without, showed reward-related activity in the nucleus accumbens that was positively correlated with self-reported yearning when confronted with photos of their deceased mother. This suggests that persistent activation of reward areas in the brain is a biological correlate of PGD/CG. Apart from these biological correlates, several psychological dysfunctions have been identified as having a specific linkage with PGD/CG symptoms. These include impairments in the ability to retrieve specific memories following loss (Chapter 13) and negative thinking and avoidance behaviors (Chapter 16).

The syndrome is not primarily a result of social deviance or conflicts with society

This point is an important consideration more than a defining criterion of mental or psychiatric disorder (Stein et al., 2010). It cautions that the PGD/CG label should never be used when grief reactions are consistent with cultural and religious norms. The importance of cultural diversity in the expressions and manifestations of grief is recognized in recent proposals of grief-related disorders for DSM-5 (discussed below) that include the criterion that "the bereavement reaction must be out of proportion or inconsistent with cultural or religious norms" to qualify as disordered (APA, 2011). Notably though, consistent psychometric performance of PGD/CG symptom criteria has been observed across different non-Western cultures, suggesting that it is not purely a "Western" construct (e.g., Fujisawa et al., 2010; Morina et al., 2011).

The syndrome has diagnostic validity

The syndrome should have diagnostic validity in terms of prognostic significance, psychobiological disruption, and response to treatment. The prognostic significance and underlying psychobiological disruptions of PGD/CG have been discussed above. With respect to treatment, there is growing evidence that treatments specifically designed to target PGD/CG symptoms are efficacious. Shear et al. (2005) found complicated grief treatment to be more effective in the treatment of PGD/CG than interpersonal psychotherapy originally designed for the treatment of depression. Boelen, de Keijser, van den Hout, and van den Bout (2007; see also Chapter 16) found cognitive–behavioral grief therapy to be more effective than supportive counseling. Thus, in these studies, interventions focusing on underlying mechanisms of PGD/CG were more effective than non-specific interventions also used for the treatment of other disorders. This indicates that, if not adequately diagnosed, a person with PGD/CG may receive a treatment that has insufficient effect for PGD/CG, whereas, if adequately identified, he or she can be referred to an effective treatment.

The syndrome has clinical utility

Inclusion of PGD/CG in DSM-5 has benefits in terms of clinical utility: It aids in the identification and treatment of a significant minority of bereaved people who were thus far not identified at all, or diagnosed with the wrong label. Illustrative are Shear et al.'s (2011) findings that 85% of a large sample seeking treatment for PGD/CG had made multiple attempts to receive adequate help before receiving effective PGD/CG-targeted psychotherapy. Clinical utility of PGD/CG is nonetheless an important area for further study (see First et al., 2004). Accordingly, research is now being prepared that addresses the acceptability of standardized PGD/CG criteria and their impact on clinical decision making and treatment.

No definition perfectly specifies boundaries for the concept "mental/ psychiatric disorder"

As with the criterion that "The syndrome is not primarily a result of social deviance or conflicts with society" (above) this point is an important consideration more than a defining feature of mental/psychiatric disorder (Stein et al., 2010) and – as such – applies no more or less to PGD/CG than to other syndromes in DSM. It could be taken as an encouragement to continue research on the nature, duration, and severity of grief symptoms defining the boundaries between normal/ uncomplicated grief and PGD/CG.

Diagnostic validators and clinical utility should help to differentiate the syndrome from "nearest neighbors"

Factor analytic studies support the differential diagnosis of PGD/CG. In many different samples PGD/CG symptoms have been found to be distinct from, rather than loading on a single dimension with, symptoms of depression, anxiety, and other nearest neighbors (Bonanno et al., 2007; Prigerson, Frank, et al., 1995). Moreover, as noted, PGD/CG is associated with many adverse outcomes when controlling for these symptoms, providing further evidence that it is distinct from its nearest neighbors.

Potential benefits of adding a new syndrome to DSM-5 should outweigh potential harms

Two frequently reported concerns about inclusion of PGD/CG in DSM-5 include the risk of medicalization of normal/uncomplicated grief and the stigmatization of those receiving the diagnosis. The risk of medicalization of normality is inherent to the DSM as a categorical system. That is, all signs and symptoms of all mental/ psychiatric disorders in DSM can also occur in "normal" individuals and they point at a disorder only when they are present in particular combinations, at particular levels of duration and severity. Because the boundaries between normality and psychopathology are hard to draw, there is always a risk of inflated rates of false positive diagnosis when normal signs and symptoms are falsely labeled as markers of some mental/psychiatric disorder. All this applies to grief: PGD/CG symptoms resemble reactions seen in normal/uncomplicated grief and there is indeed a risk of false positive diagnosis of PGD/CG. To some extent, pathologization of normal grief can be avoided by making a careful distinction between PGD/CG *symptoms* and PGD/CG *caseness*. If someone has PGD/CG symptoms, this does not necessarily mean that he or she has a mental/psychiatric disorder; this is so only when these symptoms are present at particular levels of duration and severity.

The risk of stigmatization is also not specific to PGD/CG. Although being diagnosed with any DSM label presents such a risk, this does not imply that these labels are not valid. In the case of grief, not including PGD/CG in DSM would leave a significant minority of afflicted individuals undiagnosed. The choice of words is important here: The label should be used to indicate not that some people grieve "abnormally" according to some rule, but, instead, that their suffering is so intense and causes so much distress and disability that it requires professional care. Concerns about stigmatization have not been supported by research: in a recent study, 98.5% of a community-based sample of bereaved people noted that they would be willing to receive help for PGD/CG if they were diagnosed with this condition and a similar percentage would be relieved to know they had a recognizable condition (Johnson et al., 2009).

Recent proposals of criteria for DSM-5

In light of the research findings reviewed above, three criteria sets have recently been proposed for inclusion in DSM-5: criteria for *Prolonged Grief Disorder* put forth by Prigerson et al. (2009), criteria for *Complicated Grief* from Shear et al. (2011), and criteria for *Adjustment Disorder (AD) Related to Bereavement* and *Bereavement Related Disorder* recently proposed by the DSM-5 Anxiety Disorder Working Group (APA, 2012).

Prolonged Grief Disorder

Prigerson developed a diagnostic algorithm for PGD. The 1999 consensus criteria (Prigerson et al., 1999) and criteria proposed by Horowitz et al. (1997) formed the starting point for this endeavor. Validation of the criteria proceeded through a series of analyses, using data from 291 mostly spousally bereaved people, who were all interviewed using the rater version of the ICG (Prigerson, Maciejewski, et al., 1995).

In the first phase of the analyses, methods from item response theory (IRT) were used to examine properties of 22 candidate PGD symptoms. In these analyses, six items were removed because they had poor *discriminative ability*, meaning that they were unable to distinguish reliably between different levels on the latent dimension of PGD severity. Another four items were removed because they showed *differential item functioning*, meaning that they were endorsed differently by people from different subgroups (e.g., men and women) who had similar scores on the underlying PGD dimension.

In the second phase, a criterion standard for PGD "caseness" was determined. Because, obviously, no such standard was available at this stage, the authors decided to define "caseness" as the score on the PGD dimension that had the greatest agreement with an expert clinician's judgment of whether or not a person represented a true case of PGD.

In Phase 3 the most parsimonious combination of symptoms that best distinguished between "cases" and "non-cases" of PGD was determined. Yearning was specified as a mandatory symptom, because this is a hallmark symptom of grief and, indeed, was among the items with the strongest ability to distinguish between low and high scores on the underlying dimension of PGD severity. Using combinatorics, a mathematical approach to study the performance of different combinations of items, almost 5,000 different algorithms were tested. The optimal, most efficient algorithm included yearning and at least five of nine additional symptoms, described under criterion C in Table 7.1.

In Phase 4 the predictive validity for three temporal subtypes of PGD was determined: *acute PGD* (meeting criteria for caseness at 0–6 months, but not at 6–12 months), *delayed PGD* (caseness at 6–12 months but not at 0–6 months), and *persistent PGD* (caseness at 0–6 months and 6–12 months). Findings revealed that delayed and persistent PGD, but not acute PGD, were related to adverse health outcomes at 12–24 months (including depression and PTSD, suicidal ideation, and poor quality of life). This phase thus provided evidence that PGD symptoms should not be labeled as a disorder when present in the first 6 month post loss. In the next phase, the formulation of the criteria was finalized with the addition of criterion D, requiring that symptoms were present to a disabling degree.

The predictive validity of the proposed criteria was examined in the sixth and last phase of the analyses. These analyses showed that those meeting criteria for PGD at 6–12 months post loss but not meeting criteria for concomitant depression, PTSD, or generalized anxiety disorder had a significantly greater chance than non-cases of suffering one of these disorders, suicidal ideation, functional disabilities, and reduced quality of life at 12–24 months post loss.

Complicated Grief

Shear et al. (2011; see also Simon et al., 2011) developed another set of standardized criteria for CG. To inform this process, the authors gathered data from three groups who all completed the ICG: bereaved healthy controls ($n = 95$), patients diagnosed with a mood or anxiety disorder ($n = 369$), and a group of patients presenting for treatment of CG ($n = 318$) that included 288 people identified as "cases" of CG. Cases were those who had a score of at least 30 on the ICG and who were identified as such by expert clinicians. The authors then conducted IRT, factor, and sensitivity/specificity analyses on these data to inform their proposal for CG criteria.

In the first step of their analyses, factor analysis on data of the full sample ($n = 782$) showed that ICG items represented a single underlying dimension. In the second step, IRT methods were used to explore the performance of items. These analyses showed that "feeling that life is empty," "loneliness," and "feeling

Table 7.1 Criteria for prolonged grief disorder, complicated grief, and bereavement related disorder

Prolonged Grief Disorder (Prigerson)	Complicated Grief (Shear)	Bereavement Related Disorder (DSM proposal)
A **Event:** Bereavement (loss of a significant other)	A The person has been bereaved, i.e. experienced the death of a loved one, for at least 6 months	A The person experienced the death of a close relative or friend at least 12 months earlier
B **Separation distress:** The bereaved person experiences yearning (e.g., craving, pining, or longing for the deceased; physical or emotional suffering as a result of the desired, but unfulfilled, reunion with the deceased) daily or to a disabling degree	B At least one of the following symptoms of persistent intense acute grief has been present for a period longer than is expected by others in the person's social or cultural environment: 1. Persistent intense yearning or longing for the person who died 2. Frequent intense feelings of loneliness or as if life is empty or meaningless without the person who died 3. Recurrent thoughts that it is unfair, meaningless, or unbearable to have to live when a loved one has died, or a recurrent urge to die in order to find or to join the deceased 4. Frequent preoccupying thoughts about the person who died, e.g., thoughts or images of the person intrude on usual activities or interfere with functioning	B Since the death at least one of the following symptoms is experienced on more days than not and to a clinically significant degree: 1. Persistent yearning/longing for the deceased 2. Intense sorrow and emotional pain because of the death 3. Preoccupation with the deceased person 4. Preoccupation with the circumstances of the death
C **Cognitive, emotional, and behavioral symptoms:** The bereaved person must have five (or more) of the following symptoms experienced daily or to a disabling degree: 1. Confusion about one's role in life or diminished sense of self (i.e., feeling that a part of oneself has died) 2. Difficulty accepting the loss 3. Avoidance of reminders of the reality of the loss	C At least two of the following symptoms are present for at least a month: 1. Frequent troubling rumination about circumstances or consequences of the death, e.g., concerns about how or why the person died, or about not being able to manage without their loved one, thoughts of having let the deceased person down, etc. 2. Recurrent feeling of disbelief or inability to accept the death, as if the person cannot believe or accept that their loved one is really gone 3. Persistent feeling of being shocked, stunned, dazed or emotionally numb since the death	C Since the death at least six of the following symptoms are experienced on more days than not and to a clinically significant degree: *Reactive distress to the death* 1. Marked difficulty accepting the death 2. Feeling shocked, stunned, or emotionally numb over the loss 3. Difficulty in positive reminiscing about the deceased 4. Bitterness or anger related to the loss 5. Maladaptive appraisals about oneself in relation to the deceased or the death (e.g., self-blame)

4. Inability to trust others since the loss
5. Bitterness or anger related to the loss
6. Difficulty moving on with life (e.g., making new friends, pursuing interests)
7. Numbness (absence of emotion) since the loss
8. Feeling that life is unfulfilling, empty, or meaningless since the loss
9. Feeling stunned, dazed or shocked by the loss

D **Timing:** Diagnosis should not be made until at least 6 months has elapsed since the death

E **Impairment:** The disturbance causes clinically significant impairment in social, occupational, or other important areas of functioning (e.g., domestic responsibilities)

F **Relation to other mental disorders:** The disturbance is not better accounted for by major depressive disorder, generalized anxiety disorder, or posttraumatic stress disorder

---

4. Recurrent feelings of anger or bitterness related to the death
5. Persistent difficulty trusting or caring about other people or feeling intensely envious of others who have not experienced a similar loss
6. Frequently experiencing pain or other symptoms that the deceased person had, or hearing the voice of or seeing the deceased
7. Experiencing intense emotional or physiological reactivity to memories of the person who died or to reminders of the loss
8. Change in behavior due to excessive avoidance or the opposite, excessive proximity seeking, e.g., refraining from going places, doing things, or having contact with things that are reminders of the loss, or feeling drawn to reminders of the person, such as wanting to see, touch, hear, or smell things to feel close to the person who died. (Note: sometimes people experience both of these seemingly contradictory symptoms.)

D The duration of symptoms and impairment is at least 1 month

E The symptoms cause clinically significant distress or impairment in social, occupational, or other important areas of functioning, where impairment is not better explained as a culturally appropriate response

---

6. Excessive avoidance of reminders of the loss (e.g., avoiding places or people associated with the deceased)
Social/identity disruption
7. A desire not to live in order to be with the deceased
8. Difficulty trusting other people since the death
9. Feeling alone or detached from other people since the death
10. Feeling that life is meaningless or empty without the deceased, or the belief that one cannot function without the deceased
11. Confusion about one's role in life or a diminished sense of one's identity (e.g., feeling that a part of oneself died with the deceased)
12. Difficulty or reluctance to pursue interests since the loss or to plan for the future (e.g., friendships, activities)

D The disturbance causes clinically significant distress or impairment in social, occupational, or other important areas of functioning

E Mourning shows substantial cultural variation; the bereavement reaction must be out of proportion or inconsistent with cultural or religious norms

stunned/dazed" discriminated best between high and low scores on the underlying CG dimension, whereas the items "experiencing pain as deceased," "avoidance," and "feeling drawn to things associated with deceased" emerged as poor indicators of CG.

Then, in a third step, the authors performed factor analysis on ICG scores obtained in the subsample of CG cases. The 19 items clustered into six underlying factors: (1) yearning and preoccupation, (2) anger and bitterness, (3) shock and disbelief, (4) estrangement from others, (5) hallucinations of the deceased, and (6) behavior change. This factor structure was used to inform the proposed criteria (see Table 7.1). For instance, the five ICG items that clustered into the first factor were grouped into four "symptoms of persistent intense acute grief" under criterion B. The two ICG items of factor 2 were combined in criterion C4.

In a fourth step, the authors examined the sensitivity (proportion of actual CG cases identified as such) and specificity (proportion of non-cases of CG identified as such) of separate ICG items and combinations of items. Of the individual items, "yearning and longing" was the most sensitive one, confirming its centrality to CG. Additional analyses showed that the presence of at least one symptom from the "yearning and preoccupation" cluster yielded the largest sensitivity, whereas the presence of at least one symptom from the "hallucinations" cluster yielded the lowest sensitivity. Then the authors examined in how many of the six clusters one symptom had to be present to optimally distinguish cases and non-cases. This analysis showed that having at least one symptom from the "yearning and preoccupation" cluster and from two other symptom clusters yielded the optimal identification of cases and non-cases.

In a next step, Shear et al. (2011) added several items to the CG criteria that were not included in their quantitative analyses. First, based on evidence for an association between CG and suicidal thinking, "suicidality" was added as part of the separation distress criterion (criterion B). Secondly, "rumination" was added as one of the symptoms under criterion C "because there is data for importance of this symptom" (pp. 108–109). Finally, "emotional or physical reactivity to reminders of the loss" was added under criterion C, because it proved important in studies by Bonanno et al. (2007).

In keeping with Prigerson's proposal, a time criterion described that the diagnosis should not be made in the first 6 months post loss. In keeping with the ICG instruction asking for symptom presence in the preceding month, a timeframe of at least 1 month of symptoms was required. Finally, a distress and disability criterion was added (criterion E).

Adjustment Disorder Related to Bereavement and Bereavement Related Disorder

The DSM-5 has embraced the idea that a disorder of grief should be included. The current state of affairs (April 2012) is that two disorders of grief have been proposed by the Anxiety Disorder Working Group. The first is called *AD Related to Bereavement* in the main body of the DSM-5. The second is called *Bereavement Related Disorder*, proposed for inclusion in its Appendix.

AD related to bereavement is defined as present when the person experiences on more days than not "intense yearning/longing for the deceased, intense sorrow and emotional pain, or preoccupation with the deceased or the circumstances of the death, at least 12 months following the death of a close relative or friend" (APA, 2012). Other symptoms that may qualify as indicative of the disorder are "difficulty accepting the death, intense anger over the loss, a diminished sense of self, a feeling that life is empty, or difficulty planning for the future or engaging in activities or relationships" (APA, 2012).

Criteria for Bereavement Related Disorder have been proposed for the Appendix – a part of the DSM where "unofficial disorders" are described that still need further study. Criteria are listed in Table 7.1. Criteria for this disorder are met if, at least 12 months after the death of the loved one, the person experiences one symptom placed under criterion B, and 6 of 12 symptoms representing "reactive distress" and "social/identity disruption" placed under criterion C, which cause significant distress and impairment.

Discussion

We summarized evidence that PGD/CG meets criteria for being included as a new condition in DSM-5. Working groups preparing DSM-5 have embraced this idea. Although this is an important step toward recognition of a distinct disorder of grief, critical comments can be made about the proposals for AD Related to Bereavement and Bereavement Related Disorder. Most importantly, no studies are yet available that have examined the validity, reliability, or dimensionality of criteria for the proposed two criteria sets. For instance, looking at criteria for Bereavement Related Disorder, there is no empirical validation for the 12-month time criterion, for the distinction between symptoms of "reactive distress" and "social/identity disruption," and for the requirement that 6 of 12 symptoms from criterion C need to be present to optimally identify cases.

Important also is that criteria for both proposed disorders differ considerably from the ones that have so far been used in clinical practice and research. Thus, their inclusion in DSM-5 will cause a significant discontinuity in clinical practice and research (see First et al., 2004). That is, in clinical practice, those who meet criteria for AD Related to Bereavement or Bereavement Related Disorder, based on the proposed criteria, differ from those who were thus far diagnosed with PGD/ CG, based on Prigerson's or Shear's criteria, or the frequently used cut-off of a score of > 25 on the ICG. Moreover, none of the research findings regarding the prevalence, risk factors, and treatment of PGD/CG are directly applicable to AD Related to Bereavement and Bereavement Related Disorder.

These problems could be averted if an empirically examined criterion set were included in DSM-5, such as the ones proposed by Prigerson et al. (2009) or Shear et al. (2011). This is not to say that these proposals require no further study. For instance, criteria from Prigerson et al. are based on a relatively small sample, mainly consisting of elderly bereaved spouses, and thus require replication. Criteria from Shear et al. (2011) seem complex (see below) and are not clearly linked to empirical research. For instance, it is not clear what data justify inclusion of unstudied criteria (e.g., rumination). Notable too is that several items have proven to have poor psychometric properties in prior studies; for instance, the identification and hallucinatory symptoms represented in criterion C6 proved to be poor indicators of PGD/CG in an earlier study by Prigerson et al. (1999). Further, the specification that the grief is present "longer than is expected by others in the person's social or cultural environment" (criterion B) would seem difficult to determine in a standardized and sufficiently reliable way.

An alternative would be to include in DSM-5 only symptom criteria that have been assessed in prior research. For instance, if DSM-5 criteria relied on symptoms assessed with the ICG, this would allow for re-analyses of the many data sets that have been collected with this scale in different countries, with different bereaved groups. Given that symptoms such as suicidality, positive reminiscing, or self-blame, which are all part of the criteria for Bereavement Related Disorder, are not included in the ICG or other scales used in prior studies, there is no chance that re-analyses of data could be helpful in testing the now proposed criteria.

Irrespective of their precise form, there is a need for standardized criteria for PGD/CG. Such criteria would enable clinicians to identify and treat the condition, and to receive reimbursement for this treatment. Moreover, standardized criteria would enable researchers to study causes, consequences, and treatment of this condition, and to compare findings between studies. Comparison of research findings has so far been difficult, given that researchers have not relied on the exact same criteria to define PGD/CG across studies. The time criterion, for instance, has changed. This does not diminish the value of studies supporting the diagnostic validity and clinical utility of the PGD/CG construct summarized in this chapter, particularly because most of these studies used the same measure (the ICG) and investigated PGD/CG as a continuous rather than a categorical construct. However, the variation in descriptions of PGD/CG in prior research should be considered in the process toward standardization of criteria and, at the same time, emphasizes the importance of achieving such standardization.

There are many topics that need further study. For instance, researchers should continue to search for diagnostic algorithms that best distinguish between bereaved individuals who are and those who are not at risk for persistent health impairments, with a time criterion that optimally balances false positives and negatives. This algorithm should be examined across heterogeneous groups of mourners. It is also important to strive for criteria that are parsimonious, even though these should cover the many different forms the clinical picture of PGD/CG may take. For example, the B3 criterion from Shear et al.'s (2011) criteria is not a good example in this respect because it encompasses four distinct symptoms that should be disaggregated. The algorithm of symptoms should be parsimonious as well: needing to have only two of eight criteria (Shear) is simpler to diagnose (and thus has stronger inter-rater reliability) than 6 of 12 criteria (Bereavement Related Disorder). Moreover, the latter proposal produces many more variations than the former one. Yet still, the former criteria may be too easy to meet and thereby inflate prevalence rates. Regardless, these are all empirical issues that can be investigated.

It is also important to distinguish symptoms of PGD/CG from the causes and consequences of these symptoms. For instance, in accord with the broader literature (also see Chapter 12 in this volume), rumination, included in Shear's criteria, is perhaps better seen as a cause than a symptom of PGD/CG. Suicidality is perhaps more a consequence than a symptom of PGD/CG.

Notwithstanding these considerations, it seems timely to include a formal category for PGD/CG in DSM-5. This would facilitate empirical research and would imply recognition of the suffering of a significant minority of mourners who experience difficulties in their process of recovery. Inclusion of a disorder of grief in DSM-5 would imply not a pathologization of something normal but, instead, a normalization of something that mostly is not, but sometimes is, indeed, pathological.

References

APA. (2000). *Diagnostic and statistical manual of mental disorders* (4th edn. Text Revision). Washington, DC: American Psychiatric Association.

APA. (2012). *Proposed revision for adjustment disorder*. Retrieved April 23, 2012, from http://www.dsm5.org/ProposedRevisions/Pages/proposedrevision.aspx?rid=367.

Boelen, P. A., & van den Bout, J. (2008). Complicated grief and uncomplicated grief are distinguishable constructs. *Psychiatry Research, 157*, 311–314.

Boelen, P. A., van den Bout, J., de Keijser, J., & Hoijtink, H. (2003). Reliability and validity of the Dutch version of the Inventory of Traumatic Grief. *Death Studies, 27*, 227–247.

Boelen, P. A., de Keijser, J., van den Hout, M. A., & van den Bout, J. (2007). Treatment of complicated grief: A comparison between cognitive behavioral therapy and supportive counseling. *Journal of Consulting and Clinical Psychology, 75*, 277–284.

Bonanno, G. A., Wortman, C. B., Lehman, D. R., Tweed, R. G., Haring, M., Sonnega, J., et al. (2002). Resilience to loss and chronic grief. *Journal of Personality and Social Psychology, 83*, 1150–1164.

Bonanno, G. A., Neria, Y., Mancini, A. D., Coifman, D., Litz, B., & Insel, B. (2007). Is there more to complicated grief than depression and PTSD? A test of incremental validity. *Journal of Abnormal Psychology, 116*, 342–351.

Faschingbauer, T. R., Zisook, S., DeVaul, R. (1987). The Texas Revised Inventory of Grief. In Zisook, S. (Ed.), *Biopsychosocial aspects of bereavement* (pp. 127–138). Washington, DC: APA Press.

First, M. B., Pincus, H. A., Levine, J. B., Williams, J. B., Ustun, B., & Peele, R. (2004). Clinical utility as a criterion for revising psychiatric diagnoses. *American Journal of Psychiatry, 161*, 946–954.

Fujisawa, D., Miyashita, M., Nakajima, S., Ito, M., Kato, M., & Kim, Y. (2010). Prevalence and determinants of complicated grief in the general population. *Journal of Affective Disorders, 127*, 352–358.

Hogan, N., Worden, J. W., & Schmidt, L. (2004). An empirical study of proposed complicated grief disorder criteria. *Omega, 48*, 263–277.

Holland, J. M., Neimeyer, R. A., Boelen, P. A., & Prigerson, H. G. (2009). The underlying structure of grief: A taxometric investigation of prolonged and normal reactions to loss. *Journal of Psychopathology and Behavioral Assessment, 31*, 190–201.

Horowitz, M. J., Bonanno, G. A., & Holen, A. (1993). Pathological grief: Diagnosis and explanation. *Psychosomatic Medicine, 55*, 260–273.

Horowitz, M. J., Siegel, B., Holen, A., Bonanno, G. A., Milbrath, C., & Stinson, C. H. (1997). Diagnostic criteria for complicated grief disorder. *American Journal of Psychiatry, 154*, 904–910.

Johnson, J. G., First, M. B., Block, S., Vanderwerker, L. C., Zevin, K., Zhang, B. H., & Prigerson, H. G. (2009). Stigmatization and receptivity to mental health services among recently bereaved adults. *Death Studies, 33*, 691–711.

Kersting, A., Brähler, E., Glaesmer, H., & Wagner, B. (2011). Prevalence of complicated grief in a representative population-based sample. *Journal of Affective Disorders, 131*, 339–343.

Morina, N., Von Lersner, U., & Prigerson, H. G. (2011). War and bereavement: Consequences for mental and physical distress. *PLoS One, 6*, e22140.

O'Connor, M. F., Wellisch, D. K., Stanton, A. L., Eisenberger, N. I., Irwin, M. R., & Lieberman, M. D. (2008). Craving love? Enduring grief activates brain's reward center. *Neuroimage, 42*, 969–972.

Prigerson, H. G., Frank, E., Kasl, S. V., Reynolds, C. F., Anderson, B., Zubenko, G. S., Houck, P. R., George, C. J., & Kupfer, D. J. (1995). Complicated grief and bereavement-related depression as distinct disorders: Preliminary empirical validation in elderly bereaved spouses. *American Journal of Psychiatry, 152*, 22–30.

Prigerson, H. G., Horowitz, M. J., Jacobs, S. C., Parkes, C. M., Aslan, M., Goodkin, K., et al. (2009). Prolonged Grief Disorder: Psychometric validation of criteria proposed for DSM-V and ICD-11. *PLoS Medicine, 6*(8): e1000121.

Prigerson, H. G., & Jacobs, S. C. (2001). Traumatic grief as a distinct disorder: A rationale, consensus criteria, and a preliminary empirical test. In Stroebe, M. S., Hansson, R. O., Stroebe, W., & Schut, H. (Eds.), *Handbook of bereavement research: Consequences, coping, and care* (pp. 613–647). Washington, DC: APA Press.

Prigerson, H. G., & Maciejewski, P. K. (2008). Grief and acceptance as opposite sides of the same coin: setting a research agenda to study peaceful acceptance of loss. *British Journal of Psychiatry, 193*, 435–437.

Prigerson, H. G., Maciejewski, P. K., Reynolds, C. F., Bierhals, A. J., Newsom, J. T., Fasiczka, A., et al. (1995). Inventory of Complicated Grief: A scale to measure maladaptive symptoms of loss. *Psychiatry Research, 59*, 65–79.

Prigerson, H. G., Shear, M. K., Jacobs, S. C., Reynolds, C. F., Maciejewski, P. K., Davidson, J., et al. (1999). Consensus criteria for traumatic grief. *British Journal of Psychiatry, 174*, 67–73.

Reynolds, C. F. III, Miller, M. D., Pasternak, R. E., Frank, E., Perel, J. M., Cornes, C., et al. (1999). Treatment of bereavement-related major depressive episodes in later life. *American Journal of Psychiatry, 156*, 202–208.

Robins, E., & Guze, S. B. (1970). Establishment of diagnostic validity in psychiatric illness: Its application to schizophrenia. *American Journal of Psychiatry, 126*, 983–987.

Shear, K., Frank, E., Houck, P. R., Reynolds, C. F. III. (2005). Treatment of complicated grief: A randomized controlled trial. *JAMA, 293*, 2601–2608.

Shear, M. K., Simon, N., Wall, M., Zisook, S., Neimeyer, R., Duan, N., et al. (2011). Complicated grief and related bereavement-issues for DSM-5. *Depression and Anxiety, 28*, 103–117.

Simon, N. M., Wall, M. M., Keshaviah, A., Dryman, M. T., LeBlanc, N. J., & Shear, M. K. (2011). Informing the symptom profile of complicated grief. *Depression and Anxiety, 28*, 118–126.

Stein, D. J., Phillips, K. A., Bolton, D., Fulford, K. W. M., Zadler, J. Z., & Kendler, K. S. (2010). What is a mental/psychiatric disorder? From DSM-IV to DSM-V. *Psychological Medicine, 40*, 1759–1785.

8 Is complicated/prolonged grief a disorder?

Why the proposal to add a category of complicated grief disorder to the DSM-5 is conceptually and empirically unsound

Jerome C. Wakefield

Should prolonged intense grief be classified as a mental disorder in DSM-5? This is what two research groups studying "prolonged grief disorder" (PGD) or "complicated grief disorder" (CG) have proposed (Prigerson et al., 2009; Shear et al., 2011). Rather than considering prolonged intense grief generally to be a painful but normal-range phenomenon that is on the upper end of the continuum of grief severity, and rather than seeing such severity as reflecting normally varying factors such as closeness of the lost relationship and the griever's circumstances and temperament, existential nature, and history, these researchers argue that grief that satisfies certain symptom and duration criteria should be considered in and of itself a psychiatric disorder.

Any biologically designed response can malfunction, so it is plausible that there exist some grief disorders. The question is whether the proposed CG diagnostic criteria identify a class of such disorders with reasonable validity.

There are many versions of the CG proposal, with varying mixes of symptom criteria and with duration requirements ranging from 2 months to 14 months. Recent articles have tended to defend a 6-month duration, and I will focus on these proposals. However, the DSM-5 workgroup has recently placed on the APA website a proposed CG-like variant of adjustment disorder with a 12-month duration requirement. In addition to the standard requirements for adjustment disorder, the bereavement-related variant is defined as follows:

> *[Adjustment Disorder] Related to Bereavement:* For at least 12 months following the death of a close relative or friend, the individual experiences on more days than not intense yearning/longing for the deceased, intense sorrow and emotional pain, or preoccupation with the deceased or the circumstances of the death. The person may also display difficulty accepting the death, intense anger over the loss, a diminished sense of self, a feeling that life is empty, or difficulty planning for the future or engaging in activities or relationships. Mourning shows substantial cultural variation; the bereavement reaction must be out of proportion or inconsistent with cultural or religious norms. (American Psychiatric Association, 2010a)

These criteria appear to require only one symptom, such as yearning for the lost person (the symptoms in the first sentence are disjunctively linked by "or," and the symptoms in the second sentence "may" also be present but apparently need not be). The rationale offered on the DSM-5 website for thus pathologizing grief lasting more than 12 months as an adjustment disorder notes "a need for a diagnosis to characterize an individual who is having clinically significant distress as a result of the death of a loved one" (American Psychiatric Association, 2010b), but offers no evidence or systematic argument that these conditions are in fact disorders. Instead, it refers to the research literature on grief: "This matter has been the subject of considerable research on abnormal mourning which has been named, in some circles, 'prolonged grief' and as 'complicated grief' by other researchers" (American Psychiatric Association, 2010b). This reference circularly takes it as given that the grief researchers are correct in claiming that what they are studying is abnormal mourning rather than intense normal mourning.

The DSM-5 also proposes for further study a separate bereavement related disorder, defined using symptoms similar to other recent proposals. Diagnosis of bereavement related disorder would be warranted if, at least 12 months after the loss, the individual continued to experience yearning, intense sorrow, or continued preoccupation with the lost individual or the circumstances of the loss, plus at least six out of the following symptoms relating to the death that cause distress or role impairment beyond what is culturally expected: difficulty accepting the death; feeling shocked or stunned; difficulty positively reminiscing about the deceased; bitterness or anger related to the loss; self-blame; avoidance of reminders of the loss; desire not to live in order to be with the deceased; difficulty trusting other people; feeling alone or detached; feeling life is meaningless or empty; confusion about one's role in life; difficulty pursuing one's interests.

The bereavement related disorder proposal includes the same 12-month duration requirement and the same sorts of symptoms as the bereavement-related adjustment disorder proposal, but with a much more demanding symptom threshold. Anyone who qualified as disordered under "bereavement related disorder" or similar CG proposals would certainly qualify as disordered under "adjustment disorder related to bereavement." So, the DSM-5 plans to pathologize all those cases that would be pathologized as "complicated grief" and more. The question of whether the specified conditions are really disorders is thus now of more than theoretical interest.

I review here the arguments for the disordered status of these likely newly pathologized conditions. Regarding terminology, the DSM-5's label of "bereavement related disorder" is insufficiently specific because there are many disorders other than disordered grief itself that can be related to bereavement, ranging from major depression to heart failure. Consequently, I use the term "complicated grief" (CG).

Bowlby's warning

John Bowlby's work set the stage for most current work on loss, and CG researchers cite his attachment theory as a framework for thinking about grief (Shear et al., 2007; Shear & Shair, 2005). I preface my discussion of recent grief research with a reminder of Bowlby's warning about seeing normal grief as briefer or less severe than it is.

Bowlby was concerned that clinicians and researchers might misconstrue the potential severity and duration of normal grief and thus pathologize this gradual and difficult process. He thus cautioned:

> Loss of a loved person is one of the most intensely painful experiences any human being can suffer . . . [T]here is a tendency to under-estimate how intensely distressing and disabling loss usually is and for how long the distress, and often the disablement, commonly lasts. Conversely, there is a tendency to suppose that a normal healthy person can and should get over bereavement not only fairly rapidly but also completely. Throughout this volume I shall be countering those biases. Again and again emphasis will be laid on the long duration of grief. (Bowlby, 1980, p. 8)

What did Bowlby have in mind when he emphasized "the long duration of grief"? According to Bowlby, widows who fully recover:

> are more likely to take two or three years to do so than a mere one . . . I emphasize these findings, distressing though they are, because I believe that clinicians sometimes have unrealistic expectations of the speed and complete-ness with which someone can be expected to get over a major bereavement. (p. 101)

As I will show, current grief researchers seem to have forgotten Bowlby's warning.

Three arguments based on the DSM's definition of mental disorder

I begin by briefly considering three arguments for the pathological status of pro-longed grief that are linked in one way or another to the DSM's definition of mental disorder.

Impairment as the criterion for disorder

Prigerson and colleagues sometimes claim that the essence of disorder is impair-ment (e.g., "Thus, impairment is the criterion for determining pathology"; Prigerson & Maciejewski, 2006, p. 15). This criterion is so invalid that it would imply that sleep and pregnancy are disorders. Moreover, normal grief can be highly distressing and role impairing, so impairment alone cannot distinguish normal from disordered grief. In support of the impairment claim, Prigerson and Maciejewski cite the DSM's definition of mental disorder, which requires that, to be a disorder, a condition must be "associated with present distress (e.g., pain-ful symptom) or disability (i.e., impairment in one or more important areas of functioning)" (American Psychiatric Association, 2000, p. xxi). However, this is presented by the DSM as a necessary condition for disorder, not as sufficient by itself. Prigerson and Maciejewski fail to cite the definition's additional requirements (see below).

Disorder as statistical deviance

Those arguing that CG is a disorder frequently fall back on statistical criteria that rely on the degree of severity of grief symptoms as a "gold standard" supporting disorder attributions, whether setting the threshold at the upper 50% (Horowitz et al., 1997) or 20% (Prigerson et al., 1997, 2009). Yet it is plainly a fallacy to identify statistical deviance with disorder (Stroebe et al., 2000; Wakefield, 1992a). Deviant features need not be disorders (even normal grief is "deviant" relative to typical functioning, and those with greater intensity of normal responses will always by definition be statistically deviant from the majority), and common features need not be normal.

The statistical approach may be inspired by the DSM's statement in its definition of disorder that, for a condition to be a disorder, it "must not be merely an expectable and culturally sanctioned response to a particular event, for example, the death of a loved one" (American Psychiatric Association, 2000, p. xxxi). This clause eliminates certain socially sanctioned, expectable conditions from disorder status, but it does not imply that every unexpectedly intense response is a disorder.

There is an especially powerful reason for dismissing the statistical argument in the CG debate. The alternative hypothesis to the CG disorder claim is that the identified conditions are by and large simply the upper end of the severity continuum of normal grief. Consequently, the statistical argument begs the question, because the competing hypotheses – the normal and the disordered construal of the identified conditions – equally assert that the specified conditions are statistically deviant.

The argument that CG satisfies DSM's definition of mental disorder

Prigerson's group repeatedly claims that CG satisfies the DSM's definition of mental disorder, and quotes chapter and verse. The problem is that these quotations consistently leave out a crucial sentence in the definition that states the "dysfunction" requirement that a harmful (impairing, distressing) condition, to be a disorder, must result from a dysfunction: "Whatever its original cause, it must currently be considered a manifestation of a behavioral, psychological, or biological dysfunction in the individual" (p. xxi). The centrality of the dysfunction requirement and an elaboration of "dysfunction" as failure of biologically designed processes to perform their functions is pursued in my "harmful dysfunction" analysis of disorder (Wakefield, 1992b, 1999, 2006).

So, to satisfy the DSM's definition of mental disorder, the CG proposal's fundamental challenge is to show that the conditions identified as CG are due to dysfunction. CG researchers have attempted to meet this challenge. I consider the three most prominent arguments they offer for the dysfunction etiology of CG: the distinctive symptom argument, the derailment of grieving argument, and the predictive validity argument.

CG as categorical pathology: the distinctive symptom argument

It is sometimes claimed that CG's symptoms are qualitatively different phenomena from those of normal grief, lending plausibility to the claim that its symptoms are pathognomonic for a disorder with a distinct etiology. However, this appealing notion has not turned out to fit the facts. Misleading statements suggestive of such distinct symptoms continue to appear in the literature (e.g., "CG is characterized by a unique pattern of symptoms following bereavement"; Lichtenthal, Cruess, & Prigerson, 2004, p. 637), but CG researchers have mostly come to acknowledge that there is no clear qualitative difference between the symptoms of CG and normal grief and have consequently rejected this as a test of validity: "The issue is not whether the symptoms sort themselves into seemingly pathological versus seemingly normal symptom clusters" (Prigerson & Maciejewski, 2006, p. 15).

A glance at the proposed DSM diagnostic criteria above, ranging from yearning and disbelief to lack of interest in usual activities, reveals that all of the proposed symptoms of CG occur in intense acute grief. In 1998, a panel of experts acknowledged that there are no "smoking gun" symptoms revealing a pathological grief process: "The panel acknowledged that a wide range of 'symptoms' that occur after a loss could be considered within normal limits" (Prigerson et al., 1999, p. 68). For example, when Prigerson et al. (1997) used a symptom intensity criterion for CG that identified the top 20% at 6 months post loss as disordered, they found that 57% of the grief-stricken met the criterion at 2 months post loss.

Shear and Mulhare (2008) claim that CG differs qualitatively from normal grief in being accompanied by rumination and avoidance (Table 2, p. 664). However, these symptoms are not in fact unique to CG. Shear and Mulhare's definition of rumination is extraordinarily broad (even worrying about your prolonged grieving qualifies), and their list of normal-grief symptoms includes the rumination-like item "thoughts and memories of the deceased are prominent and preoccupying." Regarding avoidance, grieving individuals normally use avoidance to regulate the degree of painful sadness (Stroebe & Schut, 1999), and research indicates that avoidance occurs during acute stages of grief (Bonanno, Papa, Lalande, Zhang, & Noll, 2005, Figure 3, p. 92).

The view that CG cannot be symptomatically distinguished from acute grief was confirmed by a recent taxometric study by a group of leading CG researchers. They concluded: "As a whole, these taxometric analyses offered little support for a categorical conceptualization of normal grief and PGD" (Holland, Neimeyer, Boelen, & Prigerson, 2009, p. 198).

CG as derailed grief: the interminability argument

Grief varies enormously from individual to individual and according to circumstances. Recent research challenges traditional stage models of grief and suggests that grief is an idiosyncratic process of integrating a loss (Bonanno & Kaltman, 1999), suggesting that any durational and intensity CG cut-off points are arbitrary. Those with lengthier grieving processes may be dealing with closer relationships or deeper existential issues, for example, and simply experiencing longer integration trajectories rather than suffering from dysfunctions.

CG proponents have come up with an ingenious and powerful reply to this objection. They argue that, as a matter of empirical fact, once grief goes on for the specified 6- to 12-month duration, then it goes on more or less indefinitely. According to this argument, normal grief surely should have a trajectory of recovery over time to be normal, so interminable intense grief strongly suggests that something has gone wrong with the grief process: It has been "derailed" from its biologically designed course. Such "derailment" implies internal dysfunction that is blocking the natural course of the recovery process, and thus justifies attribution of disorder:

> Complicated grief, unlike normal or uncomplicated grief, is not a self-limited process. (Prigerson et al., 1995, p. 23)

> In some bereaved individuals . . . the intense pain and distress festers, can go on interminably (as "complicated grief") . . . Once established, complicated grief tends to be chronic and unremitting. (Zisook & Shear, 2009, pp. 67, 69)

> CG entails harmful dysfunction in that a normal healing process has been derailed. (Shear et al., 2011, p. 105)

According to this argument, the primary reason for the validity of the 6-month or 12-month duration threshold for complicated grief is that symptoms that exist intensely at 6 or 12 months tend to persist indefinitely after that rather than to diminish with time, on account of a derailed or frozen or otherwise malfunctioning grieving process. The alternative hypothesis is simply that at 6 or 12 months, although there may be some cases of frozen grief processes, most symptoms are part of a longer but still normal grieving process that is moving towards resolution at a slow pace. The question is: What do the data actually show? Do they confirm or falsify the "derailment/interminability" hypothesis?

The "interminability" claim is bewildering in light of the history of grief research. As Bowlby makes clear, many individuals continue to heal after 6 months or a year. Case after case in classic texts portrays individuals with severe grief reactions at 1 or 2 years grappling with deep issues triggered by the loss and eventually progressing to recovery.

For example, Parkes and Weiss (1983) describe the difficult course of grief of Mrs. Webley, a woman in her early thirties with a 9-year-old daughter, whose husband, on whom she was greatly dependent, died of diabetes. Her acute grief immediately after the death was severe, including disbelief, intense yearning, and difficulty with usual chores. Mrs. Webley's situation was less acute but not much improved a year after the loss: "When we saw Mrs. Webley at the end of the first year of her bereavement [i.e., 13 months post loss], she appeared depressed and apathetic . . . Despite the passage of the year, her husband was constantly in Mrs. Webley's thoughts." Although she had gotten over the disbelief ("I have got myself to knowing now that he's gone"; p. 140), she was despairing ("You're in a lost world") and unmotivated ("I don't feel like working any more. I go in because I force myself to go in"; p. 140), and still missed and thought about her husband frequently ("But I do miss him terribly. I'm still involved with him too much . . . I keep saying, Why did you have to go?"; pp. 140–141). Yet she was gradually experimenting with greater autonomy: "I know the decisions are wrong, but I'm trying to learn how to do it myself" (p. 141).

Mrs. Webley at 1 year without doubt would have met currently proposed criteria for complicated grief. Did she have an interminable mental disorder in which the grieving progress was derailed? Or was she simply dealing with greater and deeper challenges than most? Parkes and Weiss continue:

> We saw Mrs. Webley again at three years after her husband's death, two years after the interview in which she made the comments quoted above. Much had happened in her life. She had begun seeing another man, had become pregnant by him, and had given birth to a second daughter. She hoped the man she was seeing would marry her . . . Mrs. Webley was no longer lonely. She still at times thought of her husband, but she no longer did so constantly. (pp. 141–142)

Mrs. Webley clearly needed a relationship to feel happy. The loss of her husband left her not only bereaved, but lonely and adrift, experiencing chronic distress. Is it a disorder to be lonely and to desperately need to find someone with whom to share your life, and to dwell meanwhile on the past? She had the capacity to change and succeeded in doing so, but it took a few years and she was still in intense grief at the 13-month mark. Perhaps the critical point was not her suffering but the degree of progress she had made, and the beginnings of growth that were discernible. Although Mrs. Webley might have benefited from more support and therapeutic help, it seems doubtful that she or other individuals with such trajectories are best served by pathologizing their experiences and placing them within the category of the mentally disordered. Indeed, it is possible that such an approach could "derail" such individuals from the hard work they need to do to change their circumstances and themselves to create a new life.

To mention a more famous example, Viederman (1995) notes that the 29-year-old Richard Feynman, later to become a Nobel laureate in physics, wrote to his beloved former wife, then 2 years dead, that he was unable to experience anything for other women. He subsequently remarried happily and lived an extraordinarily productive life with a well-known contagious *joie de vivre* (p. 2).

These are not isolated cases. The interminability argument is falsified by the very research data on which CG proponents rely. No doubt there are some interminable cases of intense grief. Shear's group, although supporting a 6-month durational threshold for CG (Shear et al., 2011), reports that the mean time post-loss of the clinical sample recruited to refine its criteria was 5.5 years (Simon et al., 2011). The evidence indicates that the proposed criteria for CG do not in fact identify such an interminably grieving group.

For example, Horowitz et al. (1997) measured 30 symptoms of grief at 6 months and 14 months post loss in a sample of 70 bereaved individuals. Rather than symptoms at 6 months being persistent, results indicated that "The frequency of these symptoms declined significantly in the interval between 6 months and 14 months after the death of a significant other" (Horowitz et al., 1997, p. 909). For example, here are the changes from 6 to 14 months in the percentages of the sample judged to have severe levels of six symptoms from Horowitz et al.'s criteria: unbidden memories, 72% vs. 42%; strong yearning, 58% vs. 35%; emotional spells, 47% vs. 20%; feeling alone and empty, 59% vs. 38%; avoids reminders of the deceased, 44% vs. 17%; and loss of interest in important activities, 62% vs. 19%. In another study, Prigerson et al. (2008; see also Maciejewski, Zhang, Block, & Prigerson, 2007) analyzed longitudinal data on grief and depressive symptoms, documenting the rise and fall of various symptoms over time. The results reveal gradually decreasing levels of symptoms over the first 18 months of grieving (see Fig. 8.1 in Prigerson et al. 2008, p. 169). For example, 5–6 months post loss the average occurrence of yearning is almost daily; after a year, about every other day; after almost 2 years, weekly. Prigerson et al. (2008) attempt to explain their rationale for calling the CG cases "chronic" and "persistent" despite decreasing symptom levels:

> [T]hose diagnosed with PGD revealed persistently high levels of grief that did not drop to the level of those without PGD throughout the study observation period . . . Thus, the PGD diagnosis after 6 months postloss identified a group of bereaved individuals who would remain persistently grief stricken. (p. 172)

However, the fact that the most symptomatically severe at 6 months remained higher in symptoms over time than those who were less symptomatic at 6 months just shows that those higher in symptoms at 6 months tend to stay higher in symptoms later on as well. They are the more intense responders. This form of "persistence" does not imply lack of improvement in symptoms over time. It just implies lack of change of relative position as the group overall improves.

Prigerson et al. also claim that, because indicators of grief peak at about 6 months, after that the symptoms are likely to represent pathology. This is a bewildering claim. After the point of greatest average intensity of normal symptoms, there inevitably will be a period as the normal symptoms gradually subside – but the symptoms remain predominantly normal. This absurd argument would imply that every individual taller than the 5′9″ average height must be suffering from a growth hormone pathology.

In sum, the available data decidedly falsify the "persistence" claim for those having CG-level symptoms at 6–18 months. Beyond that interval, persistence remains relatively unstudied. The "derailment" and "interminability" claims as applied to 6- to 12-month-threshold CG are scientific myths.

CG as risk factor: the predictive validity argument

Predictive validity is currently Prigerson and colleagues' central argument for CG being a pathology:

> [T]he symptoms of CG are associated with and predictive of substantial morbidity (e.g., depression, suicidal ideation, high blood pressure), adverse health behaviors (e.g., increased smoking, alcohol consumption, poor sleep), and quality of life impairments. Thus, the symptoms are indicative of pathology . . . What our results demonstrate is that the set of CG symptoms that we have identified . . . are predictive of many negative outcomes and that is the basis for distinguishing them from normal grief symptoms. (Prigerson & Maciejewski, 2006, p. 15)

Prigerson et al. in their definitive 2009 study attempt to show not only that CG differs from intense normal grief (the issue on which I focus), but also that CG is different from other common disordered responses to loss and stress, particularly major depressive disorder (MDD), posttraumatic stress disorder (PTSD), and generalized anxiety disorder (GAD). Prigerson et al. in their final predictive validity analyses eliminate individuals with one or more of these other disorders, and test the predictive validity of "pure" CG (only 3.3% of the bereaved sample). I focus on these analyses as most relevant, so henceforth *CG* will refer to "pure" CG.

In their bereaved sample, Prigerson et al. (2009) compare the risk for four negative outcomes at 12–24 months of those who qualify for CG at 6–12 months (i.e., they have the most severe symptoms) with those who do not. For CG versus other grievers at 6–12 months, the outcomes at 12–24 months are other mental disorders (MDD, GAD, PTSD), 28.6% vs. 3.4%; suicidal ideation, 57.1% vs. 10.1%; functional disability, 71.4% vs. 35.9%; and poor quality of life, 83.3% vs. 14.7%, respectively (Table 4, p. 9). Note that the initial 6- to 12-month baseline levels of the predicted variables are not controlled or reported in these comparisons. Before evaluating these empirical results, I comment on the conceptual status of the predictive validity argument.

Conceptual problems with the predictive validity argument

Prigerson et al. argue that, if CG predicts statistically heightened negative outcomes, then it must be pathological. This is a grossly invalid inference; later negative outcomes are not always evidence of earlier disorder. The fact that individuals who grieved more intensely had increased negative outcomes no more implies that their grief was disordered than does the fact that there are heightened risks with pregnancy imply that pregnancy itself is a disorder. Risk permeates life and does not itself imply dysfunction. Risk management to avoid negative outcomes is one thing, diagnosis and treatment of disorder another, and confusing the two spuriously pathologizes life's many difficulties.

In mounting a "risk" argument for CG's disordered status, Prigerson et al. (2009) might be construed as relying on the "risk" clause of the DSM's definition of mental disorder, which states that a disorder must be associated either with present distress or impairment "or with a significantly increased risk of suffering death, pain, disability, or an important loss of freedom" (American Psychiatric Association, 2000, p. xxxi). However, the definition does not say that risk is sufficient for disorder. In addition, the risk must be caused by a dysfunction. Because risk is omnipresent in life, risk is evidence of disorder only if the presence of a dysfunction can be independently supported.

Using predictive validity for disorder validation has the inherent weakness that both disorders and non-disorders can have negative outcomes of similar kinds. For example, bad marriages with resultant chronic high stress are known to predict various later physical ailments, but that has not moved the DSM to accept bad marriages as mental disorders. Shortness and homeliness within their normal-range domains are known to have negative impacts on a variety of outcomes, yet neither is a disorder.

Another limitation of predictive validity is that the statistical associations on which claims of predictive validity for a group are based are sometimes due to relatively small numbers of individuals within the group experiencing negative outcomes. It is then questionable whether pathologizing the entire group is justified based on associations due to a minority. For example, coughing is statistically associated with an increased likelihood of tuberculosis, but no one suggests pathologizing everyone who is coughing, because most coughing is a normal biologically designed adaptive response to abnormal environmental factors such as dust in the air. The statistical association between coughing and tuberculosis is based on a few individuals whose coughs are due to tuberculosis. Those individuals – not necessarily the others – suffer from pathology. To support the case for CG at 6–12 months being a disorder, the negative outcomes measured at 12–24 months must plausibly imply that the condition at 6–12 months involved a dysfunction of grief processes, not just intense normal grief.

The use of risk of negative outcomes to support disorder attribution is sufficiently problematic that a committee considering DSM-5 revision of the definition of mental disorder proposed eliminating the "risk" clause:

> Regarding the phrase pertaining to "increased risk", risk factors are important to bear in mind and perhaps even to treat . . . At the same time, we would note that disorder and risk factors should not be conflated . . . We therefore tentatively suggest simplifying this criterion by omitting the phrase on risk. (Stein et al., 2010, p. 1762)

Prigerson's "risk" argument suffers from precisely the fallacy identified by the committee. "Treatment" of risk factors may be warranted, but raises different issues from treatment of disorder. The DSM lists non-disordered conditions that are frequently targets of clinical intervention under what have come to be known as the "V Codes" because of their diagnostic codes in the manual, and risk without dysfunction belongs there.

Mortality

Turning to negative outcomes of CG, Prigerson et al. (2009) mention in passing a CG-as-disorder argument not addressed in their data, namely the mortality associated with grief. However, they assume without evidence that CG will encompass the majority of such deaths. To the contrary, it is known that the most significant mortality increase occurs in the first days and weeks post loss, decreasing almost to population levels by about 6 months post loss (Buckley, McKinley, Tofler, & Bartrop, 2010). That is before CG would be diagnosed. Some continued excess mortality may be related to pre-existing physical conditions or lifestyle tendencies exacerbated by stress, not requiring a CG disorder explanation (Parkes & Prigerson, 2010).

Physical disorders

Some studies have shown that CG predicts small increases in some later physical problems, such as high blood pressure or cardiovascular disease and even cancer. These results are based on few cases, and causality has not been established. Moreover, all mental and physical stresses are risk factors for such disorders. Running for a bus and having a marital argument both raise the risk of a heart attack, yet neither is a disorder. There is no reason to attribute such outcomes to disordered grief as opposed to intense normal grief.

Other mental disorders

Of four outcomes examined in the 2009 paper, I set aside development of another mental disorder. The identified mood and anxiety disorders are of high prevalence (their validity can be questioned as well; Horwitz & Wakefield, 2007), and have many high-stress predictors that are not disorders. The fact that CG, like many other stressful circumstances, contains a risk of developing these stress-related disorders does not make it a disorder, any more than losing a job and marital dissolution, which also increase risk for these disorders, are themselves disorders.

Functional impairment and quality of life

By definition, those qualifying for CG had higher symptom severity than those with non-CG at 6–12 months. As noted, one can expect the more intense responders with highest 6- to 12-month grief symptoms generally to stay highest at 12–24 months, even if symptoms subside on a lengthy trajectory. Thus, in considering whether 12- to 24-month outcomes support an inference to 6- to 12-month dysfunction, the "dysfunction" hypothesis must be compared with the alternative hypothesis that higher grief severity at 6–12 months can explain the results at 12–24 months.

Prigerson et al.'s (2009) measures for functional impairment and quality of life were intentionally formulated with low thresholds to maximize the chances of finding an effect. For example, "Individuals with at least 'some difficulty' with at least one of the 14 tasks (e.g., bathing) were considered functionally impaired in order to make the measure sensitive to impairment in a highly functioning sample" (p. 3). So, if an individual sometimes did not engage in just one activity (e.g., walking a mile) because of grief symptoms, that was enough to qualify as functionally impaired. This is problematic because normal grief symptoms are often moderately impairing as a result of withdrawal, reduced energy and motivation, and focus on grieving.

Moreover, one would expect those higher in grief symptoms, disordered or not, to experience a lower quality of life. Quality of life in itself is a dubious indicator of disorder, especially among those emotionally affected by death of a loved one. Bonanno et al. (2005) show that the related measure of self-perceived health status increases dramatically from 4 to 18 months as grief distress decreases. One would expect quality of life to track grief distress as well.

So, the quality of life and functional impairment outcomes might mean nothing more than that the CG group, having had higher grief intensity at 6–12 months, still had high enough intensity at 12–24 months to display negative outcomes generally associated with emotional suffering, including lower subjective quality of life and moderate functional impairment. The modest thresholds for being "positive" on these outcomes are consistent with normal grief and do little to address the disorder question.

Suicidal ideation

The outcome variable most often cited as evidence of CG pathology is suicidal ideation. As noted, of CG versus non-CG at 6–12 months, 57.1% versus 10.1%, respectively, were positive for suicidal ideation at 12–24 months. To measure this variable, "Positive responses to one or more of the four Yale Evaluation of Suicidality screening questions were categorized as having suicidal ideation" (Prigerson et al., 2009, p. 3). The study's measure of suicidal ideation was aimed at maximizing sensitivity; any positive (non-zero) responses to questions concerning feelings about living versus dying, wish to live, wish to die, and thoughts of killing oneself were considered "positive" for suicidal ideation (Holly Prigerson, personal communication, November 5, 2010).

The preamble to the questions notes that "Sometimes people with [grief] feel that this experience has affected their feelings about living." Such reaching for positive responses would be justified in a screening instrument where sensitivity is paramount, but this study attempts to validate the presence of disorder, and reaching for positive responses regarding, for example, "feelings about living" is straying far from clearly pathological terrain. A weaker will to live in the face of real loss and sustained emotional suffering is not the same as suicidal ideation indicative of pathology. One would expect individuals with higher levels of feelings of meaninglessness, lack of role clarity, impoverished friendship networks and interests, and yearning for their lost loved one (all CG symptoms) to be more likely to entertain the thought that life may not be worth living, quite aside from any pathology.

However, the most serious validity problem in inferring earlier disorder from later suicidal ideation arises from the wording of the one question asking directly about suicidal ideation: "In light of [the loss], have you ever had thoughts of killing yourself?", with possible positive replies "yes" or "possibly." An "ever" question logically implies that the positives will increase with time, because one never exits from a positive answer that one has "ever" had such thoughts. As time goes on, those who continue to have intense suffering and who thus may transiently think about whether suicide would be preferable are added to the number of positives. (The number who already had such thoughts at 6–12 months is not presented.) Indeed, a "positive" on this question does not indicate current suicidal ideation at all; someone whose only suicidal ideation was 6 months earlier would still appropriately answer "yes."

The likelihood of false positives for suicidality is increased even further by "possibly" being a positive response, encompassing those who have only transiently or vaguely entertained the notion of ending it all. Many people under stress entertain such thoughts. For example, in one high school screening for suicidal thoughts over the past 3 months, 10% responded positively, yet the stability of such answers over a mere 8-day test–retest period was low. The designers of the instrument observed that "Poor test–retest reliability could be related to the ephemeral nature of suicidal ideation and depressive feelings among teens" (Shaffer et al., 2004, p. 77). The same is likely to be true of those suffering from grief, and the "possibly" option exacerbates the problem. So, the increased "suicidal ideation" among the CG-diagnosed group could be a near-tautologous result of the way this question is phrased plus the CG group's greater distress and the inevitable desperate thoughts that occur during lengthy periods of suffering. Taking all the problems together with this and the other outcomes, there are no grounds for plausibly inferring an earlier disorder from these outcome measures.

Conclusion

I identified several arguments presented to support the claim that intense grief lasting 6–12 months or more is pathological, rather than a severe normal variant, and thus that CG should be added as a new category of disorder to the DSM-5. These arguments fail either because of conceptual flaws or because they are contrary to the research evidence. The current CG proposals are thus scientifically unwarranted.

Granting that in principle there are grief disorders, my analysis suggests the need for far more stringent diagnostic criteria than those proposed, if massive false positive diagnoses are to be avoided. The proposals' relabeling of millions of intensely grieving individuals as disordered is serious enough, but a much greater false positives problem would occur subsequently when the diagnosis is on the books and out of the research setting, and general practitioners are treating grief in a public sensitized by pharmaceutical advertising to think about grief as a disorder.

The research effort supporting the CG proposal, clearly motivated by compassion for the grief-stricken, has been a win–win gamble for grief studies. The research has highlighted clinical phenomena previously ignored or marginalized, and added immeasurably to our understanding of grief's symptoms and trajectory. The contributions of the Prigerson and Shear CG research groups is a watershed in grief studies, irrespective of the merits or the outcome of the proposal to add CG as a new category of disorder to DSM-5.

References

American Psychiatric Association. (2000). *Diagnostic and statistical manual of mental disorders, DSM-IV-TR* (4th edn., text revision). Washington, DC: APA.

American Psychiatric Association. (2010a). *Adjustment disorders*. Retrieved April 28, 2011, from http://www.dsm5.org/ProposedRevisions/Pages/proposedrevision.aspx?rid=367.

American Psychiatric Association (2010b). *Adjustment disorders: Rationale*. Retrieved April 28, 2011, from http://www.dsm5.org/ProposedRevisions/Pages/proposedrevision.aspx?rid=367#.

Bonanno, G. A., & Kaltman, S. (1999). Toward an integrative perspective on bereavement. *Psychological Bulletin, 126*(6), 760–776.

Bonanno, G. A., Papa, A., Lalande, K., Zhang, N., & Noll, J. G. (2005). Grief processing and deliberate grief avoidance: A prospective comparison of bereaved spouses and parents in the United States and the People's Republic of China. *Journal of Consulting and Clinical Psychology, 73*, 86–98.

Bowlby, J. (1980). Loss. *Sadness and depression* (Attachment and loss, Vol. 3). New York: Basic Books.

Buckley, T., McKinley, S., Tofler, G., & Bartrop, R. (2010). Cardiovascular risk in early bereavement: A literature review and proposed mechanisms. *International Journal of Nursing Studies, 47*(2), 229–238.

Holland, J. M., Neimeyer, R. A., Boelen, P. A., & Prigerson, H. G. (2009). The underlying structure of grief: A taxometric investigation of prolonged and normal reactions to loss. *Journal of Psychopathology and Behavioral Assessment, 31*, 190–231.

Horowitz, M. J., Siegel, B., Holen, A., Bonanno, G. A., Milbrath, C., & Stinson, C. H. (1997). Diagnostic criteria for complicated grief disorder. *American Journal of Psychiatry, 154*, 904–910.

Horwitz, A. V., & Wakefield, J. C. (2007). *The loss of sadness: How psychiatry transformed normal sorrow into depressive disorder*. New York: Oxford University Press.

Lichtenthal, W., Cruess, D., & Prigerson, H. G. (2004). A case for establishing complicated grief as a distinct mental disorder in DSM-V. *Clinical Psychology Review, 24*, 637–662.

Maciejewski, P., Zhang, B., Block, S., & Prigerson, H. (2007). An empirical examination of the stage theory of grief. *Journal of the American Medical Association, 297*(7), 716–722.

Parkes, C. M., & Prigerson, H. G. (2010). *Bereavement*. New York: Routledge.

Parkes, C. M., & Weiss, R. S. (1983). *Recovery from bereavement*. New York: Basic Books.

Prigerson, H. G., Bierhals, A. J., Kasl, S. V., Reynolds, C. F., Shear, M. K., Day, N., et al. (1997). Traumatic grief as a risk factor for mental and physical morbidity. *American Journal of Psychiatry, 154*, 616–623.

Prigerson, H. G., Frank, E., Kasl, S. V., Reynolds, C. F., Anderson, B., Zubenko, G. S., et al. (1995). Complicated grief and bereavement-related depression as distinct disorders: Preliminary empirical validation in elderly bereaved spouses. *American Journal of Psychiatry, 152*, 22–30.

Prigerson, H. G., Horowitz, M. J., Jacobs, S. C., Parkes, C. M., Aslan, M., Goodkin, K., et al. (2009). Prolonged grief disorder: Psychometric validation of criteria proposed for DSM-V and ICD-11. *PLoS Medicine, 6*(8), e1000121.

Prigerson, H. G., & Maciejewski, P. K. (2006). A call for sound empirical testing and evaluation of criteria for complicated grief proposed for DSM-V. *Omega, 52*, 9–19.

Prigerson, H. G., Shear, M. K., Jacobs, S. C., Reynolds, C. F., Maciejewski, P. K., Davidson, J. R. T., et al. (1999). Consensus criteria for traumatic grief: A preliminary empirical test. *British Journal of Psychiatry, 174*(1), 67–73.

Prigerson, H. G., Vanderwerker, L. C., & Maciejewski, P. K. (2008). A case for inclusion of prolonged grief disorder in DSM-V. In Stroebe, M. S., Hansson, R. O., Schut, H., & Stroebe, W. (Eds.), *Handbook of bereavement research and practice: Advances in theory and intervention* (pp. 165–186). Washington, DC: American Psychological Association.

Shaffer, D., Scott, M., Wilcox, H., Maslow, C., Hicks, R., Lucas, C. P., et al. (2004). The Columbia Suicide Screen: Validity and reliability of a screen for youth suicide and depression. *Journal of the American Academy of Child and Adolescent Psychiatry, 43*, 71–79.

Shear, M. K., Monk, T., Houck, P., Melhem, N., Frank, E., Reynolds, C., & Sillowash, R. (2007). An attachment-based model of complicated grief including the role of avoidance. *European Archive of Psychiatry and Clinical Neuroscience, 257*, 453–461.

Shear, M. K., & Mulhare, E. (2008). Complicated grief. *Psychiatric Annals, 38*(10), 662–670.

Shear, M. K., & Shair, H. (2005). Attachment, loss, and complicated grief. *Developmental Psychobiology, 47*, 253–267.

Shear, M. K., Simon, N., Wall, M., Zisook, S., Neimeyer, R., Duan, N., et al. (2011). Complicated grief and related bereavement issues for DSM-5. *Depression and Anxiety, 28*, 103–117.

Simon, N. M., Wall, M. M., Keshaviah, A., Dryman, M. T., LeBlanc, N. J., & Shear, M. K. (2011). Informing the symptom profile of complicated grief. *Depression and Anxiety, 28*(2), 118–126.

Stein, D. J., Phillips, K. A., Bolton, D., Fulford, K. W. M., Sadler, J. Z., & Kendler, K. S. (2010). What is a mental/psychiatric disorder? From DSM-IV to DSM-V. *Psychological Medicine, 40*(11), 1759–1765.

Stroebe, M., & Schut, H. (1999). The dual process model of coping with bereavement: Rationale and description. *Death Studies, 23*(3), 197–224.

Stroebe, M., van Son, M., Stroebe, W., Kleber, R., Schut, H., & van den Bout, J. (2000). On the classification and diagnosis of pathological grief. *Clinical Psychology Review, 20*, 57–75.

Viederman, M. (1995). Grief: Normal and pathological variants. *American Journal of Psychiatry, 152*(1), 1–4.

Wakefield, J. C. (1992a). The concept of mental disorder: On the boundary between biological facts and social values. *American Psychologist, 47*, 373–388.

Wakefield, J. C. (1992b). Disorder as harmful dysfunction: A conceptual critique of DSM-III-R's definition of mental disorder. *Psychological Review, 99*, 232–247.

Wakefield, J. C. (1999). Evolutionary versus prototype analyses of the concept of disorder. *Journal of Abnormal Psychology, 108*, 374–399.

Wakefield, J. C. (2006). The concept of mental disorder: Diagnostic implications of the harmful dysfunction analysis. *World Psychiatry, 6*, 149–156.

Zisook, S., & Shear, K. (2009). Grief and bereavement: What psychiatrists need to know. *World Psychiatry, 8*, 67–74.

9 Lessons from PTSD for complicated grief as a new DSM mental disorder

Jan van den Bout and Rolf J. Kleber

Introduction

In 1980 Post-Traumatic Stress Disorder (PTSD) was introduced as a diagnostic category in the *Diagnostic and Statistical Manual of Mental Disorders* (3rd Edition) (DSM-III; American Psychiatric Association, 1980). It is the only disorder in the current DSM nomenclature in which a cause of the disorder is included, namely a (psycho)trauma (or more than one). The proposed DSM-5 disorders Prolonged Grief Disorder (Prigerson et al., 2009) and Complicated Grief (CG; Shear et al., 2011) resemble PTSD in that a necessary cause is also specified, namely the loss of a significant other, in particular the death of a loved one. Both could fit in a general rubric of event-related disturbances, as was already argued in the 1990s (Brom, Kleber, & van den Bout, 1993). For that reason it is illuminating to review what the scientific, clinical, and societal consequences have been of the introduction of PTSD in the DSM system. What have been the pros and cons of the construct PTSD since its inclusion in DSM? And, after more than three decades of research and clinical work, what lessons are there to be learnt for the concepts of prolonged grief disorder and complicated grief, in case one of them (or an amalgam of these) is 'canonized' in DSM-5?

PTSD and DSM

The introduction of PTSD in 1980 in DSM-III has undoubtedly led to an impressive bulk of empirical research covering a wide range of traumatic experiences. As the editor of the *Journal of Traumatic Stress* Paula Schnurr (2010) mentioned, the number of publications on trauma grew over ninefold between 1980–1984 and 1995–1999 (from 930 to 8,606). Not only in absolute figures, but also relatively speaking, publications on trauma became more frequent: within the anxiety disorders literature between 1981 and 1985, 16% of the publications were on trauma, growing to 38% between 2000 and 2005 (Boschen, 2008).

Before going into detail on the vicissitudes of the construct PTSD in science (specifically in psychiatry and [clinical] psychology) and in society (including persons who experienced a traumatic event), we first provide a short historical account of the introduction of this construct.

A historical note on the introduction of PTSD in DSM

A system like the DSM does not fall from heaven nor is it a 'necessary' conse-quence of scientific findings. Rather, it is the result of human endeavour and is ultimately created through consensus meetings with experts. In these consensus meetings scientific findings of course play a role, but frequently other concerns are decisive, sometimes because there simply are no scientific data to rely on. PTSD is in this respect a nice illustration: the experts were to a large extent influenced by the *Zeitgeist*. What were these societal influences that led to the introduction of PTSD in DSM?

In the 1960s and 1970s, the USA fought a long war in Vietnam, a war that was far from popular in the home country. During many years numerous anti-war demonstrations were organized. When U.S. veterans returned to their home com-munities, they did not receive a warm welcome (as the veterans of the Second World War had received). For instance, they were often called 'baby killers'. Partly as a result of this unfriendly welcome and the idea of having fought for nothing (the USA ultimately lost this war), a substantial number of veterans suffered from chronic distress, severe feelings of malaise, marital problems, alcoholism, and social instability after discharge from the army. A group of anti-war psychiatrists (most notably Chaim Shatan and Robert Lifton, who earlier had written about the victims of the atomic bombs on Hiroshima and Nagasaki) and Vietnam veterans (most notably Charles Figley) proposed a relatively new view on these problems: the veterans exhibited a 'post-Vietnam Syndrome' (a term first used by Shatan in 1972). That is, their health problems were the result of the traumatic experi-ences in Vietnam. The central new assumption was that '– in contrast to standard psychiatric opinion – problematic temperaments, personalities, and behaviours were not shaping a subject's response to trauma but were products of it' (McHugh & Treisman, 2007, p. 215). In short, the atrocities experienced during combat in Vietnam were considered as the main cause of the veterans' difficulties, but one should realize that the poor homecoming climate and the lack of recognition reinforced the problems.

At the same time, the American Psychiatric Association (APA) was working on a fundamental revision of the DSM system, a revision in the direction of a revival of nosological entities (van Praag, 2000). Thus emphasis was laid on a description of concrete symptoms belonging to a circumscribed disorder. The 'post-Vietnam Syndrome' ideally fulfilled the criteria for such a disorder: it appeared to be a clear disorder with highly identifiable symptoms. In an effective lobby of the Vietnam Veterans Working Group of psychiatrists the editorial committees of DSM (most notably Nancy Andreasen) were persuaded to adopt the concept as a new disorder.

Once this was accomplished, three groups worked together to let the diagnosis grow after it had been adopted (see McHugh & Treisman, 2007). Psychiatrists realized that not only the atrocities in Vietnam but also civilian traumata could lead to a similar disorder: they were also 'victims of [traumatic] stress'. Vietnam veterans realized that a diagnosis of war-caused disorder was more honourable than a personality disorder, substance abuse, or an adjustment disorder. Somewhat later this was also realized by victims of other severe events, such as rape, physical abuse, and accidents. Finally, the Veterans Administration was eager to embrace the diagnosis as an excellent justification for its work with Vietnam veterans.

Essential for the conceptual formulation of PTSD was the scientific work of the psychiatrist Mardi Horowitz. He conducted a series of elegant experiments in the early 1970s, in which he analysed the central responses to traumatic events. In 1976 he published his seminal book *Stress Response Syndromes* (Horowitz, 2003), in which he formulated disordered forms of coping with traumatic stress. This work formed the basis for the content of the PTSD concept.

To conclude: primarily societal developments (a draining war that was finally lost, resulting in veterans with, among others, severe feelings of malaise) led to the introduction of PTSD in DSM-III.

Critical voices on the mental disorder PTSD

As already indicated, the introduction of PTSD gave rise to much research. Consequently, we now know much more about traumatic stressors and their negative consequences. Theoretical models on the origin and maintenance of posttraumatic symptomatology have been formulated and tested. Posttraumatic pathology has become one of the important foci of psychology and psychiatry, leading to more funding of research on trauma. Effective therapy methods for PTSD have been developed and tested, and much has been learnt about the possibilities as well as limitations (including noxious effects) of prevention and treatment (e.g. debriefing). These scientific and societal accomplishments have been accompanied by the foundation of societies for professionals in the trauma field, such as the International Society for Traumatic Stress Studies (ISTSS), with branches in nearly all continents. In addition, there are specialized trauma journals, such as the *Journal of Traumatic Stress* and the *European Journal of Psychotraumatology*. By and large, in view of the just-mentioned accomplishments, one can state that the introduction of PTSD in DSM has been a nearly unprecedented success.

However, during the 30 years of its existence there have been dissenting voices, which seem to become only louder with the coming of DSM-5. These critical voices relate to the characterization of traumatic events and resulting symptoms and to the suggestion that PTSD may be primarily a product of social construction (Young, 2004). In a rather sceptical review, Rosen and Lilienfeld (2008) stated that virtually all core assumptions of the construct of PTSD lack compelling or consistent empirical support. Other authors (for example, McNally, 2004, 2009) have also analysed the conceptual limitations. In the next paragraphs we will discuss the most salient issues raised by PTSD critics. These issues are also highly relevant to a future inclusion of complicated grief in DSM-5.

The stressor criterion

The central tenet of the concept of PTSD is that a special class of events (criterion A: the stressor criterion) is causally related to a certain set of reactions (criteria

B–D: the symptom criteria). It is evident that criterion A events are not a sufficient cause for PTSD (because even the most severe traumatic events do not always lead to PTSD), but these events are seen as a *necessary* condition for PTSD. To put it simply: the concept of PTSD implies that there can be no PTSD without having experienced traumatic events. However, what does research show about this relation?

People can show the full range of PTSD symptoms without having experienced criterion A events. These symptoms appear after non-criterion A events such as marital disruption. As an illustration: Mol et al. (2005) conducted an open population study among nearly 1,500 respondents. They found that non-traumatic life events can generate at least as many PTSD symptoms as 'traumatic' events, casting doubt on the specificity of traumatic events as a cause of PTSD. It thus appears that full-blown PTSD can develop in the absence of the occurrence of a criterion A event. This result could be caused by the fact that several PTSD symptoms are rather generally defined. Nevertheless, the specificity of the concept of trauma (defined as extreme experiences of powerlessness and disruption) is lost.

Dose–response relationship between traumatic stressors and symptoms

A corollary of the foregoing is the assertion that the more 'heavy' the event is ('traumatic' or otherwise), the 'heavier' the symptoms are. Research shows that this hypothesis has not always been corroborated (see Rosen & Lilienfeld, 2008). Factors other than the event per se may be more important. Traumatic events are often not the largest contributor to outcome. Thus, criterion A events are not necessary and surely not sufficient to instigate PTSD; but, in addition, factors extraneous to the traumatic event may contribute more variance to clinical outcome than the event itself.

Changes in the stressor criterion

In DSM-III the stressor criterion A was relatively simple: 'Existence of a recognizable stressor that would evoke significant symptoms of distress in almost everyone' (American Psychiatric Association, 1980, p. 238). In later editions the objective part of the stressor criterion was expanded, while at the same time a subjective criterion was added. In DSM-IV it reads:

> The person has been exposed to a traumatic event in which both of the following were present: (1) the person experienced, witnessed, or was confronted with an event or events that involve actual or threatened death or serious injury, or a threat to the physical integrity of self or others (2) the person's response involved intense fear, helplessness, or horror. (American Psychiatric Association, 1994, p. 427)

'Confronted with' could mean 'hearing about', and thus the implications of this expansion were considerable. Watching television and being confronted with a disaster or hearing or reading narratives of survivors could potentially lead to PTSD. This led to quite a lot of debate. Spitzer, First, and Wakefield (2007) plead for more stringent criteria in the interest of 'Saving PTSD from itself'. Most likely, this indirect confrontation will be dropped from the criterion definition in DSM-5.

A consequence of this change in criterion A for the relation between PTSD and CG can be illustrated with the results of a community survey in Detroit by Breslau et al. (1998). Criterion A stipulates: 'confronted with . . . the actual . . . death'. Of the total 2,181 respondents, 60% indicated that they had experienced the sudden, unexpected death of a friend or relative. No fewer than 31% of the persons with PTSD had experienced such a sudden loss. So, loss became more or less part of the PTSD definition. One could comment that with this change in criterion A the clinical picture of PTSD has changed dramatically: to a large extent PTSD now also consists of grief phenomena, ignoring salient differences between posttraumatic and grief reactions (Boelen, van den Hout, & van den Bout, 2006; Raphael, Martinek, & Wooding, 2004; see also Chapter 10 of this volume).

The issue of comorbidity

One of the appealing aspects of PTSD is that it strikes mental health practitioners and laymen (including patients) as a self-evident syndrome: traumatic stressors can be so vehement and intruding that 'flashbacks' and forms of avoidance and denial are only 'natural'. However, research has clearly shown that a person confronted with a traumatic experience can suffer from more mental disorders than PTSD. There is substantial comorbidity observed, so much that a 'pure' PTSD disorder appears to be a rarity. So, is PTSD simply a sort of amalgam of other disorders and is the diagnosis of PTSD, although appealing, in fact redundant? For instance, one third to one half of those suffering from PTSD also show a clinical depression (Keane, Marshall, & Taft, 2006). That someone may suffer from depression at the same time is not surprising when one looks at the symptoms that are listed for both PTSD and depression: loss of interests, social indifference, trouble sleeping, and difficulty concentrating. Other concomitant disorders regularly occurring with PTSD are substance abuse disorders, complicated grief, and generalized anxiety disorder.

Overemphasis or simulation of complaints?

If a patient reports having experienced a traumatic experience, most health care practitioners usually will not check whether this event actually happened. However, it was found among Vietnam veterans in the United States suffering from combat-induced PTSD that some of them had experienced no combat in Vietnam and that some of them had not even been in Vietnam (McNally, 2004). The symptoms were heavily emphasized, exaggerated, or even simulated. Undoubtedly, the legal possibility of financial compensation for combat-related PTSD played a large role. As mentioned before, PTSD is the only diagnosis in DSM in which an external cause is mentioned. Therefore it is a diagnosis that can be used to get (financial) compensation. It might have secondary gains. The extent of this problem is not known; it occurs probably more after experiences for which objective data about the (f)acts are not easily available.

Society and trauma/PTSD

The term *(psycho)trauma* has become very popular in society. The concept of (psycho)trauma and, in its vestige the disorder PTSD, has been enormously popularized, even to the extent that nowadays *PTSD* is a term that is known by many readers of newspapers. Also, most people now 'know' and realize that very distressing events can lead to severe mental effects. In some countries the official mental disorder of PTSD has led to the possibility of compensation for damage for clients with PTSD. Among professionals working with 'traumatized' clients the mental disorder PTSD has led to more status (and to more funding). However, the enormous popularity of the terms *trauma* and *PTSD* has some consequences that might be or may become problematic, for laymen without traumata as well as for people who experienced traumatic events. These effects may also occur after the introduction of a diagnosis of complicated grief.

First of all, there is the danger of 'trauma inflation'. The term *trauma* is often used in everyday speech to point to almost every negative event, such as the transition from kindergarten to elementary school. This inflation is hardly present in scientific and professional literature (the *Journal of Traumatic Stress* publishes mainly about war, disasters, and abuse). Nevertheless, the term has crept into common usage as a label for minor problems and daily hassles as well. The focus on severe events and their long-lasting and serious disturbances is lost and the term runs the risk of becoming meaningless.

Perhaps more importantly, by and large the phrase *posttraumatic stress disorder* seems to imply that a traumatic event is the main determinant of the (stress) reactions and malfunctioning of a person (or client/patient). Above we saw that such a link is far from self-evident. The danger is that such a diagnosis obscures other possible pathogenic features (Rosen & Lilienfeld, 2008) that might be important, such as prior and current vulnerabilities, which could therapeutically be targeted. Admittedly, for some clients such a presentation is pleasant: they can attribute their emotional problems to an external event (and one might speculate that this is a major reason for the popularity of the term *trauma*). However, it is questionable whether such a notion is beneficial for them: their own responsibility for and influence on their prior and current emotional problems no longer seem at stake.

Somewhat paradoxically, recent developments in the field of traumatic stress underline the point that is made here. More and more emphasis is laid on the finding that some people do quite well under 'traumatic' circumstances: they are resilient (Bonanno, 2004; Brom & Kleber, 2009; see also Chapter 5 of this volume). In fact these resilient people are the best proof of the assertion that it is not a traumatic event itself, but the way a person conceptualizes and reacts to a 'traumatic' event, that determines his or her emotions and behaviours.

DSM: a pragmatic system with drawbacks

Do we really need elaborate and precise definitions of mental disorders? In psychiatric epidemiology some decades ago, a strong movement arose to come to unequivocal descriptions of mental disorders. Researchers needed unambiguous criteria to assess mental disorders, especially in the case of collaborative research in different countries. Also for mental health practitioners across countries it became desirable to use the same diagnostic phrases for the same mental phenomena. Thus, both research diagnostic criteria and classification systems for mental disorders were formulated (or revised).

As noted earlier, characteristic of the third edition of DSM in 1980 was a revival of the nosological way of looking at psychiatric problems. Subsequently, DSM-IV went further along those lines. The nosological disease model holds that 'psychiatric disorders are characterised by a particular symptomatology, course, outcome, treatment response . . .' (van Praag, 2000, p. 151). Van Praag rightly stresses that for mental health problems/disorders '[t]his disease model is a premise, not an empirically based concept. The premise holds that disturbances of the psychic "apparatus" manifest themselves as discrete entities' (ibid.). In the DSM-IV the very first feature of the definition of mental disorder is: 'A clinically significant behavioral or psychological syndrome or pattern that occurs in an individual'. We note that *pattern* seems a much weaker expression than *syndrome*, whereas the word *syndrome* appears weaker than *disorder*, the term that is commonly used in the case of somatic disorders. Recently Stein et al. (2010) reviewed the DSM-IV definition of mental disorder and proposed some changes with an eye on the coming DSM-5. They explicitly state that no definition perfectly specifies precise boundaries for the concept of mental disorder. Nevertheless, the current diagnostic criteria for the mental disorders are quite strict.

The DSM system, originally primarily a tool for researchers, who of course need some form of categorization and classification, has subsequently been used as a tool for mental health professionals assessing their clients. It is a tool that is prototypical for the medical model: there is a disorder or there is no disorder. It is also a tool with severe implications: only when a disorder has been established should reimbursed help be given. In other words: a mental health professional can bill the insurance company only in cases where there is a diagnostic code, which thus requires a diagnosis in terms of some form of 'official' disorder.

The strict focus on having to decide whether a particular client/patient 'has' a disorder (or syndrome or pattern) or not is understandable in some settings (a yes or no decision makes sense in various insurance, medical, or forensic contexts), but it also has disadvantages. Tucker wrote in an editorial in the *American Journal of Psychiatry* some words which almost every clinician will recognize:

> by using DSM, sometimes clinicians are treating the diagnosis and not the patient . . . We are not looking at or studying the patient's phenomenology any more, but are looking for the symptoms needed to make the diagnosis . . . Accurate observation and the story of the patient must be included in our

diagnostic processes. All are necessary for the effective care of our patients, which in the long run, is what it is all about. (Tucker, 1998, p. 161)

Cooper (2004; see also Chapter 2, this volume) has argued cogently that the answer to the question 'what is a (mental) disorder?' is determined not only by scientific findings but also by social factors (such as the perceived need that people with severe emotional problems should get help) and financial factors (such as – a consideration of the mental health practitioner – the wish to make it easier for patients to obtain reimbursement, or – a consideration of the insurance companies – the wish to restrict the number of patients who qualify), irrespective of the question whether their mental problems fall within the definition of a mental disorder. She gives several examples to underline her argument, one from a (former) DSM Working Group on PTSD which noted that 'requiring a minimum duration before a diagnosis of PTSD could be made might reduce help-seeking behaviour as well as reimbursement for treatment' (Davidson, Foa, et al., 1996; cited in Cooper, 2004). Cooper stresses also that social factors (such as the perceived need that people with severe emotional problems should get help) are determinants for including certain severe emotional problems within DSM, which reflects a widespread conviction among many health practitioners: the DSM should furnish a licence for doing reimbursed interventions with clients who need psychotherapeutic help, and undoubtedly there are intensely grieving people for whom this is the case.

To recapitulate: (1) although a precise definition of mental disorder is lacking, the diagnostic criteria for the separate mental disorders are quite strict; (2) there are clear indications that the very focus on classification issues (consisting of two steps: is there a disorder and, if so, what is the disorder?) may hinder the diagnostic and the therapeutic process; and (3) social, clinical, and financial factors influence what is considered a disorder and/or influence what is included in the DSM or not. Hence, a consideration for including CG within the DSM could be that almost all grief experts are of the opinion that some form(s) of complicated grief exist(s), but they have as yet dissenting opinions on the issue of whether the currently proposed DSM-5 grief disorders cover their ideas on CG adequately.

More generally speaking, one should perhaps go a step further. Perhaps less attention and effort should be paid to deciding whether something is a disorder or not. Instead, the efforts and skills and time of clinicians should rather be devoted to alleviating human mental suffering, irrespective of the answer to the question whether this suffering is an indication of a mental disorder or not (see also Bolton, 2008, for a philosophical treatise on this subject). Additionally, it should be remembered that, if there is an official disorder, there is frequently no one-to-one relation between a certain disorder and intervention. For example, for the large majority of Axis I disorders (including the frequent mood and anxiety disorders) the intervention of choice is mainly cognitive–behavioural therapy. This being the case one could wonder what the merits are of all the efforts towards classification, when the chosen intervention hardly has a relation with the classification, possibly because 'transdiagnostic' processes are more important than previously thought. An additional consideration is that, in the case of some 'official' disorders, hardly anything can be done, whereas in cases where no 'official' disorder has been diagnosed there are frequently effective intervention activities available. Also, most mental health practitioners assess whether a patient 'has' a DSM disorder primarily for administrative reasons (partly resulting from the insurance system), not for therapeutic reasons.

Complicated grief and DSM-5: explorations

We now return to our main question: what lessons are to be learnt for the disorder complicated grief from the adventures of PTSD in the 30 years since its inception? In our section on critical voices on the mental disorder PTSD we discussed issues that have a clear relevance to a possible introduction of CG in DSM-5. Should complicated grief (or whatever other term might be chosen) be included in the DSM system or not? If the answer is yes: what can be predicted about the future of this new disorder? Let us try to extrapolate from the findings about PTSD to the eventual inclusion of CG in DSM.

Acknowledgement of suffering

The inclusion of the mental disorder of PTSD led to much research. The field of traumatic stress is booming in science. The same can be said of society: trauma(tic stress) is a much discussed topic in the media and among the public. That traumatic events sometimes can lead to severe mental problems is now common wisdom in society, and some victims acquire a set of symptoms that can be labelled as PTSD. Although we are not aware of research on this matter, persons with PTSD seem not to be stigmatized for having this psychiatric label. On the contrary, there is nowadays recognition of the (pathological) effects of traumatic events. Similarly, for patients with severe mental problems in the aftermath of severe events, the 'official' disorder PTSD has made reimbursement for psychotherapeutic help possible.

Including CG in the DSM might have similar consequences. Currently, the dominant attitude towards grief appears to be: grief is part of life, so please restrict the whining. Inclusion of CG would lead to the realization that complications in grief are a serious matter, which can take the form of a real disorder and need special care. Such a label provides patients with acknowledgement. They will be taken (more) seriously by professionals.

Growth of effective interventions

Since 1980 numerous controlled studies have been published on interventions for PTSD. In the literature, the suggestion has repeatedly been made that experts on grief interventions should look at what has been found and accomplished in the field of interventions for PTSD. This suggestion is somewhat ironic, because before 1980 there were already grief intervention studies that were in fact proto-typic for the later studies on PTSD (e.g. Ramsay, 1977). However, in the decades since 1980 far fewer controlled intervention studies have been published on CG than on PTSD. Based on the experiences with PTSD, it seems safe to conclude that an official mental disorder in DSM would lead to more and better-suited interven-tion approaches for people suffering from CG. In addition, it will probably also lead to better guidelines about whether one should refrain from intervention. For instance, some acute interventions after trauma (such as emotional debriefing) that originally appeared to be sensible have been found inadvisable (Bisson, Brayne, Ochberg, & Everly, 2007). The parallel between grief and trauma is intriguing in this respect: treatments of disorders have been found to be effective, but brief forms of preventative counselling have not always been found to be effective (Schut & Stroebe, 2010).

Above we mentioned that in the case of a mental disorder in which the cause is implied (PTSD) there is the danger that such a diagnosis obscures prior and current vulnerabilities, which could be targeted therapeutically. By implication, this would possibly also apply for CG. However, just as this possible danger de facto is no problem in concrete therapeutic activities (because psychotherapy is always about changeable factors within a person), it is to be expected that this will not be a problem for the treatment of CG either.

The introduction of a disorder as self-fulfilling prophecy

As noted earlier, since the inclusion of PTSD in DSM-III, public attention to trauma and the consequences of traumatic experiences has grown enormously. From a societal perspective, PTSD's inclusion has led to consequences that gen-erally seem more positive than negative. However, scientifically speaking, the picture is less positive. Robert Spitzer, one of the main protagonists of the (new) DSM approach in 1980, wrote with two noted scholars: 'Since its introduction into DSM-III in 1980, no other DSM diagnosis . . . has generated so much contro-versy in the field as to the boundaries of the disorder, diagnostic criteria, central assumptions, clinical utility, and prevalence in various populations' (Spitzer, First, & Wakefield, 2007, p. 233). The question arises: if we had known then what we now know about the construct of PTSD, would PTSD have been accepted as an official mental disorder? The answer to this question may possibly be yes, but we are not certain. However, the paradox is: we know what we know now, for the very reason that PTSD was introduced as a disorder (resulting in much research). And the paradox goes even further: because of its societal success and impact, the somewhat ramshackle construct PTSD will undoubtedly survive in the DSM-5.

In addition, the case of PTSD has shown that its inclusion in DSM has led to research that eventually led to changes in PTSD criteria. Along similar lines, one could predict that inclusion of CG in DSM with (some amalgam of) the proposed diagnostic criteria could lead to fruitful research, on the basis of which better diagnostic criteria could be formulated.

Although grief is part of human life, the phenomena of normal and abnormal grief are hardly known among laypeople, medical and health professionals, or clergy (Wortman & Silver, 2001). The introduction in DSM of some form of CG will undoubtedly lead to more knowledge among professionals and laypeople about normal and pathological grief (see also Stroebe et al., 2000). However, it will also lead to more demand for 'services' for people with CG, be it by means of psychotherapy or by medication, and thus to more reimbursements. On the other hand, as Kendler (2010) rightly notes, assessing a DSM disorder provides the possibility, but by no means the requirement, that treatment should be started. Sometimes it is more appropriate to wait (and perhaps eventually abstain) than to begin with interventions.

Blurring normal and abnormal adaptation to trauma: the danger of medicalization

One unfortunate result of the introduction of PTSD was that all consequences of extreme events were primarily considered from the perspective of PTSD, in short, from a psychopathology perspective. However, only a minority of the persons who experience a traumatic event develop PTSD. For instance, prevalence rates of PTSD vary in studies of natural and technological disasters between 2% and 45% (Neriah, Nandi, & Galea, 2008). The reported percentages vary on account of differences in event characteristics, instruments, and length of time since the event. Unfortunately, as a result of the focus on pathology, normal reactions to traumatic events have hardly been examined. Therefore, some authors even spoke of a 'tyranny' of PTSD (e.g. Kleber, 1995). This risk may also occur after the introduction of the concept of complicated grief; it may be beneficial for people suffering from disturbances, but not for the majority of people confronted with loss.

There is the risk that normal reactions will be considered as mental problems or disorders that need professional help. Some have raised concerns about the possibility that normal grief would be medicalized as a consequence of a DSM disorder CG (Stroebe et al., 2000). However, this argument holds not only or in particular for normal grief, but for almost any mental problem or disorder. 'Normal' social anxiety runs the risk of becoming labelled social phobia, 'normal rumination' runs the risk of becoming labelled generalized anxiety disorder (GAD), problems with eating may change into 'eating disorders'.

A related concern is the possibility that the family will withdraw if a treatment for CG is being carried out. De Keijser (1997) reported that the social network appears to withdraw when a family member makes use of grief counselling; this finding is in need of further exploration. Bereaved seem not to envisage such a reaction: Prigerson and Vanderwerker (2005) report that none of their CG respondents expected that, if they met criteria for CG, their family members would be less understanding of their distress.

The stressor criterion

Earlier we mentioned that research suggests that full-blown PTSD might develop in the absence of the occurrence of any 'traumatic' event. As a corollary, it can be expected that the symptom pattern of CG (such as yearning about what has been lost) will be found in absence of the loss of a loved one. This is to be expected because grief is about the dissolution of bonds, but in the grief literature it is hardly stressed that people have bonds not only with other people (and animals), but also with other (non-)material objects, such as one's work situation or one's culture. For example, people who suddenly lose their jobs, after many years of having made personal investments for their employers, may show grief symptoms, which occasionally are even more intense and long-standing than the grief symptoms as a result of, for example, the loss of one's partner. The same applies for losing 'objects' such as one's mental health. For example, there are reports (Appelo et al., 1993) suggesting that some of the characteristic symptoms of schizophrenia are primarily grief symptoms, arising from the realization that one's life perspective has been broken and that one has a pervasive, life-long illness. This suggests that grief (with possible disordered forms) is a much more all-embracing phenomenon than thought before.

Epilogue

Without any doubt, the growth of the PTSD field has been multifaceted: massive, impressive, and successful as well as complicated, questionable, and sometimes unconvincing. In spite of the criticisms, PTSD will most definitely remain in DSM-5. To be fair, the critical arguments apply also to other well-known disorders such as depression and schizophrenia. In these fields there are also debates about the weak and strong boundaries of these disorders. It is wise to make use of all the PTSD-related pros and cons in the development (and lobbying) with regard to the future diagnosis of CG. Many issues with regard to PTSD hold true for a future disorder of CG. Perhaps the main lesson is: try – for the sake of persons with enduring intense grief problems – to include CG in DSM, but be careful and do not overstretch the significance of the concept.

References

American Psychiatric Association. (1980). *Diagnostic and statistical manual of mental disorders* (3rd edn.). Washington DC: APA.

American Psychiatric Association. (1994). *Diagnostic and statistical manual of mental disorders* (4th edn.). Washington DC: APA.

Appelo, M. T., Slooff, C. J., Woonings, F., Carson, J., & Louwerens, J. (1993). Grief: Its significance for rehabilitation in schizophrenia. *Clinical Psychology and Psychotherapy, 1*, 53–59.

Bisson, J. I., Brayne, M., Ochberg, F. M., & Everly, G. S. Jr. (2007). Early psychosocial intervention following traumatic events. *American Journal of Psychiatry, 164*, 1016–1019.

Boelen, P. A., van den Hout, M., & van den Bout, J. (2006). A cognitive–behavioral conceptualization of complicated grief. *Clinical Psychology: Science and Practice, 13*, 109–128.

Bolton, D. (2008). *What is mental disorder?* Oxford: Oxford University Press.

Bonanno, G. A. (2004). Loss, trauma, and human resilience: Have we underestimated the human capacity to thrive after extremely aversive events. *American Psychologist, 59,* 20–28.

Boschen, M. J. (2008). The growth of PTSD in anxiety disorder research. *Psychiatry Research, 138,* 262–264.

Breslau, N., Kessler, R. C., Chilcoat, H. D., Schultz, L. R., Davis, G. C., & Andreski, P. (1998). Trauma and posttraumatic stress disorder in the community: The 1996 Detroit area survey of trauma. *Archives of General Psychiatry, 55,* 626–632.

Brom, D., & Kleber, R. J. (2009). Resilience as the capacity for processing traumatic experiences. In Brom, D., Path-Horenczyk, R., & Ford, J. D. (Eds.), *Treating traumatized children: Risk, resilience and recovery* (pp. 133–149). New York: Routledge.

Brom, D., Kleber, R. J., & van den Bout, J. (1993). Loss and trauma: Unity and diversity. In Malkinson, R., Rubin, S. S., & Witztum, E. (Eds.), *Loss and bereavement in Jewish society in Israel* (pp. 39–50). Jerusalem: Cana Publishing House.

Cooper, R. (2004). What is wrong with the D.S.M.? *History of Psychiatry, 15,* 5–25.

Davidson, J., Fox, E., & Blank, A. (1996). Post traumatic stress disorder. In Widiger, T., Frances, A., Pincus, H., Ross, R., First, M., Davis, W., & Kline, M. (Eds.), *DSM-IV sourcebook, vol. 2* (pp. 577–605). Washington, DC: American Psychiatric Association.

Horowitz, M. J. (2003). *Stress response syndromes* (4th edn.). San Francisco: Jossey-Bass.

Keane, T. M., Marshall, A. D., & Taft, C. T. (2006). Posttraumatic stress disorder: Etiology, epidemiology and treatment outcome. *Annual Review of Clinical Psychology, 2,* 161–197.

de Keijser, J. (1997). *Sociale steun en professionele begeleiding bij rouw* [Social support and professional counselling for the bereaved]. Amsterdam: Thesis Publishers.

Kendler, K. S. (2010). *Mood disorders*. Retrieved March 22, 2011, from DSM-5 website: http://www.dsm5.org/about/Documents/grief%20exclusion_Kendler.pdf.

Kleber, R. J. (1995). Epilogue: Towards a broader perspective of traumatic stress. In Kleber, R. J., Figley, C. R., & Gersons, B. P. R. (Eds.), *Beyond trauma: Cultural and societal dimensions* (pp. 299–306). New York: Plenum.

McHugh, P. R., & Treisman, G. (2007). PTSD: A problematic diagnostic category. *Journal of Anxiety Disorders, 21,* 211–222.

McNally, R. J. (2004). Conceptual problems with the DSM-IV criteria for posttraumatic stress disorder. In Rosen, G. M. (Ed.), *Posttraumatic stress disorder: Issues and controversies* (pp. 1–14). Chichester, UK: John Wiley & Sons.

McNally, R. J. (2009). The cutting edge: Can we fix PTSD in DSM-V? *Depression and Anxiety, 26,* 597–600.

Mol, S. S., Arntz, A., Metsemakers, J. F., Dinant, G. J., Vilters-van Montfort, P. A., & Knottnerus, J. A. (2005). Symptoms of post-traumatic stress disorder after non-traumatic events: Evidence from an open population study. *British Journal of Psychiatry, 186,* 494–499.

Neria, Y., Nandi, A., & Galea, S. (2008). Posttraumatic stress disorder following disasters: A systematic review. *Psychological Medicine, 38,* 467–480.

van Praag, H. M. (2000). Nosologomania: A disorder of psychiatry. *World Journal of Psychiatry, 1,* 151–158.

Prigerson, H. G., Horowitz, M. J., Jacobs, S. C., Parkes, C. M., Aslan, M., Goodkin, K., et al. (2009). Prolonged Grief Disorder: Psychometric validation of criteria proposed for DSM-V and ICD-11. *PLoS Medicine, 6*(8): e1000121.

Prigerson, H. G., & Vanderwerker, L. C. (2005). Final remarks. *Omega, 52,* 91–94.

Ramsay, R. W. (1977). Behavioural approaches to bereavement. *Behaviour Research and Therapy, 15,* 131–135.

Raphael, B., Martinek, N., & Wooding, S. (2004). Assessing traumatic bereavement. In Wilson, J. P., & Keane, T. M. (Eds.), *Assessing psychological trauma and PTSD* (2nd edn., pp. 492–510). London: Guilford.

Rosen, G. M., & Lilienfeld, S. O. (2008). Posttraumatic stress disorder: An empirical evaluation of core assumptions. *Clinical Psychology Review, 28*, 837–868.

Shear, M. K., Simon, N., Wall, M., Zisook, S., Neimeyer, R., Duan, N., et al. (2011). Complicated grief and related bereavement-issues for DSM-5. *Depression and Anxiety, 28*, 103–117.

Schnurr, P. P. (2010). PTSD 30 years on. *Journal of Traumatic Stress, 23*, 1–2.

Schut, H. A. W., & Stroebe, M. S. (2010). Effects of social support, counselling, and therapy before and after the loss: Can we really help bereaved people? *Psychologica Belgica, 50*, 89–102.

Spitzer, R. J., First, M. B., & Wakefield, J. C. (2007). Saving PTSD from itself in DSM-V. *Journal of Anxiety Disorders, 21*, 233–241.

Stein, D. J., Phillips, K. A., Bolton, D., Fulford, K. W. M., Sadler, J. Z., & Kendler, K. S. (2010). What is mental/psychiatric disorder? From DSM-IV to DSM-V. *Psychological Medicine, 40*, 1759–1765.

Stroebe, M., van Son, M. J. M., Stroebe, W., Kleber, R. J., Schut, H. A. W., & van den Bout, J. (2000). On the classification and diagnosis of pathological grief. *Clinical Psychology Review, 20*, 57–75.

Tucker, G. J. (1998). Putting DSM-IV in perspective. *American Journal of Psychiatry, 155*, 159–161.

Wortman, C., & Silver, R. (2001). The myths of coping with loss revisited. In Stroebe, M., Hansson, R., Stroebe, W., & Schut, H. (Eds.), *Handbook of bereavement research: Consequences, coping, and care* (pp. 405–429). Washington, DC: American Psychological Association.

Young, A. (2004). When traumatic memory was a problem: On the historical antecedents of PTSD. In Rosen, G. M. (Ed.), *Posttraumatic stress disorder: Issues and controversies* (pp. 127–146). Chichester, UK: John Wiley & Sons.

10 Complicated grief in the context of other psychiatric disorders

PTSD

Beverley Raphael, Jennifer Jacobs, and Jeff Looi

Introduction

The consideration of the possibility of "pathologies" of grief has a substantial history in literature, reflected in prolonged and debilitating mourning overwhelming the bereaved's life: they live on, as it were, in their continuing relationship with the deceased to the exclusion of other life. Freud (1917), in "Mourning and Melancholia," discussed the potential for grief to lead to depression. "Traumatic" grief has also been considered as a possible entity (Raphael, 1983). Recent research has highlighted the distinction between complicated grief, depression, and posttraumatic stress disorder (PTSD) as separate syndromes (Boelen, van de Schoot, van den Hout, de Keijser, & van den Bout, 2010; Golden & Dalgleish, 2010).

The comorbidity of complicated grief and PTSD, the phenomena of reactions to the stressors of loss and trauma, the possible etiology identified in scientific studies to date, and implications for management will be the focus of this chapter.

The potential for trauma syndromes such as PTSD to sit alongside, interact with, or contribute to complicated grief is a challenge for multiple reasons. First, early in the development of the concept "Traumatic Stress," theory identified bereavement or loss of a loved one as a stressor. It has subsequently been difficult to disengage loss and define it as a distinct stressor and "bereavement" as a distinct entity. It has been and still is, to a major degree, included by many workers in the field as a "traumatic" stressor. Second, "Complicated Grief" was also at times referred to as "traumatic grief," as in the original development of this concept and its evolution into "Prolonged Grief Disorder." The progressive development of the understanding of "traumatic grief" as the coexistence of grief and trauma phenomena has come with studies which have better clarified the different reactive phenomena that may follow these different stressor experiences. The attention to violent deaths, particularly those associated with human malevolent intent such as homicide or terrorism, has further contributed to recognition of the trauma of the loss as well as the grief (Neria & Litz, 2003; Rynearson & McCreery, 1993). Traumatic bereavement could lead to a mixture of trauma and grief, or indeed complicated grief disorder and comorbid trauma symptoms to the level of PTSD. Thus PTSD could result from the way a loved one died, or other co-occurring traumatic stressors.

Phenomena of traumatic stress reactions and bereavement reactions in children and adults

Important early studies of children by Pynoos and colleagues (Pynoos, Frederick, et al., 1987; Pynoos, Nada, Frederick, Ginda, & Stuber, 1987) examined reactions in a group of school children who experienced a sniper attack, in which several children were killed. The researchers developed a Traumatic Stress Reaction Index (16 items) and a Grief Reaction Index (nine items). Severity of exposure to life threat was correlated with high levels of traumatic stress reactive phenomena and symptoms. The children more closely associated with a child who died showed higher levels of grief reactive phenomena on the Grief Reaction Index. Furthermore, the traumatic stress reaction phenomena were more likely to be associated with the development of PTSD, whereas loss/bereavement phenomena were more likely to be associated with depression. This work has extended to current studies with children so affected, and intervention strategies to address this pathology have been developed. For instance, Pynoos, Steinberg, and Brymer (2007) have developed and tested a model of postdisaster intervention that identifies "traumatic bereavement" and recommends strategies, school-based or other, to address this. Researchers and clinicians have increasingly recognized the coexistence of traumatic stress and grief phenomena for children experiencing certain losses, and developed models to assess and manage this (Cohen & Mannarino, 2008).

Studies examining bereavement phenomena over time have assessed patterns of reaction for adult populations of bereaved community members following the death of a loved one (Byrne & Raphael, 1993; Middleton, Moylan, Raphael, & Martinek, 1998). These are non-clinical samples and so represent the spectrum of potential reactions. The reactive phenomena demonstrate patterns of progressive decline in levels in the early months after a major bereavement. About 9% were found to continue in a "chronic" pattern for 6 months or more, with high levels of acute grief phenomena reported in the populations studied, representing patterns like those of prolonged grief disorder or complicated grief (Raphael & Minkov, 1999).

The decline in levels of reactive phenomena or "symptoms" after exposure to the stressor of loss of a loved one is similar to the patterns of traumatic stress reactive phenomena or symptoms over time. If symptom patterns reach the level of dysfunction or disorder, they have the potential to meet criteria for complicated grief and PTSD after a specific period.

Both these sets of phenomena relate directly and specifically to the stressors experienced. Studies have included clear, systematic, and validated measures of the specific phenomena; for instance, for bereavement, the Core Bereavement Items scale (CBI) (Burnett, Middleton, Raphael, & Martinek, 1997) and traumatic stress measures such as the reliable and valid items of PTSD checklists. The specific stressors, as opposed to reactive phenomena, are, however, infrequently measured systematically and consistently, thus complicating comparison across different studies in these fields.

Clinical observations of phenomena

Characteristic reactions of grief and posttraumatic stress (PTS) reactions are important in demonstrating specificity of reactive phenomena as well as similarities. These can be considered in terms of:

- cognitive phenomena;
- affective phenomena;
- avoidance phenomena;
- arousal phenomena;
- other related phenomena.

These have been reported previously (Raphael, Martinek, & Wooding, 2004). They have been considered to be useful themes in clinical assessment, and could also be considered as potential domains in research studies. These phenomena are presented in Tables 10.1 and 10.2.

Bereavement and pathology: complicated grief, PTSD, depression

The potential for the loss of a loved one to lead to complicated or prolonged grief is widely discussed in this volume, as are criteria for such a syndrome or disorder. Conceptually this syndrome is strongly related to attachment theory, and suggests an ongoing, complicated attachment of the bereaved to the person who is now deceased. The stressor is the disruption of the attachment, its loss. There is considerable research examining the relationship between loss and depression, and other complications after bereavements. It is only recently that studies have specifically included the potential for the distinct entity PTSD as a comorbidity.

It is of note that many of the more recent studies considering bereavement, complicated grief, and PTSD have been of populations affected by disaster or terrorism. In some of these studies, recording the potential for loss syndromes has been considered chiefly because there are concurrently multiple deaths and losses. The stressors of life threat, as indicated in criterion A of DSM-IV, have also been investigated, as has their contribution to the subsequent development of PTSD. High mortality rates have been found to be associated with higher levels of psychopathology, for instance, explaining 20% of the variance in disaster effect size in a well-controlled meta-analysis (Norris & Wind, 2009). This probably relates to the fact that bereavement is an additional stressor, as well as to the fact that many of those surviving are likely to have been exposed to severe life-threatening circumstances themselves, with associated heightened risk of PTSD. In addition they may have been exposed to the multiple, possibly mutilating, deaths of others.

Studies after September 11, 2001 (9/11), such as those of Galea et al. (2002), reported that, at 5–8 weeks, having a friend or relative who had been killed, that is, a bereavement stressor, was associated with depression, not PTSD. Complicated grief was not measured. However, a subsequent study of primary care patients

Table 10.1 Phenomena of posttraumatic reactions and bereavement

Posttraumatic phenomena	Bereavement phenomena
Cognitive phenomena	
Intrusions of *scene of trauma* (e.g., death) not associated with yearning or longing	Image of *lost person* constantly comes to mind (unbidden or bidden)
Associated with distress, anxiety at image	Associated with yearning or longing
Preoccupation with the *traumatic event* and circumstances of it	Distress that person is not there
Memories usually of the *traumatic* scene	Preoccupation with the *lost person* and intense images of him or her
Re-experiencing of threatening aspects of the event	*Memories of person* associated with affect relevant to memory (often positive)
	Re-experiencing of *person's presence*, as though he or she were still there (e.g., hallucinations of sound, touch, sight)
Affective phenomena	
Anxiety	
Anxiety is the principal affect	Anxiety, when present, is *separation* anxiety
And is *general* and generated by threat	Is specific and generated by separation from lost person
Fearful of *threat/danger*	
Precipitated by reminders, intrusions	Is generated by imagined future without lost person
	Precipitated by his or her *failure to return*
Yearning/longing	
These are not prominent features	Yearning for lost person is a core grief phenomenon
Not person oriented; if occurs, is for things to have been as they were before – for the return of "innocence of death" and for the sense of personal invulnerability	Is person oriented, intense, painful, profound, triggered by reminders of him or her; yearning for him or her to return, to be there
Sadness	
Sadness not commonly described	Sadness frequent and profound
Nostalgia for event not described	Feelings of nostalgia common and persistent
Avoidance phenomena	
Avoids reminders of events, including places	May search for and *seek out* places of familiarity, *treasured objects* (e.g., linking objects, photos and images)
Attempts to lessen affect; numbing, lessened feelings generally	May try to *avoid reminders of the absence* of the lost person; may try to *mitigate* pangs of grief but only temporarily, including distracting, but also seeks to express grief as normal
May have great difficulty talking of event during avoidance times, although at others may be powerfully driven to talk of the experience (but not person)	May be very driven to talk of lost relationship and lost person
Withdrawal from others (protective of self)	May seek others for support or to talk of deceased
Arousal phenomena	
Oriented to threat and danger	Oriented to lost person
General scanning and alertness to danger, fearfulness	General *scanning* of *environment for lost one or cues* of him or her
Exaggerated startle response (i.e., response to minimal threat)	Arousal drives *searching* behavior
Overresponse to cues of trauma	Overresponse to cues of lost person

Source: Adapted from Raphael et al. (2004).

Table 10.2 Other phenomena: signs of reactive process

Posttraumatic phenomena	Bereavement phenomena
Occur on witnessing something horrific, torture, etc., fear and threat	"Contraction of the grief muscles . . . Appears to be common to all the races of mankind" (p. 185)
"probably that horror would generally be accompanied by *strong contraction of the brow*, but as far as fear is one of the elements, the *eyes and mouth* would be *opened,* and the *eyebrows raised* – as far as antagonistic action of the corrugations permitted this movement" (pp. 322–323)	*Obliquity of the eyebrows;* contraction of central fascia of frontal muscle Inner ends of eyebrows (p. 188) puckered into bunch Transverse furrows across the middle parts of the forehead
"*Contraction of platysma* does add greatly to the expression of fear" (p. 317) Eyes somewhat staring Pupils may be dilated	*Depression of corners of mouth* Mouth closed Corners drawn downward and outward (pp. 201–202) Curved mouth concavely downward

Note: Page numbers are from Darwin (1872/1998).

who knew someone who died in the attack found that they were twice as likely to report problems in functioning, work, and social and family life, and at least one mental disorder (Neria et al., 2008). Although depression was the most prevalent condition, the stressor experience reported was most strongly connected with PTSD. In another study, Neria et al. (2007) used a web-based survey to study the long-term grief reactions of 704 adults bereaved after 9/11 at 2.5–3.5 years after the attack. They specifically assessed complicated grief as a distinct syndrome, and found that it was often comorbid with depression and PTSD. Whereas most of the participants reported some complicated grief symptoms, 43% met study criteria for complicated grief as a diagnosis.

A comprehensive study of bereaved Norwegians who had lost loved ones in the 2004 South East Asian tsunami was carried out, assessing those who had been directly exposed to the disaster and those not so exposed (Kristensen, Weisaeth, & Heir, 2009). The authors used diagnostic criteria interviews to diagnose PTSD and major depressive disorder and a self-report scale to measure prolonged grief disorder (PGD). Rates of psychiatric disorders were twice as high in those directly exposed. They reported that loss of a child and low education correlated with PGD whereas exposure correlated with PTSD. Each disorder was independently correlated with functional impairment.

Stressor exposures, PTSD, and bereavement

Multiple studies have highlighted the complexity of etiological processes that might contribute to comorbidity of PTSD and complicated grief. Questions arise whether this is related to traumatic circumstances of the death, life threat exposures for the bereaved, or other concurrent stressors. This is not clearly identifiable in the methodologies and findings of many studies – particularly the degree to which "circumstances of the death" is the identified stressor, vis-à-vis the multiple other potential life threat circumstances that may occur in association with loss. There is also the possibility of PTSD being the initial condition, with associated effects on attachment relationships being a factor contributing to the development of complicated grief. Other vulnerabilities, such as past trauma and loss, children's developmental trauma, or multiple concurrent adversities could also increase the risk of complicated grief.

The potential ways people have died may be "traumatic," as described in the stressor criterion A of PTSD, and be associated with greater risk of PTSD for those so bereaved. This could be the case if, for example (as per criterion A of PTSD), the person witnessed, or was confronted with, an event or events that involved actual or threatened death or serious injury or threat to the physical integrity of the self or others, and the person's response involved intense fear responses, helplessness, and horror.

Anderson, Arnold, Angus, and Bryce (2008) have studied complicated grief and PTS in family members of patients in an intensive care clinic. Family members were enrolled when their loved one was still alive in intensive care, and assessed at three time points: enrolment, 1 month, and 6 months. Interviews and assessment covered anxiety, depression, PTS, and complicated grief. This study found that complicated grief was not associated with anxiety or depression at any time point. Forty-six percent of the bereaved participants had complicated grief. Thirty-five percent of participants had PTS symptoms according to the cut-off point on the Impact of Event Scale (IES), which indicates probable PTSD, and this correlated with pre-existing and concurrent anxiety scores. Of significance, however, was the finding that all the bereaved participants with high levels of PTS (IES score > 30) also had complicated grief. The authors expressed concern at the high prevalence of "post-traumatic stress" in this cohort of family members, because of the "profound impact of such disorders on physical and mental health and social functioning" (p. 1874).

In a study of adults who had lost first-degree relatives to war-related violence (Kosovo), Morina, Rudari, Bleichhardt, and Prigerson (2009) examined the rates of PGD or complicated grief disorder and its association with PTSD and major depressive disorder (MDD). This preliminary investigation is of interest in that the particular stressors were assessed as well as symptoms/syndrome patterns, for instance if there was an immediate threat to one's own life, and other ongoing "strains." The loss of a loved one was associated with PGD, which affected 38% of this sample of 60 bereaved people; PTSD was associated with immediate threat to one's own life and affected 55% of this population. Major depressive disorder was predicted by ongoing strains and occurred in 38%. Prolonged grief disorder was significantly associated with MDD, anxiety symptoms, sleeping difficulties, and feelings of embitterment. Whereas two thirds (65%) of the participants with PGD also met criteria for PTSD, 49% of those with PTSD did not meet criteria for PGD. There was no significant relationship between PTSD and PGD, nor between PGD or PTSD and MDD. These findings would suggest that, even though these bereavements were likely to have been very traumatic in terms of the circumstances of the way people died, the PTSD in this study was specifically related to the extent of personal life threat. The PTSD and PGD were two distinct entities, highlighting the etiological and phenomenological distinctions, despite the prevalence and overlap of comorbidities. Of particular concern, as noted by these authors, was that "even seven years after the war, 73.3% of the participants fulfilled criteria for PGD, PTSD or MDD" (p. 7). They also note that a major area of psychopathology, that related to complicated or prolonged grief disorder, would not have been addressed if bereavement-related pathology had not been included. Benedek and Ursano (2006) describe related issues with military communities.

The nature of bereavement through death by homicide has been studied in detail and reported in a review drawing together many of these themes (Rynearson, 2006). Rynearson's early work in this field highlighted the traumatic nature of such deaths, even for those not present when the death occurred. They could be tormented by images and flashbacks of such potential circumstances of death, as well as the complexity and intensity of their grief (Rynearson & McCreery 1993; see also Chapter 20 in this volume). In a recent national study of mental health correlates of losing a loved one to homicide, Zinzow, Rheingold, Hawkins, Saunders, and Kilpatrick (2009) found heightened risks for PTSD (odds ratio 1.88), major depressive episode (odds ratio 1.64), and drug use dependence (odds ratio 1.77). Unfortunately, complicated grief was not considered in this study.

Suicide deaths have been studied in terms of those who survive such family losses. Brent, Melhelm, Donohoe, and Walker (2009) studied the incidence and course of depression in bereaved youths 21 months after the death of a parent by suicide, accident, or natural death, and also examined sequelae of such deaths for caregivers (surviving parent) (Melhelm, Walker, Moritz, & Brent, 2008). They reported an increased risk for both depression and PTSD above and beyond other vulnerability factors. In terms of the "sudden" deaths studied, being bereaved by suicide was not associated with heightened risk compared with other acute deaths. This study is of interest in that a specific measure of "Circumstances of Exposure to Death" had been developed and tested in a prior related study (Brent et al., 1992). Complicated grief was assessed using the Inventory of Complicated Grief (Prigerson et al., 1995). Both risk and protective factors that might influence the impact of bereavement were also assessed, such as family cohesion, social support, self-esteem, and coping styles, plus pre-existing psychopathology as reported for the deceased, the surviving parent, and offspring. This comprehensive study thus addressed a significant variable in the circumstances of the death, and it also examined specific types of sudden death that, in and of themselves, may have contributed to increased risk of adverse bereavement outcomes. Complicated grief was found in 32% of the suicide caregivers, 25% of accident caregivers, and 31% of sudden natural death caregivers, as a new-onset psychiatric condition. In terms of the offspring complicated grief was reported in 21% of suicide bereaved, 18% of accident bereaved, and 19% of those bereaved by natural sudden death. This study found that caregiver and offspring symptoms of depression, anxiety, PTSD, suicidal ideation, and complicated grief were correlated. The study examined correlations of new-onset of PTSD in the bereaved offspring, finding that prior psychiatric history (odds ratio 9.4), bipolar disorder in the deceased parent (odds ratio 1.9), and family history of PTSD (odds ratio 6.8) were predictors. It is of particular significance that type of death per se was not a significant predictor of PTSD, but that "being at the scene when the death occurred" (odds ratio 8.3) (Melhelm et al., 2008, p. 407) was. As will be discussed below, this may be a better indicator of the potential impact of "circumstances of the death" as a possible traumatic stressor exposure. Brent et al. (2009) interviewed the initial cohort described above approximately 9 months after the loss. This second study reported on subsequent data with interviews about a year later, that is, 21 months after the death. Compared with the non-bereaved control group, the bereaved young people had higher rates of major depression or alcohol or substance use problems. Post hoc correlates indicated that the level of complicated grief was higher in young people whose parents had died by accident. The centrality of depression as a pathological outcome, with onset associated with bereavement, was further demonstrated in the cumulative incidence and course of depression in bereaved compared with non-bereaved control youths. Cumulative incidence and course of PTSD in those bereaved was highest in the first 9 months, about 8.5%, but not in the subsequent period. Remission was common. The authors conclude that the "direct effect of bereavement on incident depression and PTSD was limited to the first 9 months after the loss" (p. 791).

Shocking, horrific ways of dying may be the consequence of different life threats, including homicide, mass disaster, terrorism, or war, where criterion A of PTSD may be met. All may lead to suffering, profound agony, helplessness, grief, and the specific suffering associated with the deaths of children. September 11, 2001, exemplifies this, the effects of which were increased by extensive media depiction and amplification, that is, witnessing, often repeatedly, horrific deaths. It is likely that such circumstances would encompass both trauma and loss. This and other terrorist or similar shocking and deliberate perpetrations of mass death and destruction could lead to the potential for traumatic exposures as well as loss and grief. Shear, Jackson, Essock, Donahue, and Felton (2006) screened people presenting to Project Liberty community counseling outreach services after 9/11. These researchers found that, at 1.5 years after the event, 44% of the counseling recipients who knew someone who had been killed in the attacks screened positive for complicated grief. Positive screening, which was highest amongst those who had lost a family member, was associated with functional impairment and subthreshold or diagnostic levels of major depression and PTSD. These authors highlighted the complex interfaces of trauma and grief pathologies, in that the symptoms of complicated grief with separation anxiety may interact with threat anxiety aspects of PTSD. Higher PTS symptom scores and higher grief scores were associated with higher levels of functional impairment, and neither grief alone nor PTSD alone correlated with such impairment.

Assessment and management: complicated grief with trauma syndromes as comorbidity

The issues discussed above constitute a complex and sensitive challenge to management. This is the more so because of overlapping symptom patterns, as with many such comorbidities, the extra burden that may result for the person who is affected, and the skills required for treatment. Shear et al. (2001) conducted a pilot study and subsequently a randomized controlled trial of a manualized but sensitive treatment for complicated grief (Shear, Frank, Houck, & Reynolds, 2005). They have contributed a very important set of strategies for this field.

The potential adaptations of this model to treat comorbid trauma syndromes are well exemplified in the development of a protocol for the treatment of complicated grief and substance use disorders. This study (Zuckoff et al., 2006) included the set of the complicated grief strategies, but also had the goal of helping patients "to achieve sufficient initial improvement in substance use behaviours" (p. 207). They would then learn skills for managing intense emotions safely so that these would not, if evoked in the grief therapy, lead to relapse of substance use behaviors related to this emotional response. The model developed was called CGSUT (Complicated Grief Substance Use Treatment). It combined components for achieving abstinence from substances; enhanced tolerance for emotional reactiveness (including motivational interviewing and emotion coping skills); and the established treatment for complicated grief. Two of the strategies, those for enhancing recognition and management of distressing emotions and skills for communicating feelings and empathy for others, are likely to be of use across other comorbidities such as PTSD. This small open trial, the authors suggest, "is promising" and "a grief focussed treatment, combined with MI [motivational interviewing] and skills building for emotion coping and communication" constitutes a feasible model for further study (Shear et al., 2007, p. 209). A challenge lies in the fact that comorbidity is frequently entrenched, particularly years after the loss, so that studies of early intervention (e.g., Fiegelman, Jordan, & Gorman, 2009) should be considered of particular importance. Longer therapies (e.g., 24 sessions) also challenge commitment.

Hensley (2006) took up the earlier conceptualization of complicated grief as traumatic grief, and considered comorbid depression, again demonstrating the difficulties of terminology in this field. From this review she suggested that treatment may require "specific psychotherapeutic techniques addressing the trauma and separation distress central to this disorder" (p. 124).

The increasing focus on cognitive–behavioral therapies (CBT) that are trauma focused, as a treatment for trauma syndromes, has provided a basis for the use of this type of intervention in the management of such comorbidity. Nevertheless there is significant overlap with complicated grief treatment elements. This is particularly likely if the trauma stressor is directly related to the circumstances of the death, the way the person died, whereby emotional responsiveness, fear reactions, anger, and distress may be intense. The management of these emotional aspects is likely to be critical. In the first author's experience with clinical management of these issues, the discussion of the death itself, what actually happened, can be facilitated with empathy, so that the exposure component is progressively managed and is a less dominating element of the pathology, that is, "the story of the death" is told.

Shear et al. (2007) further examined the attachment aspect of complicated grief and highlighted the significance of the avoidance theme in management in this context. The reviewing of the bonds of the bereaved person to the lost person, and the capacity to review memories and deal with the dependent and ambivalent aspects of the relationship with the deceased, may be part of therapeutic exposure or confrontation processes. Having a more real set of memories of the relationship may help the bereaved. Attachment issues and the ways in which they contribute to complicated grief need clinical and research clarification. Furthermore, the significance of the attachment theme needs to be more specifically researched in therapy models and clinical trials.

The role of pharmacotherapy in the management of complicated grief and PTSD comorbidity remains to be established. Simon et al. (2008) describe the association of "naturalistic" pharmacotherapy use in the treatment trial of Shear et al. (2005). They found that those having such antidepressant pharmacotherapy were more likely to complete the full course of therapy sessions for complicated grief treatment than those undergoing the control intervention psychotherapy treatment. Pharmacotherapy could be indicated for comorbid PTSD. The pharmacological rationale behind any such interventions should also be clarified.

Stroebe, Schut, and Stroebe (2005) looked at grief counseling more broadly, showing in their review that there was little evidence that the emotional disclosure aspect of counseling facilitated adjustment to loss in normal bereavement, and the same issues are also relevant for trauma syndromes. This further emphasizes the importance of research addressing vulnerabilities and possible protective factors with the aim of lessening the risk of complicated grief disorder, related comorbidities such as trauma syndromes, substance use disorders, and depression, and other adverse health or behavioral outcomes. Prevention and early intervention strategies have been suggested (Zhang, El-Jawahri, & Prigerson, 2006) and some earlier studies (randomized controlled trials) demonstrated that interventions with high-risk bereaved persons could potentially lead to improved outcomes (Raphael, 1977).

The needs of children and adolescents with complicated grief and trauma syndromes have been increasingly recognized, particularly in disaster-affected populations, or among children affected in other ways by grief and trauma. Cohen, Mannarino, and Starlon (2006) have described this work in their studies of child traumatic grief, a mixture of unresolved grief symptoms and trauma symptoms. They used modularized approaches to deal with grief problem symptoms, and trauma-focused CBT for trauma symptoms. They also provided program components for parents or caregivers to assist them to deal with their children's needs and possibly their own difficulties.

The model of complicated grief therapy used by Shear for adults, the modifications developed for complicated grief and substance use, and the modularized formats for children have all been shaped by research and applied as clinically relevant to the assessed phenomena of complicated grief and any associated comorbidities. The therapeutic descriptions suggest both adaptation of frameworks and responsiveness to particular patterns in these complex sets of comorbid phenomena and grief problems. The clinical programs described are forming and developing the evidence base. Such evolution is of value, as are the currently available trials and conceptualizations. A more comprehensive research framework could also build on emerging literature on Internet-based therapies (Stroebe et al., 2005; Wagner & Maercker, 2008) and the potential role of pharmacotherapies. The various models with children and their families will also require further research development (Cohen & Mannarino, 2008). The progressive evolution, translation, and implementation of such scientifically developed programs is critically important to meet real-world needs for those affected by complicated grief, PTSD, and other comorbidities. This is the more so when the difficulties of retaining people in some of the trials highlights the barriers to care delivery and the potential benefits that evaluation of the translated program can add to research and knowledge development. This is clear with the model of Pynoos et al. (2007), which has translated screening and interventions into program models for trauma and grief, taking into account developmental issues. As in all psychotherapies, the context, the significant others, and being attuned to the person's experience of grief and trauma should inform therapeutic management. Genuineness, empathy, and warmth are still central, particularly for those who have experienced the tragic loss of a primary attachment figure in traumatic circumstances. The role of consoling, human touch, and healing rituals also need to be further researched. The processes of grieving are core human adaptations, and should be valued, respected, and understood. They are shaped in their expression by enduring cultural processes. Their core biological underpinnings are being progressively explored. The problems, "diseases" of grief, are also being described. However, the underlying power and "magic" of human bonds in times of loss and grief should be seen for what they are: the core of family, the fabric of society.

References

American Psychiatric Association. (2000). *Diagnostic and statistical manual of mental disorders* (4th edn., text revision). Washington, DC: Author.

Anderson, W., Arnold, R., Angus, D., & Bryce, C. (2008). Posttraumatic stress and complicated grief in family members of patients in the intensive care unit. *Journal of General Internal Medicine, 23*, 1871–1876.

Benedek, D. & Ursano, R. (2006). Mass violent death and military communities: Domains of response in military operations, disaster and terrorism. In Rynearson, E. (Ed.), *Violent death: Resilience and intervention beyond the crisis* (pp. 295–310). New York: Routledge.

Boelen, P., van de Schoot, R., van den Hout, M., de Keijser, J., & van den Bout, J. (2010). Prolonged grief disorder, depression and posttraumatic stress disorder as distinguishable syndromes. *Journal of Affective Disorders, 125*, 374–378.

Brent, D., Melhelm, N., Donohoe, M., & Walker, M. (2009). The incidence and course of depression in bereaved youth 21 months after the loss of a parent to suicide, accident or a sudden natural death. *American Journal of Psychiatry, 166*, 786–794.

Brent, D., Perdper, J., Moritz, G., Allman, C., Friend, A., Schweers, J., Roth, C., Balach, L., & Harrington, K. (1992). Psychiatric effects of exposure to suicide among the friends and acquaintances of adolescent suicide victims. *Journal of the American Academy of Child and Adolescent Psychiatry, 31*, 629–639.

Burnett, P., Middleton, W., Raphael, B., & Martinek, N. (1997). Measuring core bereavement phenomena. *Psychological Medicine, 24*, 411–421.

Byrne, G., & Raphael, B. (1993). A longitudinal study of bereavement phenomena in recently widowed elderly men. *Psychological Medicine, 27*, 49–57.

Cohen, J., & Mannarino, A. (2008). Disseminating and implementing trauma-focused CBT in community settings. *Trauma, Violence, Abuse, 9*, 214–226.

Cohen, J., Mannarino, A., & Starlon, V. (2006). A pilot study of modified cognitive behavioural therapy for childhood traumatic grief (CBT-CTG). *Journal of the American Academy of Child and Adolescent Psychiatry, 45*, 1465–1473.

Darwin, C. (1872/1998). *The expression of emotions in men and animals* (3rd edn.). London: HarperCollins.

Fiegelman, W., Jordan, J., & Gorman, B. (2009). How they died, time since loss, and bereavement outcomes. *Omega, 58*, 251–273.

Freud, S. (1917). Mourning and melancholia. *Standard Edition, 14*, 243–258.

Galea, S., Ahern, J., Resnick, H., Kilpatrick, D., Bucuvalas, M., Gold, J., & Vlahov, D. (2002). Psychological sequelae of the September 11 terrorist attacks in New York City. *New England Journal of Medicine, 346*, 982–987.

Golden, A., & Dalgleish, T. (2010). Is prolonged grief distinct from bereavement-related posttraumatic stress? *Psychiatry Research, 178*, 336–341.

Hensley, P. (2006). Treatment of bereavement-related depression and traumatic grief. *Journal of Affective Disorders, 92*, 117–124.

Kristensen, P., Weisaeth, L., & Heir, T. (2009). Psychiatric disorders among disaster bereaved: An interview study of individuals directly or not directly exposed to the 2004 tsunami. *Depression and Anxiety, 26*, 1127–1133.

Melhelm, N., Walker, M., Moritz, G., & Brent, D. (2008). Antecedents and sequelae of sudden parental death in offspring and surviving caregivers. *Archives of Paediatric and Adolescent Medicine, 162*, 403–410.

Middleton, W., Moylan, A., Raphael, B., & Martinek, N. (1998). A longitudinal study comparing bereavement phenomena in recently bereaved spouses, adults, children and parents. *Australian and New Zealand Journal of Psychiatry, 32*, 235–241.

Morina, N., Rudari, V., Bleichhardt, G., & Prigerson, H. (2009). Prolonged grief disorder, depression, and posttraumatic stress disorder among bereaved Kosovar civilian war survivors: A preliminary investigation. *International Journal of Social Psychiatry, 56*, 288–297.

Neria, Y., Gross, R., Litz, B., Maguen, S., Insel, B., Seirmarco, G., et al. (2007). Prevalence and psychological correlates of complicated grief among bereaved adults 2.5–3.5 years after September 11th attacks. *Journal of Traumatic Stress, 20*, 251–262.

Neria, Y., & Litz, B. (2003). Bereavement by traumatic means: The complex synergy of trauma and grief. *Journal of Loss and Trauma, 9*, 73–87.

Neria, Y., Olfson, M., Gameroff, M., Wickramaratne, P., Gross, R., Pilowsjy, D., et al. (2008). The mental health consequences of disaster-related loss: Findings from primary care one year after the 9/11 terrorist attacks. *Psychiatry, 71*, 339–348.

Norris, F., & Wind, L. (2009). The experience of disaster: Trauma, loss, adversities, and community effects. In Neria, Y., Galea, S., & Norris, F. (Eds.) *Mental health and disasters* (pp. 29–44). London: Cambridge University Press.

Prigerson, H., Maciejewski, P., Newson, J., Reynolds, C., Bierhals, A., Miller, M., & Doman, J. (1995). Inventory of Complicated Grief: A scale to measure maladaptive symptoms of loss. *Psychiatry Research, 59*, 65–79.

Pynoos, R., Frederick, C., Nada, K., Arroyo, W., Steinberg, A., Eth, S., et al. (1987). Life threat and posttraumatic stress in school-aged children. *Archives of General Psychiatry, 44*, 1057–1063.

Pynoos, R., Nada, K., Frederick, C., Ginda, L., & Stuber, M. (1987). Grief reactions in school-aged children following a sniper attack at school. *Israeli Journal of Psychology and Related Sciences, 24*, 53–63.

Pynoos, R., Steinberg, A., & Brymer, M. (2007). Children and disasters: Public mental health approaches. In Ursano, R. J., Fullerton, C. S., & Weisaeth, L. (Eds.) *Textbook of disaster psychiatry* (pp. 48–68). Cambridge: Cambridge University Press.

Raphael, B. (1977). Preventive intervention with the recently bereaved. *Archives of General Psychiatry, 34*, 1450–1459.

Raphael, B. (1983). *The anatomy of bereavement.* New York: Basic Books.

Raphael, B., Martinek, N., & Wooding, S. (2004). Assessing traumatic bereavement. In Wilson, J., & Keane, T. (Eds.), *Assessing psychological trauma and PTSD* (2nd edn., pp. 492–510). London: Guilford Press.

Raphael, B., & Minkov, C. (1999). Abnormal grief. *Current Opinion in Psychiatry, 12*, 99–102.

Rynearson, E. (2006). *Violent death: Resilience and intervention beyond the crisis.* New York: Routledge.

Rynearson, E., & McCreery, J. (1993). Bereavement after homicide: A synergism of trauma and loss. *American Journal of Psychiatry, 150*, 258–261.

Shear, K., Frank, E., Foa, E., Cherry, C., Reynolds, C., Vander-Bilt, J., & Masters, S. (2001). Traumatic grief treatment: A pilot study. *American Journal of Psychiatry, 158*, 1506–1508.

Shear, K., Frank, E., Houck, P., & Reynolds, C. (2005). Treatment of complicated grief: A randomised controlled trial. *Journal of the American Medical Association, 293*, 2601–2608

Shear, K., Jackson, C., Essock, S., Donahue, S., & Felton, C. (2006). Screening for complicated grief among project liberty service recipients 18 months after September 11, 2001. *Psychiatric Services, 57*, 1291–1297.

Shear, K., Monk, T., Houck, P., Melhem, N., Frank, E., Reynolds, C., & Sillowash, R. (2007). An attachment-based model of complicated grief including the role of avoidance. *European Archives of Psychiatry and Clinical Neuroscience, 257*, 453–461.

Simon, N., Shear, K., Fagiolini, A., Frank, E., Zalta, A., Thompson, E., et al. (2008). Impact of concurrent naturalistic pharmacotherapy on psychotherapy of complicated grief. *Psychiatry Research, 159*, 31–36.

Stroebe, W., Schut, H., & Stroebe, M. (2005). Grief work, disclosure and counselling: Do they help the bereaved? *Clinical Psychology Review, 235*, 395–414.

Wagner, B., & Maercker, A. (2008). An internet-based cognitive–behavioural intervention for complicated grief: A pilot study. *Giornale Italiano di Medicina del Lavoro ed Ergonomica, 30*, B47–B53.

Zhang, B., El-Jawahri, A., & Prigerson, H. (2006). Update on bereavement research: Evidence-based guidelines for the diagnosis and treatment of complicated grief. *Palliative Care Reviews, 9*, 1188–1203.

Zinzow, H., Rheingold, A., Hawkins, A., Saunders, B., & Kilpatrick, G. (2009). Losing a loved one to homicide: Prevalence and mental health correlates in a national sample of young adults. *Journal of Traumatic Stress, 22*, 20–27.

Zuckoff, A., Shear, K., Frank, E., Dales, D., Seligman, K., & Sillowash, R. (2006). Treating complicated grief and substance use disorder: A pilot study. *Journal of Substance Abuse Treatment, 30*, 205–211.

Part IV

Contemporary research on risk factors, processes, and mechanisms

11 Prospective risk factors for complicated grief

A review of the empirical literature

Laurie A. Burke and Robert A. Neimeyer

Grieving is a natural response to the loss of a loved one, one that is repeatedly experienced by most individuals during their lifetimes. Although grief is ubiquitous, research shows that responses to loss vary among grievers. Some individuals respond resiliently, by experiencing little in the way of psychological distress (Bonanno & Kaltman, 2001), others experience acute grief for as long as 1–2 years (Bonanno & Mancini, 2006), and still others experience severe, debilitating, and sometimes life-threatening grief for a protracted length of time – a condition known as complicated grief (CG; Prigerson, Frank, et al., 1995) or prolonged grief disorder (PGD; Prigerson et al., 2009). Therefore, because of the increased precision with which we can identify the distinct characteristics of CG (Holland, Neimeyer, Boelen, & Prigerson, 2009), better scales with which to measure it (Prigerson, Frank, et al., 1995), and improved therapies with which to treat it (Shear, Frank, Houch, & Reynolds, 2005), isolating prospective risk factors is crucial. Our primary goal in this chapter is to identify empirically supported factors that predict subsequent susceptibility to the full range of responses to loss, from common to complicated grief, that merit further scientific and clinical attention.

CG as a distinct risk

Although depression and other forms of general psychopathology are important components of bereavement distress (Bonanno & Mancini, 2006), some researchers maintain that grief-specific distress can be expressed on a continuum of responses to loss. On one end is resilience, such that psychological equilibrium is regained fairly quickly after the loss (Bonanno & Kaltman, 2001). The middle range reflects a common response in which grievers suffer moderate distress (e.g., shock, anguish, sadness), but over time are able to adapt to the loss. The most serious expression – CG – appears at the far end of the spectrum, and is characterized by a state of protracted grieving, reflected in profound separation distress, emotionally disconcerting and invasive memories of the deceased, emptiness and meaninglessness, an inability to accept the loss, and considerable difficulty continuing to live life in the absence of the loved one (Holland et al., 2009). Other researchers view CG as a distinct entity from normative grief, so that measured symptom counts that exceed a normed cut-off score on a scale assessing CG (e.g., the Inventory of Complicated Grief, ICG; Prigerson, Maciejewski, et al., 1995) are considered to be categorically different from lower ones and, thus, constitute the presence of a discrete disorder (i.e., CG or prolonged grief disorder; Prigerson, Frank, et al., 1995; Prigerson et al., 2009).

CG has demonstrated construct validity as a condition that predicts serious medical and psychological outcomes, beyond those predicted by depression, PTSD, or anxiety (Lichtenthal, Cruess, & Prigerson, 2004). Historically, most studies have investigated samples of older Caucasian widows, with middle to upper socioeconomic status, bereaved by natural deaths, who have a normative response to their loss. However, recent studies have assessed CG in a variety of samples (e.g., multiple races, Goldsmith, Morrison, Vanderwerker, & Prigerson, 2008; parents, Keesee, Currier, & Neimeyer, 2008; survivors of terrorism, Shear, Jackson, Essock, Donahue, & Felton, 2006; African Americans bereaved by homicide, McDevitt-Murphy, Neimeyer, Burke, & Williams, 2012), in which CG may be more prevalent than originally thought and predicted by specific risk factors.

The present review

Although earlier reviews have been informative (see Sanders, 1988; M. Stroebe, Schut, & Stroebe, 2007; W. Stroebe & Schut, 2001), they necessarily failed to include the burgeoning recent literature on intense and prolonged grief. Lobb and colleagues (2010) reviewed studies on CG, and grouped risk factors into categories associated with childhood, issues of dependency, caregiving, cognitive and behavioral conceptualizations, traumatic death, and serious mental illness. They found that insecure attachment, excessive dependency, negative interpretations of grief reactions, a lack of meaning making, a lack of preparedness for the death, perception that the loved one suffered while dying, low social support, caregiver burden, and a history of psychopathology exacerbate grief. Though useful, Lobb et al.'s (2010) review and others combined genuinely *prospective predictors*, per se, with contemporaneous predictors that may actually represent *correlates* or *consequences* of CG. Thus, there remains a need for an empirical review of risk factors associated with grief-specific distress in the recent literature, with fine-grained reporting of results from studies that explored the relation of risk factors to common grief and CG.

We limited our review to independent variables that (a) preceded the loss (e.g., kinship relationship to deceased), (b) were related to the death itself (e.g., cause of death), (c) were static at the time of the loss or during bereavement (e.g., demographic factors, such as race or gender), or (d) were measured at a minimum of two time points (e.g., Time 1, social support, predicted Time 2, CG), excluding cognitive–behavioral factors (e.g., rumination, meaning making) that could be correlates or consequences of CG, except when their predictive power was explored in longitudinal studies. We further restricted dependent variables to assessments of common grief and CG, excluding other negative and positive outcomes (e.g., depression and posttraumatic growth, respectively). Our rationale for including common grief in our review was that (a) prior to the creation of a reliable, standardized, and validated measurement of protracted and maladaptive grief responses (e.g., ICG; Prigerson, Maciejewski, et al., 1995) researchers were reliant upon less specialized scales to assess grief in survivors, and (b) contemporary research suggests that grief can be evaluated on a continuum, ranging from low-level normative grief to a severe grief disorder (Holland et al., 2009). As a result, assessment of severity of grief across its full range can draw upon measures of both normative and complicated grief symptomatology.

Procedure

We accessed articles using the PsycINFO and PsycARTICLES online databases by using the search terms *loss*, *death*, *grief*, *complicated grief*, *bereavement*, *mourning*, *risk factor*, and *predict*. We also used book chapters, our library of grief-related articles, and the reference lists of other germane studies that emerged in our search. Studies we included were (a) empirical, (b) quantitative, and (c) published in English, in a peer-reviewed journal, between 1980 and 2010 (and earlier seminal work). Although the genesis of CG cannot be firmly established from non-experimental studies, in order to strengthen inferences related to causality, we limited our analysis of independent variables to stable factors (e.g., age, ethnicity) found in cross-sectional studies, or to longitudinal studies measuring independent variables at one time point that predict later grief. Because people's mood states could affect their report of psychological factors associated with the loss, variables assessing coping behaviors or other cognitive, emotional, or social processes were included only when studies that examined them used a truly prospective design.

Data for risk factors were analyzed by recording (a) the number of studies that examined each factor, (b) the number that found it to be a statistically significant predictor, (c) its relation to grief, and (d) its grouping into one of six categories, as described below.

Results

Initial analyses

Using 43 studies to explore risk factors of grief, we found that 16 studies measured only CG using the ICG (Prigerson, Maciejewski, et al., 1995), or its revised version, the ICG-R (Prigerson & Jacobs, 2001), 21 measured only grief more generally using a scale or items designed to measure more normative responses to loss such as the Core Bereavement Items (Burnett, Middleton, Raphael, & Martinek, 1997), and six measured both using a version of the ICG *and* at least one other scale measuring normative responses to loss. A total of 60 distinct independent variables met our inclusion criteria for risk factors. Of these, 37 risk factors were statistically significant in predicting grief or CG in at least one study. Risk factors were collated into the following distinct categories: *survivor's background* (e.g., gender), *death- and bereavement-related* (e.g., cause of death), *relationship to the deceased* (e.g., kinship), *intrapersonal* (e.g., attachment style), *religion/belief* (e.g., worldview), and *interpersonal* (e.g., social support).

When analyzed in groups, the death- and bereavement-related, relation to deceased, and intrapersonal categories had the most statistically significant risk factors ($n=8$ in each), followed by *survivor's background* ($n=5$), and *interpersonal*, and *religion/belief* ($n=4$ in each). When analyzed individually, 14 factors emerged as strong indicators of CG (see Table 11.1). These were ranked in order of the ratio of number of studies finding a given variable significant relative to the number that explored the variable. In these terms, being female emerged as the most prominent risk factor for CG, followed by being a spouse or parent (especially a mother) of the deceased, violent death, low levels of social support, the deceased's age (both younger and older), younger age of the bereaved, suddenness/unexpectedness of the death, being non-Caucasian, anxious, avoidant, or having insecure attachment style, discovering or identifying the body (in cases of violent death), high pre-death marital dependence, high levels of neuroticism, less education, prior losses, lower income, problematic relationship with the deceased, recency of the death, and lack of family cohesion.

Subsequent analyses

To increase confidence in our results, we also considered the literature using even more stringent criteria: *confirmed risk factors* of CG were each explored in at least three studies and were found statistically significant more than 50% of the time. Six such confirmed risk factors emerged: (1) low social support, (2) anxious/avoidant/insecure attachment style, (3) discovering or identifying the body (in cases of violent death), (4) being the spouse or parent of the deceased, (5) high pre-death marital dependence, and (6) high neuroticism. Thirty-two variables were identified as *potential risk factors* (explored in fewer than three studies or found to be statistically significant less than half of the time). These included being non-Caucasian, younger age of the bereaved, being female, less education, low income, violent death, sudden/unexpected death, perception of death as preventable, prior losses, lack of anticipatory grieving, searching for meaning, less importance of religion, regular church attendance, lack of spiritual beliefs, prior mental health counseling, pre-existing psychological condition, lack of technological connectedness (no use of email, Internet, cell phone), little time spent talking about the loss, frequent pre-death contact with the deceased, belief in professional counseling, subjectively close relationship with the deceased, problematic relationship with the deceased, recency of the death, lack of family cohesion, deceased's age (both younger and older), deceased's gender opposite of bereaved's, good pre-death health of deceased, length of illness of deceased (too long or too short), and negative cognitions related to self, life, the future, and threatening interpretations of one's own grief. Although the scope of this chapter precludes reporting on every risk factor in every study, the following review describes a sampling of risk factors nested within categories.

Table 11.1 Top risk factors of common grief and complicated grief in order of number of studies in which they were explored

Risk factors	Number of studies explored	Number of studies statistically significant	Percentage of studies statistically significant	Rank according to percentage	Risk factor type[a]
Younger age of bereaved	20	(5)	21	10	P
Being female	19	(8)	42	7[b]	P
Violent death	17	(6)	35	8	P
Deceased's age (both younger/older)	12	(5)	42	7[b]	P
Sudden, unexpected death	12	(5)	42	7[b]	P
Less education	12	(2)	17	11[b]	P
Spouse or parent of deceased (especially a mother)	11	(7)	64	5	C
Being non-Caucasian	8	(4)	50	6	P
Low social support	7	(6)	86	2	C
Low income, experienced prior losses, problematic relationship with deceased, recency of loss	6	(2)	33	9[c]	P
Lack of family cohesion	6	(1)	17	11	P
Anxious/avoidant/insecure attachment style	5	(4)	80	3	C
Found, saw, or identified the body in cases of violent death, or issues related to death notification	3	(3)	100	1	C
High pre-death marital dependency, high neuroticism	3	(2)	67	4[c]	C

Notes
a   C, confirmed risk factor; P, potential risk factor.
b   Risk factors share ranking.
c   Ranking represents multiple risk factors.

Survivor's background

GENDER[1]

Nineteen out of 43 (44%) studies explored the role of gender in grieving. Eight (42%) found that it was significant. For example, Lang and Gottlieb's (1993)

study of 57 parents bereaved of infants found that mothers suffered more than fathers in terms of grief. Spooren, Henderick, and Jannes (2000) found in their sample of 85 mothers and fathers bereaved by motor vehicle accidents that men and women did not differ in terms of their general psychological distress. Gender did, however, predict CG, with women suffering greater complications. Likewise, Prigerson et al.'s (2002) study found higher rates of CG among 151 female Pakistani psychiatric patients than among male Pakistani psychiatric patients. In Keesee et al.'s (2008) study of 157 parents, mothers reported more common grief than fathers but not more CG. More complex interactions of gender with other variables have also occasionally been reported, as in Callahan's (2000) study of 210 people bereaved by suicide in which women who found their loved one's body had more grief. However, other studies have found gender to be unrelated to grief, as in Momartin, Silove, Manicavasagar, and Steel's (2004) evaluation of 126 Bosnian refugees in Australia. Nonetheless, when gender differences are observed, as they often are, evidence indicates that women are more susceptible to intense and complicated grief reactions than men.

RACE

Half of the studies (four out of eight) exploring race reported significant results. Goldsmith et al. (2008) investigated two samples – 316 bereaved individuals and 222 cancer patients and their caregivers – whereas Neimeyer, Baldwin, and Gillies (2006) studied a sample of 506 young adults, both finding that African Americans experienced more grief than Caucasian Americans. Tarakeshwar, Hansen, Kochman, and Sikkema (2005) compared groups in a sample of 252 HIV-infected grievers and found that minorities (African Americans and Hispanics) reported more grief than Caucasians. Likewise, Laurie and Neimeyer's (2008) study of 1,672 bereaved college students found that being African American predicted CG, even when controlling for other variables (e.g., length of bereavement and cause of death). Evaluating grieving parents ($n=52$) and spouses ($n=90$) in the United States and the People's Republic of China (PRC) longitudinally at 4 and 18 months post loss, Bonanno, Papa, Lalande, Zhang, and Noll (2005) found that initially the PRC sample had higher grief than the U.S. sample, but later Chinese participants had lower grief than their American counterparts. This suggests the need to evaluate ethnic variations in bereavement beyond the narrow spectrum of North American culture and across a longer period, to determine whether certain ethnic groups are at greater risk of prolonged grief disorder and, if so, what might account for this effect. Still, it is worth emphasizing that 50% of the studies found that race is not a risk factor of CG. For example, Carr (2004) compared African Americans ($n=33$ widowed persons and 12 controls) and Caucasians ($n=177$ widowed persons and 75 controls) in the Changing Lives of Older Couples (CLOC) study and found no difference in levels of yearning or grief, just as Cruz and colleagues (2007) found no differences in African Americans ($n=19$) and Caucasians ($n=19$) presenting for CG therapy.

Death- and bereavement-related factors

CAUSE OF DEATH[2]

Many studies (18) examined this risk factor, and over a third of them (7; 39%) found cause of death to be related to subsequent grief. Most used cross-sectional designs, except where noted. Prigerson et al.'s (2002) investigation found that violent death (murder vs. illness, accident, and drowning) did not predict CG in 151 bereaved psychiatric patients. However, of those studies in which cause of death was a predictor, violent death was consistently found to produce more intense and complicated grief than death due to illness. Cleiren (1993) examined this factor over time and found that unnatural deaths (suicide or motor vehicle accident [MVA] vs. extended illness) led to greater grief in 309 parents and spouses, and that suicide bereaved were the most preoccupied with their loss. At Time 1 (T1; 4 months post loss), families bereaved by MVAs had more grief than those bereaved by suicide or illness, but at T2 (14 months) cause of death was no longer a risk factor. Gamino, Sewell, and Easterling (2000) compared 85 people bereaved by illness, homicide, suicide, and accident, and found that traumatic deaths produced more grief. Likewise, Currier, Holland, Coleman, and Neimeyer's (2007) cross-sectional investigation of 1,723 bereaved college students indicated that people bereaved by violent death (accident, suicide, and homicide) had more severe grief than those experiencing a loss through natural, anticipated death or natural, sudden death. Specifically, in terms of CG, they found no statistically significant difference among accident, suicide, and homicide, but scores were higher for violent deaths than for natural, anticipated deaths, and homicide and accident deaths produced more CG than did natural sudden deaths. In terms of common grief, they found that homicide produced substantially higher scores than all other types of deaths. Looking at both common grief and CG, Keesee et al. (2008) found higher grief in 94 violently bereaved parents than in 63 parents bereaved by other means. Finally, Momartin et al.'s (2004) examination of 126 Bosnian refugees indicated that the traumatic loss of a family member was the strongest risk factor for CG.

PERI-EVENT VARIABLES

One hundred percent of the small number of cross-sectional studies (three) examining peri-death variables found a relation with grief. To illustrate, Spooren et al. (2000) assessed the support that 85 parents bereaved by MVAs received after the death, and found that dissatisfaction with material help and with information given about the event predicted CG. With 540 suicidally bereaved parents, Feigelman, Jordan, and Gorman (2009) found that survivors who saw or found the body had significantly greater grief than those who did not view the body prior to the funeral. In fact, discovering the body proved to be the strongest risk factor of grief. In another suicide study ($n = 210$), seeing the body at the scene of the death intensified grief, as did being the one to find it – especially for women (Callahan, 2000). However, stepwise analyses revealed that *finding* the body was not more grief producing than simply *seeing* the body, and viewing the deceased's body at the funeral did not increase grief. Nor was the specific weapon type or suicide method (e.g., hanging) associated with grief outcomes, even when comparing the use of guns (the most common method; 47%) with seven other methods.

Relationship to the deceased

KINSHIP

Fully two thirds of studies of kinship (e.g., spouse, parent, child) demonstrated a link to intensified grief (e.g., Boelen, van den Bout, & van den Hout, 2003). For example, Laurie and Neimeyer's (2008) cross-sectional sample of 1,670 bereaved college students reported a main effect for kinship in predicting CG, such that students bereaved of immediate family had more grief than those bereaved of more distant relationships. In Cleiren's (1993) longitudinal study ($n=309$), kinship proved the strongest predictor of grief, explaining 15% of the variance in T2 (14 months post loss) scores, such that parents and spouses grieved more severely than did adult children or siblings. Even when the ages of both the bereaved and the deceased child were controlled, grief was higher for mothers at 4 and 14 months post loss, and recovery was slower. Differences among kinship categories are sometimes observed as well. For example, Prigerson and colleagues' (2002) cross-sectional examination found that spouses and parents ($n=151$) were far more likely (22 and 11 times, respectively) to have CG than other kinship types. Bonanno et al.'s (2005) longitudinal assessment found no differences in spouse ($n=90$) and parent ($n=52$) grieving at T1 (4 months); but, at T2 (14 months), parents' scores were higher than spouses'. Occasionally studies qualify this general trend linking kinship with higher risk of intense grief, as in the finding by van der Houwen and colleagues (2010) in their longitudinal study of 195 bereaved individuals, which showed that partner loss predicted emotional loneliness, but kinship did not predict grief more generally.

MARITAL DEPENDENCY

Two out of three longitudinal studies found a relation between the mourner's pre-loss dependency upon his or her spouse and subsequent grief. However, both studies with significant results used the CLOC data ($n=205$ and 210 widowed persons), so that this finding stands in need of replication. Bonanno et al. (2002) found that pre-loss spousal dependency was associated with subsequent chronic grieving as opposed to resilience, and Carr (2004) found that spousal dependency was a risk factor for despair, a specific dimension of grief. Cleiren's (1993) study of 309 survivors of MVA loss, on the other hand, yielded null findings.

Intrapersonal factors

ATTACHMENT STYLE (AVOIDANT, ANXIOUS, INSECURE)

Although too infrequently studied, attachment styles were associated with grief in three out of four of the longitudinal studies we reviewed. For example, van der Houwen et al.'s (2010) final statistical model in their study of 195 bereaved individuals indicated that avoidant but not anxious attachment predicted higher levels of CG. Using the CLOC data ($n = 103$), Brown, Nesse, House, and Utz (2009) found that pre-loss insecure attachment style and grief were related at 6, 24, and 48 months. In two studies of 219 bereaved parents, Wijngaards-de Meij and colleagues (2007a, 2007b) showed that avoidant and anxious attachment styles explained 13% of the variance in CG scores. On the other hand, results are not fully consistent. Bonanno et al. (2002) examined avoidant and dismissive attachment in a study of 205 conjugally bereaved people and found that both were unrelated to grief.

NEUROTICISM

Similarly, two out of three studies linked neuroticism with grief. For instance, in their final regression analysis of their longitudinal study of 195 grievers, van der Houwen et al. (2010) found a statistically significant relation between neuroticism and CG. In Wijngaards-de Meij et al.'s (2007a) study with 219 bereaved parents, attachment coupled with neuroticism explained 22% of the variance in CG scores, with neuroticism alone accounting for 18% of the total variance. Yet Bonanno and colleagues (2002) found no association between neuroticism and grief in their longitudinal study of 205 elderly spouses.

SEARCHING FOR MEANING AND SENSE MAKING

Coleman and Neimeyer (2010) used the CLOC study's prospective design to show that engaging in a search for meaning predicted both concurrent and prospective grief in a sample of bereaved spouses ($n = 250$). Specifically, those who struggled to make sense of the loss 6 and 18 months post loss had higher subsequent grief scores fully 4 years after the death. Interestingly, however, sense making, when it did occur, emerged as a strong positive predictor of subsequent well-being (e.g., interest, excitement, accomplishment), rather than an inverse predictor of grief symptomatology per se.

NEGATIVE COGNITIONS

Including a sample of 97 mourners in their longitudinal study, Boelen, van den Bout, and van den Hout (2006) found that bereavement-associated negative cognitions at T1 (1–4 months post loss) related to the griever's *self, life, future,* or *threatening interpretations of grief* (e.g., "If I fully realized what the death of ____ means, I would go crazy") each individually predicted CG at T2 (7–10 months post loss), even after controlling for background variables and CG symptomatology at T1. Additionally, the *future* subscale (e.g., "In the future, I will never become really happy any more") was the only subset of negative cognitions at T1 that enduringly predicted CG at T3 (16–19 months post loss), with an interaction of *threatening interpretations* × *avoidance of the reality of the loss* likewise prospectively predicting CG at T3 in hierarchical multiple regressions.

Religion/belief factors

IMPORTANCE OF RELIGION

The few prospective studies conducted on the importance of religion yielded inconsistent evidence for its relation to grief. For example, Brown et al. (2009) used the CLOC data to monitor grief in 103 spouses. They found that assigning greater importance to religious/spiritual beliefs pre-loss predicted less grief at 6 and 18 months post loss, although high church attendance was unrelated. Conversely, when Kersting et al. (2007) compared grief in 62 women who had terminated their pregnancy with 65 women who birthed a full-term baby, they found that those who placed higher import on faith grieved the hardest, possibly reflecting guilt or regret about their decision to abort the fetus.

SPIRITUAL BELIEF OR WORLDVIEW

These risk factors produced equivocal results across two studies. In Bonanno et al.'s (2002) prospective study (*n* = 205) bereaved spouses who were the most resilient also had greater acceptance and believed in a just world. However, no connection between chronic grief and a dysfunctional worldview was discovered. Yet Easterling, Gamino, Sewell, and Stirman (2000) found in their cross-sectional study of 85 bereaved individuals that spiritual beliefs about one's relationship with God or events that increase belief in God's existence were related to less grief.

Interpersonal factors

SOCIAL SUPPORT

Six out of seven (86%) longitudinal studies found that low levels of social support predicted intensified grief (e.g., Bonanno et al., 2002). Vanderwerker and Prigerson (2004) prospectively examined 293 older people and found that higher social support at 6 months post loss forecast less CG near the end of the first year. However, Gamino, Sewell, and Easterling's (1998) cross-sectional study found that grief and social support were unrelated in a sample of 74 mourners.

Discussion

The multidimensional nature of adaptation to loss poses challenges to the identification of risk factors predicting prolonged and intense grieving. One specific challenge concerns the basic understanding of CG as a construct. According to those who conceptualize CG as existing on a continuum, differences between grievers whose response to loss warrants treatment and those whose does not are reflected in the duration and intensity of symptoms and levels of impairment, not in distinctive symptoms. Nevertheless, lacking a genuine cut-point where grief responses are considered in need of treatment, researchers and clinicians must make personal or consensual judgments about a given griever's level of impairment and distress. On the other hand, finer discrimination of distress that spans the range of grief responses provides sensitivity that may be lost in models that insist on bifurcation of high-/low-distress respondents.

Likewise, the contrasting view held by some researchers that common grief and CG are symptomatically different carries implications for understanding of the grieving process. On the one hand, assessing grief in this way may blur variability in responses that represent different points on the same continuum. This view also carries the potential for social and personal stigma in suggesting that some individuals are grieving in a diagnosably disordered manner. Conversely, this model's clear identification of cases of CG could simplify communication among mental health professionals and more readily specify who is or is not in need of treatment.

Viewing grief in dimensional terms, we systematically sought out studies that explored antecedents and predictors of CG, and were limited only by the types of factors explored in the primary studies. We identified more consistent prospective predictors of intense grieving, as well as those that were potential factors in forecasting grief outcomes. Risk factors that emerged as most salient included low levels of social support, avoidant/anxious/insecure attachment style, discovering the body (in cases of violent death) or dissatisfaction with death notification, being a spouse or a parent of the deceased, high levels of pre-death marital dependency, and high levels of neuroticism. Inasmuch as CG is conceptualized as an attachment-based disorder, with symptomatology indicative of separation distress and preoccupation with the deceased, it is understandable that mourners who are vulnerable to feeling abandoned and alone, who suffer from excessive anxiety or obsession, and who lose a security-enhancing or care-providing relationship, under conditions of minimal support, and perhaps in circumstances that leave them struggling with posttraumatic imagery, would be especially prone to the development of CG.

In addition to these primary conclusions, studies further suggest that being young, being non-Caucasian, having less education, little income, prior losses, or losing a child of any age to a violent, sudden death tends to predict prolonged and intense grief. Unfortunately, few of those potential risk factors are modifiable in the context of therapy. This highlights the importance of studying those predictors of poor outcome that in principle are modifiable, as intervention could focus usefully on strengthening social integration of the bereaved (Burke, Neimeyer, & McDevitt-Murphy, 2010), facilitating the use of their spiritual or secular philosophies as a psychological resource (Park & Halifax, 2011), challenging their dysfunctional interpretations or predictions about themselves and the future (Boelen et al., 2006), joining them in their quest for meaning in a senseless loss (Neimeyer, Burke, Mackay, & van Dyke-Stringer, 2010), and strengthening their continuing bond with the deceased so as to enhance their attachment security (Field & Wogrin, 2011). Fortunately, empirically informed therapies that pursue such goals are currently being developed (Neimeyer, Harris, Winokuer, & Thornton, 2011).

Limitations to this review

Generally speaking, research on risk factors is rife with complexity. For instance, because we sought to include only truly prospective factors in our review, potentially modifiable variables included only in correlational studies were excluded (although static variables in the same studies might be included). Other challenges included collating the variety of measures and items used for assessing grief, interpreting poorly defined variables, and deciphering vague reporting of results, all of which required some level of subjective judgment.

Moreover, some variables represented in this review are likely to have equal relevance in predicting grief and more general symptomatology (e.g., depression, suicidality), whereas other factors may differentially predict grief and non-grief outcomes in ways that could not be addressed in this review. For instance, some studies have shown that men suffer more depression than women following spousal loss (Stroebe & Stroebe, 1983), in contrast to findings reviewed above implicating female gender with greater grieving. Furthermore, the search for universal risk factors also can be complicated by the different cultural, economic, and political contexts in which studies are conducted. For example, concern for health care disparities experienced by different ethnicities could make investigation of racial differences in CG a high priority in the United States, whereas in some European countries such practices could be considered inappropriate.

To strengthen causal inferences, we excluded risk factors that were likely to change as a result of the loss, or that were simply correlated with grief, focusing instead on longitudinal designs and stable independent variables (e.g., gender of the mourner). These exclusions meant that most studies on coping strategies, cognitions, or meaning making in bereavement – factors that are perhaps the most malleable and amenable to therapeutic intervention – were given little attention, simply because the majority of research to date on these factors utilized cross-sectional designs. We were similarly limited by the paucity of studies exploring mediators or moderators of grief,[3] and by the equivocal findings across studies, which probably result from variations in methodological standards and measurement tools. Use of state-of-the-science measures and consideration of moderator variables could yield more precise findings in future research. Finally, we were further restricted by our exclusion of qualitative studies that may have suggested a richer understanding of the CG experience.

Although we have made a concerted attempt to isolate and categorize prospective risk factors that predict an intense grieving process in order to make definitive statements about who is susceptible to CG, a meta-analytical review of risk factor effect sizes would be desirable. Perhaps most informative of all would be one that includes other relevant bereavement outcomes (e.g., depression, post-traumatic stress), both longitudinal and cross-sectional, including samples diverse in age, ethnicity, and nationality. A more comprehensive analysis along these lines would provide a broader picture of why some people are more likely than others to develop intense and sustained difficulties in bereavement, as opposed to grief symptoms alone.

Clinical implications and future directions for research

A systematic empirical review of this sort is valuable for many reasons. First, although CG is concerning in itself, it is often not the final outcome in mourning gone awry; rather, CG can function as a risk factor for even more dire psychological and physical health problems. For example, CG subsequently predicts cardiovascular illness (Prigerson et al., 1997), suicidality (Latham & Prigerson, 2004), substance abuse, depression, anxiety, and overall life disruption (Ott, 2003; Shear et al., 2011).

Moreover, identification of CG predictors enables clinicians to provide proactive assistance, especially to individuals facing expected deaths (e.g., of a loved one with cancer), or to those at special risk in the wake of a widespread trauma or disaster. For example, Rando (1983) found in her study of 54 parents bereaved by their child's cancer that, when anticipatory grieving was done prior to the death, less disordered grieving occurred afterward. Additionally, identification of modifiable risk factors can guide the development of relevant secondary or tertiary interventions. For instance, armed with the knowledge that poor social support poses risks to bereavement adaptation (Burke et al., 2010), health care professionals in end-of-life contexts could assess families' social support before bereavement begins, with an eye toward preventive intervention.

Finally, the argument for a continuing focus on risk factors of CG in bereavement research is, perhaps, made more evident in terms of the tremendous need for more widespread understanding of this life-vitiating condition. As a whole, medical and mental health professionals, clergy, and society alike are woefully uninformed about CG, its predictors, or its treatment. Disseminating knowledge to frontline workers and to the grievers themselves could be a first step toward prevention and treatment of a life-limiting response to loss.

Acknowledgment

The authors gratefully acknowledge the invaluable help of Natalie L. Davis in this work.

Notes

1 Comparisons of mothers versus fathers were reported in the *gender* category rather than under *kinship,* which compared several relationship types (i.e., parents, siblings, spouses).
2 See Chapter 20 in this volume for commentary on the definition and categorization of violent versus non-violent death loss.
3 An exception to this was Boelen and colleagues' (2006) study that examined negative thoughts/beliefs, cognitive–behavioral avoidance strategies, and interactions between the two.

References

Boelen, P. A., van den Bout, J., & van den Hout, M. A. (2003). The role of negative interpretations of grief reactions in emotional problems after bereavement. *Journal of Behavior Therapy and Experimental Psychiatry, 34*, 225–238.

Boelen, P. A., van den Bout, J., & van den Hout, M. A. (2006). Negative cognitions and avoidance in emotional problems after bereavement: A prospective study. *Behavior Research and Therapy, 44*, 1657–1672.

Bonanno, G. A., & Kaltman, S. (2001). The varieties of grief experience. *Clinical Psychology Review, 21*, 705–734.

Bonanno, G. A., & Mancini, A. D. (2006). Bereavement-related depression and PTSD: Evaluating interventions. In Barbanel, L., & Sternberg, R. J. (Eds.), *Psychological interventions in times of crisis* (pp. 37–55). New York: Springer.

Bonanno, G. A., Papa, A., Lalande, K., Zhang, N., & Noll, J. G. (2005). Grief processing and deliberate grief avoidance: A prospective comparison of bereaved spouses and parents in the United States and the People's Republic of China. *Journal of Counseling and Clinical Psychology, 73*(1), 86–98.

Bonanno, G. A., Wortman, C. B., Lehman, D. R., Tweed, R. G., Haring, M., Sonnega, J., et al. (2002). Resilience to loss and chronic grief. *Journal of Personality and Social Psychology, 83*, 1150–1164.

Brown, S. L., Nesse, R. M., House, J. S., & Utz, R. L. (2009). Religion and emotional compensation: Results from a prospective study of widowhood. *Society for Personality and Social Psychology, 30*, 1165–1174.

Burke, L. A., Neimeyer, R. A., & McDevitt-Murphy, M. E. (2010). African American homicide bereavement: Aspects of social support that predict complicated grief, PTSD and depression. *Omega, 61*, 1–24.

Burnett, P., Middleton, W., Raphael, B., & Martinek, N. (1997). Measuring core bereavement phenomena. *Psychological Medicine, 27*, 49–57.

Callahan, J. (2000). Predictors and correlates of bereavement in suicide support group participants. *Suicide and Life Threatening Behavior, 30*, 104–124.

Carr, D. S. (2004). African American/Caucasian differences in psychological adjustment to spousal loss among older adults. *Research on Aging, 26*, 591–622.

Cleiren, M. (1993). *Bereavement and adaptation: A comparative study of the aftermath of death.* Washington, DC: Hemisphere.

Coleman, R. A., & Neimeyer, R. A. (2010). Measuring meaning: Searching for and making sense of spousal loss in later life. *Death Studies, 34*, 804–834.

Cruz, M., Scott, J., Houck, P., Reynolds, C. F. III., Frank, E., & Shear, M. K. (2007). Clinical presentation and treatment outcome of African Americans with complicated grief. *Psychiatric Services, 58*, 700–702.

Currier, J. M., Holland, J., Coleman, R., & Neimeyer, R. A. (2007). Bereavement following violent death: An assault on life and meaning. In Stevenson, R., & Cox, G. (Eds.), *Perspectives on violence and violent death* (pp. 175–200). Amityville, NY: Baywood.

Easterling, L. W., Gamino, L. A., Sewell, K. W., & Stirman, L. S. (2000). Spiritual experience, church attendance, and bereavement. *Journal of Pastoral Care, 54*, 263–275.

Feigelman, W., Jordan, J. R., & Gorman, B. S. (2009). How they died, time since loss, and bereavement outcomes. *Omega: Journal of Death and Dying, 58*, 251–273.

Field, N. P., & Wogrin, C. (2011). The changing bond in therapy for unresolved loss. In Neimeyer, R. A., Harris, D., Winokuer, H., & Thornton, G. (Eds.), *Grief and bereavement in contemporary society* (pp. 37–46). New York: Routledge.

Gamino, L. A., Sewell, K. W., & Easterling, L. W. (1998). Scott & White Grief Study: An empirical test of predictors of intensified mourning. *Death Studies, 22*, 333–355.

Gamino, L. A., Sewell, K. W., & Easterling, L. W. (2000). Scott & White grief study phase 2: Toward an adaptive model of grief. *Death Studies, 24*, 633–660.

Goldsmith, B., Morrison, R. S., Vanderwerker, L. C., & Prigerson, H. (2008). Elevated rates of prolonged grief disorder in African Americans. *Death Studies, 32*, 352–365.

Holland, J. M., Neimeyer, R. A., Boelen, P. A., & Prigerson, H. G. (2009). The underlying structure of grief. *Journal of Psychopathology and Behavioral Assessment, 31*, 190–201.

van der Houwen, K., Stroebe, M., Stroebe, W., Schut, H., van den Bout, J., & Wijngaards-de Meij, L. (2010). Risk factors for bereavement outcome: A multivariate approach. *Death Studies, 34*, 195–220.

Keesee, N. J., Currier, J. M., & Neimeyer, R. A. (2008). Predictors of grief following the death of one's child: The contribution of finding meaning. *Journal of Clinical Psychology, 64*, 1–19.

Kersting, A., Kroker, K., Steinhard, J., Ludorff., K., Wesselmann., U., & Ohrmann, P. (2007). Complicated grief after traumatic loss: A 14-month follow-up study. *European Archive of Psychiatry Clinical Neuroscience, 257*, 437–443.

Lang, A., & Gottlieb, L. (1993). Parental grief reactions and marital intimacy following infant death. *Death Studies, 17*, 233–255.

Latham, A., & Prigerson, H. (2004). Suicidality and bereavement. *Suicide and Life Threatening Behavior, 34*, 350–362.

Laurie, A., & Neimeyer, R. A. (2008). African Americans and bereavement: Grief as a function of ethnicity. *Omega, 57*, 173–193.

Lichtenthal, W. G., Cruess, D. G., & Prigerson, H. G. (2004). A case for establishing complicated grief as a distinct mental disorder in DSM-V. *Clinical Psychology Review, 24*, 637–662.

Lobb, E. A., Kristjanson, L. J., Aoun, S. M., Monterosso, L., Halkett, G. K. B., & Davies, A. (2010). Predictors of complicated grief: A systematic review of empirical studies. *Death Studies, 34*, 673–698.

McDevitt-Murphy, M. E., Neimeyer, R. A., Burke, L. A., & Williams, J. L. (2012). Assessing the toll of traumatic loss: Psychological symptoms in African Americans bereaved by homicide. *Psychological Trauma: Theory, Research, and Policy, 4*, 303–311.

Momartin, S., Silove, D., Manicavasagar, V., & Steel, Z. (2004). Complicated grief in Bosnian refugees. *Comprehensive Psychiatry, 45*, 475–482.

Neimeyer, R. A., Baldwin, S. A., & Gillies, J. (2006). Continuing bonds and reconstructing meaning: Mitigating complications in bereavement. *Death Studies, 30*, 715–738.

Neimeyer, R. A., Burke, L., Mackay, M., & van Dyke-Stringer, J. (2010). Grief therapy and the reconstruction of meaning: From principles to practice. *Journal of Contemporary Psychotherapy, 40*, 73–83.

Neimeyer, R. A., Harris, D., Winokuer, H., & Thornton, G. (Eds.). (2011). *Grief and bereavement in contemporary society: Bridging research and practice*. New York: Routledge.

Ott, C. H. (2003). The impact of complicated grief on mental and physical health at various points in the bereavement process. *Death Studies, 27*, 249–272.

Park, C., & Halifax, J. (2011). Religion and spirituality in adjusting to bereavement. In Neimeyer, R. A., Harris, D., Winokuer, H., & Thornton, G. (Eds.), *Grief and bereavement in contemporary society* (pp. 355–364). New York: Routledge.

Prigerson, H., Ahmed, I., Silverman, G. K., Saxena, A. K., Maciejewski, P. K., Jacobs, et al. (2002). Rates of risks of complicated grief among psychiatric clinic patients in Karachi, Pakistan. *Death Studies, 26*, 781–792.

Prigerson, H. G., Beirhals, A. J., Kasl, S. V., Reynolds, C. F., Shear, K., Day, N., et al. (1997). Traumatic grief as a risk factor for mental and physical morbidity. *American Journal of Psychiatry, 154*, 616–623.

Prigerson, H. G., Frank, E., Kasl, S., Reynolds, C., Anderson, B., Zubenko, G. S., et al. (1995). Complicated grief and bereavement related depression as distinct disorders. *American Journal of Psychiatry, 152*, 22–30.

Prigerson, H. G., Horowitz, M. J., Jacobs, S. C., Parkes, C. M., Aslan, M., Goodkin, K., et al. (2009). Prolonged grief disorder: Psychometric validation of criteria proposed for DSM-V and ICD-11. *PLoS Medicine, 6*(8), 1–12.

Prigerson, H. G., & Jacobs, S. C. (2001). Traumatic grief as a distinct disorder: A rationale, consensus criteria, and a preliminary empirical test. In Stroebe, M. S., Hansson, R. O., Stroebe, W., & Schut, H. (Eds.), *Handbook of bereavement research* (pp. 613–645). Washington, DC: American Psychological Association.

Prigerson, H. G., Maciejewski, P., Reynolds, C. F., Beirhals, A. J., et al. (1995). Inventory of Complicated Grief: A scale to measure maladaptive symptoms of loss. *Psychiatry Research, 59*, 65–79.

Rando, T. A. (1983). An investigation of grief and adaptation in parents whose children have died of cancer. *Journal of Pediatric Psychology, 8*, 3–20.

Sanders, C. M. (1988). Potential risk factors in bereavement outcome. *Journal of Social Issues, 44*, 97–111.

Shear, K., Frank, E., Houch, P. R., & Reynolds, C. F. (2005). Treatment of complicated grief: A randomized controlled trial. *Journal of the American Medical Association, 293*, 2601–2608.

Shear, M. K., Jackson, C. T., Essock, S. M., Donahue, S. A., & Felton, C. J. (2006). Screening for complicated grief among Project Liberty service recipients 18 months after September 11, 2001. *Psychiatric Services, 57*, 1291–1297.

Spooren, D. J., Henderick, H., & Jannes, C. (2000). Survey description of stress of parents bereaved from a child killed in a traffic accident. *Omega, 42*, 171–185.

Stroebe, M., Schut., H., & Stroebe, W. (2007). Health outcomes in bereavement. *The Lancet, 370*, 1960–1073.

Stroebe, M. S., & Stroebe, W. (1983). Who suffers more? Sex differences in health risks of the widowed. *Psychological Bulletin, 93*, 279–301.

Stroebe, W., & Schut, H. (2001). Risk factors in bereavement outcome: A methodological and empirical review. In Stroebe, M. S., Hansson, R. O., Stroebe, W., & Schut, H. (Eds.), *Handbook of bereavement research: Consequences, coping and care* (pp. 349–371). Washington, DC: American Psychological Association.

Tarakeshwar, N., Hansen, N., Kochman, A., & Sikkema, K. J. (2005). Gender, ethnicity and spiritual coping among bereaved HIV-positive individuals. *Mental Health, Religion, & Culture, 8*, 109–125.

Vanderwerker, L. C., & Prigerson, H. G. (2004). Social support and technological connectedness as protective factors in bereavement. *Journal of Loss and Trauma, 9*, 45–57.

Wijngaards-de Meij, L., Stroebe, M., Schut, H., Stroebe, W., van den Bout, J., & Heijden,
P. G. M. (2007). Neuroticism and attachment insecurity as predictors of bereavement
outcome. *Journal of Research and Personality, 41*, 498–505.

Wijngaards-de Meij, L., Stroebe, M., Schut, H., Stroebe, W., van den Bout, J., & Heijden,
P. G. M. (2007). Patterns of attachment and parents' adjustment to the death of their
child. *Personality and Social Psychology Bulletin, 33*, 537.

12 Repetitive thought

Rumination in complicated grief

Edward R. Watkins and Michelle L. Moulds

Repetitive thought (RT) is defined as the 'process of thinking attentively, repetitively or frequently about one's self and one's world' and has been proposed to form 'the core of a number of different models of adjustment and maladjustment' (Segerstrom, Stanton, Alden, & Shortridge, 2003, p. 3). Repetition is a property that is common to a range of thought processes that have implications for self-regulation, psychopathology, and mental and physical health, including worry, rumination, cognitive processing, rehearsal, reflection, and problem-solving. Watkins (2008) argued that organizing our knowledge of these different processes around the generic construct of RT provides a means to integrate a number of disparate literatures, without being limited by preconceptions or different terminology. Importantly, RT encompasses processes that are relevant to both normal and pathological grief.

Thus, RT includes *depressive rumination*, which is defined as 'passively and repetitively focusing on one's symptoms of distress and the circumstances surrounding these symptoms' (Nolen-Hoeksema, McBride, & Larson, 1997, p. 855). Rumination prospectively predicts the onset and maintenance of depression (Nolen-Hoeksema, 2000), and is hypothesized to be a maladaptive process that prolongs grief reactions (Bonanno, Papa, Lalande, Zhang, & Noll, 2005; M. Stroebe et al., 2007). RT may also occur within more adaptive processes, such as *cognitive processing*; that is, actively thinking about a stressor, the thoughts and feelings it evokes, and its implications for one's life and future (Bower, Kemeny, Taylor, & Fahey, 1998; Greenberg, 1995). Cognitive processing accounts hypothesize that, in response to a stressful experience, people think repetitively about the event in order to integrate and incorporate it into their existing meaning structures (e.g. Janoff-Bulman, 1992).

As this comparison highlights, a key question within the study of normal and pathological grief is whether RT about loss has unconstructive versus constructive consequences. We review the relevant theories and evidence concerning the different consequences of RT following bereavement. We then propose an integrative solution to this question that we frame within a recent theory that hypothesizes that the consequences of RT vary according to its content (positive versus negative) and the way in which individuals engage in RT (abstract versus concrete; Watkins, 2008).

Repetitive thought and grief: theory

The leading cognitive conceptualization of RT is based on control theory approaches that propose that rumination is triggered by a discrepancy in goal progress. Within this account, RT serves the function of facilitating progress towards the desired goal by increasing awareness and focus on the unresolved issue (Martin & Tesser, 1996). RT continues either until the goal is met or until the individual disengages from and abandons the goal. Increased focus on the discrepancy will be constructive if the individual makes progress towards the goal, but will only highlight the discrepancy and increase distress if the discrepancy cannot be resolved (e.g. if the goal is unrealistic/unattainable and cannot be altered). This process also applies to discrepancies that result from events that do not fit into an individual's mental models of the world. Moreover, the discrepancies that initiate RT are often a consequence of loss events. Since bereavement is one of the most common and yet most personally significant loss events, this theory proposes that RT will be a common response to bereavement.

The grief literature also suggests that RT is an important process in grieving, with a similar debate about whether it is constructive or unconstructive. Historically, 'grief work' models have argued that it is necessary to work through the negative emotions, thoughts, and memories associated with loss in order to facilitate adjustment (e.g. Bowlby, 1980). These approaches by definition implicate RT about the deceased and the loss in the process of recovery. These theories have been challenged for having unspecified operationalizations of 'working through' and because there is limited evidence that confronting feelings and grief-related memories in a non-structured way is adaptive (e.g. Bonanno & Kaltman, 1999; W. Stroebe, Schut, & M. Stroebe, 2005). Nonetheless, more recent cognitive processing accounts (e.g. Bower et al., 1998; Lepore, Silver, Wortman, & Wayment, 1996) and cognitive–behavioural accounts of grieving (e.g. Boelen, van den Hout, & van den Bout, 2006b) propose a role for RT in integrating the loss into existing mental structures.

More specifically, Bonanno and colleagues have postulated the *grief work as rumination hypothesis*, which proposes that grief processing involves pathological RT about the loss that exacerbates rather than ameliorates grief-related distress (e.g. Bonanno, Papa, & O'Neill, 2002; Bonanno et al., 2005). In the dual-process model, M. Stroebe and Schut (1999) propose that grief processing, presumably including RT about the loss, may be adaptive, but only when balanced with avoidance and other restoration-coping responses. By implication, this account suggests that there is an optimal amount of RT: too little will prevent effective adjustment, whereas too much will exacerbate distress.

We propose that, rather than adopt an all-or-nothing view of the consequences of RT, it better reflects the evidence on the effects of RT (Watkins, 2008), as well as evidence that RT is both a normal response within non-pathological grief and a characteristic symptom of complicated grief (CG), to hypothesize that RT in the aftermath of loss can have constructive or unconstructive consequences. In the initial months following bereavement, nearly all individuals, including those who do not develop chronic difficulties, report rumination and daily thoughts about the deceased (Bonanno & Kaltman, 2001; Bonanno, Wortman, & Neese, 2004). Nonetheless, the majority of bereaved individuals (85–90%) adapt to their bereavement in the initial months, such that they no longer experience distress about the loss (Bonanno & Kaltman, 2001; Bonanno et al., 2004). Thus, for the majority of people who respond adaptively to bereavement, RT experienced in the initial months of normal grief cannot have a powerful unconstructive effect: it is an epiphenomenon with little impact on outcome, or it has a beneficial effect on outcome, or it may be the result of another process. Nonetheless, elevated levels of RT about the loss have been identified in the 10–15% of individuals with chronic grief symptoms (e.g. Bonanno et al., 2004), that is, diagnosed with CG (also prolonged grief or traumatic grief). CG is characterized by a persistent sense of yearning for the deceased, difficulty accepting or believing the loss, bitterness, lack of trust, and loss of perceived meaning in life. To receive a CG diagnosis, symptoms must be present for at least 6 months and cause functional impairment (e.g. Lichtenthal, Cruess, & Prigerson, 2004; Prigerson et al., 2009). Yearning for or preoccupation with the deceased is a key symptom of CG (Prigerson et al., 2009).

Repetitive thought and grief: evidence

Unconstructive effects of RT following bereavement

There is growing evidence that RT can have negative consequences for adjustment to a bereavement. The strongest evidence comes from longitudinal prospective studies in which RT at an initial assessment predicted negative outcomes such as depression at a subsequent assessment. Unfortunately, no studies have directly examined whether RT prospectively predicts specific CG symptoms such as yearning. Evidence that RT prospectively predicts depression is consistent with the hypothesis that RT is involved in contributing to chronic, dysfunctional patterns of grief, although it needs to be treated cautiously given evidence that CG is distinctive and distinguishable from depression (e.g. Bonanno et al., 2004; Prigerson et al., 2009).

Nolen-Hoeksema, Parker, and Larson (1994) examined 253 adults who lost a family member to a terminal illness, and found that individuals with a more depressive ruminative style (using the Response Styles Questionnaire, RSQ) at 1 month post loss were more depressed 6 months later, controlling for baseline depression and demographic variables. Similarly, Nolen-Hoeksema et al. (1997) found that, in 30 gay men whose partners had recently died from AIDS, codings of RT from interview transcripts prospectively predicted levels of distress 1 year later, although this effect was lost after controlling for baseline symptoms. Lepore et al. (1996) found that high levels of RT in the first 3 weeks after the death of an infant child predicted mothers' later depression, but only for those mothers who perceived social constraints about talking about their loss.

Bonanno et al. (2005) prospectively examined measures of grief processing, deliberate grief-related avoidance, and distress at 4 and 18 months post-bereavement in individuals from the USA and China who had experienced the death of a spouse or child. The grief-processing measure included an assessment of the frequency of RT about the deceased. Consistent with the grief work as rumination hypothesis, independent of 4-month post-bereavement distress, grief processing and deliberate avoidance at 4 months predicted distress 18 months later in the U.S. sample. Similarly, Bonanno et al. (2004) found that, for widows who were not already depressed before their bereavement, more frequent talking and thinking about their loss 6 months post-bereavement predicted elevated depression at 18 months post-bereavement. However, neither of these studies included a pure index of RT, so it is unknown which element of the grief-processing construct predicted increasing symptoms. Moreover, there is a question concerning the selection of the timing of the follow-up assessments. It is possible that beneficial grief processing, and, by extension, constructive forms of RT, might be more common in the first 1–4 months of bereavement.

Finally, several cross-sectional studies have examined the relationship between RT, coping responses, and symptoms following bereavement. These studies are limited by their correlational nature, leaving unresolved the direction of the causal relationship between RT and symptoms. In a Japanese study of parents who had experienced the loss of a child, RT was significantly associated with the onset of major depression, after controlling for demographic variables (Ito et al., 2003). Michael and Snyder (2005) found that increased RT was associated with reduced well-being in bereaved students. Davis, Lehman, Wortman, Silver, and Thompson (1995) reported that RT following uncontrollable and traumatic events, such as sudden infant death, was associated with a greater level of distress.

In a prospective study, Boelen, van den Bout, and van den Hout (2006a) examined the relationship between cognitive and behavioural avoidance and the symptoms of CG. The avoidance measure included items that assessed RT (e.g. 'I ruminate about the question why he/she died'). Although avoidance was associated with concurrent CG symptoms, it did not predict subsequent CG symptoms after baseline symptoms were controlled. However, since the measure assessed other aspects of avoidance as well as RT, we cannot be confident that the pattern of findings reflects assessment of RT.

Also relevant is the extensive evidence that RT in response to loss or trauma events can have unconstructive consequences (Watkins, 2008). The response to bereavement theoretically fits within this broader class of loss and traumatic events, and we propose that the same mechanisms and processes should be relevant. This evidence includes the finding that RT about a traumatic event predicts the persistence of posttraumatic stress disorder (PTSD) in prospective longitudinal studies from 6 months to 3 years later (e.g. Ehlers, Mayou, & Bryant, 1998; Mayou, Ehlers, & Bryant, 2002). Taken together, the theoretical overlap between cognitive–behavioural accounts of PTSD and CG (e.g. Ehlers, 2006) and evidence of the link between RT and poor psychological adjustment are consistent with the hypothesis that RT may be unconstructive following bereavement.

Constructive effects of RT

Only a few studies have demonstrated that RT following bereavement has constructive consequences. Nonetheless, we need to be careful that the 'absence of evidence' is not falsely interpreted as 'evidence of absence', especially given the wider evidence that RT can in fact have constructive consequences, including recovery from traumatic events, and reducing anxiety and depression (Watkins, 2008).

First, in a prospective study that examined the health outcomes of HIV-seropositive men who had experienced an AIDS-related bereavement, RT was associated with finding more meaning in the loss over the next 2–3 years. In turn, this outcome was associated with better immune responses and reduced AIDs-related mortality over a 7-year follow-up (Bower et al., 1998). Finding meaning was operationalized as a major shift in values, priorities, or perspectives in response to the loss, and included developing new personal growth goals, an enhanced sense of living in the present, and the development of new perspectives (e.g. views such as *life is precious*). These changes are examples of 'finding benefit', which is defined as positive appraisals about the meaning of the event. In two prospective longitudinal studies that examined responses to bereavement, Davis, Nolen-Hoeksema, and Larson (1998) and Stein, Folkman, Trabasso, and Richards (1997) reported that finding benefit predicted better psychological adjustment and more adaptive responses to loss. Combined with the results of Bower et al.'s (1998) study, these findings suggest that RT following bereavement may be adaptive when it focuses on positive benefits or values learnt as a result of the loss.

Second, cross-sectional studies have provided evidence that the extent to which individuals engage in RT after a traumatic or stressful event is positively associated with more posttraumatic growth, as indexed by self-reported increases in relating to others, discovering new possibilities and personal strength, and increased appreciation of life. Tedeschi and Calhoun (2004) found that RT (defined as automatic or deliberate thinking about the traumatic event) immediately after a child's death was associated with posttraumatic growth in bereaved parents, whereas RT that occurred later after the death was not.

Third, there is extensive evidence from experimental and longitudinal prospective studies that RT can lead to constructive consequences in response to similar events (e.g. loss, trauma) and on symptom clusters related to CG, such as depression (see Watkins, 2008). For example, RT prospectively predicted reduced levels of depression in several longitudinal studies (e.g. Treynor, Gonzalez, & Nolen-Hoeksema, 2003; Yamada, Nagayama, Tsutiyama, Kitamura, & Furukawa, 2003). Moreover, experimental studies have suggested that certain variants of RT can have constructive consequences in response to loss and trauma events. These studies have manipulated whether participants think repetitively in either an abstract (thinking about the causes, meanings, implications, and ends of an event and why it occurred, e.g. 'Why do you feel this way?') or a concrete way (imagining the concrete, sensory, and contextual details of what is happening in a situation and focusing on the process and means of how it occurred, e.g. 'How do you feel moment by moment?'). Relative to manipulations to engage in abstract RT, manipulations that instructed participants to engage in concrete RT produced faster recovery of negative affect and reduced intrusions after a previous negative induction (Ehring, Szeimies, & Schaffrick, 2009; Watkins, 2004). Similarly, individuals who were trained to think about emotional events in a concrete way had reduced emotional reactivity to a subsequent experimental stressor (failure) relative to those trained to think in an abstract way (Watkins, Moberly, & Moulds, 2008). These results suggest that there are more constructive forms of RT, characterized by a concrete thinking style, in contrast to unconstructive forms of RT, characterized by an abstract style. Given the broad applicability of theories that address responses to stressful situations, it is reasonable to assume that similar constructive consequences of RT apply following bereavement.

Accounting for constructive versus unconstructive effects of RT

Moderators of the consequences of RT

Reviewing the literature on RT, Watkins (2008) noted that a number of properties could account for the distinct helpful versus unhelpful consequences of RT: (a) the valence (positive versus negative) of thought content, with more positive thought content leading to more constructive consequences (e.g. 'finding benefit', Bower et al., 1998; Segerstrom et al., 2003); (b) the context in which RT occurs (e.g. intrapersonal context such as mood and self-beliefs, such that more negative beliefs about the self produce more unconstructive RT; situational context, such as difficult life events, such that more stressful events produce more unconstructive RT); (c) the style of thinking adopted, with abstract RT having more unconstructive consequences than concrete RT, at least when focused on negative content. Each of these factors is relevant to responses to bereavement. Bonanno and Kaltman (1999, 2001) reviewed evidence relevant to the issue of how positive thought content can be beneficial in the aftermath of grief, and noted that the context of the bereavement may be important. Moreover, Bonanno et al. (2002) hypothesized that focusing on concrete aspects of the self may be one means to maintain identity continuity and, thus, maintain resilience following bereavement.

A control theory account of RT

These moderators are predicted from an elaboration of the control theory account of RT (Watkins, 2008). Within control theory, representations of events, behaviours, or goals can be arranged in a hierarchy of means and ends in which subordinate, concrete goals, or means, serve to achieve the more abstract, superordinate goals, or ends. A particular level in the hierarchy may be functionally and operationally superordinate at any moment in time, reflecting whether the individual is focusing attention and awareness on a more abstract or concrete level, and thereby representing reference values (goals, expectations) and perceptual signals (e.g. events and actions in the world) in a more abstract or concrete manner (Carver

& Scheier, 1982; Vallacher & Wegner, 1987; Watkins, 2008). Abstract process-ing involves representing the reasons why an action is performed or an event occurred, its meaning and implications, and elements that are common across multiple situations. Concrete processing represents how an event unfolded and how a behaviour is performed, and reflects contextual and sensory details that are specific to a particular situation. Thus, following an unexpected death of a loved one, abstract processing may include existential questions ('Why me? Why did it happen to them?'), global negative self-evaluations ('I am weak'), and negative generalizations ('Life is unfair'), whereas processing at a concrete level would focus on recalling the details of the final days of the deceased, specific memories of his or her life, and plans for what to do next.

Effective self-regulation requires flexible and balanced coordination between the different levels within the goal hierarchy, such that the superordinate level of control adaptively varies in response to situational and task demands. Depending on context, a level of control that is too abstract or too concrete, or that fails to link abstract levels to concrete levels, is hypothesized to be detrimental (Carver & Scheier, 1998).

Within control theory, abstract processing (a) insulates an individual from the specific context, making him or her less responsive to the environment, (b) gener-ates inferences across different situations beyond available data, enabling transfer of learning from one situation to another, and (c) represents events and actions in terms of their implications for more abstract goals (i.e. more personally meaning-ful ends). When there is extensive, relevant procedural knowledge that specifies the links between the abstract ends and the concrete means necessary to achieve them (e.g. when an activity or situation is familiar), these effects make abstract processing more adaptive, because they make the individual less distractible and impulsive, enable consistency and stability of goal pursuit across time, and afford useful generalizations about the world, along with effective action. However, abstract processing will be unconstructive when there is no extensive procedural knowledge, such as during unexpected, difficult, or stressful circumstances (e.g. the loss of a loved one). In such situations, abstract processing makes the indi-vidual less responsive to the environment and situational change, and provides fewer specific guides to action and problem-solving. In addition, because abstract representations are linked to personal identity, goals represented at an abstract level are harder to relinquish when progress is difficult, increasing the risk of being trapped in chronic, unhelpful RT. Under these circumstances, concrete processing is hypothesized to be constructive. Consistent with this, experimental manipulations of processing style have demonstrated that concrete processing facilitates more effective problem-solving than the abstract style (Watkins & Baracaia, 2002; Watkins & Moulds, 2005).

RT and autobiographical memory

Moreover, abstract RT results in the recall of other related events, such that the individual is no longer focused on a discrete event but rather on a number of related difficult events or a category of similar events (Watkins & Teasdale, 2001).

Theoretical accounts suggest that it will be easier to organize and make one single event coherent rather than to process multiple events simultaneously. Specifically, multiple memories interfere with the processing of one another and consume more central executive resources (Foa & Kozak, 1986) and, further, include more disparate material that does not easily fit into the sequence that is necessary to create a coherent story; coherent story making is hypothesized to be essential to effectively working through upsetting events (Pennebaker & Seagal, 1999; Smyth, True, & Souto, 2001). Thus, it is hypothesized that abstract thinking would make it difficult to emotionally process upsetting events in an effective way, consistent with experimental findings (e.g. Ehring et al. 2009; Watkins, 2004). This process is especially pertinent to CG because it could result in poor integration of the loss with existing autobiographical knowledge about the self and one's relationship with the deceased person, which is hypothesized to contribute to difficulties in acknowledging the loss, as well as associated searching behaviours that are characteristic of CG (Boelen et al., 2006b; Ehlers, 2006).

RT as avoidance

Abstract RT is also hypothesized to have maladaptive effects because it is conceptualized as a form of avoidance. Rumination is conceptualized as an escape and avoidance behaviour that has been negatively reinforced by the removal of aversive experience or because it has perceived or actual functions (Martell, Addis, & Jacobson, 2001; Nolen-Hoeksema, Wisco, & Lyubomirsky, 2008; Watkins et al., 2007). Hypothesized and clinically observed functions of rumination include (a) avoiding the risk of failure/humiliation by thinking about rather than implementing behaviour, (b) attempting to problem solve or to understand current problems but without a concrete plan of action, (c) avoiding and minimizing criticism by anticipating potential negative responses from others, (d) controlling unwanted feelings, and (e) avoiding unwanted attributes by motivating oneself (e.g. 'keeping me on my toes'). These functions parallel those that have been hypothesized to maintain and reinforce pathological worry (Borkovec & Roemer, 1995). Following bereavement, similar avoidant functions of RT might include (a) attempts to understand unexpected loss, (b) focusing on the anger felt at the deceased to minimize feelings of guilt (or vice versa), and (c) concerns that not thinking about the deceased indicates a lack of respect and love for them, or might lead to forgetting them, such that RT serves the function of avoiding being an 'uncaring' person. This functional analytic approach to RT suggests that an idiosyncratic assessment and treatment plan is required for each individual patient.

Critically, it has been proposed that abstract RT (e.g. worry), by distancing an individual from specific details and increasing verbal–conceptual thinking at the expense of emotionally vivid imagery, may avoid intense affect and/or reduce physiological arousal (Borkovec, Ray, & Stöber, 1998; Stöber & Borkovec, 2002). Likewise, individuals with PTSD engage in RT about their trauma and its sequelae but do so in an abstract, vague way (e.g. 'why did this happen to me?'). Such thinking about the causes and consequences of a trauma avoids direct reliving of the event and re-experiencing of the distress associated with recall, which in turn prevents the successful emotional processing that is critical to recovery (Foa & Kozak, 1986). Consistent with an avoidant conceptualization of rumination, in the context of depression, there is evidence that rumination is associated with measures of avoidance (Cribb, Moulds, & Carter, 2006; Moulds, Kandris, Starr, & Wong, 2007).

Recent conceptualisations have argued that RT following bereavement also serves to avoid recalling painful memories and experiencing the emotions associated with them (Boelen et al., 2006a; M. Stroebe et al., 2007). As noted above, focusing on the reasons and implications of the loss would take an individual away from direct contact with specific memories of the event, which may be negatively reinforced in the short term by reducing negative affect but in the longer term would prevent effective habituation to such memories. Despite the conceptualization of RT as avoidance in the context of grief, there is currently limited empirical support for this hypothesis. Boelen et al. (2006a) found that items that indexed RT (e.g. 'I keep on pondering about who is to blame for the loss') were correlated with items that assessed behavioural avoidance in patients with CG. However, we need to be cautious when interpreting correlations between RT and avoidance because we cannot determine that rumination functions as avoidance; the correlation could reflect a common factor such as a passive coping style, or even that increased avoidance leads to more RT. Finally, the findings of Bonanno et al. (2005) are of note here. Consistent with avoidance being problematic in resolving grief but inconsistent with RT functioning as avoidance, Bonanno et al. (2005) reported that grief processing (including assessment of RT) and grief avoidance were uncorrelated but that each process independently prospectively predicted distress.

Summary of hypotheses and relevant evidence

Thus, for both theoretical and empirical reasons, we hypothesize that there are specific and distinct subtypes of RT within grief, with distinct functional consequences. In particular, we hypothesize that concrete RT during situations of stress, such as following bereavement, is adaptive because it improves problem solving, focuses attention on the immediate environment, facilitates abandoning unachievable goals or unrealistic expectations, and aids habituation. We hypothesize that adaptive variants of RT will be characterized by finding benefit following a loss or processing grief-related events in a concrete way. We also hypothesize that there is a more pathological variant of RT characterized by an abstract focus on the meanings or implications of the bereavement, which contributes to CG. Moreover, we hypothesize that the normal process of grieving that is experienced by the majority of individuals is characterized by the adaptive variant of RT. Consistent with this hypothesis, there is extensive evidence that individuals tend (by default) to adopt more abstract processing, yet, when faced with difficult, novel, or complex situations, move towards more concrete processing (Watkins, 2008). Further, the lack of evidence that unsystematic grief work, expressive writing, or counselling is beneficial for the majority of bereaved individuals (W. Stroebe et al., 2005) is consistent with normal grief already involving adaptive responses to the loss. Because concrete RT facilitates coping and adaptation, and reduces the discrepancy between the loss and the individuals' existing mental models, we further hypothesize that it is necessarily self-limiting and thus short-lived.

In contrast, we hypothesize that the pathological forms of grieving (exemplified by CG) involve maladaptive abstract RT, which (because it prevents the resolution of the discrepancy between the loss and the individual's prior mental models) is self-perpetuating and prolongs distress. Thus, we hypothesize that constructive and unconstructive forms of RT can be distinguished on the basis of their degree of abstract versus concrete processing. Preliminary support for this hypothesis comes from findings that (a) healthy adjustment over the first 2 years following a spouse's death was associated with self-evaluations focused on concrete actions and behaviours rather than on abstract evaluations focused on character traits (Bauer & Bonanno, 2001), (b) narratives from the first month of bereavement that focused on concrete goals and plans predicted healthier outcomes 1 year later (Stein et al., 1997), and (c) bereaved individuals who report not searching for meaning (i.e. not adopting an abstract style) are more resilient and have better outcomes (Bonanno et al., 2004; Davis, Wortman, Lehman, & Silver, 2000).

Relevant to this analysis, we note that several of the measures employed to index RT following bereavement are more consistent with the conceptualization of abstract RT (e.g. RSQ, Nolen-Hoeksema et al., 1994; Boelen et al., 2006a), which could account for the asymmetry of findings towards RT having unconstructive outcomes. Other measures index only frequency of thoughts about the deceased (e.g. Bonanno et al., 2005), which cannot discriminate between adaptive and maladaptive RT, and this indicates the value of employing more sensitive measures.

A key test of the proposed hypothesis would be to examine whether a measure of RT that focused on concrete processing of the loss (e.g. recalling the detailed sensory and emotional aspects without dwelling on its meaning: thinking about *how* rather *why* it happened) predicts better adjustment in a longitudinal study. Further, this account predicts that those who show more normal grief reactions would focus on the loss in a more concrete way than those who become stuck in more protracted grief. The hypothesis could be further tested by adapting previous experimental studies that have examined the effect of abstract versus concrete manipulations in response to distressing events to the response to the death of a loved one (e.g. through an expressive writing design). Similarly, given evidence that training dysphoric individuals to repeatedly practise thinking in a concrete way reduces rumination and depression relative to a no-training control condition (Watkins, Baeyens, & Read, 2009), the current analysis predicts that such a treatment approach may be beneficial for individuals with CG.

Treatment implications

Our hypothesis that concrete processing of memories may promote an adaptive grief response accords with recent treatment developments in the CG field.

Although treatments for CG have not directly addressed RT about the loss per se, recently developed exposure-based approaches are relevant to our argument. Two recent randomized controlled trials indicated that CBT therapies that involved imaginal exposure – in which patients repeatedly relive the story of their loved one in order to process the content of grief-related memories – had significantly better outcomes for patients with CG than interpersonal psychotherapy (Shear, Frank, Houck, & Reynolds, 2005) or supportive counselling (Boelen, de Keijser, van den Hout, & van den Bout, 2007). Given that imaginal exposure involves the repeated and direct step-by-step reliving of the detail of distressing memories and their associated affect (rather than RT about why the distressing event occurred and what it means), these outcomes are consistent with the hypothesis that concrete RT may facilitate adjustment after the loss of a loved one (although we note that reliving was not the only element in these treatment packages).

Our hypothesis suggests that directly training individuals with CG to be more concrete (Watkins et al., 2009) or shift to more adaptive forms of RT (Watkins et al., 2007) could be effective treatments in CG in their own right or as adjuncts to imaginal exposure. A trial of concrete training versus a control condition would provide a test of proof-of-principle for the causal role of processing style on the maintenance of grief-related symptoms.

Implications for CG

Our review has focused on evidence regarding the role of RT in grief, given the lack of direct evidence in CG. Nonetheless, the evidence reviewed and hypotheses proposed have a number of implications for CG. First, the wider literature on RT suggests the hypothesis that abstract RT will be involved in the development and maintenance of CG, and that abstract RT about the bereavement may contribute to an ongoing preoccupation with the deceased. As noted earlier, abstract processing leads to RT that is less constructive, more prolonged, and harder to abandon. Second, abstract RT soon after the bereavement, relative to more concrete RT, may indicate an individual at risk for developing CG. Third, treatment interventions that explicitly and directly target abstract RT (rumination), whether through direct concreteness training, structured exposure, or problem solving, are hypothesized to be more effective at treating CG.

References

Bauer, J., & Bonanno, G. A. (2001). Being and doing well (for the most part): Adaptive patterns of narrative self-evaluation during bereavement. *Journal of Personality, 69*, 451–482.

Boelen, P. A., van den Bout, J., & van den Hout, M. A. (2006a) Negative cognitions and avoidance in emotional problems after bereavement: A prospective study. *Behaviour Research and Therapy, 44*, 1657–1672.

Boelen P. A., van den Hout, M. A., & van den Bout, J. (2006b). A cognitive–behavioral conceptualization of complicated grief. *Clinical Psychology: Science and Practice, 13*, 109–128.

Boelen, P. A., de Keijser, J., van den Hout, M. A., & van den Bout, J. (2007). Treatment of complicated grief: A comparison between cognitive–behavioral therapy and supportive counselling. *Journal of Consulting and Clinical Psychology, 75*, 277–284.

Bonanno, G. A., & Kaltman, S. (1999). Toward an integrative perspective on bereavement. *Psychological Bulletin, 125*, 760–776.

Bonanno, G. A., & Kaltman, S. (2001). The varieties of grief experience. *Clinical Psychology Review, 21*, 705–734.

Bonanno, G., Papa, A., & O'Neill, K. (2002). Loss and human resilience. *Applied and Preventative Psychology, 10*, 193–206.

Bonanno, G., Papa, A., Lalande, L., Zhang, N., & Noll, J. (2005). Grief processing and deliberate grief avoidance: A prospective comparison of bereaved spouses and parents in the United States and the People's Republic of China. *Journal of Consulting and Clinical Psychology, 73*, 86–98.

Bonanno, G. A., Wortman, C. B., & Neese, R. M. (2004). Prospective patterns of resilience and maladjustment during widowhood. *Psychology and Aging, 19*, 260–271.

Borkovec, T. D., Ray, W. J., & Stöber, J. (1998). Worry: A cognitive phenomenon intimately linked to affective, physiological, and interpersonal behavioral processes. *Cognitive Therapy and Research, 22*, 561–576.

Borkovec, T. D. & Roemer L. (1995) Perceived functions of worry among generalized anxiety disorder subjects: distraction from more emotionally distressing topics? *Journal of Behaviour Therapy and Experimental Psychiatry, 26*, 25–30.

Bower, J. E., Kemeny, M. E., Taylor, S. E., & Fahey, J. L. (1998). Cognitive processing, discovery of meaning, CD4 decline, and AIDS-related mortality among bereaved HIV-seropositive men. *Journal of Consulting and Clinical Psychology, 66*, 979–986.

Bowlby, J. (1980) *Attachment and loss, vol. 3: Loss: Sadness and depression*. London: Hogarth Press.

Carver, C. S., & Scheier, M. F. (1982). Control-theory: A useful conceptual-framework for personality-social, clinical, and health psychology. *Psychological Bulletin, 92*, 111–135.

Carver, C. S., & Scheier, M. F. (1998). *On the self-regulation of behavior*. Cambridge: Cambridge University Press.

Cribb, G., Moulds, M. L., & Carter, S. (2006). Rumination and experiential avoidance in depression. *Behaviour Change, 23*, 165–176.

Davis, C. G., Lehman, D. R., Wortman, C. B., Silver, R. C., & Thompson, S. C. (1995). The undoing of traumatic life events. *Personality and Social Psychology Bulletin, 21*, 109–124.

Davis, C. G., Nolen-Hoeksema, S., & Larson, J. (1998). Making sense of loss and benefiting from the experience: Two construals of meaning. *Journal of Personality and Social Psychology, 75*, 561–574.

Davis, C. G., Wortman, C. B., Lehman, D. R., & Silver, R. C. (2000). Searching for meaning in loss: Are clinical assumptions correct? *Death Studies, 24*, 497–540.

Ehlers, A. (2006). Understanding and treating complicated grief: What can we learn from post-traumatic stress disorder. *Clinical Psychology Science and Practice, 13*, 135–140.

Ehlers, A., Mayou, R. A., & Bryant, B. (1998). Psychological predictors of chronic posttraumatic stress disorder after motor vehicle accidents. *Journal of Abnormal Psychology, 107*, 508–519.

Ehring, T., Szeimies, A.-K., & Schaffrick, C. (2009). An experimental analogue study into the role of abstract thinking in trauma-related rumination. *Behaviour Research and Therapy, 47*, 284–293.

Foa, E., & Kozak, M. J. (1986). Emotional processing of fear: Exposure to corrective information. *Psychological Bulletin, 99*, 20–35.

Greenberg, M. A. (1995). Cognitive processing of traumas: The role of intrusive thoughts and reappraisals. *Journal of Applied Social Psychology, 25*, 1262–1296.

Ito, T., Tomita, T., Hasui, C., Otsuka, A., Katayama, Y.,, Kawamura, Y., et al. (2003). The link between response styles and major depression and anxiety disorders after child loss. *Comprehensive Psychiatry, 44*, 396–403.

Janoff-Bulman, R. (1992). *Shattered assumptions: Towards a new psychology of trauma.* New York: Free Press.

Lepore, S. J., Silver, R. C., Wortman, C. B., & Wayment, H. A. (1996). Social constraints, intrusive thoughts, and depressive symptoms among bereaved mothers. *Journal of Personality and Social Psychology, 70*, 271–282.

Lichtenthal, W. G., Cruess, D. G., & Prigerson, H. G. (2004). A case for establishing complicated grief as a distinct mental disorder in DSM-V. *Clinical Psychology Review, 24*, 637–662.

Martell, C. R., Addis, M. E., & Jacobson, N. S. (2001). *Depression in context: Strategies for guided action.* New York: Norton.

Martin, L. L., & Tesser, A. (1996). Some ruminative thoughts. In Wyer, R. S. (Ed.), *Advances in social cognition, Vol. 9: Ruminative thoughts* (pp. 1–47). Hillsdale, NJ: Lawrence Erlbaum Associates.

Mayou, R. A., Ehlers, A., & Bryant, B. (2002). Posttraumatic stress disorder after motor vehicle accidents: 3-year follow-up of a prospective longitudinal study. *Behaviour Research and Therapy, 40*, 665–675.

Michael, S., & Snyder C. (2005) Getting unstuck: The roles of hope, finding meaning, and rumination in the adjustment to bereavement among college students. *Death Studies, 29*, 435–458.

Moulds, M. L., Kandris, E., Starr, S., & Wong, A. C. M. (2007). The relationship between rumination, avoidance and depression in a non-clinical sample. *Behaviour Research and Therapy, 45*, 251–261.

Nolen-Hoeksema, S. (2000). The role of rumination in depressive disorders and mixed anxiety/depressive symptoms. *Journal of Abnormal Psychology, 109*, 504–511.

Nolen-Hoeksema, S., McBride, A., & Larson, J. (1997). Rumination and psychological distress amongst bereaved partners. *Journal of Personality and Social Psychology, 72*, 855–862.

Nolen-Hoeksema, S., Parker, L. E., & Larson, J. (1994). Ruminative coping with depressed mood following loss. *Journal of Personality and Social Psychology, 67*, 92–104.

Nolen-Hoeksema, S., Wisco, B. E., & Lyubomirsky, S. (2008). Rethinking rumination. *Perspectives on Psychological Science, 3*, 400–424.

Pennebaker, J. W., & Seagal, J. D. (1999). Forming a story: The health benefits of narrative. *Journal of Clinical Psychology, 55*, 1243–1254.

Prigerson, H. G., Horowitz, M. J., Jacobs, S. C., Parkes, C. M., Aslan, M., Goodkin, K., et al. (2009). Prolonged grief disorder: Psychometric validation of criteria proposed for DSM-V and ICD-11. *PLoS Med 6*(8): e1000121.

Segerstrom, S. C., Stanton, A. L., Alden, L. E., & Shortridge, B. E. (2003). A multidimensional structure for repetitive thought: What's on your mind, and how, and how much? *Journal of Personality and Social Psychology, 85*, 909–921.

Shear, K., Frank, E., Houck, P. R., & Reynolds, C. F. (2005). Treatment of complicated grief: A randomized controlled trial. *Journal of the American Medical Association, 293*, 2601–2608.

Smyth, J., True, N., & Souto, J. (2001). Effects of writing about traumatic experiences: The necessity for narrative structuring. *Journal of Social and Clinical Psychology, 20*, 161–172.

Stein, N., Folkman, S., Trabasso, T., & Richards, T. A. (1997). Appraisal and goal processes as predictors of psychological well-being in bereaved caregivers. *Journal of Personality and Social Psychology, 72*, 872–884.

Stöber, J., & Borkovec, T. D. (2002). Reduced concreteness of worry in generalized anxiety disorder: Findings from a therapy study. *Cognitive Therapy and Research, 26*, 89–96.

Stroebe, M., Boelen, P. A., van den Hout, M., Stroebe, W., Salemink, E., & van den Bout, J. (2007). Ruminative coping as avoidance: a reinterpretation of its function in adjustment to bereavement. *European Archives of Psychiatry and Clinical Neuroscience, 257*, 462–472.

Stroebe, M., & Schut, H. (1999). The dual-process model of coping with bereavement: Rationale and description. *Death Studies, 23*, 174–184.

Stroebe, W., Schut, H., & Stroebe M. (2005) Grief work, disclosure and counselling: Do they help the bereaved? *Clinical Psychology Review, 25*, 395–314.

Tedeschi, R. G. & Calhoun, L. G. (2004). Posttraumatic growth: Conceptual foundations and empirical evidence. *Psychological Inquiry, 15*, 1–18.

Treynor, W., Gonzalez, R., & Nolen-Hoeksema, S. (2003). Rumination reconsidered: A psychometric analysis. *Cognitive Therapy and Research, 27*, 247–259.

Vallacher, R. R., & Wegner, D. M. (1987). What do people think they're doing? Action identification and human behavior. *Psychological Review, 94*, 3–15.

Watkins, E. (2004). Adaptive and maladaptive ruminative self-focus during emotional processing. *Behaviour Research and Therapy, 42*, 1037–1052.

Watkins, E. R. (2008). Constructive and unconstructive repetitive thought. *Psychological Bulletin, 134*, 163–206.

Watkins, E., & Baracaia, S. (2002). Rumination and social problem-solving in depression. *Behaviour Research and Therapy, 40*, 1179–1189.

Watkins, E. R., Baeyens, C. B., & Read, R. (2009). Concreteness training reduces dysphoria: Proof-of-principle for repeated cognitive bias modification in depression. *Journal of Abnormal Psychology, 118*, 55–64.

Watkins, E R.., Moberly, N. J., & Moulds, M. L. (2008). Processing mode causally influences emotional reactivity: Distinct effects of abstract versus concrete construal on emotional response. *Emotion, 8*, 364–378.

Watkins, E., & Moulds, M. (2005). Distinct modes of ruminative self-focus: Impact of abstract versus concrete rumination on problem solving in depression. *Emotion, 5*, 319–328.

Watkins, E., Scott, J., Wingrove, J., Rimes, K., Bathurst, N., Steiner, H., et al. (2007). Rumination-focused cognitive–behaviour therapy for residual depression: A case series. *Behaviour Research and Therapy, 45*, 2144–2154.

Watkins, E., & Teasdale, J. D. (2001). Rumination and overgeneral memory in depression: Effects of self-focus and analytic thinking. *Journal of Abnormal Psychology, 110*, 353–357.

Yamada, K., Nagayama, H., Tsutiyama, K., Kitamura, T., & Furukawa, T. (2003). Coping behavior in depressed patients: A longitudinal study. *Psychiatry Research, 121*, 169–177.

13   Autobiographical memory processes in complicated grief

Ann-Marie J. Golden

What is autobiographical memory (AM) and overgeneral memory (OGM) bias and its importance?

When we talk of memory we all know what we mean: we lay down memories of our everyday experiences and then later on we attempt to recall instances from this databank. According to Baddeley (1997) the memory system consists of three closely interlinked stages of processing: first *encoding*, an initial and highly selective processing of new information; second *storage*, a limited capacity retention of encoded information over time; and third *retrieval*, the attempts to access the encoded/stored information. Memory is usually thought to consist of two 'stores': semantic (i.e. general factual information) and episodic (i.e. information about past personal life experiences). In this chapter we are only interested in the storage and retrieval of autobiographical 'episodic' memories. These are essential for self-descriptions, emotions, and the phenomenology of an individual across time and life-time experience, which contributes to an individual's sense of self (Conway & Pleydell-Pearce, 2000) and inevitably carries related physical, social, and emotional stamps.

So why is it of any value to understand autobiographical memory? Because it is related to our major goals in life, is embroidered with powerful affective states, and impacts our personal meanings. Bluck, Alea, Haberman, and Rubin (2005) suggested that autobiographical memory serves three broad functions: a *directive function*, because we use our past experiences as a reference for disentangling current problems and as a guide for confronting new challenges; a *social function*, because memories help us with development, maintenance, and nurturing of social relationships by providing material for social interactions; and a *self-representative function*, because personal memories help us to generate and sustain a self-identity that is coherent over a period of time. An additional, *adaptive function* is that the retrieval of positive personal experiences may be used as a maintenance tool of desirable moods or to modify unwanted moods (Williams, Conway, & Cohen, 2008).

In this domain of memory and affect, retrieval of personal memories using cue words has been investigated for many decades (Teasdale & Fogarty, 1979), resulting in the robust conclusion that mood-related memory biases (whether natural or induced) can contribute to and/or maintain affective disorder (e.g. the more depressed an individual, the slower his or her latency, and the greater difficulty he or she has, in the recall of positive memories). Williams and Broadbent (1986) also noted that when they asked depressed and suicidal individuals to retrieve personal memories, to a series of emotion-related cue words as part of the Autobiographical Memory Test (AMT), they tended to be general rather than specific memories (in comparison with normal controls). This finding shifted the research to include the degree of specificity, not just the speed or content of retrieval with which events are recollected.

Since this prototypical study, and over the last two decades, research has shown that individuals suffering from a range of clinical conditions such as depression (Kuyken & Dalgleish, 1995) and posttraumatic stress disorder (PTSD) (McNally et al., 1995) generally have relative difficulties retrieving specific autobiographical memories. This has been called an overgeneral memory (OGM) bias (for reviews see Moore & Zoellner, 2007; Sumner, Griffith, & Mineka, 2010; Williams et al., 2007) – that is, the tendency to recollect the past in terms of regularities across multiple experiences as opposed to specific events. OGM is also a characteristic of complicated grief (CG; Golden, Dalgleish & Mackintosh, 2007): a debilitating condition arising when, following the death of a significant other, an individual presents with a range of symptoms that cause significant impairment in day-to-day functioning for 6 months or more, including yearning, pining, guilt, bitterness or anger, intrusive distress, preoccupation with and thoughts relating to the deceased, and a difficulty in moving on (e.g. Prigerson & Maciejewski, 2005). This chapter focuses on the mechanisms involved in OGM bias and studies that address autobiographical memory and CG.

Why is this bias towards overgeneralizing memories so important to CG and why does it warrant further attention? So far we know that OGM is a trait-like characteristic that may serve as a vulnerability factor for depression (Williams et al., 2007) and plays a role in the maintenance of depression (Gibbs & Rude, 2004; Williams et al., 2006) and range of disorders (and as such OGM is an excellent example of a transdiagnostic process; Harvey, Watkins, Mansell, & Shafran, 2004). In addition to this, research has shown that individuals who exhibit this OGM bias:

1 have impaired problem solving and increased cognitive reactivity to changes in mood (i.e. easier reactivation of patterns of negative thinking) (Williams, Barnhofer, Crane, & Beck, 2005);
2 exhibit hopelessness and a diminished ability to imagine future events (Dickson & Bates, 2006);
3 have ruminative tendencies (Ramponi, Barnard, & Nimmo-Smith, 2004);
4 are at risk of developing symptomatology following stressful life events (Bryant, Sutherland, & Guthrie, 2007).

Therefore an impaired ability to retrieve specific memories from one's past may impede integration of an existing situation and thus delay recovery (see Ehlers & Clark, 2000; Williams et al., 2006).

The methodology and limitations of the Autobiographical Memory Test (AMT)

The OGM bias is usually assessed using the AMT whereby cue words that vary in emotional valence (e.g. negative, positive, and neutral) are presented and participants are instructed to retrieve an event that the given word reminds them of. The event could be important or trivial, recent or from a long time ago, but it should be a specific event (i.e. something that happened *at a particular time on a particular day and lasted for a day or less*). Participants are typically allowed 30 seconds to 1 minute for each cue word for retrieval of a specific memory. They are given an example of what is meant by specific (to the word *enjoy*, it would be inappropriate to say 'I always enjoy a good party' because that does not mention a particular time, but it would be fine to say 'Jane's party last Friday'), followed by three practice trials to ensure that they have understood the instructions.

Memories generated are coded according to the criteria laid down by Williams and Dritschel (1991). Non-specific memories include *extended memories* (events that lasted for longer periods of time) and *categoric memories* (events that occurred repeatedly over a period of time). Failure to recall, or giving opinions about the cue instead of a memory, is classed as 'no memory'.

No methodology comes without limitations and the same can be said for the AMT. Williams et al. (2007) reviewed these limitations in detail and emphasized that there are five methodological constraints that may limit the conclusions drawn from AMT studies: the number of words used as cues; general intelligence; confounding of depression and trauma history; retrospective assessment of trauma; and scarce longitudinal studies.

The psychological mechanisms in OGM bias in relation to CG research

Several mechanisms have been proposed to explain OGM bias, such as truncated search patterns in clinical groups (Williams & Dritschel, 1988); hierarchical autobiographical memory structures (Conway, 1996) with specific (and potentially aversive) memories at the lowest level; and poor executive control (Dalgleish et al., 2007). These have been integrated within the CaRFAX (capture and rumination, functional avoidance, and executive control) model (Williams, 2006). In terms of CG the most relevant processes are the three factors (rumination, functional avoidance, and executive control) of the CaRFAX model; the more recent immunity hypothesis (Golden et al., 2007); emerging grief theories (discussed elsewhere in detail: Boelen, van den Hout, & van den Bout, 2006; Shear & Shair, 2005); and the importance of the self in autobiographical memories (Conway & Pleydell-Pearce, 2000). These will be the subject of further discussion in this chapter.

Rumination and OGM bias

Rumination consists of the repetitive and intrusive revisiting of the causes, consequences, and symptoms of one's negative affective state (Nolen-Hoeksema,

1991). There is persuasive evidence for a close link between rumination and OGM bias. Watkins and Teasdale (2001) specifically identified that it is the analytical aspect of self-focused rumination that is associated with OGM bias. Dalgleish et al. (2003) further hypothesized that self-analytical processing may be activated by negative self-schemata. Grief researchers have emphasized that negative cognitions and avoidance, that is, rumination, play an important role in the development and maintenance of CG (Boelen et al., 2006) and also mediate the effect of risk factors in bereaved individuals (van der Houwen et al., 2010).

Functional avoidance and OGM bias

According to Williams, Stiles, and Shapiro (1999), trauma-exposed individuals develop a reduced capability to access specific memories as a form of 'functional avoidance' (Williams et al., 2007) of the distress associated with remembering the specific details of their traumatic experiences. They suggest that this avoidance operates through the truncation of an effortful, hierarchical search of the self-memory system (SMS), so-called generative retrieval (Conway & Pleydell-Pearce, 2000), at the level of categorical autobiographical descriptors, which gives rise to reduced recall of specific memories. Instances of trauma memory recollection generalize to the whole domain of autobiographical recollection, resulting in the classic reduced specificity effect (OGM bias) on the AMT. Therefore individuals who have been involved in traumas show this classic OGM bias on the AMT.

Kuyken and Brewin (1995) showed a significant association between OGM bias and trauma and confirmed that OGM bias not only is related to a clinical condition such as depression but is also a function of people's exposure to trauma and to previous related distress. This association between a history of trauma and OGM bias has now been replicated several times and following traumatic experiences other than abuse (e.g. Dalgleish et al., 2003). These findings suggest that OGM bias in trauma-exposed samples plays a key role in the onset and maintenance of posttraumatic stress and it is not simply a cognitive epiphenomenon associated with the acute clinical state. In terms of CG this is further examined in the 'immunity hypothesis' (Golden et al., 2007), which is discussed later.

Executive control and OGM bias

Autobiographical knowledge is thought to be mediated through executive control processes (Baddeley, 1986; Conway & Pleydell-Pearce, 2000). Executive resources are assumed to be required for keeping focused on task, inhibiting incorrect responses, and searching downwards through the hypothetical hierarchical database (e.g. Dalgleish et al., 2007; Dalgleish, Rolfe, Golden, Dunn, & Barnard, 2008). Considering that memory retrieval in its earlier stages is effortful and uses executive capacity, deficits in executive processing resources are also thought to be involved in OGM bias (Dalgleish et al., 2007). Williams (1996) proposed that OGM bias results when working memory is compromised during 'mnemonic interlock' (when the search process is cut short at an upper, general level). Some experimental studies have demonstrated that cognitive deficits and reduction in working memory capacity are linked with difficulties retrieving specific memories (e.g. Birch & Davidson, 2007). A number of studies have indicated that difficulties in specific retrieval may arise as a result of depletion of cognitive capacity caused by intrusive cognitions that are associated with clinical disorders (Kuyken & Brewin, 1995). Research in CG awaits studies looking at executive resources and OGM bias.

Immunity and OGM bias

Experiencing intrusive recollections about traumatic events is a key feature of clinical states such as acute stress disorder, adjustment disorder, and posttraumatic stress disorder (American Psychiatric Association, 1994). Distressing intrusions also play a part in CG; however, in CG the dominant emotion is sadness, pining, and yearning, whereas in PTSD it is fear and horror (Dalgleish & Power, 2004). There is an interesting paradox here since trauma victims, although exhibiting an OGM bias on the AMT trauma, report intrusions full of detailed and specific memories about their trauma (Brewin, Dalgleish, & Joseph, 1996; McNally, 2003). If OGM bias is a form of affect regulation then it seems to be acting somewhat inefficiently on individuals' day-to-day intrusive memories of the trauma, as these remain highly specific.

This raises the question whether memories associated with the source of the person's distress are somehow not susceptible, that is, are immune and resistant to the OGM bias (hence 'immunity hypothesis'). One explanation for this paradoxical 'immunity' may be that, because these 'recurrent intrusive' memories are explicitly concerned with the source of person's distress, they are sufficiently prepotent to be directly accessed in the autobiographical database (Conway & Pleydell-Pearce, 2000) in a way that does not require the effortful, hierarchical search of the autobiographical memory system. Perhaps this search, or 'generative retrieval', is circumvented and memories related to the loss and bereavement (or trauma) are being retrieved by a very direct route.

Golden et al. (2007) hypothesized that if, because of their intrusive and recurrent nature, memories related to the source of an individual's distress are habitually directly retrieved as a function of their pre-priming/prepotency, then it should be possible to demonstrate this using the cue word AMT task. This was important in order to elucidate whether OGM bias as a form of affect regulation is indeed impotent in this way with regard to memories tied to the source of an individual's distress, indicating that reducing specificity is a somewhat ineffective method of psychological defence – less a form of 'functional avoidance' (Williams et al., 2007, p. 122) than a form of dysfunctional avoidance.

Golden et al. (2007) explained that, in terms of PTSD, one could constrain the search parameters of the AMT and ask participants to respond only with trauma-related memories, that is, use a trauma-only AMT (see Figure 13.1). If trauma memories were directly retrieved, this constraint would have produced significant attenuation or elimination of the usual OGM bias associated with the

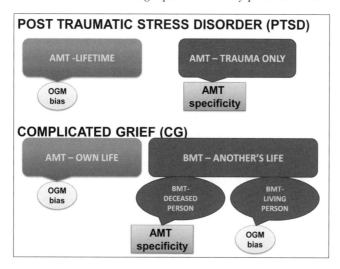

Figure 13.1 OGM bias in PTSD and CG: the comparisons between Autobiographical Memory Test (AMT) and Biographical Memory Test (BMT).

task. However, there is a clear methodological confound associated with using a trauma-only AMT. If the search parameters of the AMT were restricted to a narrowly constrained set of experiences such as traumas only, then individuals would have fewer opportunities for any generative, hierarchical search process to become truncated. First, such a search would require less navigation of the memory system and, second, establishing such a search set would additionally prime a number of specific events (i.e. the relevant trauma experiences). This would have inevitably lead to high levels of specificity in terms of the memories recalled relative to an unrestricted AMT.

The standard and trauma-only AMT are, therefore, not comparable like-for-like, and CG provided a really good vehicle to investigate this interesting question about OGM bias. In their day-to-day life, individuals with CG experience intrusive memories as part of their diagnostic symptomatology. These intrusive memories are linked to the aetiology of the individual's distress (i.e. memories about the deceased). As such these memories about the deceased are sourced from a rich database of specific events: the lifetime of the deceased person, as opposed to one or more discrete traumas (Dalgleish & Power, 2004). Intrusive memories are experienced as involuntary and highly affect-laden (Boelen et al., 2006; Dalgleish & Power, 2004). In individuals with CG, this characteristic provided an excellent opportunity to examine whether recollection targeted at the source of a person's distress becomes markedly less or more specific when the relevant memories are prompted using the cue word methodology of the AMT.

As shown in Figure 13.1, individuals with CG retrieved memories about their own life (standard AMT) as well as memories from the life of the deceased person (called BMT-Deceased). It is possible that differences between these conditions could simply be a result of comparison between an autobiographical and bio-graphical version of the test. To control for this, individuals with CG also retrieved memories from the lifetime of someone who had not died: someone whom they knew as well and as long as the deceased (called BMT-Living). It was expected that the standard OGM bias would be present since, according to Williams et al. (2007), the overgenerality mode develops as a way of avoiding distress and it then generalizes to other conditions. The introduction of BMT-Deceased and BMT-Living (Golden et al., 2007) was the first time that the cue word methodology has been extended to interrogate memories from the lifetime of someone other than the self, and it reflected a growing trend to examine memory specificity outside the strict boundaries of the standard AMT (e.g. Rottenberg, Hildner, & Gotlib, 2006).

In Figure 13.2 the findings of the study by Golden et al. (2007) show that for both positive and negative cues the standard AMT condition was as predicted: participants with CG were less specific than the controls (i.e. showing OGM bias). This finding was reversed on the BMT-Deceased: the CG group retrieved far more specific memories about the life of the person who died than did the bereaved controls. It seems that because these memories are about the source of distress, and are somehow immune, individuals are actually spared from the OGM bias. On the BMT-Living there was the same pattern of OGM bias as found on the standard AMT. Therefore this finding was not simply a function of BMT-Deceased being about somebody else. These interactions and relevant paired comparisons were statistically significant for the negative cues only. The pattern for positive cues was similar but the effects were not significant.

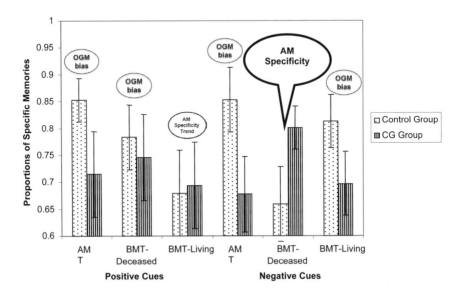

Figure 13.2 Proportions of specific memories retrieved to positive and negative cues across the two groups (error bars are +1 standard error). (Adapted from Golden, Dalgleish, & Mackintosh, 2007.)

A number of other studies have looked at CG and OGM. Boelen, Huntjens, van Deursen, and van den Hout (2010) investigated the specificity of autobiographical memories and symptomatology of CG, depression, and PTSD in 109 bereaved participants with no formal diagnosis of CG using standard AMT and trait AMT (McNally et al., 1995) (i.e. participants are presented with five positive and five negative trait adjectives and asked to recall a specific memory of when they displayed each trait). An important difference from previous studies is that the AMT tasks were conducted over the telephone and participants were given only 30 seconds to produce a specific memory. Their findings confirmed that the presence of OGM bias was significantly associated with symptom levels of CG but not with depression and PTSD. They also identified that only the symptom levels of CG and PTSD were associated with preferential retrieval of specific memories that were related to the loss or lost person on the standard AMT, whereas all three symptom measures were associated with preferential retrieval of loss-related specific memories on the trait AMT. These findings on a trait AMT are in accord with Golden et al.'s (2007) immunity hypothesis. Maccallum and Bryant (2008) and Boelen et al. (2010) showed that memories retrieved in the trait AMT were associated more with loss-related distress (these memories included the deceased person and were part of the self-relevant autobiographical information) than memories that were retrieved in the standard AMT (these memories included the lost person within more general autobiographical knowledge). These additional studies have further highlighted the importance of OGM bias in CG.

CG research studies and self and OGM bias

Whereas the CaRFAX model primarily focused on the quality of autobiographical remembering, Conway and Pleydell-Pearce (2000) proposed the self memory system (SMS), which focuses more on the content of remembering. This places an individual's sense of self at the core of memory construction and retrieval. Autobiographical memories are produced to serve the goals of the self; in other words 'the working self' is a set of active goals that reflect the concerns of the dominant self concept. So, following the death of a loved person, self-identity is somewhat reconstructed and new life goals need to be found (e.g. Neimeyer, 1998). The degree to which a bereaved individual is able to reconstruct him- or herself in the absence of the loved one, and to find a new purpose and meaning in life, is assumed to be connected with recovery (Neimeyer, Baldwin, & Gillies, 2006). The SMS in relation to CG would predict that, given that there are strong feelings of preoccupation and persistent yearning, the individual's self-identity would be related to the deceased, so the death of a loved person would be a self-defining event. Recently Boelen (2009) showed that individuals who exhibited a more severe form of CG also experienced loss as more central to their everyday inferences, their self-identity, and their perception of their own life story.

The loss of a loved one can be a challenge to one's identity because the processing of such loss may actively disrupt attachments with others and may also stimulate changes in life roles as well as life goals that are already established. Maccallum and Bryant (2008) examined the links and any distinctive patterns between autobiographical memory and self-identity. They tested self-defining memories in 20 participants with CG and 20 control participants and found that participants with CG provided more self-defining memories involving the deceased. Although both CG and non-CG groups reported a loved one's death as a self-defining moment, the non-CG group showed more evidence of finding benefit in their memory narratives and experienced less negative emotion on recall. Interestingly, fewer than half of participants with and without CG reported the death as a self-defining memory. Maccallum and Bryant (2008) suggest that this may reflect lack of integration into the autobiographical memory database due to preferential retrieval of loss-related memories or avoidance of the reality of the death; they further suggest that individuals who have successfully adapted to the loss may never had loss/death as their self-constructing pivotal event.

Reported goals are also related to personal memories and to an individual's self-construct (e.g. Moberly & MacLeod, 2006). Maccallum and Bryant (2010), using the standard AMT, set out to examine the relationship between autobiographical memory and personal goals in 24 individuals with CG and 21 bereaved controls without CG. Their results showed that individuals with CG exhibited impaired retrieval of specific autobiographical memories in response to both positive and negative cues. In addition they found that individuals with CG were more likely to retrieve memories related to their loss and there was a positive relationship between the proportion of loss-related memories recalled and the proportion of grief-related goals held by individuals after controlling for symptom level. They showed that autobiographical retrieval in CG is shaped by individual goals.

To recap, CG and the psychological mechanisms involved in OGM bias in relation to rumination and executive resources are yet to be empirically explored. Based on other clinical disorders they are likely to play an important role and it is possible that rumination may impact on retrieval style through associations with depression and symptoms of severe grief. OGM bias, as in the retrieval of categorical memories, is very likely to contribute to complications in emotionally processing and integrating the experience of death/loss. It may also have implications for pre-existing knowledge structures about the self, as this is emphasized as a core component of grief resolution. Golden et al. (2007) demonstrated standard OGM bias in a sample with CG and also revealed that retrieval of memories that are related to the source of an individual's distress (BMT-Deceased) are immune to OGM bias – an effect that has been replicated. This finding questions theoretical accounts of OGM bias as a form of affect regulation. Maccallum and Bryant (2008, 2010) showed that self-identity and goals are important for individuals with CG.

The clinical relevance of OGM bias

Should OGM bias be targeted in therapy? Considering that this bias is associated with problem-solving difficulties, an intervention that aims to help individuals to access their store of specific memories may prove beneficial. In terms of bereaved individuals and/or those with current CG diagnosis, this is particularly relevant since they should be able to retrieve memories that are not related to the deceased. This may help them, in turn, retrieve other positive specific memories and manage the issues that living without the deceased may cause.

There are some studies showing that OGM bias may be experimentally modifiable in depressed individuals. Watkins, Teasdale, and Williams (2000) showed that decentring and distraction methods reduced OGM bias in depressed individuals. Watkins and Teasdale (2001) showed that once the rumination levels are reduced then the OGM bias is also reduced, and this leads to retrieval of more specific autobiographical memories.

Through CG resolution theories, the literature has emphasized that the emotional processing of the loss is highly important (Boelen et al., 2006; Shear & Shair, 2005) and individuals with CG exhibiting OGM bias may have their recovery further hindered by delaying the emotional processing of loss. So the most obvious clinical implication is to incorporate techniques or strategies within existing cognitive therapy that may increase the specificity of memory retrieval. For example, preliminary findings from a 4-week group-based intervention entitled MEmory Specificity Training (MEST; Raes, Williams, & Hermans, 2009) have shown that as memory specificity increases individuals become better at problem solving and additionally their rumination levels decrease.

There is also preliminary evidence from a treatment study conducted by Williams, Teasdale, Segal, and Soulsby (2000) showing that mindfulness-based cognitive therapy (MBCT; Segal, Williams, and Teasdale, 2002) reduces OGM bias in individuals who are not currently depressed but have had at least two previous episodes of depression. Van der Houwen et al. (2010) suggested that mindfulness could be added to various aspects of grief therapy. Mindfulness – paying attention on purpose and non-judgmentally to what is happening around and within us – when applied to grief facilitates turning towards the grief process and being connected to all the processes that are unfolding. Through mindful attention, grieving individuals can discover and further process that grief is not their identity – that is, grief is not who they are. Kumar (2005) described in detail different aspects of mindfulness that can be used when working with the bereaved, in an interactive book entitled *Grieving Mindfully*. Additionally, there are aspects of compassion-focused therapy (CFT; Gilbert, 2009) for individuals who experience self-criticism and shame since they struggle to feel reassurance or safety and these could be further examined in bereaved individuals with CG.

Recently, Maccallum and Bryant (2011) found that OGM bias can be modified by a 10-week CBT programme in treatment-seeking individuals with CG. As symptoms of CG reduced after CBT, positive cue word memory specificity increased. However changes in memory specificity to negative cue words were not associated with a reduction in CG symptomatology. Further investigations could be tailored to add some of the aspects that specifically target OGM bias.

However, the findings by Golden et al. (2007) suggest that, for a bereaved individual with CG, being able to retrieve specific memories that are related to the loss of the loved one does not reflect an adaptive or a functional response. This ongoing focus on the individual's loss and his or her recall of specific memories related to the lost person prolongs avoidance of the reality of the loss. Training individuals with CG to retrieve specific memories related to their life and the lives of others may, by incorporating other aspects of their life, prove to be more useful and supportive of emotional processing of their loss.

Maccallum and Bryant (2010) showed that there is a significant relationship between grief-related goals and retrieval of grief-related memories; when the current working self is focused on grief and loss goals, this may reinforce dysfunctional grief processes. They also suggested that individuals with CG would benefit from the development of an alternative goal focus. Boelen's (2009) findings also emphasized that bereaved individuals with more severe symptomatology of CG experienced their loss as more central to their self-identity and life story. So introducing alternative but still life-relevant practical activities may be a way forward without making closure the main goal to be achieved.

Future research

It is clear that factors that seem to prompt and probe autobiographical memories and in turn prolong negative affective states following loss of a loved individual need further examination. There are many issues that the future studies will hopefully address, and conducting longitudinal studies and focusing on issues surrounding comorbidity are paramount. Specifically it is important to address to what degree OGM bias is modifiable within the bereaved population using MEST, CBT, MBCT, and CFT. Some other avenues of examination may be:

- whether the rumination, avoidance, and executive resources are differentially involved in the OGM bias in CG;
- what difference (if any) instructing participants to retrieve memories that are either loss or non-loss related and/or to set limits to the content (self/deceased/living) of a participant's recall may make to the outcome;
- assessment of memory content and levels of specificity with a longer post-treatment interval to overcome recency effects;
- comparing the content, rather than simply ascertaining the presence, of responses on the memory tasks, in particular the BMT-Deceased, with the content of the intrusions that participants with CG experience in day-to-day life.

This chapter has shown that OGM bias is present in individuals with complicated grief and that a way forward would be to incorporate targeting this OGM bias as part of their treatment package. This would, in turn, enable bereaved individuals to incorporate loss into their current schema; that is, eventually to accept the loss and be able to deal with the future challenges that life may bring about. There are, as with everything, other issues that may be considered in relation to bereavement (e.g. cultural values, attachment), and these are discussed elsewhere in this book.

References

American Psychiatric Association. (1994). *Diagnostic and statistical manual of mental disorders* (4th edn.). Washington, DC: American Psychiatric Association.

Baddeley, A. D. (1986). *Working memory*. Oxford: Clarendon Press.

Baddeley, A. D. (1997). *Human memory: Theory and practice* (revised edn.). Hove, UK: Psychology Press.

Birch, L. S., & Davidson, K. M. (2007). Specificity of autobiographical memory in depressed older adults and its relationship with working memory and IQ. *British Journal or Clinical Psychology, 46*, 175–186.

Bluck, S., Alea, N., Haberman, T., & Rubin, D. C. (2005). A tale of three functions: The self-reported uses of autobiographical memory. *Social Cognition, 23*, 91–117.

Boelen, P. A. (2009). The centrality of a loss and its role in emotional problems among bereaved people. *Behaviour Research and Therapy, 47*, 616–622.

Boelen, P. A., van den Hout, M. A., & van den Bout, J. (2006). A cognitive–behavioral conceptualization of complicated grief. *Clinical Psychology-Science and Practice, 13*, 109–128.

Boelen, P. A., Huntjens, R. J. C., van Deursen, D. S., & van den Hout, M. A. (2010). Autobiographical memory specificity and symptoms of complicated grief, depression, and posttraumatic stress disorder following loss. *Journal of Behaviour Therapy and Experimental Psychiatry, 41*, 331–337.

Brewin, C. R., Dalgleish, T., & Joseph, S. (1996). A dual representation theory of post-traumatic stress disorder. *Psychological Review, 103*, 670–686.

Bryant, R. A., Sutherland, K., & Guthrie, R. M. (2007). Impaired specific autobiographical memory as a risk factor for posttraumatic stress after trauma. *Journal of Abnormal Psychology, 116*, 837–841.

Conway, M.A (1996). Autobiographical memories and autobiographical knowledge. In Rubin, D. C. (Ed.), *Remembering our past: Studies in autobiographical memory* (pp. 67–93). Cambridge: Cambridge University Press.

Conway, M. A., & Pleydell-Pearce, C. W. (2000). The construction of autobiographical memories in the self-memory system. *Psychological Review, 107*, 261–288.

Dalgleish, T., & Power, M. J. (2004). Emotion-specific and emotion-non-specific components of Posttraumatic Stress Disorder (PTSD): Implications for a taxonomy of related psychopathology. *Behavior Research and Therapy, 42*, 1069–1088.

Dalgleish, T., Rolfe, J., Golden, A.-M., Dunn, B., & Barnard, P. J. (2008). Reduced autobiographical memory specificity and posttraumatic stress: Exploring the contributions of impaired executive control and affect regulation. *Journal of Abnormal Psychology, 117*, 236–241.

Dalgleish, T., Tchanturia, K., Serpell, L., Hems, S., Yiend, J., de Silva, P., & Treasure, J. (2003). Self-reported parental abuse relates to autobiographical memory style in patients with eating disorders. *Emotion, 3*, 211–222.

Dalgleish, T., Williams, J. M. G., Golden, A.-M., Perkins, N., Barrett, L. F., Barnard, P. J., et al. (2007). Reduced specificity of autobiographical memory and depression: The role of executive control. *Journal of Experimental Psychology: General, 136*, 23–42.

Dickson, J. M., & Bates, G. W. (2006). Autobiographical memories and views of the future: In relation to dysphoria. *International Journal of Psychology, 41*, 107–116.

Ehlers, A., & Clark, D. M. (2000). A cognitive model of posttraumatic stress disorder. *Behaviour Research and Therapy, 38*, 319–345.

Gibbs, B. R., & Rude, S. S. (2004). Overgeneral autobiographical memory as depression vulnerability. *Cognitive Therapy and Research, 28*, 511–526.

Gilbert, P. (2009). Introducing compassion-focused therapy. *Advances in Psychiatric Treatment, 15*, 199–208.

Golden, A-M., Dalgleish, T., & Mackintosh, B. (2007). Levels of specificity of autobiographical memories and of biographical memories of the deceased in bereaved individuals with and without complicated grief. *Journal of Abnormal Psychology, 116*, 786–795.

Harvey, A., Watkins, E., Mansell, W., & Shafran, R. (2004). *Cognitive behavioural processes across psychological disorders: A transdiagnostic approach to research and treatment.* Oxford: Oxford University Press.

van der Houwen, K., Stroebe, M., Stroebe, W., Schut, H., van den Bout, J., & Wijngaards-de Meij, L. (2010). Risk factors for bereavement outcome: A multivariate approach. *Death Studies, 34*, 195–220.

Kumar, S. M. (2005). *Grieving mindfully: A compassionate spiritual guide to coping with loss.* Oakland, CA: New Harbinger Publications.

Kuyken, W., & Brewin, C. R. (1995). Autobiographical memory functioning in depression and reports of early abuse. *Journal of Abnormal Psychology, 104*, 585–591.

Kuyken, W., & Dalgleish, T. (1995). Autobiographical memory and depression. *British Journal of Clinical Psychology, 33*, 89–92.

Maccallum, F., & Bryant, R. A. (2008). Self-defining memories in complicated grief. *Behaviour Research and Therapy, 46*, 1311–1315.

Maccallum, F., & Bryant, R. A. (2010). Impaired autobiographical memory in complicated grief. *Behaviour Research and Therapy, 48*, 328–334.

Maccallum, F. & Bryant, R. A. (2011). Autobiographical memory following cognitive behaviour therapy for complicated grief. *Journal of Behaviour Therapy and Experimental Psychiatry, 42*, 26–31.

McNally, R. J. (2003). *Remembering trauma.* Cambridge, MA: Harvard University Press.

McNally, R. J., Lasko, N. B., Macklin, M. L., & Pitman, R. K. (1995). Autobiographical memory disturbance in combat-related post-traumatic stress disorder. *Behaviour Research and Therapy, 33*, 619–630.

Moberly, N. J., & MacLeod, A. K. (2006). Goal pursuit, goal self-concordance, and the accessibility of autobiographical knowledge. *Memory, 14*, 901–915.

Moore, S. A., & Zoellner, L. A. (2007). Overgeneral autobiographical memory and traumatic events: An evaluative review. *Psychological Bulletin, 133*, 419–437.

Neimeyer, R. A. (1998). *Lessons of loss: A guide to coping.* New York: McGraw Hill.

Neimeyer, R. A., Baldwin, S. A., & Gillies, J. (2006). Continuing bonds and reconstructing meaning: Mitigating complications in bereavement. *Death Studies, 30*, 715–738.

Nolen-Hoeksema, S. (1991). Responses to depression and their effects on the duration of depressive episodes. *Journal of Abnormal Psychology, 100*, 569–582.

Prigerson, H. G., & Maciejewski, P. K. (2005). A call for sound empirical testing and evaluation of criteria for Complicated Grief proposed for DSM-V. *Omega-Journal of Death and Dying, 52*, 9–19.

Raes, F., Williams, J. M. G., & Hermans, D. (2009). Reducing cognitive vulnerability to depression: A preliminary investigation of Memory Specificity Training (MEST) in inpatients with depressive symptomatology. *Journal of Behaviour Therapy and Experimental Psychiatry, 40*, 24–38.

Ramponi, C., Barnard, P., & Nimmo-Smith, I. (2004). Recollection deficits in dysphoric mood: An effect of schematic models and executive mode? *Memory, 12*, 655–670.

Rottenberg, J., Hildner, J. C., & Gotlib, I. H. (2006). Idiographic autobiographical memories in major depressive disorder. *Cognition & Emotion, 20*, 114–128.

Segal, Z. V., Williams, J. M. G., & Teasdale, J. D. (2002). *Mindfulness-based cognitive therapy for depression: A new approach for preventing relapse*. New York: Guilford Press.

Shear, K. M., & Shair, H. (2005). Attachment, loss, and complicated grief. *Developmental Psychobiology, 47*, 253–267.

Sumner, J. A., Griffith, J. W., & Mineka, S. (2010). Overgeneral autobiographical memory as a predictor of the course of depression: A meta-analysis. *Behaviour Research and Therapy, 48*, 614–625.

Teasdale, J. D., & Fogarty, S. J. (1979). Differential effects of induced mood on retrieval of pleasant and unpleasant memories from episodic memory. *Journal of Abnormal Psychology, 88*, 248–257.

Watkins, E., & Teasdale, J. D. (2001). Rumination and overgeneral memory in depression: Effects of self-focus and analytic thinking. *Journal of Abnormal Psychology, 110*, 353–357.

Watkins, E., Teasdale, J. D., & Williams, R. M. (2000). Decentring and distraction reduce over general autobiographical memory in depression. *Psychological Medicine, 30*, 911–920.

Williams, H. L., Conway, M. A., & Cohen, G. (2008). Autobiographical memory. In Cohen, G., & Conway, M. A. (Eds.), *Memory in the real world* (3rd edn., pp. 21–90). Hove, UK: Psychology Press.

Williams, J. M. G. (1996). Depression and the specificity of autobiographical memory. In Rubin, D. C. (Ed.), *Remembering our past: Studies in autobiographical memory* (pp. 244–267). New York: Cambridge University Press.

Williams, J. M. G. (2006). Capture and rumination, functional avoidance, and executive control (CaRFAX): Three processes that underlie overgeneral memory. *Cognition and Emotion, 20*, 548–568.

Williams J. M. G., Barnhofer T., Crane C., & Beck A. T. (2005). Problem solving deteriorates following mood challenge in formerly depressed patients with a history of suicidal ideation. *Journal of Abnormal Psychology, 114*, 421–431.

Williams, J. M. G., Barnhofer, T., Crane, C., Hermans, D., Raes, F., Watkins, E., & Dalgleish, T. (2007). Autobiographical memory specificity and emotional disorder. *Psychological Bulletin, 113*, 122–148.

Williams, J. M. G., & Broadbent, K. (1986). Autobiographical memory in suicide attempters. *Journal of Abnormal Psychology, 95*, 144–149.

Williams J. M. G., Chan S., Crane C., Barnhofer T., Eade J., & Healy H. (2006). Retrieval of autobiographical memories: The mechanisms and consequences of truncated search. *Cognition & Emotion, 20*, 351–382.

Williams, J. M. G., & Dritschel, B. H. (1988). Emotional disturbance and the specificity of autobiographical memory. *Cognition and Emotion, 2*, 221–234.

Williams, J. M. G., & Dritschel, B. (1991). Categoric and extended autobiographical memories. In Conway, M., Rubin, H., Spinnler, W., & Wagennar, W. (Eds.), *Theoretical perspectives on autobiographical memory* (pp. 391–409). Dodrecht: Kluwer Academic Publishers.

Williams, J. M. G., Stiles, W. B., & Shapiro, D. (1999). Cognitive mechanisms in the avoidance of painful and dangerous thoughts: Elaborating the assimilation model. *Cognitive Therapy and Research, 23*, 285–306.

Williams, J. M. G., Teasdale, J. D., Segal, Z. V., & Soulsby, J. (2000). Mindfulness-based cognitive therapy reduces overgeneral autobiographical memory in formerly depressed patients. *Journal of Abnormal Psychology, 109*, 150–155.

14 Attachment insecurities and disordered patterns of grief

Mario Mikulincer and Phillip R. Shaver

As everyone with an interest in bereavement knows, Bowlby's (1980) extension of attachment theory into the realm of bereavement and grieving was a major component of his now massively influential theoretical work. In countless articles and many books, including a recent integration of the literature by Bowlby's long-time colleague Parkes (2006), Bowlby's ideas have been tested, challenged, applied clinically, and extended. In the present chapter we offer a brief overview of the theory and its relevance to complicated, or disordered, grieving; its tests in our and other contemporary investigators' studies; and the potential applications of our research to clinical interventions for individuals suffering from complicated or disordered grief.

We begin with an overview of attachment theory and explain the theory's perspective on loss, bereavement, and both normative and complicated grieving. We then review empirical evidence demonstrating how attachment insecurities are involved in complicated patterns of grief. At the end of the chapter we offer a brief, but we hope seminal, research-based perspective on ways to prevent and treat complicated grief.

Overview of attachment theory

Bowlby (1982) claimed that human beings are born with an innate psychobiological system (which he called the *attachment behavioral system*) that motivates them to seek proximity to supportive others (*attachment figures*) in times of need. He also (Bowlby, 1973) delineated important individual differences in attachment-system functioning, which he attributed mainly to the history of interactions with attachment figures, beginning in infancy. Interactions with attachment figures who are available, sensitive, and responsive in times of need promote the normal functioning of the attachment system and encourage the development of a stable sense of security and positive mental representations of self and others, which Bowlby (1973) called *internal working models*. Unfortunately, when a person's attachment figures have not been reliably available, sensitive, and supportive, negative working models of self (as not sufficiently lovable) and others (as unaccepting and unresponsive) are likely to have developed.

When studying individual differences in attachment-system functioning in adults, attachment research has focused mainly on *attachment orientations*: a person's chronic pattern of relational expectations, emotions, and behaviors resulting from the internalization and memory of a particular attachment history (Fraley & Shaver, 2000). Specifically, many recent studies of adult attachment (reviewed by Mikulincer & Shaver, 2007a) have found that individual differences in attachment orientations can be measured along two continuous dimensions of *attachment anxiety* and *avoidance* (Brennan, Clark, & Shaver, 1998), which are roughly orthogonal. Attachment *anxiety* reflects the degree to which a person worries that relationship partners will not be available in times of need and is afraid of being rejected or abandoned. Attachment-related *avoidance* reflects the extent to which a person distrusts relationship partners' goodwill and strives to maintain independence and emotional distance from partners. People who score low on both dimensions are said to be secure, or secure with respect to attachment. The two dimensions can be measured with reliable and valid self-report scales (e.g., Brennan et al., 1998) and are associated in theoretically predictable ways with many aspects of mental health and relationship quality (see Mikulincer & Shaver, 2007a, for a review).

We (Mikulincer & Shaver, 2007a) have proposed that a person's location in the two-dimensional space defined by attachment anxiety and avoidance reflects both the person's sense of attachment security and the ways in which he or she deals with threats and stressors. People who score low on these dimensions are generally secure and tend to employ constructive and effective affect-regulation strategies. Those who score high on either attachment anxiety or avoidance, or both (a condition called fearful avoidance), suffer from attachment insecurities and tend to use secondary attachment strategies (Cassidy & Kobak, 1988) in an effort to cope with threats, frustrations, losses, and insecurities. People who score high on attachment anxiety rely on hyperactivating strategies: energetic attempts to achieve support and love combined with a lack of confidence that these resources will be provided and with feelings of anger and despair when they are not provided (Cassidy & Kobak, 1988). In contrast, people who score high on avoidant attachment tend to use deactivating strategies: trying not to seek proximity to others when threatened, denying vulnerability and a need for other people, and avoiding closeness and interdependence in relationships. Research has consistently shown that attachment anxiety and avoidance can be viewed as risk factors for emotional and behavioral problems (see Mikulincer & Shaver, 2007a, for an extensive review of results).

An attachment perspective on loss and grief

According to attachment theory, the loss of an attachment figure is a profound blow that triggers intense distress and a predictable series of responses, which Bowlby (1982) originally called *protest*, *despair*, and *detachment*. In childhood, the initial response to separation from an attachment figure is protest: The child very actively resists separation by crying, calling, searching, and clinging in an attempt to regain contact. If protest fails to restore proximity, as is obviously the case following the death of an attachment figure, these vigorous reactions eventually wane and anxiety and anger give way to pervasive despair, including depressed mood, pained expressions, decreased appetite, and disturbed sleep. Over time, despair usually gives way to what Bowlby (1982) called "detachment": apparent recovery and gradual renewal of interest in other activities and new relationship partners.

Bowlby (1980) viewed adult romantic, or pair-bond, relationships as the primary attachment bonds in adulthood and assumed that adults who lose their long-term romantic, or marital, partner will undergo a series of reactions similar to those observed in infants (see also Parkes & Weiss, 1983; Shaver & Fraley, 2008). Like infants, bereaved adults react with strong protest, anger, calling, and yearning for reunion. When a person fully realizes that his or her partner will not return, despair and disorganization can ensue, accompanied by sleeping and eating disturbances, social withdrawal, intense sorrow, and loneliness (Weiss, 1991). In the case of adult bereavement, Bowlby (1980) preferred to call the final phase of grief responses "reorganization" rather than "detachment," because adults often transfer their proximity seeking, at least partly, to new relationship partners without fully detaching from the lost partner. According to Bowlby (1980), adults can rearrange their attachment representations so that the deceased can continue to serve as a symbolic source of protection while new relationships with living partners are formed on new foundations.

According to Bowlby (1980), "reorganization" is the optimal resolution of the bereavement process. It involves two major psychological tasks: (1) accepting the death of the lost partner, returning to mundane activities, and forming new relationships, and (2) maintaining some kind of symbolic bond to the deceased and integrating the lost relationship within a new reality. These tasks require an "editing" of the hierarchy of attachment figures in a process that resembles the replacement of parents by peers as primary attachment figures during adolescence (e.g., Hazan & Zeifman, 1999; Weiss, 1991). Psychologically successful mourners can maintain a symbolic bond to the deceased while adjusting to real circumstances, and restore and even enhance their sense of security and well-being based on both the continuing attachment bond with the deceased and new attachment bonds with living companions.

Bowlby's (1980) reasoning fits well with the various dual-process models of bereavement (e.g., Rubin, 1991; Stroebe & Schut, 1999). For instance, Stroebe and Schut (1999) viewed adjustment to loss as a dynamic oscillation between loss orientation and restoration orientation. Loss orientation includes yearning, rumination, separation distress, and reappraisal of the meaning and implications of the loss. Restoration orientation includes attending to life changes, doing new things, distracting oneself from grief, denying or suppressing grief, and forming new relationships. In this model, oscillation between these two orientations brings about a gradual reorganization of life and mind, such that the deceased is integrated into the bereaved individual's identity and he or she establishes new relationships and finds new meanings in life.

Attachment insecurities and disordered patterns of grief

Beyond describing the normative processes of bereavement and coping with the loss of a close relationship partner, Bowlby (1980) proposed a framework for conceptualizing disordered patterns of mourning and suggested that attachment insecurities can sometimes complicate grief. Anxiously attached individuals are unwilling or unable to handle many life tasks on their own and to suppress or inhibit painful feelings, thoughts, and memories related to a deceased partner, thereby making attachment reorganization impossible. Avoidant individuals are unwilling or unable to experience thoughts, feelings, and memories related to a deceased partner, which makes it difficult to create meaning from the loss and integrate the lost relationship into a new reality. In both cases, attachment-related worries and defenses may interfere with attachment reorganization and complicate the grief process.

Bowlby (1980) suggested that attachment insecurities contribute to two major forms of disordered mourning: "chronic mourning" and "prolonged absence of conscious grieving" (p. 138). Chronic mourning is characterized by overwhelming anxiety and sadness, prolonged difficulty in re-establishing normal functioning and forming new relationships, preoccupation with the deceased partner, and maintenance of intense emotional bonds with the deceased. In contrast, prolonged absence of grief is characterized by lack of overt expressions of sadness or distress, detachment from the deceased partner, and continuation of normal life without major disruptions. Most clinicians agree with Bowlby's conceptualization of these two forms of disordered mourning, although they tend to label the absence of grief "delayed grief," "inhibited mourning," or "absent mourning" (see Stroebe, Hansson, Stroebe, & Schut, 2001). According to Bowlby (1980), whereas attachment anxiety underlies chronic mourning, attachment-related avoidance contributes to the absence of grief.

Anxious attachment and chronic mourning

Even when their relationship partners are alive, attachment-anxious people are preoccupied with their responsiveness and supportiveness, likely to make intrusive demands for greater love and attention, and eager for support and reassurance (Shaver, Schachner, & Mikulincer, 2005). Not surprisingly, therefore, when they lose a relationship partner to death, they are likely to experience intense preoccupation with the deceased, yearn inconsolably for the lost source of protection and support, fail to accept the loss, and have difficulty establishing new relationships. These are some of the core features of chronic mourning.

Another characteristic of chronic mourning is that the bereaved person is frequently overwhelmed by painful memories of the deceased and is unable to cope with or manage them effectively (e.g., Boelen, van den Hout, & van den Bout, 2006). This inability to control the flow of painful memories is one of the most salient characteristics of attachment-anxious adults. For example, Mikulincer and Orbach (1995) found that anxiously attached individuals had very fast access to painful memories and that these memories spread like wildfire throughout their cognitive system. Using the Adult Attachment Interview, Roisman, Tsai, and Chiang (2004) found similar signs of emotional dysregulation when anxiously attached individuals were asked to talk about their emotional experiences (i.e., they exhibited facial expressions of sadness or anger even they were speaking about neutral or positive childhood experiences). We believe that this is the same kind of confusion and disorganization that occurs when anxiously attached mourners are bombarded with intrusive images, feelings, and memories related to the deceased person, although it is likely to be even more intense in the case of bereavement.

Another characteristic of chronic mourning is the pervasive presence of negative beliefs about the self and the future (e.g., Boelen, van den Bout, & van den Hout, 2003). According to Foa and Rothbaum (1998), these negative beliefs can be particularly resistant to change when the loss confirms negative views of the self, hopeless beliefs, and catastrophic cognitions that were present before the loss. This is more likely to be the case when a person was already anxiously attached. There is extensive evidence that anxiously attached individuals tend to possess negative views of self, to exaggerate even fairly minor threats, and to hold pessimistic beliefs about managing distress (see Mikulincer & Shaver, 2007a, for a review).

Avoidant attachment and the absence of grief

Avoidant people habitually deal with stress and distress by denying attachment needs, suppressing attachment-related thoughts and emotions, and inhibiting unwanted urges to seek proximity or support (Mikulincer & Shaver, 2007a). Following the death of an attachment figure, avoidant people are likely to use their deactivating defenses to inhibit anxiety and despair, downplay the importance of the loss, and try to steer clear of thoughts and memories focused on the deceased. This is what Bowlby (1980) meant by the absence of grief. He considered this to be a defensive reaction involving redirection of attention away from painful thoughts and feelings ("defensive exclusion") and the segregation or dissociation of memories of the deceased which nevertheless continue to influence emotions and behaviors without the individual's awareness of their effects.

Bowlby (1980) thought the prolonged absence of grief could eventually lead to difficulties in mental and physical health. He expected that people who fail to mourn would have difficulties integrating losses meaningfully into their working models and schemas. Since a bereaved person is likely to have engaged in many daily activities with the now-deceased partner, each of these activities or the places where they occurred becomes an unwanted reminder of the loss and a further source of either distress or the need to suppress thoughts and feelings.

Of course, the negative emotional and physical consequences of "absence of grieving" are most likely to emerge in cases where the bereaved individual was deeply attached to the lost partner. If an avoidant person was able to avoid closeness and interdependence with a partner while he or she was alive, he or she may experience less anxiety and despair following the death of this partner even without strenuous attachment deactivation. In such cases, the absence of grieving may reflect a real absence of distress because there was no strong emotional bond between the bereaved individual and the deceased. Compatible with this idea, many people who show few signs of grief immediately after the death of a partner do not exhibit heightened distress and emotional problems months or years later (see Bonanno, 2001, for a review).

It may be difficult, in particular cases, to tell the difference between successful but very active suppression, on one hand, and a true absence of anything to suppress, on the other. For several years, our own research was unclear about the existence of this difference. Now, however, Bowlby's (1980) ideas about avoidant people's defensive suppression of memories, thoughts, and feelings concerning separations and losses have been well supported in a series of experiments conducted in our laboratories.

Fraley and Shaver (1997) asked participants to write about whatever thoughts and feelings they were experiencing while being allowed to think about anything except thoughts about their long-term relationship partner leaving them for someone else. Findings indicated that avoidant attachment was associated with both less frequent thoughts of loss following the suppression task and lower skin conductance during the task, suggesting that avoidant people may be able to block unwanted thoughts and to prevent the emotional arousal these thoughts might otherwise cause. A subsequent study used functional magnetic resonance imaging (fMRI) to observe brain processes during this same suppression task (Gillath, Bunge, Shaver, Wendelken, & Mikulincer, 2005) and found that avoidant attachment was associated with a particular pattern of activation and deactivation in brain regions involved in suppression.

Avoidant people's ways of dealing with losses are also manifested in what Fraley, Garner, and Shaver (2000) called *preemptive* defenses, for example, directing attention away from loss-related information, or encoding it in a shallow way. Fraley et al. (2000) asked participants to listen to a genuinely emotional interview about the loss of a close relationship partner and then to recall details of the interview, either soon after hearing it or at various delays ranging from half an hour to 21 days. Whereas avoidant people initially encoded less loss-related information, they did not differ from more secure participants in the rate of forgetting the encoded information. It therefore seems that avoidant people defend from loss-related information preemptively, by blocking threatening material from awareness before it is fully encoded.

Although these findings imply that avoidant people are effective in suppressing painful memories and thoughts, Mikulincer, Dolev, and Shaver (2004) found that avoidant people can nevertheless be disturbed by the unwanted resurgence of suppressed thoughts. In two studies, participants were asked to think about a painful relationship breakup, were either instructed or not instructed to suppress thoughts about this separation, and then performed a Stroop color-naming task under conditions of low or high cognitive load. In the Stroop task, participants were asked to indicate the color in which words related to the painful separation (Study 1) or negative and positive self-traits (Study 2) were printed. Longer color-naming latencies implied greater accessibility to suppressed thoughts of separation or to self-related traits. In this way, Mikulincer et al. (2004) examined whether avoidant defenses are capable of inhibiting the post-suppression rebound effect and the intrusion of self-related worries (heightened access to negative self-traits) even when other cognitive demands draw upon limited psychological resources.

Under low cognitive load, findings of the two studies revealed that avoidant people were able to suppress thoughts related to the breakup and had poorer access to such thoughts and enhanced access to *positive* self-representations in the Stroop task following suppression. However, the effectiveness of avoidant defenses was significantly impaired when a high cognitive load taxed the mental resources needed to maintain thought suppression. Under a high cognitive load, avoidant people exhibited greater automatic activation of thoughts of separation and *negative* self-traits following suppression. In other words, their defenses collapsed when mental resources were too scarce to maintain them, and this collapse was associated with a spread of activation from unwanted separation-related thoughts to formerly suppressed negative self-representations. Studies showing that avoidant people do sometimes experience strong negative emotions in response to chronic, uncontrollable, and severely distressing events also suggest a breakdown of defenses when the mental load includes not just cognitive processes but intense stress as well (e.g., Berant, Mikulincer, & Shaver, 2008). In line with Bowlby's (1980) analysis, these findings indicated that avoidant individuals' attempts to suppress painful thoughts concerning a loss fail to eliminate the distress, and the suppressed material can resurface in experience and action when high cognitive or emotional demands are encountered.

Empirical evidence on the links between attachment insecurities and complicated grief

A few studies have directly examined the associations between a history of insecure attachment experiences in childhood (separation anxiety, childhood abuse, parental death) and bereavement in adulthood and found that such a history was associated with complicated patterns of grief (e.g., Silverman, Johnson, & Prigerson, 2001; Vanderwerker, Jacobs, Parkes, & Prigerson, 2006). In addition, adult attachment studies have consistently found that self-reports of attachment anxiety are positively associated with complicated grief reactions (e.g., Field & Sundin, 2001; Fraley & Bonanno, 2004; Jerga, Shaver, & Wilkinson, 2011; Wayment & Vierthaler, 2002; Wijngaards-de Meij et al., 2007a, 2007b). For example, Field and Sundin (2001) found that anxious attachment, assessed 10 months after the death of a spouse, predicted higher levels of psychological distress 14, 25, and 60 months after the loss, and Fraley and Bonanno (2004) found that attachment anxiety assessed 4 months after the loss of a spouse predicted higher levels of anxiety, depression, grief, trauma-related symptoms, and alcohol consumption 18 months following the loss.

There is also evidence concerning the association between attachment anxiety and difficulties in attachment reorganization. Field and Sundin (2001), for example, found that higher scores in attachment anxiety were associated with more positive thoughts about a deceased spouse 14 months after the loss, perhaps reflecting a continuing emotional investment in an idealized figure. This kind of idealization was also evident in Nager and De Vries's (2004) qualitative study of the contents of memorial websites created by adult daughters in memory of their deceased mothers. Using the Continuing Bonds Scale, Waskowic and Chartier (2003) found that, although secure and anxious people scored relatively high on the scale, anxious people scored higher than their secure counterparts on rumination about and preoccupation with a lost spouse.

With regard to avoidant attachment, studies have generally found no significant association between this attachment orientation and depression, grief, or distress following the death of a relationship partner (Field & Sundin, 2001; Fraley & Bonanno, 2004; Wayment & Vierthaler, 2002). However, Wayment and Vierthaler (2002) found that avoidance was associated with higher levels of somatic symptoms following the death of spouse, and Wijngaards-de Meij et al. (2007a, 2007b) found that avoidant people exhibited higher levels of grief and depression following the death of their child than secure people.

Recently, Jerga et al. (2011) reviewed previous studies that failed to find significant associations between avoidant attachment and complicated grief and concluded that the failure might have occurred for four methodological reasons. First, although past studies assessed grief symptoms, they failed to assess symptoms of prolonged or complicated grief (Prigerson et al., 2009). Second, participants in previous studies were aware, when they agreed to participate, that the study was designed to investigate loss and grief, perhaps biasing the sample and causing people who were struggling with their loss, or were using an avoidant strategy to keep from thinking about it, to choose not to participate. Third, previous research did not always control for the closeness or strength of the relationship with the deceased, so avoidant people may have reported losses of a less significant nature than the ones described by other participants. Fourth, previous studies often involved small samples and may have had insufficient statistical power to detect a link between avoidant attachment and complicated grief.

To begin to deal with these methodological problems, Jerga et al. (2011) conducted a cross-sectional study with a large sample, measuring both manifestations of typical grief and symptoms of prolonged grief, assessing attachment-related avoidance both generally and with respect to the lost partner, disguising the nature of the study in the beginning to avoid sampling biases, and controlling statistically for relationship closeness and strength. The researchers found that global avoidant attachment was positively associated with prolonged grief symptoms but not with typical or normative grief symptoms. That is, people who are generally avoidant in close relationships experience long-term difficulties adjusting to the death of a relationship partner, even though they do not necessarily experience more intense typical grief symptoms.

Interestingly, Jerga et al. (2011) also found that relationship-specific avoidance was negatively associated with both typical and prolonged grief symptoms. However, Jerga et al. (2011) showed that this association disappeared when measures of relationship closeness and strength were statistically controlled, suggesting that avoidant individuals may maintain relatively weak and emotionally distant relationships with the deceased, which in turn leaves them with less to grieve about. In other words, it is not avoidant attachment per se that protects avoidant individuals from grief symptoms; it is rather the weakness of the emotional bonds they have to contend with when a relationship partner dies. Overall, these findings emphasize that researchers should take seriously Bowlby's (1980) cautions about assessing grief responses among avoidant people, because "in all studies except those using the most sophisticated of methods, it is easy to overlook such people and to group them with those whose mourning is progressing in a genuinely favorable way" (p. 211).

An attachment perspective on grief resolution and counseling

If attachment insecurities are risk factors for complicated grief, then the initiation, maintenance, or restoration of a sense of attachment security should increase resilience and facilitate attachment reorganization and a more optimal resolution of the grief process. According to attachment theory, interactions with available and supportive attachment figures impart a sense of safety, arouse positive emotions (e.g., relief, love), and provide psychological resources for dealing with problems and adversities (Bowlby, 1988). Hundreds of cross-sectional and longitudinal studies reviewed by Mikulincer and Shaver (2007a) have found that secure individuals are likely to remain relatively unperturbed in times of stress, to recover rapidly from periods of distress, and to experience relatively long stretches of positive affectivity, which can increase resilience and mental health following the loss of a relationship partner.

Bowlby (1988) also suggested that attachment security, which can be either dispositional or rooted in a lost relationship, facilitates attachment reorganization and makes healthy adjustment to loss more likely. Secure individuals can recall and think about a lost partner without extreme difficulty, can acknowledge feelings of love and grief, and can talk about the loss without being overwhelmed by distress and pain (Stroebe, Schut, & Stroebe, 2005). In addition, secure individuals' positive models of others allow them to continue to think positively about the deceased, whereas their positive models of self allow them to cope with the loss and begin to form new relationships. They can therefore be open to new relationships and invest emotionally in new partners without defensively detaching from the deceased partner.

Attachment research has shown that self-reports of dispositional attachment security are associated with better emotional adjustment following the loss of a relationship partner (e.g., Fraley & Bonanno, 2004; van Doorn, Kasl, Beery, Jacobs, & Prigerson, 1998; Waskowic & Chartier, 2003; Wayment & Vierthaler, 2002). For example, Fraley and Bonanno (2004) found that people classified as securely attached 4 months after the loss of a spouse reported relatively low levels of bereavement-related anxiety, grief, depression, and posttraumatic distress concurrently (at 4 months) and 18 months after the loss.

In some of our studies we examined effects of increased security on various indicators of mental health by experimentally activating mental representations of supportive attachment figures (e.g., Mikulincer, Hirschberger, Nachmias, & Gillath, 2001). Although none of these studies examined the effects of momentary activation of the sense of attachment security on the grief process, they provide clues that might guide and enrich future bereavement studies. Using several research techniques (which we refer to as "security priming"; Mikulincer & Shaver, 2007b), including subliminal exposure to names of people designated by participants as security-enhancing attachment figures and visualization of the faces of security-enhancing attachment figures, we have consistently found that security priming improved participants' moods even in threatening contexts (e.g., Mikulincer et al., 2001) and mitigated cognitive symptoms of posttraumatic stress disorder and eating disorders (Admoni, 2006; Mikulincer, Shaver, & Horesh, 2006).

In a recent laboratory experiment, we (Cassidy, Shaver, Mikulincer, & Lavy, 2009) took another step forward by showing that a momentary increase in the sense of attachment security can mitigate hyperactivating and deactivating affect-regulation strategies that are likely to complicate the process of grieving. Participants completed a measure of dispositional attachment anxiety and avoidance and wrote a description of an incident in which a close relationship partner hurt them. Participants then completed a short computerized task in which they were repeatedly exposed subliminally (for 22 milliseconds) to either a security-enhancing prime word (love, affection) or a neutral prime (lamp, staple). Immediately after the priming trials, participants were asked to think again about the hurtful event they had described and to rate how they would react to such an event if it happened in the future: how rejected they would feel, how they would feel about themselves, and how well each of nine action descriptions fitted the way they would react (various defensive and hostile reactions, various constructive reactions, and crying).

In the neutral priming condition, the findings conformed to the usual deactivating and hyperactivating strategies of avoidant and anxious people. Avoidance scores were associated with less negative appraisals of the hurtful episode, less intense feelings of rejection, less crying, and more defensive/hostile reactions. In the neutral priming condition, attachment anxiety was associated with more intense feelings of rejection, more crying, and more negative emotions. These typical correlational findings were dramatically reduced in size (most approached zero) in the security-priming condition. In other words, security priming reduced the tendency of avoidant people to rely on deactivating defenses and the tendency of anxious people to react hyperactively to hurtful episodes and psychological pain.

These findings may be useful in planning future bereavement research and may assist in developing interventions for complicated grief. When a person is already secure, based on a history of supportive relationships, he or she can deal constructively with the loss of a relationship partner. When a person has a history of unreliable, unpredictable attachment figures and is dispositionally anxious as a result, he or she is likely to intensify distress and cope badly with a loss. However, this habitual hyperactivating response can be notably softened by a boost in felt security accomplished through symbolic sources (as in our studies). We also believe that actual interactions with a security provider (e.g., a counselor or therapist) may also boost felt security and then soften habitual hyperactivating responses. In contrast, people who have had to deal, historically, with cool, consistently unsupportive attachment figures and have developed a defensively avoidant pattern of relating to others may be somewhat protected from the pain and distress usually caused by a loss. However, this benefit may come at the expense of considerable problems in attachment reorganization and meaning construction following a loss. This habitual protective armor can be at least temporarily softened by an infusion of felt security, which seems to allow an avoidant person to become more open to inner pain (Cassidy et al., 2009). This openness may provide an opening for exploring the loss experience and learning more about the importance of relationships and their relevance for finding meaning in life.

These ideas fit with Bowlby's (1988) notion that therapeutic change begins with the formation of a secure attachment bond with a therapist. Basically, therapists need to provide what attachment theory calls a safe haven and secure base for a client, which are prerequisites for boldly exploring painful experiences, reworking mental representations of self and others, and learning new approaches to behaving within relationships. These beneficial effects of enhanced attachment security have already been documented in studies of treating clients with mood disorders. For example, in a study based on data from the multi-site NIMH (National Institute of Mental Health) Treatment of Depression Collaborative Research Program, Zuroff and Blatt (2006) found that a client's positive views of his or her therapist's sensitivity and supportiveness predicted relief from depression and maintenance of therapeutic benefits over an 18-month period. Future research should examine whether the formation of a secure attachment bond with a therapist has beneficial effects in therapeutic interventions with people suffering from complicated grief.

References

Admoni, S. (2006). *Attachment security and eating disorders*. Unpublished doctoral dissertation, Bar-Ilan University, Ramat Gan, Israel.

Berant, E., Mikulincer, M., & Shaver, P. R. (2008). Mothers' attachment style, their mental health, and their children's emotional vulnerabilities: A seven-year study of children with congenital heart disease. *Journal of Personality, 76*, 31–66.

Boelen, P. A., van den Bout, J., & van den Hout, M. A. (2003). The role of cognitive variables in psychological functioning after the death of a first degree relative. *Behavior Research and Therapy, 41*, 1123–1136.

Boelen, P. A., van den Hout, M. A., & van den Bout, J. (2006). A cognitive–behavioral conceptualization of complicated grief. *Clinical Psychology: Science and Practice, 13*, 109–128.

Bonanno, G. (2001). Grief and emotion: A social-functional perspective. In Stroebe, M., Stroebe, W., Hansson, R. O., & Schut, H. A. W. (Eds.), *Handbook of bereavement research: Consequences, coping, and care* (pp. 493–515). Washington, DC: American Psychological Association.

Bowlby, J. (1973). *Attachment and loss, vol. 2. Separation: Anxiety and anger.* New York: Basic Books.

Bowlby, J. (1980). *Attachment and loss, vol. 3. Sadness and depression.* New York: Basic Books.

Bowlby, J. (1982). *Attachment and loss, vol. 1. Attachment* (2nd edn.). New York: Basic Books.

Bowlby, J. (1988). *A secure base: Clinical applications of attachment theory.* London: Routledge.

Brennan, K. A., Clark, C. L., & Shaver, P. R. (1998). Self-report measurement of adult romantic attachment: An integrative overview. In Simpson, J. A., & Rholes, W. S. (Eds.), *Attachment theory and close relationships* (pp. 46–76). New York: Guilford Press.

Cassidy, J., & Kobak, R. R. (1988). Avoidance and its relationship with other defensive processes. In Belsky, J., & Nezworski, T. (Eds.), *Clinical implications of attachment* (pp. 300–323). Hillsdale, NJ: Erlbaum.

Cassidy, J., Shaver, P. R., Mikulincer, M., & Lavy, S. (2009). Experimentally induced security influences responses to psychological pain. *Journal of Social and Clinical Psychology, 28,* 463–478.

van Doorn, C., Kasl, S. V., Beery, L. C., Jacobs, S. C., & Prigerson, H. G. (1998). The influence of marital quality and attachment styles on traumatic grief and depressive symptoms. *Journal of Nervous and Mental Disease, 186,* 566–573.

Field, N. P., & Sundin, E. C. (2001). Attachment style in adjustment to conjugal bereavement. *Journal of Social and Personal Relationships, 18,* 347–361.

Foa, E. B., & Rothbaum, B. O. (1998). *Treating the trauma of rape: Cognitive–behavior therapy for PTSD.* New York: Guilford Press.

Fraley, R., & Bonanno, G. A. (2004). Attachment and loss: A test of three competing models on the association between attachment-related avoidance and adaptation to bereavement. *Personality and Social Psychology Bulletin, 30,* 878–890.

Fraley, R. C., Garner, J. P., & Shaver, P. R. (2000). Adult attachment and the defensive regulation of attention and memory: Examining the role of preemptive and postemptive defensive processes. *Journal of Personality and Social Psychology, 79,* 816–826.

Fraley, R. C., & Shaver, P. R. (1997). Adult attachment and the suppression of unwanted thoughts. *Journal of Personality and Social Psychology, 73,* 1080–1091.

Fraley, R. C., & Shaver, P. R. (2000). Adult romantic attachment: Theoretical developments, emerging controversies, and unanswered questions. *Review of General Psychology, 4,* 132–154.

Gillath, O., Bunge, S. A., Shaver, P. R., Wendelken, C., & Mikulincer, M. (2005). Attachment-style differences in the ability to suppress negative thoughts: Exploring the neural correlates. *Neuroimage, 28,* 835–847.

Hazan, C., & Zeifman, D. (1999). Pair-bonds as attachments: Evaluating the evidence. In Cassidy, J., & Shaver, P. R. (Eds.), *Handbook of attachment: Theory, research, and clinical applications* (pp. 336–354). New York: Guilford.

Jerga, C., Shaver, P. R., & Wilkinson, R. B. (2011). Attachment insecurities and identification of at-risk individuals following the death of a loved one. *Journal of Social and Personal Relationships, 28,* 891–914.

Mikulincer, M., Dolev, T., & Shaver, P. R. (2004). Attachment-related strategies during thought-suppression: Ironic rebounds and vulnerable self-representations. *Journal of Personality and Social Psychology, 87,* 940–956.

Mikulincer, M., Hirschberger, G., Nachmias, O., & Gillath, O. (2001). The affective component of the secure base schema: Affective priming with representations of attachment security. *Journal of Personality and Social Psychology, 81*, 305–321.

Mikulincer, M., & Orbach, I. (1995). Attachment styles and repressive defensiveness: The accessibility and architecture of affective memories. *Journal of Personality and Social Psychology, 68*, 917–925.

Mikulincer, M., & Shaver, P. R. (2007a). *Attachment in adulthood: Structure, dynamics, and change.* New York: Guilford Press.

Mikulincer, M., & Shaver, P. R. (2007b). Boosting attachment security to promote mental health, prosocial values, and inter-group tolerance. *Psychological Inquiry, 18*, 139–156.

Mikulincer, M., Shaver, P. R., & Horesh, N. (2006). Attachment bases of emotion regulation and posttraumatic adjustment. In Snyder, D. K., Simpson, J. A., & Hughes, J. N. (Eds.), *Emotion regulation in families: Pathways to dysfunction and health* (pp. 77–99). Washington, DC: American Psychological Association.

Nager, E. A., & de Vries, B. (2004). Memorializing on the World Wide Web: Patterns of grief and attachment in adult daughters of deceased mothers. *Omega, 49*, 43–56.

Parkes, C. M. (2006). *Love and loss: The roots of grief and its complications.* London: Routledge.

Parkes, C. M., & Weiss, R. S. (1983). *Recovery from bereavement.* New York: Basic Books.

Prigerson, H. G., Horowitz, M. J., Jacobs, S. C., Parkes, C. M., Aslan, M., Goodkin, K., et al. (2009). Prolonged grief disorder: Psychometric validation of criteria proposed for DSM-V and ICD-11. *PLoS Med, 6*(8), 20. Retrieved February 3. 2010, from http://www.plosmedicine.org/article/info:doi%2F10.1371%2Fjournal.pmed.1000121.

Roisman, G. I., Tsai, J. L., & Chiang, K. H. S. (2004). The emotional integration of childhood experience: Physiological, facial expressive, and self-reported emotional response during the Adult Attachment Interview. *Developmental Psychology, 40*, 776–789.

Rubin, S. S. (1991). Adult child loss and the two-track model of bereavement. *Omega, 24*, 183–202.

Shaver, P. R., & Fraley, R. C. (2008). Attachment, loss, and grief: Bowlby's views and current controversies. In Cassidy, J., & Shaver, P. R. (Eds.), *Handbook of attachment: Theory, research, and clinical applications* (2nd edn., pp. 48–77). New York: Guilford Press.

Shaver, P. R., Schachner, D. A., & Mikulincer, M. (2005). Attachment style, excessive reassurance seeking, relationship processes, and depression. *Personality and Social Psychology Bulletin, 31*, 1–17.

Silverman, G. K., Johnson, J. G., & Prigerson, H. G. (2001). Preliminary explorations of the effects of prior trauma and loss on risk for psychiatric disorders in recently widowed people. *Israel Journal of Psychiatry and Related Sciences, 38*, 202–215.

Stroebe, M., Hansson, R. O., Stroebe, W., & Schut, H. A. W. (2001) (Eds.) *Handbook of bereavement research: Consequences, coping, and care.* Washington, DC: American Psychological Association.

Stroebe, M., & Schut, H. A. W. (1999). The dual process model of coping with bereavement: Rationale and description. *Death Studies, 23*, 1–28.

Stroebe, M., Schut. H. A. W., & Stroebe, W. (2005). Attachment in coping with bereavement: A theoretical integration. *Review of General Psychology, 9*, 48–66.

Vanderwerker, L. C., Jacobs, S. C., Parkes, C. M., & Prigerson, H. G. (2006). An exploration of associations between separation anxiety in childhood and complicated grief in later-life. *Journal of Nervous and Mental Diseases, 194*, 121–123.

Waskowic, T. D., & Chartier, B. M. (2003). Attachment and the experience of grief following the loss of a spouse. *Omega, 47*, 77–91.

Wayment, H. A., & Vierthaler, J. (2002). Attachment style and bereavement reactions. *Journal of Loss and Trauma, 7*, 129–149.

Weiss, R. S. (1991). The attachment bond in childhood and adulthood. In Parkes, C. M., Stevenson-Hinde, J., & Marris, P. (Eds.), *Attachment across the life cycle* (pp. 66–76). London: Tavistock.

Wijngaards-de Meij, L., Stroebe, M., Schut, H., Stroebe, W., van den Bout, J., van der Heijden, P. G., & Dijkstra, I. (2007). Neuroticism and attachment insecurity as predictors of bereavement outcome. *Journal of Research in Personality, 41*, 498–505.

Wijngaards-de Meij, L., Stroebe, M., Schut, H., Stroebe, W., van den Bout, J., van der Heijden, P. G., & Dijkstra, I. (2007). Patterns of attachment and parents' adjustment to the death of their child. *Personality and Social Psychology Bulletin, 33*, 537–548.

Zuroff, D. C., & Blatt, S. J. (2006). The therapeutic relationship in the brief treatment of depression: Contributions to clinical improvement and enhanced adaptive capacities. *Journal of Consulting and Clinical Psychology, 74*, 199–206.

15 Physiological mechanisms and the neurobiology of complicated grief

Mary-Frances O'Connor

Complicated grief (CG) is a disorder of significant impact, as described in other chapters of this book. In addition to the mental anguish accompanying this disorder, new evidence suggests that concurrent physiological changes occur and these could impact physical health. This chapter will begin by reviewing selective theories that incorporate physiological aspects of general bereavement (i.e., attachment theory and physiological co-regulation), and will then review theories that incorporate physiological changes in CG specifically. Next, the empirical evidence for the health effects of CG and physiological mechanisms are reviewed.

A discussion of the advantages of studying the physiology and neurobiology of CG follows. Health outcomes are one piece of evidence of physiological mechanisms in CG. However, the use of physiology in research designs to distinguish aspects of psychological phenomena will be discussed below as a useful reason to include physiology in research studies of CG. For example, the underlying aspects of the body's stress response hint at distinctions between CG and post-traumatic stress disorder (PTSD), or simply CG and non-complicated grief (non-CG). Finally, the chapter ends with a summary of the research that has begun, and, importantly, demonstrates the gaps in knowledge of the neurobiological and physiological aspect of CG.

In an attempt to be clear regarding the operationalization of CG, each of the studies reviewed has included a description of how the investigators measured CG. In addition, the studies reviewed have not included participants with comorbid major depression, unless explicitly stated.

Models and theories of general bereavement

In addition to documenting empirical evidence of a physiological component to CG, developing theories about *why* there would be a physiological component to CG will assist the field in moving forward. These theories will inform what hypotheses are developed and tested, and ultimately may lead to an understanding of how we may improve treatment for CG. This section will review attachment theory, and the consequences of separation: a disorganized protest response to the withdrawal of the attachment figure, and an organized physiological stress response.

One theory that general bereavement research has found very useful is attachment theory (see Chapter 14). This theory states that the bonds between parent and child, and between romantic partners, are a product of behavioral conditioning whereby an association is developed between the attachment figure and (1) a reduction in distress and (2) the generation of pleasure (Bowlby, 1980). This conditioning explains a variety of behaviors, such as the maintenance of close proximity between bonded individuals, the development of mental schemas, or working models, that provide comfort during absence of the attachment figure, and distress that is generated upon separation from the attachment figure (for a review of these behaviors in adults, see Hazan, Gur-Yaish, & Campa, 2004). Attachment theory has specific predictions for bereavement: the process of bereavement includes a gradual extinction of this conditioning, in which the regulatory benefits conferred by mental representations of the attachment figure diminish slowly over time. Bowlby (1980) described the end point of successful mourning as a psychological reorganization of one's thoughts and feelings about a deceased attachment figure (for review, see Sbarra & Hazan, 2008).

Added to the original attachment theory is an emphasis on the role of the attachment figure in *physiological*, as well as psychological, regulation. Thus, repeated social contact with a particular person results in a conditioned response whereby this attachment figure is reliably associated with a state of psychological security and physiological calm (Depue & Morrone-Strupinsky, 2005). Much of the original work on physiological co-regulation came from a series of studies by Myron Hofer (1984). These studies were designed to isolate different aspects of what exactly was lost when a rat pup was separated from its mother. For example, warmth and milk are two very different aspects of the loss. Separate experiments were conducted to test the impact of the different aspects that were lost, and to determine which physiological systems were impacted in the pup by the loss of the individual aspects. Hofer theorized that the diverse responses to loss could be understood in terms of the removal of "maternal regulators" (p. 12), which were physiological. He drew analogies to human separation and bereavement, indicating that human bereavement also included the loss of physiological regulators, rather than only psychological stress.

Sbarra and Hazan (2008) theorized that the response to separation (or bereavement) in fact has two unrelated (though usually co-occurring) physiological components. First, there is a general stress response (termed *organized* by Sbarra and Hazan). Second, there is an attachment-specific stress response (termed *disorganized* by Sbarra and Hazan) driven by the loss of the rewarding aspects of attachment. These two aspects of response will be discussed, followed by their relationship to CG.

General stress response

First, bereavement provokes a general stress response (termed *organized* by Sbarra and Hazan). This is the physiological stress response that psychologists refer to as the "fight-or-flight" response. When an event triggers a fear reaction, accompanying changes allow the person to be physically prepared to fight or flee from the thing that has triggered the fear. This reaction, however, occurs in a wide range of circumstances that feel threatening, even when there is not a clear "thing" that can be fought or fled. The physical reactions happen in physiological systems that allow for increased blood flow to muscles, increased attention to the environment, and increased metabolism. The systems include the cardiovascular system, which shows increased heart rate and increased chemicals used by the cardiovascular system, called catecholamines (e.g., epinephrine). The systems also include the hypothalamic–pituitary–adrenal (HPA) axis, from which the stress hormone cortisol is made. Cortisol helps to metabolize food quickly into blood sugar, to provide increased energy to the body.

General bereavement research has demonstrated increases in catecholamines and cortisol in the early stages of bereavement (Gerra et al., 2003; Hofer, Wolff, Friedman, & Mason, 1972; Jacobs et al., 1987; Jacobs, Mason, et al., 1986), and higher heart rate and blood pressure in the first 2 weeks after the loss (Buckley et al., 2011). However, this general physiological stress response to bereavement is not distinct from the response to other stressful life events (e.g., stress of job loss, stress associated with man-made disasters).

Attachment-specific stress response

In addition to the general stress response, there is an attachment-specific stress response (termed *disorganized* by Sbarra and Hazan) driven by the loss of the rewarding aspects of attachment (Insel, 2003; Kovacs, Sarnyai, & Szabo, 1998; Panksepp, Knutson, & Burgdorf, 2002). Physiological systems respond to the removal of the conditioned pleasure and soothing associated with the attachment figure. Sbarra and Hazan (2008) use the term *co-regulation* to describe the physiological aspect of the feelings of security that an attachment figure provides.

The physiological systems responsible for this attachment-specific stress response include the dopamine system (Depue & Morrone-Strupinsky, 2005), the opioid system (Nelson & Panksepp, 1998; Panksepp, Nelson, & Bekkedal, 1997), and the oxytocin system (Lim & Young, 2006; Young & Wang, 2004). The dopamine system is important in the experience of motivation to seek our rewards, both wanting and, quite literally, moving toward a desired object. Dopamine is one of the neurotransmitters that is fundamental in conditioning, in associating the experience of reward with specific objects (Berridge, Robinson, & Aldridge, 2009). In the present discussion, this conditioning specifically creates the attachment to a *particular* figure. Dopamine is important in pursuing rewards, and opioids are important in the enjoyment of those rewards (Depue & Morrone-Strupinsky, 2005). Opioids are another group of neurochemicals made endogenously by the body, and they are also released under a variety of social interactions, including gentle physical touch. Oxytocin is a neurohormone important in birthing and nursing in all mammals, but in humans it has also been linked to suppression of anxiety during psychosocial stress and to the enhancement of trust (Heinrichs, Baumgartner, Kirschbaum, & Ehlert, 2003; Kosfeld, Heinrichs, Zak, Fischbacher, & Fehr, 2005).

Data about the effect of bereavement or separation on these attachment-specific systems are primarily from rodent and primate research, although empirical data in human bereavement have documented an increase in β-endorphins (one type of opioids) (Gerra et al., 2003) in the first weeks after the loss.

Models and theories of CG

It is important to pause at this point and reflect on the fact that the models and theories described so far apply to bereavement generally. These are not models that specifically explain why some individuals develop CG in response to the death of a loved one and others adjust resiliently.

A biopsychosocial model of CG has been put forward by Shear and Shair (2005). They posit first that the symptoms of *acute* grief result from a temporary failure of biobehavioral regulatory functions resulting from the mental representation of the deceased person, much like what has been described above. In most cases, this acute grief resolves as the bereaved person assimilates the finality of the loss and this knowledge is integrated into attachment-related long-term memory and mental schemas. This allows an effective attachment system to function again, and there is a reduction of overwhelming and intense sadness.

Although acute grief is usually followed by resilient adjustment (Bonanno et al., 2002), Shear and Shair (2005) suggest that adjustment to the death may become complicated by maladaptive attitudes and behaviors (and, this author adds, perhaps physiological constraints of the neurobiological attachment system). In Shear and Shair's model, based on prior work by Myron Hofer and Mardi Horowitz:

> CG is viewed as a stress response syndrome that results from failure to integrate information about death of an attachment figure into an effectively functioning secure base schema and/or inability to effectively re-engage the exploratory system in a world without the deceased. (Shear et al., 2007, p. 453)

The difficulty with creating a neurobiological model of CG is that it is currently unknown whether, at a basic level, CG represents merely a person with acute grief whose process of adaptation has been interrupted, or a wholly other process than non-complicated adaptation. For example, CG may stem from a pre-existing individual difference, which is already present at the time of the death of the attachment figure. However, it may require the removal of the attachment figure for this pre-existing condition to be revealed in behavior.

The two portions of Shear and Shair's model of CG may be roughly mapped onto the two types of physiological stress responses that have been discussed above. The general stress response (e.g., the fight-or-flight response) may be seen as similar to CG diagnostic criteria that include efforts to avoid thoughts of the deceased, feeling stunned, dazed, or shocked, and excessive irritability or anger (Prigerson et al., 2009; Shear et al., 2011).[1] The failure to integrate the reality of the death may lead to a continuously realized acute grief, prolonging the acute grief experience.

The attachment-specific stress response, driven by the loss of the rewarding aspects of attachment, might be seen as analogous to CG diagnostic criteria that include yearning for the deceased, feeling as if life is empty or meaningless without the person who died, frequent preoccupying thoughts about the person who died, and persistent difficulty trusting or caring about other people (Prigerson et al., 2009; Shear et al., 2011). The ability to re-engage with the social world following the death of an attachment figure may require the affiliative aspects of attachment system to explore new relationships and turn to existing ones for support.

In the next section, the empirical work supporting the role of physiology and neurobiology in CG will be reviewed in detail.

Studies of the physiology and neurobiology of CG

Crying

Crying is a canonical sign of grief, and is clearly a physiological event. Crying is also a very complex behavior, influenced by gender, culture, personality characteristics, and the social environment (Romans & Clarkson, 2008). There is some evidence that early in a crying episode there is high arousal in the cardiovascular system, but that across the episode there is an increase in the regulation of system, and heart rate slows again (Hendriks, Rottenberg, & Vingerhoets, 2007). Early work that examined the difference in symptoms between CG and bereavement-related depression found that crying was more strongly related to other CG symptoms than to other depression symptoms (Prigerson, Frank, et al., 1995).

Hypertension and heart rate

The most convincing early empirical evidence that there was a physiological component to bereavement came from studies of morbidity and mortality associated with bereavement (sometimes referred to as the "broken-heart phenomenon"; Stroebe, 1994). Work on that topic has been reviewed elsewhere (Buckley, McKinley, Tofler, & Bartrop, 2009; Stroebe, Schut, & Stroebe, 2007), but newer studies have developed this line of research by investigating the relationship between morbidity and mortality and the subgroup of bereaved individuals who have CG.

For instance, CG symptoms[2] and blood pressure were measured in bereaved participants at 6, 13, and 25 months (Prigerson et al., 1997). High blood pressure was operationalized as systolic blood pressure over 140 mm Hg, and CG was measured using the Grief Measurement Scale (Jacobs, Kasl, et al., 1986), modified to reflect only items from the 19-item Inventory of Complicated Grief (ICG;

Prigerson, Maciejewski, et al., 1995). CG symptoms at 6 months were associated with increased risk of high blood pressure at 13 months. In addition, self-reported incidence of cancer has been shown in two studies to be higher in those with CG (Prigerson et al., 1997; Prigerson, Maciejewski, et al., 1995).

The mechanisms that account for these health changes have not yet been robustly examined in CG,[3] although there is a great deal of evidence regarding changes in physiological mechanisms in general bereavement. A study by Bonanno, Neria, Mancini, Coifman, Litz, and Insel (2007) examined the heart rate changes associated with recalling events related to the loss (i.e., the participant's relationship to the deceased). This recall was done at approximately 4 months post-death and again at approximately 18 months. CG symptoms were measured using eight items (Horowitz et al., 1997). CG symptoms were only slightly and non-significantly associated with baseline heart rate, but significantly associated with decreased heart rate from 4 months to 18 months (Bonanno et al., 2007). The authors interpret these data in light of both animal and human studies demonstrating a withdrawal upon separation from attachment figures. In contrast to the negative correlation of CG symptoms and heart rate, PTSD symptoms in this study were seen to correlate positively with heart rate, such that higher PTSD symptoms were associated with a higher baseline heart rate and an increased heart rate across the two recall sessions.

Neurobiology

Several studies have now been conducted using functional magnetic resonance imaging (fMRI) as a modality in bereavement research. However, most of them have investigated general bereavement. If CG is a distinct phenomenon from non-CG, there should be differences in the neurobiological correlates. To the author's knowledge, only one study has investigated group differences between bereaved persons with CG and non-CG using fMRI (O'Connor et al., 2008).

Participants in this study were 23 women, each with a female family member who had died of breast cancer in the prior 18 months. This group was chosen because of the prevalence of CG among women with a family history of breast cancer. These women have often lost multiple female family members, often when the family member was still very young, and the survivors identify very strongly with them, because of their own increased risk.

CG was diagnosed with a structured clinical interview (Prigerson & Jacobs, 2001), with a cut-off for CG extrapolated from an ICG of ≥ 30 (Prigerson, Maciejewski, et al., 1995). The participants included 11 women with CG and 12 women with non-CG. Exclusion criteria included Axis I psychiatric disorders (including current depression) and medical disorders.

Participants provided a photograph of their deceased loved one, which was matched with a photo of a stranger. Grief-related words were taken from an interview about the death event (e.g., *collapse, funeral, loss*) and were matched with neutral words (e.g., *announce, ceiling, list*). These words were embedded into the photos to create composites. These picture–word composites resulted in a 2 × 2 factorial design: (1) deceased + grief word, (2) stranger + grief word, (3) deceased + neutral word, (4) stranger + neutral word. Sixty composites were shown, in a manner comparable to a slide show. This task had previously been validated in the scanner with participants' skin conductance responses and subjective grief ratings in response to each slide (Gündel, O'Connor, Littrell, Fort, & Lane, 2003).

Analyses revealed that, in response to reminders of the deceased, CG participants showed greater activation than those with non-CG in a subcortical area of the brain called the nucleus accumbens. To be clear, this means not that this was the only area of the brain that was active during the mental processing of the picture–word composites, but that it was more active in those with CG than in those with non-CG, above a statistical threshold of $p < 0.001$ (uncorrected for multiple comparisons).

Research on both animals and humans clearly demonstrates that the nucleus accumbens is active during the processing of rewards. In this use of the term *reward*, the reference is to the psychological construct of reward as a reinforcer (i.e., as opposed to punishment), rather than a positive, experiential feeling of reward. Reward can be decomposed into "wanting" and "liking," and elegant experimental designs have shown that the nucleus accumbens is activated when a reward is "wanted" (Knutson, Adams, Fong, & Hommer, 2001). Quotation marks are used around the terms here to distinguish the experiential aspect of wanting from the reinforcement value of "wanting" that is associated with nucleus accumbens activation.

Additional analyses were conducted to explore the correlates of activation in this region. Activation in the nucleus accumbens was not correlated with the amount of time that had passed since the death event, the participant's age, or the self-reported positive/negative affect after the scan. The nucleus accumbens activation *was* positively correlated with self-reported yearning at an interview in the week prior to the scan ($r = 0.42$, $p < 0.05$). This result is understandable, given that, when an object is reinforcing (i.e., it is "wanted"), there may also be a yearning for that object.

It is also important to recognize that knowing that this region distinguishes these two groups does not mean that the nucleus accumbens activation is causal (i.e., we do not know that this region causes impaired adaptation during grief, or whether it is a consequence of the symptoms of CG). It also does not tell us if the region is related to individual differences, or if it is part of a network of activation that changes across adaptation. In other words, one possibility is that those with CG would show distinctive activation in this region as an individual difference – perhaps even before the loss of a loved one. Alternatively, all individuals may show greater activation in this region early in adaptation to a loved one's death, and decreasing activation in this region as they adapt psychologically. These two alternatives require future research that scans each participant more than once across time, in order to observe change during adaptation.

Finally, it is not possible to know from functional neuroimaging what neurons in the nucleus accumbens region are the sources of this increased activation. For example, this brain region is rich in oxytocin, opioid, and dopamine receptors, and neurons that use one, two, or all three of these neurotransmitters may have been more active in those with CG than in those with non-CG. Thus, future research that investigates the levels of these neurotransmitters in the central nervous system (or, in cases where there is a valid method, the behavioral output of these central levels) might be a productive avenue of research in discriminating CG from non-CG.

For those with CG, reminders of the deceased activated neural reward activity, and this neural reinforcement may interfere with adapting to the loss in the present. Alternatively, the nucleus accumbens activation may simply be a neurobiological indicator of where the bereaved is in the adaptation process. Because activation of this region is also seen in fMRI studies of adults viewing photos of their living romantic partners and their children (Bartels & Zeki, 2004), it is reasonable to hypothesize that those with CG are responding subcortically to the cue as though the loved one were still alive.

Sleep

Sleep can be measured through polysomnography (PSG),[4] a comprehensive recording of the physiological changes that occur during sleep. These recordings include brain waves, eye movements, and muscle, heart, and breathing activity. PSG can identify when someone is sleeping, and also what type of sleep they are experiencing (e.g., deep sleep, rapid eye movement [REM] sleep associated with dreaming).

In the first study of sleep in CG, symptoms were measured with 13 of the 19 items on the ICG, because the study was begun prior to the publication of the ICG and not all information was available for early participants (Prigerson, Maciejewski, et al., 1995). Symptoms of CG were not associated with main effects on PSG measures although mild subjective sleep impairment was reported. In general, sleep continuity measures in subjects with CG alone were similar to data from non-bereaved healthy control subjects previously published.

Because CG symptoms showed no main effects on PSG sleep measures, it appears that CG symptoms do not entail the changes in sleep physiology seen in depression (for a review of the relationship between REM sleep and depression, see Berger & Riemann, 1993). The study did show that CG in combination with comorbid depression was associated with a higher percentage of REM sleep; however, two subjects primarily drove this effect. The authors conclude in their discussion that, based on their physiological data, CG should not be considered a form of depressive reaction to bereavement (McDermott et al., 1997).

In a second study of the physiology of sleep and circadian rhythms of widowed individuals (Monk et al., 2008), participants were assessed with the ICG, with CG caseness defined as an ICG score of 25 or greater at 6 months (Prigerson, Maciejewski, et al., 1995). Out of 18 individuals who were bereaved longer than 6 months, only four met criteria for CG. Sleep was measured through PSG in this study as well. The four CG participants were only approximately 0.5 standard deviation worse in sleep duration (total minutes of PSG-measured sleep), sleep efficiency (percentage of the night actually spent asleep), and sleep latency (the number of minutes between lights out and sleep onset) than the whole sample mean.

Another measure that was included in this study was core body temperature. This is a physiological system with a very strong circadian rhythm. Early work by Hofer and colleagues demonstrated that, when rat pups were separated from their mother, they showed overactive or depressed behavior depending on whether they were kept at the same temperature as when they were with her, or allowed to cool without her body heat, respectively (Hofer, 1994). This was one piece of evidence used to support the physiological co-regulation basis of grief.

Monk and colleagues recorded core body temperature continuously, around the clock. Core body temperature normally is lowest at 1 a.m., with a steep rise through the morning hours and a more gradual rise to mid-evening. In the pattern of core body temperature, those with CG showed a shift of half an hour earlier in circadian temperature rhythm phase. A temperature rhythm that is shifted forward can lead to early awakening. Those with CG were also 1 standard deviation worse in circadian temperature rhythm amplitude (i.e., their temperature did not have as large a rise and fall across the day). No information was provided whether the four CG participants differed in age from the other participants, which is important information, as these same changes can be seen in normal aging.

In this second study, no differences were reported for those with CG related to the percentage of sleep spent in REM, even though this variable was measured. This suggests that this sample, albeit extremely small, is a replication of the first study findings that those with CG do not show the same pattern of increased REM sleep found in depression. Clearly more data need to be collected comparing CG and depression to make a definitive statement on the role of REM sleep in these disorders.

Genetics

How might genetics affect symptoms of CG? In the field of genetics, this paradigm is referred to as a gene-by-environment interaction, abbreviated as GxE. In this case, bereavement is the environmental portion of the interaction, and likely genes are investigated to determine whether a genetic portion of the interaction exists. In other words the question is posed: What genetic vulnerabilities more often lead to CG after bereavement?

Only one study has currently been published on genetics and CG. The genetic variation that has been investigated is the gene region that contains the code for monoamine oxidase-A (MAO-A). This genetic variation functions to make more or less of the enzyme MAO-A, depending on which variation the person carries. MAO-A breaks down molecules that are familiar in psychopathology, including serotonin, dopamine, epinephrine, and norepinephrine. Thus, some people make more MAO-A and consequently they have less serotonin and dopamine (because it is broken down more quickly and therefore less available). Kersting and colleagues (2007) hypothesized that those who have the genetic variation that causes elevated MAO-A activity could have an increased vulnerability to CG.

CG is a risk factor for major depression (Boelen & Prigerson, 2007), so the study by Kersting and colleagues was done with psychiatric inpatients who were diagnosed with major depression and had a history of bereavement. To measure CG, the investigators used the ICG (Prigerson, Maciejewski, et al., 1995), categorizing those scoring 25 or above as having CG. The more active variant of the MAO-A gene was significantly associated with CG in women, whereas there was no such effect in male patients. This result means that, among depressed women, those who had the more active genetic variation and who were bereaved (i.e., GxE) were more likely to have CG. The effects of this MAO-A variation have been shown in women specifically in other psychiatric disorders, such as panic disorder and obsessive–compulsive disorder (Camarena, Cruz, de la Fuente, & Nicolini, 1998; Deckert et al., 1999).

Why study the physiology and neurobiology of CG?

As seen in this review, it is useful to consider including neurobiological and physiological markers in study designs when investigating CG, as these markers can sometimes be used to discriminate between disorders in a useful way (e.g., depression vs. CG, PTSD vs. CG), even when a clinical gestalt may be murky. Because biomarkers show promise in distinguishing CG from non-CG, it would also be useful to include them as outcome measures in treatment studies, as a multi-method way of operationalizing outcome. As with biomarkers in most affective disorders, none are yet ready to be used in a clinical setting to aid in diagnosis.

In addition, a common misconception is that the only way that a physiological understanding of CG would be used is through pharmacotherapy. However, an understanding of the physiological mechanisms in this disorder can be used in a host of ways. This includes understanding the ways in which production of neurotransmitters and activation of the body's systems are created endogenously (e.g., through warm physical contact, meditation, cognitive–behavioral therapy, rumination, suppression).

The stress of bereavement is created not just by the circumstance per se, but also by the individual's response to it. The individual's response is a psychological one and, concurrently, a physiological one. This stress response may specifically include CG symptoms. To the degree that we discover whether these symptoms are mediated by attachment (Langner & Maercker, 2005), then understanding the physiology and neurobiology of attachment will no doubt assist in treating the CG response to bereavement. Observing and documenting the physiological response to bereavement, and how it shapes and is shaped by the psychological response, may help us to improve adaptation even in the face of one of life's most stressful events.

Summary and future directions

In summary, the study of the physiology and neurobiology of CG is only at the earliest beginning, with studies nibbling around the edges of the disorder by focusing on individual variables. Self-regulation, at the psychological as well as physiological levels, may be important in coping with pangs of grief and assist in acceptance of the death of an attachment figure. Human physiology and neurobiology embody the reactivity and recovery in oscillatory waves of grief. One hypothesis is that increases in certain neurochemicals (e.g., catecholamines, oxytocin, and cortisol) following the death of a loved one may make it more likely that we reach out to other attachment figures, and make the strengthening of bonds with the living more likely during the mourning period. Another hypothesis is that a failure to mount this physiological response to the death of an attachment figure could prevent the normal social exploratory behaviors, an avoidance symptom often seen in CG.

In addition, the withdrawal of interpersonal regulators must be accommodated following the death of an attachment figure. For some, this withdrawal leads to changes in sleep, eating, concentration, and enjoyment of activities. Preliminary evidence suggests that the physiology underlying these changes is dissimilar between disorders (e.g., increased REM sleep in depression, but not in CG, and increased heart rate across time in PTSD, but not in CG). Careful comparison of these disorders is necessary to determine whether physiological markers can be useful in diagnosis, and then in differential treatment for them.

The assimilation of the reality of the death must occur in the brain for the working model of attachment to be revised. Yet another hypothesis is that if the assimilation of the new information does not occur, for psychological reasons (e.g., extreme guilt or avoidance) and/or biological ones (e.g., increased degradation of bioamines), then the adaptation to the death may be prolonged and lead to CG.

Some physiological markers of CG will correlate with a separation distress response and others will correlate with a general stress response. The physiological markers that correlate with a general stress response may occur with other stressful life events, but the physiological markers that correlate with the separation distress should be specific to the loss of an attachment figure. In addition, the physiological markers correlated specifically to the loss of an attachment figure may be pre-existing traits (endemic to the individual or to the relationship), or these physiological markers may develop, or fail to recover, across time during the adaptation process.

Most affective disorders (e.g., major depressive disorder) are better described on a continuum than as discrete categories (Prisciandaro & Roberts, 2009) and CG may well turn out to be similar in this regard. The relationship between the clinical gestalt of CG and individual biomarkers is complex. It is highly unlikely that there is a one-to-one correspondence between any particular physiological or neurobiological marker and CG. For one thing, physiological systems are multiply intertwined, and feed back information to each other, and therefore any biomarker impacts a host of other biomarkers. However, by measuring these markers, we may see what contributes to poor adaptation or what the physiological predictors of CG are. Using physiological and neurobiological variables in bereavement research as one part of a multi-method approach will only increase our understanding of the phenomena.

Notes

1 The disorder is referred to as prolonged grief disorder in the Prigerson et al. (2009) paper.
2 The disorder is referred to as traumatic grief in the Prigerson et al. (1997) paper.
3 Not reviewed here are self-reported physical health symptoms measured in some studies and found to be associated with CG symptoms or caseness.
4 Additional studies examining self-report measures of sleep in persons with CG also have been published, but the present chapter focuses solely on physiological measurements.

References

Bartels, A., & Zeki, S. (2004). The neural correlates of maternal and romantic love. *Neuroimage, 21*, 1155–1166.

Berger, M., & Riemann, D. (1993). Symposium: Normal and abnormal REM sleep regulation: REM sleep in depression – an overview. *Journal of Sleep Research, 2*, 211–223.

Berridge, K. C., Robinson, T. E., & Aldridge, J. W. (2009). Dissecting components of reward: "Liking", "wanting", and learning. *Current Opinion in Pharmacology, 9*, 65–73.

Boelen, P. A., & Prigerson, H. G. (2007). The influence of symptoms of prolonged grief disorder, depression, and anxiety on quality of life among bereaved adults: A prospective study. *European Archives of Psychiatry in Clinical Neuroscience, 257*, 444–452.

Bonanno, G. A., Neria, Y., Mancini, A., Coifman, K. G., Litz, B., & Insel, B. (2007). Is there more to complicated grief than depression and posttraumatic stress disorder? A test of incremental validity. *Journal of Abnormal Psychology, 116*, 342–351.

Bonanno, G. A., Wortman, C. B., Lehman, D. R., Tweed, R. G., Haring, M., Sonnega, J., et al. (2002). Resilience to loss and chronic grief: A prospective study from preloss to 18-months postloss. *Journal of Personality & Social Psychology, 83*, 1150–1164.

Bowlby, J. (1980). *Attachment and loss, vol. 3: Loss, sadness and depression*. New York: Basic Books.

Buckley, T., McKinley, S., Tofler, G., & Bartrop, R. (2009). Cardiovascular risk in early bereavement: A literature review and proposed mechanisms. *International Journal of Nursing Studies, 47*, 229–238.

Buckley, T., Mihailidou, A. S., Bartrop, R., McKinley, S., Ward, C., Morel-Kopp, M. C., et al. (2011). Haemodynamic changes during early bereavement: potential contribution to increased cardiovascular risk. *Heart, Lung and Circulation, 20*, 91–98.

Camarena, B., Cruz, C., de la Fuente, J. R., & Nicolini, H. (1998). A higher frequency of a low activity-related allele of the MAO-A gene in females with obsessive–compulsive disorder. *Psychiatry and Genetics, 8*, 255–257.

Deckert, J., Catalano, M., Syagailo, Y. V., Bosi, M., Okladnova, O., Di Bella, D., et al. (1999). Excess of high activity monoamine oxidase A gene promoter alleles in female patients with panic disorder. *Human Molecular Genetics, 8*, 621–624.

Depue, R. A., & Morrone-Strupinsky, J. V. (2005). A neurobehavioral model of affiliative bonding: Implications for conceptualizing a human trait of affiliation. *Behavior and Brain Science, 28*, 313–350; discussion 350–395.

Gerra, G., Monti, D., Panerai, A. E., Sacerdote, P., Anderlini, R., Avanzini, P., et al. (2003). Long-term immune-endocrine effects of bereavement: Relationships with anxiety levels and mood. *Psychiatry Research, 121*, 145–158.

Gündel, H., O'Connor, M.-F., Littrell, L., Fort, C., & Lane, R. D. (2003). Functional neuroanatomy of grief: An fMRI study. *American Journal of Psychiatry, 160*, 1946–1953.

Hazan, C., Gur-Yaish, N., & Campa, M. (2004). What does it mean to be attached? In Rholes, W. S., & Simpson, J. A. (Eds.), *Adult attachment: New directions and emerging issues* (pp. 55–85). New York: Guilford Press.

Heinrichs, M., Baumgartner, T., Kirschbaum, C., & Ehlert, U. (2003). Social support and oxytocin interact to suppress cortisol and subjective responses to psychosocial stress. *Biological Psychiatry, 54*, 1389–1398.

Hendriks, M. C., Rottenberg, J., & Vingerhoets, A. J. (2007). Can the distress-signal and arousal-reduction views of crying be reconciled? Evidence from the cardiovascular system. *Emotion, 7*, 458–463.

Hofer, M. A. (1984). Relationships as regulators: A psychobiologic perspective on bereavement. *Psychosomatic Medicine, 46*, 183–197.

Hofer, M. A. (1994). Early relationships as regulators of infant physiology and behavior. *Acta Paediatrica Supplement, 397*, 9–18.

Hofer, M. A., Wolff, C. T., Friedman, S. B., & Mason, J. W. (1972). A psychoendocrine study of bereavement. I. 17-Hydroxycorticosteroid excretion rates of parents following death of their children from leukemia. *Psychosomatic Medicine, 34*, 481–491.

Horowitz, M. J., Siegel, B., Holen, A., Bonanno, G. A., Milbrath, C., & Stinson, C. H. (1997). Diagnostic criteria for complicated grief disorder. *American Journal of Psychiatry, 154*, 904–910.

Insel, T. R. (2003). Is social attachment an addictive disorder? *Physiology & Behavior, 79*, 351–357.

Jacobs, S. C., Kasl, S. V., Ostfeld, A. M., Berkman, L., Kosten, T. R., & Charpentier, P. (1986). The measurement of grief: Bereaved versus non-bereaved. *Hospice Journal, 2*, 21–36.

Jacobs, S. C., Mason, J., Kosten, T. R., Kasl, S. V., Ostfeld, A. M., & Wahby, V. (1987). Urinary free cortisol and separation anxiety early in the course of bereavement and threatened loss. *Biological Psychiatry, 22*, 148–152.

Jacobs, S. C., Mason, J. W., Kosten, T. R., Wahby, V., Kasl, S. V., & Ostfeld, A. M. (1986). Bereavement and catecholamines. *Journal of Psychosomatic Research, 30*, 489–496.

Kersting, A., Kroker, K., Horstmann, J., Baune, B. T., Hohoff, C., Mortensen, L. S., et al. (2007). Association of MAO-A variant with complicated grief in major depression. *Neuropsychobiology, 56*, 191–196.

Knutson, B., Adams, C. M., Fong, G. W., & Hommer, D. (2001). Anticipation of increasing monetary reward selectively recruits nucleus accumbens. *Journal of Neuroscience, 21*, RC159.

Kosfeld, M., Heinrichs, M., Zak, P. J., Fischbacher, U., & Fehr, E. (2005). Oxytocin increases trust in humans. *Nature, 435*, 673–676.

Kovacs, G. L., Sarnyai, Z., & Szabo, G. (1998). Oxytocin and addiction: A review. *Psychoneuroendocrinology, 23*, 945–962.

Langner, R., & Maercker, A. (2005). Complicated grief as a stress response disorder: Evaluating diagnostic criteria in a German sample. *Journal of Psychosomatic Research, 58*, 235–242.

Lim, M. M., & Young, L. J. (2006). Neuropeptidergic regulation of affiliative behavior and social bonding in animals. *Hormones and Behavior, 50*, 506–517.

McDermott, O. D., Prigerson, H. G., Reynolds, C. F. III, Houck, P. R., Dew, M. A., Hall, M., et al. (1997). Sleep in the wake of complicated grief symptoms: An exploratory study. *Biological Psychiatry, 41*, 710–716.

Monk, T. H., Begley, A. E., Billy, B. D., Fletcher, M. E., Germain, A., Mazumdar, S., et al. (2008). Sleep and circadian rhythms in spousally bereaved seniors. *Chronobiology International, 25*, 83–98.

Nelson, E. E., & Panksepp, J. (1998). Brain substrates of infant–mother attachment: Contributions of opioids, oxytocin, and norepinephrine. *Neuroscience and Biobehavioral Review, 22*, 437–452.

O'Connor, M. F., Wellisch, D. K., Stanton, A. L., Eisenberger, N. I., Irwin, M. R., & Lieberman, M. D. (2008). Craving love? Enduring grief activates brain's reward center. *NeuroImage, 42*, 969–972.

Panksepp, J., Knutson, B., & Burgdorf, J. (2002). The role of brain emotional systems in addictions: A neuro-evolutionary perspective and new 'self-report' animal model. *Addiction, 97*, 459–469.

Panksepp, J., Nelson, E., & Bekkedal, M. (1997). Brain systems for the mediation of social separation-distress and social-reward: Evolutionary antecedents and neuropeptide intermediaries. *Annals of the New York Academy of Sciences, 807*, 78–100.

Prigerson, H. G., Bierhals, A. J., Kasl, S. V., Reynolds, C. F. III, Shear, M. K., Day, N., et al. (1997). Traumatic grief as a risk factor for mental and physical morbidity. *American Journal of Psychiatry, 154*, 616–623.

Prigerson, H. G., Frank, E., Kasl, S. V., Reynolds, C. F., III, Anderson, B., Zubenko, G. S., et al. (1995). Complicated grief and bereavement-related depression as distinct disorders: Preliminary empirical validation in elderly bereaved spouses. *American Journal of Psychiatry, 152*, 22–30.

Prigerson, H. G., Horowitz, M. J., Jacobs, S. C., Parkes, C. M., Aslan, M., Goodkin, K., et al. (2009). Prolonged grief disorder: Psychometric validation of criteria proposed for DSM-V and ICD-11. *PLoS Medicine, 6*, e1000121.

Prigerson, H. G., & Jacobs, S. C. (2001). Traumatic grief as a distinct disorder: A rationale, consensus criteria, and preliminary empirical test. In Stroebe M. S., Hansson, R. O., Stroebe, W., & Schut, H. (Eds.), *Handbook of bereavement research: Consequences, coping and care* (pp. 613–645). Washington, DC: American Psychological Association.

Prigerson, H. G., Maciejewski, P. K., Reynolds, C. F., Bierhals, A. J., Newsom, J. T., Fasiczka, A., et al. (1995). Inventory of Complicated Grief: A scale to measure maladaptive symptoms of loss. *Psychiatry Research, 59*, 65–79.

Prisciandaro, J. J., & Roberts, J. E. (2009). A comparison of the predictive abilities of dimensional and categorical models of unipolar depression in the National Comorbidity Survey. *Psychological Medicine, 39*, 1087–1096.

Romans, S. E., & Clarkson, R. F. (2008). Crying as a gendered indicator of depression. *Journal of Nervous and Mental Disease, 196*, 237–243.

Sbarra, D. A., & Hazan, C. (2008). Coregulation, dysregulation, self-regulation: An integrative analysis and empirical agenda for understanding adult attachment, separation, loss, and recovery. *Personality and Social Psychology Review, 12*, 141–167.

Shear, M. K., Monk, T., Houck, P., Melhem, N., Frank, E., Reynolds, C., et al. (2007). An attachment-based model of complicated grief including the role of avoidance. *European Archives of Psychiatry and Clinical Neuroscience, 257*, 453–461.

Shear, M. K., & Shair, H. (2005). Attachment, loss, and complicated grief. *Developmental Psychobiology, 47*, 253–267.

Shear, M. K., Simon, N., Wall, M., Zisook, S., Neimeyer, R., Duan, N., et al. (2011). Complicated grief and related bereavement issues for DSM-5. *Depression and Anxiety, 28*, 103–117.

Stroebe, M. (1994). The broken heart phenomenon: An examination of the mortality of bereavement. *Journal of Community & Applied Social Psychology, 4*, 47–61.

Stroebe, M., Schut, H., & Stroebe, W. (2007). Health outcomes of bereavement. *Lancet, 370*, 1960–1973.

Young, L. J., & Wang, Z. (2004). The neurobiology of pair bonding. *Nature Neuroscience, 7*, 1048–1054.

Part V

Treatment of complicated grief

Principles, paradigms, and procedures

16 Prolonged grief disorder

Cognitive–behavioral theory and therapy

*Paul A. Boelen, Marcel van den Hout, and
Jan van den Bout*

Introduction

For a minority of people, the death of a loved one precipitates the development of prolonged grief disorder (PGD), or complicated grief (CG) as it has also been named (e.g., Prigerson et al., 2009). PGD has been defined as a clinical condition that encompasses specific grief reactions (including separation distress and difficulties accepting the loss and moving on without the lost person) that cause significant distress and disability at least 6 months after the death occurred. Symptoms of PGD are distinct from normal grief, bereavement-related depression, posttraumatic stress disorder (PTSD), and other anxiety symptoms and syndromes, and, if left untreated, associated with significant impairments in health and quality of life (Prigerson et al., 2009; see also Chapter 7 in this volume).

Parallel to the growing recognition of PGD as a distinct disorder, increasing attention is being given to its treatment, with the most well-tested and effective recent therapies being based in cognitive–behavioral therapy (CBT). For instance, Shear, Frank, Houck, and Reynolds (2005) found "complicated grief treatment" – a 16-session treatment containing elements CBT such as imaginal exercises to revisit the death (exposure) and working toward achievement of personal goals – to be effective in reducing PGD. Wagner, Knaevelsrud, and Maercker (2006) found Internet-based CBT, including elements of confronting the loss, cognitive restructuring, and social sharing, to be effective in reducing PGD and concomitant depressive and anxious symptoms. We examined the effectiveness of a 12-session CBT for PGD, based on a cognitive–behavioral conceptualization of the condition (Boelen, de Keijser, van den Hout, & van den Bout, 2007). Compared with supportive counseling, CBT was considerably more effective in ameliorating PGD symptoms.

The present chapter addresses the theory and treatment of PGD from the perspective of cognitive–behavioral theorizing, with a focus on our own theoretical approach (Boelen, van den Hout, & van den Bout, 2006). Notably, this approach bears resemblance to other recent theoretical approaches to PGD (Shear, Boelen, & Neimeyer, 2011). Specifically, this chapter will (1) introduce a theoretical basis of CBT for PGD, (2) describe key interventions included in this approach, and (3) review research on its theoretical underpinnings and effectiveness.

Theoretical basis of CBT for PGD

One puzzling aspect of PGD is that, although people with PGD are so bound up with the loss that they have difficulty functioning, the loss continues to feel unreal. That is, for people suffering PGD, the disbelief, pangs of pain, and separation distress that normally occur intensely early after the death exacerbate rather than gradually fade. We formulated a cognitive–behavioral model that attempts to explain why, in some individuals, acute grief reactions persist and exacerbate (Boelen, van den Hout, & van den Bout, 2006). This model proposes that three interrelated processes account for this: (1) insufficient elaboration and integration of the loss within autobiographical memory; (2) negative thinking; and (3) anxious and depressive avoidance behaviors.

This model draws heavily on general cognitive–behavioral theorizing (Beck, 1976) and multirepresentational models of psychopathology, in which various forms of mental representation (cognitions, schemas, image representations, distributed networks) and behavioral and cognitive responses are combined to explain psychopathology (Dalgleish, 2004; Teasdale, 1999). This model is particularly inspired by Ehlers and Clark's (2000) cognitive model of PTSD. Next, these three processes will be described in more detail.

Insufficient elaboration and integration of the loss

Prototypically, in uncomplicated grief, explicit (i.e., consciously accessible) knowledge that the separation is irreversible gradually gets integrated with existing knowledge about the self and the lost person, which is part of the autobiographical memory base. This process is fostered by actively elaborating on the implications of the loss for the self in the past, present, and future, as well as by confronting external changes caused by the loss. Thus, through a process of (active) elaboration, explicit knowledge about the loss gradually gets connected with implicit memory knowledge about the self and the relation with the lost person. The effect of this process is that the loss becomes part of the life story of the mourner and gradually becomes a less disruptive, more normalized (albeit still painful) event (cf. Ehlers & Clark, 2000).

Our CBT model postulates that, in PGD, this process of elaboration and integration is stalled or incomplete. This has several effects. A first effect is that, because memory knowledge about the separation is disconnected from other memory knowledge, the death continues to be a very shocking, unbelievable event. At the same time, because the loss is so emotional and consequential, all kinds of stimuli easily elicit memories, thoughts, and feelings that are associated with the death such that – eventually – everything is a reminder of it. Stated differently, the lack of connectivity between memories of the loss and other knowledge is assumed to cause these memories to continue to intrude into awareness, causing PTSD-like symptoms of intrusions, and a continued sense of shock, as if the loss happened very recently rather than months or years ago (cf. Conway & Pleydell-Pearce, 2000).

A second effect is that too little adjustment of knowledge about the self takes place, as a result of which the person is left with a reduced sense of clarity about the self. Integration of the reality of the loss with knowledge about the self is a prerequisite for mourners to be able to redefine who they are without the lost person. To the extent that this integration fails, a mismatch exists between the external reality (absence of loved one) and self-knowledge (partially defined in terms of lost person). This, in turn, can lead to an impaired sense of self-clarity: a situation in which roles, goals, personal attributes, and other aspects of the self that the lost person co-defined are temporarily unclear, fragmented, and unstable (Campbell et al., 1996). This reduced self-clarity probably contributes to the wish to revert back to the pre-loss period, difficulties in accepting the loss, isolation, and a sense that life lacks meaning – symptoms that are all hallmark features of PGD (Boelen, Keijsers, & van den Hout, 2012).

The third effect is that no adjustment of the "relationship representation" takes place, so separation distress persists. Individuals form mental representations of relationship with close others as part of autobiographical memory (Bowlby, 1980; Mikulincer, 2006). These contain information about emotional (anxiety, despair) and behavioral responses (crying, searching) that are activated when the relationship is threatened and that serve to maintain proximity and felt security. When a loved one dies, a process normally unfolds in which the fact that the loss is irreversible connects with the relationship representation. This coincides with a gradual reduction of such reactions of separation distress. To the extent that there is a lack of integration of the loss with the relationship representation, the absence of the lost person will continue to generate symptoms of separation distress that are central to PGD. This notion links up with Shear and Shair's (2005) biobehavioral model of bereavement, which also proposes that "symptoms of acute grief . . . usually resolve following revision of the internalized representation of the deceased to incorporate the reality of the death. Failure to accomplish this integration results in the syndrome of complicated grief' (p. 253).

In sum, the notion that, in persons suffering from PGD, information about the separation is insufficiently connected with memory knowledge about the self and the lost person helps to explain how the loss can be experienced in different ways: how it can be thought about constantly but still feel shocking and unreal, how mourners can say that the loss has changed them, but still feel left with a reduced self-clarity, and how they rationally know that their loss is permanent but, at a less conscious level, continue to experience the separation as reversible.

Persistent negative thinking

As a second process, the CBT conceptualization proposes that, unlike people who recover from loss, individuals with PGD have rigid negative cognitions and assumptions that contribute to the maintenance and exacerbation of their acute grief symptoms (Boelen, van den Hout, & van den Bout, 2006). Two categories of cognitions are particularly important. The first includes negative global cognitions about the self ("I am a worthless person without my husband"), life ("Life has no meaning any more"), and the future ("I will certainly never find joy again"). These global negative views may develop when the loss shatters pre-existing positive views. For instance, the loss of a child may lead to negative views of self and life, when this event is strongly at odds with pre-existing positive views and the person is unable to maintain positive views taking into account the loss event. Such beliefs can also arise when the loss reactivates pre-existing negative assumptions. The death of a loving partner may reactivate negative views that one is a worthless person. The importance of global negative views of self and life in emotional problems following loss accords with earlier theories of coping with loss (Janoff-Bulman, 1992) and trauma (Foa & Rothbaum, 1998; see also Park, 2010). These theories have emphasized that recovery from such events hinges on a person's ability to maintain positive views of self and life following such events.

The second category includes catastrophic misinterpretations of one's own reactions to the loss. Bereaved people have to manage painful emotions, thoughts, and memories. Acceptance of these responses fosters emotional processing. Problems arise when people interpret these responses in a catastrophic fashion. Mourners may label the intensity of their sadness as signaling loss of control, view their numbness as announcing depression, and interpret vivid intrusions as reflecting insanity. Such misinterpretations are assumed to fuel distress and avoidance and to prevent the person from reviewing and adjusting to the loss's implications. Trauma research has shown that catastrophic interpretations of initial posttraumatic stress symptoms (e.g., "If I think back to this accident, I will go out of my mind") contribute to the development of chronic PTSD (Mayou, Ehlers, & Bryant, 2002). After bereavement, similar misinterpretations are assumed to contribute to acute grief reactions becoming chronic.

Anxious and depressive avoidance

Anxious avoidance refers to avoidance of confrontation with the reality, implications, and pain of the loss, driven by the fear that this confrontation will be intolerable and unbearable. The importance of avoidance behaviors in maintaining grief draws from early behaviorist accounts in which pathological grief was essentially seen as a phobia for normal grief reactions (Ramsay, 1977). Anxious avoidance resembles the concept of experiential avoidance, referring to attempts to alter the frequency, duration, or form of negatively evaluated private events such as thoughts, feelings, and memories (e.g., Hayes, Wilson, Gifford, Follette, & Strohsahl, 1996). It is the opposite of experiential acceptance, reflecting the willingness to endure unwanted private events without judgment and defense. Anxious avoidance can manifest itself in situational avoidance of places, pictures, and people associated with the loss. It may also take the form of cognitive avoidance behaviors, including the suppression of unwanted thoughts and memories, or rumination about events surrounding the death (e.g., "Why did the loss occur?," "How could it have been prevented?") as a means to keep thoughts and memories that are even more painful to think about out of awareness.

Anxious avoidance can be distinguished from *depressive avoidance*, which refers to withdrawal from social, occupational, and recreational activities that could be rewarding and provide a continued sense of self. The concept draws from early behavioral models of depression that implicated decreases in non-depressive, rewarding behaviors as a key maintaining factor in clinical depression (e.g., Jacobson, Martell, & Dimidjian, 2001). After bereavement, depressive avoidance can occur when the loss interrupts access to reinforcers for healthy behavior. As Ramsay (1977) put it, "A widow whose reinforcers consisted of doing everything with and for her husband suddenly finds herself left with no positive reinforcers when he dies" (p. 133). In addition, it can occur when mourners lack the skills needed to achieve valued goals in the absence of the lost person, or when they think that engaging in activities without the lost person is disrespectful to him or her. Negative cognitions are assumed to be important in depressive avoidance as well, especially those concerning the effects of engaging in potentially helpful behaviors (e.g., "Meeting friends will not make me feel better") and one's abilities to do so (e.g., "I am unable to take up new responsibilities"). The reduction of interest and competence in autonomous functioning, implicated in the concept of depressive avoidance, also results from inhibition of the biobehavioral exploratory system circuitry that occurs with the activation of attachment responses following loss (Elliot & Reis, 2003; Shear et al., 2011).

Both forms of avoidance are detrimental. For instance, anxious avoidance is detrimental because it causes distress and interferes with the elaboration and integration of the irreversibility of the loss and the implications thereof. Depressive avoidance is detrimental because it interferes with the experience of positive emotions and maintains negative views of the self, life, and future.

Interaction between, and the mediating role of, the three processes

The three processes are assumed not only to directly contribute to symptoms of PGD, but also to influence each other. For instance, elaboration of the loss, and subsequent integration of the reality of the loss with memory knowledge about the self and the lost relationship, is likely to be blocked when reviewing the consequences of the loss brings to mind negative thoughts about the self, life, and the future. Likewise, a tendency to engage in anxious avoidance is likely to prevent such integration. Negative cognitions and avoidance behaviors also have a mutual impact. For instance, negative cognitions about the self and life are likely to maintain a depressive cycle of withdrawal and inactivity. Catastrophic misinterpretations of grief reactions can contribute to anxious avoidance behaviors, which, in turn, prevent correction of such misinterpretations.

Important also is that the three processes are assumed to mediate the impact of various established risk factors for poor bereavement outcome. These include personality characteristics of the bereaved individual, such as neuroticism and insecure attachment style; features characterizing the loss, such as who died and the mode of death; and events and circumstances occurring in the aftermath (e.g., perceived social responses). Put another way, it is proposed that the three processes are intermediate mechanisms that explain why, for instance, people who are insecurely attached have an elevated chance of developing PGD (cf. Wijngaards-de Meij et al., 2007). This is so because these people are likely to have more difficulties in accepting and integrating the reality of the loss (Process 1), maintaining a positive view of self (Process 2), and engaging in helpful coping behaviors (Process 3), as a result of which they have a greater chance of developing PGD. The notion of mediation is important because it sheds light on changeable mechanisms (e.g., negative cognitions) that can be targeted in treatment, to curb the effect of more static, less easily changeable risk factors (e.g., personality features) on the development and maintenance of PGD.

Cognitive–behavioral treatment

The aim of CBT for PGD is to alleviate persisting acute grief symptoms and to help the person to achieve valued goals. To accomplish this, (1) the loss needs to be integrated with existing knowledge, (2) unhelpful thinking patterns need to be identified and altered, and (3) unhelpful avoidance strategies need to replaced by more helpful ones. Different conventional CBT interventions can be used to achieve these aims. Examples of interventions are described below.

Promoting elaboration and integration of the loss

A key intervention to directly target the lack of integration is exposure. During exposure, the person is encouraged to gradually confront the painful reality of the loss and to elaborate upon its implications. Several means can be used to achieve this aim. The person suffering from PGD can be asked to tell or write a detailed story about the events surrounding the death. This can be followed up by repeated reliving of the most painful aspects (or so-called hot spots) of the story. Such exposure is similar to revisiting the death, an intervention central to Shear's "complicated grief treatment" (Shear et al., 2005, 2011). This exercise uses a procedure similar to prolonged exposure in the treatment of PTSD (Foa & Rothbaum, 1998) and includes a reliving and subsequent further discussion of the most troubling moments surrounding the death.

Imaginal exposure or reliving can be complemented with writing assignments. People suffering from PGD can be instructed to write a detailed account of the moments surrounding the loss: a procedure that is central to Internet-based CBT for PGD (Wagner et al., 2006; Chapter 17 in this volume). In our own experience, it is particularly useful to encourage them to write a letter to the lost person, carefully reviewing what is missed most now that he or she is dead. Within-session exposure can also be complemented with exposure to situations or stimuli outside therapy. Visiting the hospital where the loved one died or visiting places the lost person always used to visit may help people with PGD to accept that the loss occurred and to put it in the past.

As applied in this manner, exposure is not used to promote emotional habituation to painful memories and emotions. Instead, it is used to identify the most painful memories that need to be confronted and worked through in treatment and the most important guilty, angry, shameful, and frightening beliefs that need to be re-evaluated. It is also used to encourage the person with PGD to fully connect with the reality of the loss and to lessen the disbelief. In addition, it is meant to help the person to experience that experiential avoidance of the loss is fruitless, that he or she has the strength to confront the loss, and that doing so lessens the pain and fosters adjustment.

Changing maladaptive cognitions and assumptions

Cognitive restructuring aims to alleviate emotional suffering by (1) identifying (maladaptive) cognitions that underlie a person's suffering in particular situations and circumstances; (2) examining the validity and utility of these cognitions; and (3) reformulating these cognitions incorporating information gathered in step 2 into cognitions that are associated with less suffering and facilitate constructive action. Cognitive restructuring focuses on the idiosyncratic meanings of the loss and its sequelae, with a particular focus on global negative views of the self, life, and the future and catastrophic misinterpretation of grief reactions. In identifying maladaptive cognitions, it is important to search for relevant cognitions. Not every negative cognition can be changed or should be changed. Instead, the therapist should look for those cognitions that are central to the problems of the person, that interfere with the achievement of valued goals, and that are falsifiable. For example, it is hard to dispute the cognition "Life is meaningless" but easier to discuss the validity of the cognition "Life has no meaning now, and I probably won't find meaning in life in the future."

When relevant cognitions are identified, both verbal and behavioral techniques can be used to change these cognitions. An example of the former one is using Socratic questioning to investigate the validity ("How do I know that what I think is true?," "What evidence is there in favor of and against this thought?") and utility ("What will happen if I continue thinking this way?," "What is the worst thing that can happen if what I think it true?") of a particular cognition.

Behavioral techniques include behavioral experiments. These are specified actions/assignments that patients undertake in order to test specific maladaptive cognitions and catastrophic misinterpretations as well as the validity of alternative, more positive predictions (cf. Bennett-Levy et al., 2004). They are particularly suitable for testing specific negative predictions (with an *If . . . , then . . .* format) that lead to negative feelings and block constructive action. For instance, a cognition such as "If I think over the implications of this loss, I will get so sad that I would go crazy" can be tested by encouraging the person to gradually review the consequences of the loss within the safe context of the therapy. A negative cognition such as "If I share my feelings about this loss, then nobody would probably respond in a supportive manner" could be tested by encouraging the person to set up a meeting with a friend to talk about how he or she has felt recently.

Writing assignments can be used to complement within-session cognitive restructuring. For instance, people suffering from PGD can be instructed to write a supporting letter to an imaginary friend who has the exact same problems, with an emphasis on trying to help this friend to re-evaluate maladaptive cognitions about the loss (see Wagner et al., 2006; Chapter 17 in this volume).

Reducing anxious and depressive avoidance

In targeting anxious avoidance, cognitive restructuring is used to identify and discuss the prediction that underlies the avoidance of particular loss-related stimuli (e.g., "If I looked at a photo of my deceased wife, the pain would be so intense that I'd turn into an emotional wreck"). Then, behavioral experiments, as described in the previous section, can be used to test the validity of the prediction further (Bennett-Levy et al., 2004). This often means that people are encouraged to confront the avoided stimuli, in order to experience that doing so alleviates rather than attenuates the suffering. Behavioral experiments resemble exposure interventions. Notably, though, behavioral experiments are explicitly meant to change specific assumptions, whereas exposure interventions can have various aims (including identification of "hot spot" memories and maladaptive cognitions, and encouraging elaboration of the loss).

Anxious avoidance may coincide with particular strategies developed to minimize distress – strategies that are reminiscent of "safety behaviors" in anxiety disorders. For instance, people suffering PGD may engage in compulsive proximity-seeking behavior (e.g., visiting the graveyard twice a day), or ruminative thinking about why the loss occurred, in order to minimize confrontation with the pain associated with the irreversibility of the death. Response prevention can be used to gradually eliminate such behavior. The procedure resembles response prevention as applied in the treatment of obsessive–compulsive disorder (OCD). Yet, unlike in the treatment of OCD, in which response prevention is used to alter predicted external threat, in PGD treatment it is used to confront valid thoughts and feelings that have to be dealt with in treatment.

Behavioral activation is an important intervention in targeting depressive avoidance. In behavioral activation, people are instructed to register activities and mood for some days or weeks, in order to experience how activity improves mood. Then, behavioral interventions are applied to help the person to re-engage in rewarding activities (Jacobson et al., 2001). In addition, treatment could focus on identification of social, occupational, or recreational goals, and planning actions necessary to achieve goals. Dependent on the nature of the goals, this can be accompanied by social skill training, problem-solving skill training, and time management training (Jacobson et al., 2001). Personal goal work is also central to "complicated grief treatment" (Shear et al., 2011); it is based on the idea that working toward the achievement of valued goals fosters the experience of positive emotions, the ability to solve problems, and the motivation to confront painful information. In behavioral activation, there is a clear focus on action, irrespective of certain aversive thoughts and mood states. A key idea behind this approach is that it is not necessary to change mood before behavior can be changed but, on the contrary, behavior change can precede improvement of mood. A further idea is that activation and working toward the achievement of valued goals can facilitate self-clarity and a continued sense of self (Ehlers, 2006).

Research on CBT theory and treatment for PGD

In this section we will review evidence that supports the CBT theory and treatment of PGD.

Theory

Because the underpinnings of CBT for PGD draw heavily on existing cognitive–behavioral theorizing (Beck, 1976; Dalgleish, 2004; Ehlers & Clark, 2000), the extensive body of evidence supporting the view that unhelpful thoughts, behaviors, and memory processes indeed work in concert, maintaining all kinds of emotional suffering, provides indirect support for the CBT approach to PGD. However, an increasing number of studies have directly investigated causes and correlates of PGD from the perspective of CBT.

For instance, earlier research findings of a linkage between grief severity and negative views about meaningfulness of the world and the worthiness of the self (Schwartzberg & Janoff-Bulman, 1991) and self-blame and other-blame (Field & Bonanno, 2001) accord with the importance of negative cognitions in grief. In several of our own studies, we found evidence for a significant linkage between negative cognitions and assumptions and PGD severity. For instance, in a prospective study, stronger endorsement of negative assumptions about the self, life, and the future in the early stages of grief predicted more severe PGD and depression across 2 years post loss (Boelen, van den Bout, & van den Hout, 2006). Furthermore, in cross-sectional and prospective studies (Boelen, van den Bout, & van den Hout, 2003, 2010), we found evidence that catastrophic misinterpretations of grief reactions were associated with more severe PGD as well as with tendencies to experientially avoid the pain of the loss. The importance of these misinterpretations in predicting PGD was also supported in a large-scale longitudinal study by Van der Houwen, Stroebe, Schut, Stroebe, and van den Bout (2010).

Research has also provided evidence for the importance of avoidance behaviors in PGD. For instance, generic measures of deliberate avoidance of loss-related stimuli have been found to be significantly associated with loss-related distress in several studies (e.g., Bonanno, Papa, Lalande, Nanping, & Noll, 2005; Shear et al., 2007). In a cross-sectional study, we found evidence that indices of situational and cognitive avoidance were associated with PGD (Boelen & van den Hout, 2008). Importantly, the strength of the association was stronger in mourners who strongly endorsed catastrophic misinterpretations, attesting to the notion that avoidance strategies interact with catastrophic misinterpretations in maintaining PGD. A further cross-sectional study showed that anxious and depressive avoidance are separate constructs having distinct associations with PGD severity (Boelen & van den Bout, 2010). Several studies have pointed at a linkage between PGD and difficulties to retrieve specific memories (e.g., Chapter 13 in this volume). Given that such difficulties are assumed to reflect avoidant tendencies, these studies also support the importance of avoidance in maintaining PGD.

Relatively few studies have as yet addressed the hypothesis that PGD is associated with a lack of connectivity between explicit knowledge of the loss and implicit memory knowledge. Although this is mainly an implicit process occurring at the level of the autobiographical memory base, it is postulated to manifest itself in at least two introspectively accessible phenomena. The first is a sense of unrealness that can be defined as a subjective sense of uncertainty or ambivalence about the irreversibility of the separation. The second is a reduced sense of clarity about the self. In a series of studies we found evidence that increased levels of PGD are indeed associated with a greater sense of "unrealness" about the loss (even when controlling for negative cognitions, avoidance, and concomitant depression) and with an impaired sense of self-clarity (Boelen, 2010; Boelen et al., 2012). Two studies by Maccallum and Bryant provided further support for a linkage between PGD and insufficient emotional processing at the level of auto-biographical memory. In the first of these, people with PGD were found to report more self-defining memories (i.e., vivid memories comprising enduring concerns about the self) related with the lost person than people without PGD (Maccallum & Bryant, 2008). This can also be taken as evidence that PGD is associated with an impairment in the adjustment of self-representational knowledge. In a second study, PGD patients were found to have an attentional bias for information related with death and separation (Maccallum & Bryant, 2010) – a finding that accords with the notion that PGD is characterized by a reduced integration of such knowledge with other autobiographical knowledge.

Two studies provided evidence for the hypothesis that a lack of integration, negative thinking, and avoidance behaviors indeed mediate the impact of established personality-related and situational risk factors on PGD severity. In a cross-sectional study, these three processes were found to mediate the associations of neuroticism and attachment insecurity with PGD severity (Boelen & Klugkist, 2011). In a longitudinal study by Van der Houwen et al. (2010), catastrophic misinterpretations were found to mediate the impact of several risk factors on PGD, including gender, neuroticism, and expectedness of the death.

Treatment

CBT has consistently been found to be an effective treatment for a wide range of disorders (Beck, 2005). Again, this indirectly supports the relevance of this approach for treating PGD. More direct evidence for the effectiveness of CBT interventions comes from early studies by Mawson, Marks, Ramm, and Stern (1981) and Sireling, Cohen, and Marks (1988). In these studies, exposure to loss-related stimuli was found to lead to reduction in symptoms of problematic forms of grief. As noted, some of the more recently conducted treatment studies have also provided evidence for the effectiveness of CBT for PGD. In a large trial, Shear et al. (2005) compared the effectiveness of "complicated grief treatment" with the effects of interpersonal psychotherapy. The former treatment was significantly more effective in terms of effect sizes and the time it took before significant reductions in CG symptoms occurred than the latter approach. Wagner et al. (2006) subjected patients with PGD to an Internet-based CBT treatment. In comparison with patients in a waiting-list control group, those who underwent the treatment experienced a greater reduction in PGD and related symptoms.

In our own treatment trial we randomly allocated 54 people with PGD to one of three treatments: one of two CBT treatments or non-directive supportive treatment (Boelen et al., 2007). The two CBT conditions consisted of six 45-minute manual-based sessions of cognitive restructuring (CR) and six sessions of exposure therapy (ET) applied in two orders (CR + ET and ET + CR). The six sessions of CR focused on explanation of the rationale of CR and learning to identify, dispute, and alter negative cognitions. ET sessions included narrating the story of the loss in detail, identification of internal and external reminders of the loss that were avoided, and gradual confrontation with these reminders. Different forms of exposure were used (e.g., exposure in vitro when patients avoided particular memories, response prevention when they engaged in compulsive proximity-seeking behaviors). Results showed that symptoms of PGD and general psychopathology declined significantly more in people allocated to the CBT treatments than in those allocated to supportive counseling. For instance, in the intention to treat analysis, pre-treatment to post-treatment effect sizes (Cohen's d) on the Inventory of Complicated Grief, a well-validated measure of PGD (Prigerson et al., 1995), were 0.87 for the CR + ET condition and 1.29 for the ET + CR condition, compared with 0.42 for the counseling condition. Effect sizes for CBT conditions are large according to conventional guidelines and resemble the effect size of 1.35 in the intention-to-treat analyses found by Shear et al. (2005) for their PGD treatment. In follow-up analyses, we found that stronger reduction in PGD severity was significantly associated with stronger reductions in negative cognitions and avoidance. Although this was not a formal test of mediation, outcomes support the relevance of targeting negative thinking and avoidance in the treatment of PGD (Boelen, de Keijser, van den Hout, & van den Bout, 2011).

Closing comments

In CBT perspectives on PGD (Boelen, van den Hout, & van den Bout, 2006; Shear et al., 2005, 2011; Wagner et al., 2006) it is hypothesized that memory processes, negative cognitions, and avoidance behaviors play a key role in the development and maintenance of PGD. As outlined in this chapter, there is increasing evidence supporting this hypothesis. Nonetheless, more work needs to be done to test basic premises of CBT perspectives on PGD. For instance, studies conducted to date have mostly relied on self-report measures. It would be relevant for future studies to use other methods to study the role of memory processes, cognitions, and behaviors in PGD, including methods based on social cognition and diary-keeping methods to map out avoidance behaviors. In addition, experimental research is needed to test the proposed directions of causality between variables.

More work obviously also needs to be done in the area of CBT treatment for PGD. Although the findings summarized in this chapter support the potential strength of CBT as a treatment of PGD, there is still ample scope for improving this treatment. For instance, in our own study (Boelen et al., 2007), only 32.6% of patients randomly assigned to the CBT conditions showed clinically significant reductions in PGD severity. This being the case, it seems important to further refine the recent promising treatments. It is important for future studies to try to disentangle the effects of specific components of treatment for specific subgroups of people suffering PGD. It is also important to enhance clarity on mechanisms of change of CBT, that is, whether or not CBT indeed produces alleviation of distress because it lessens negative cognitions and avoidance. Notwithstanding these considerations, there are reasons to be optimistic about the explanatory value and clinical usefulness of applying cognitive–behavioral theorizing to the study and treatment of persons with PGD.

References

Beck, A. T. (1976). *Cognitive therapy and the emotional disorders*. New York: International Universities Press.

Beck, A. T. (2005). The current state of cognitive therapy: A 40-year retrospective. *Archives of General Psychiatry, 62*, 953–959.

Bennett-Levy, J., Butler, G., Fennell, M. J. V., Hackmann, A., Mueller, M. & Westbrook, D. (Eds.) (2004). *The Oxford guide to behavioural experiments in cognitive therapy.* Oxford, Oxford University Press.

Boelen, P. A. (2010). A sense of "unrealness" about the death of a loved-one: An exploratory study of its role in emotional complications among bereaved individuals. *Applied Cognitive Psychology, 24*, 238–251.

Boelen, P. A., & van den Bout, J. (2010). Anxious and depressive avoidance and symptoms of prolonged grief, depression, and posttraumatic stress-disorder. *Psychologica Belgica, 50*, 49–67.

Boelen, P. A., van den Bout, J., & van den Hout, M. A. (2003). The role of negative interpretations of grief reactions in emotional problems after bereavement. *Journal of Behavior Therapy and Experimental Psychiatry, 34*, 225–238.

Boelen, P. A., van den Bout, J., & van den Hout, M. A. (2006). Negative cognitions and avoidance in emotional problems after bereavement: A prospective study. *Behaviour Research and Therapy, 44*, 1657–1672.

Boelen, P. A., van den Bout, J., & van den Hout, M. A. (2010). A prospective examination of catastrophic misinterpretations and experiential avoidance in emotional distress following loss. *Journal of Nervous and Mental Disease, 198*, 252–257.

Boelen, P. A., & van den Hout, M. A. (2008). The role of threatening misinterpretations and avoidance in emotional problems after loss. *Behavioural and Cognitive Psychotherapy, 36*, 71–88.

Boelen, P. A., van den Hout, M. A., & van den Bout, J. (2006). A cognitive–behavioral conceptualization of complicated grief. *Clinical Psychology: Science and Practice, 13*, 109–128.

Boelen, P. A., de Keijser, J., van den Hout, M. A., & van den Bout, J. (2007). Treatment of complicated grief: A comparison between cognitive behavioral therapy and supportive counseling. *Journal of Consulting and Clinical Psychology, 75*, 277–284.

Boelen, P. A., de Keijser, J., van den Hout, M. A., & van den Bout, J. (2011). Factors associated with outcome of cognitive behavioral therapy for complicated grief: A preliminary study. *Clinical Psychology & Psychotherapy, 18*, 284–291.

Boelen, P. A., Keijsers, L., & van den Hout, M. A. (2012). The role of self-concept clarity in prolonged grief disorder. *Journal of Nervous and Mental Disease, 200*, 56–62.

Boelen, P. A., & Klugkist, I. (2011). Cognitive behavioural variables mediate the associations of neuroticism and attachment insecurity with prolonged grief disorder severity. *Anxiety, Stress, & Coping, 24*, 291–307.

Bonanno, G. A., Papa, A., Lalande, K., Nanping, Z., & Noll, J. G. (2005). Grief processing and deliberate grief avoidance: A prospective comparison of bereaved spouses and parents in the United States and China. *Journal of Consulting and Clinical Psychology, 73*, 86–98.

Bowlby, J. (1980). *Attachment and loss, vol. 3: Loss: Sadness and depression*. New York: Basic Books.

Campbell J. D., Trapnell, P. D., Heine, S. J., Katz, I. M., Lavallee, LF, & Lehmann D. R. (1996). Self-concept clarity: Measurement, personality correlates and cultural boundaries. *Journal of Personality and Social Psychology, 70*, 141–156.

Conway, M. A., & Pleydell-Pearce, C. W. (2000). The construction of autobiographical memories in the self-memory system. *Psychological Review, 107*, 261–288.

Dalgleish, T. (2004). Cognitive approaches to posttraumatic stress disorder: The evolution of multirepresentational theorizing. *Psychological Bulletin, 130*, 228–260.

Ehlers, A. (2006). Understanding and treating complicated grief: What can we learn from posttraumatic stress disorder? *Clinical Psychology: Science and Practice, 13*, 135–140.

Ehlers, A., & Clark, D. M. (2000). A cognitive model of posttraumatic stress disorder. *Behaviour Research and Therapy, 38*, 319–345.

Elliot, A. J., & Reis, H. T. (2003). Attachment and exploration in adulthood. *Journal of Personality and Social Psychology, 85*, 317–331.

Field, N. P., & Bonanno, G A. (2001). The role of blame in adaptation in the first 5 years following the death of a spouse. *American Behavioral Scientist, 44*, 764–781.

Foa, E. B., & Rothbaum, B. O. (1998). *Treating the trauma of rape: Cognitive–behavioral therapy for PTSD*. New York: Guilford.

Hayes, S. C., Wilson, K. G., Gifford, E. V., Follette, V. M., & Strohsahl, K. (1996). Experiential avoidance and behavioral disorders: A functional dimensional approach to diagnosis and treatment. *Journal of Consulting and Clinical Psychology, 64*, 1152–1168.

van der Houwen, K., Stroebe, M., Schut, H., Stroebe, W., & van den Bout, J. (2010). Mediating processes in bereavement: The role of rumination, threatening misinterpretations, and deliberate grief avoidance. *Social Science and Medicine, 71*, 1669–1676.

Jacobson, N. S., Martell, C. R., & Dimidjian, S. (2001). Behavioral activation treatment for depression: Returning to contextual roots. *Clinical Psychology: Science and Practice, 8*, 255–270.

Janoff-Bulman, R. (1992). *Shattered assumptions: Towards a new psychology of trauma*. New York: Free Press.

Maccallum, F., & Bryant, R. A. (2008). Self-defining memories in complicated grief. *Behaviour Research and Therapy, 46*, 1311–1315.

Maccallum, F., & Bryant, R. A. (2010). Attentional bias in complicated grief. *Journal of Affective Disorders, 125*, 316–322.

Mayou, R. A., Ehlers, A., & Bryant, B. (2002). Posttraumatic stress disorder after motor vehicle accidents: 3-year follow-up of a prospective longitudinal study. *Behaviour Research and Therapy, 40*, 665–675.

Mawson, D., Marks, I., Ramm, E., & Stern, R. S. (1981). Guided mourning for morbid grief: A controlled study. *British Journal of Psychiatry, 138*, 185–193.

Mikulincer, M. (2006). Attachment, caregiving, and sex within romantic relationships: A behavioral systems perspective. In Mikulincer, M., & Goodman, G. S. (Eds.), *Dynamics of romantic love: Attachment, caregiving, and sex* (pp. 23–44). New York: Guilford.

Park, C. L. (2010). Making sense of the meaning literature: An integrative review of meaning making and its effects on adjustment to stressful life events. *Psychological Bulletin, 136*, 257–301.

Prigerson, H. G., Horowitz, M. J., Jacobs, S. C., Parkes, C. M., Aslan, M., Goodkin, K., et al. (2009). Prolonged Grief Disorder: Psychometric validation of criteria proposed for DSM-V and ICD-11. *PLoS Medicine 6*(8), e1000121.

Prigerson, H. G., Maciejewski, P. K., Reynolds, C. F., Bierhals, A. J., Newsom, J. T., Fasiczka, A., et al. (1995). Inventory of Complicated Grief: A scale to measure maladaptive symptoms of loss. *Psychiatry Research, 59*, 65–79.

Ramsay, R. W. (1977). Behavioural approaches to bereavement. *Behaviour Research and Therapy, 15*, 131–135.

Schwartzberg, S. S., & Janoff-Bulman, R. (1991). Grief and the search for meaning: exploring the assumptive worlds of bereaved college students. *Journal of Social and Clinical Psychology, 10*, 270–288.

Shear, M. K., Boelen, P. A., & Neimeyer, R. A. (2011). Treating Complicated Grief: Converging approaches. In Neimeyer, R. A., Harris, D. L., Winokuer, H. R., & Thornton, G. F. (Eds.), *Grief and bereavement in contemporary society: Bridging research and practice* (pp. 139–163). New York: Routledge.

Shear, K., Frank, E., Houck, P. R., & Reynolds, C. F. III. (2005). Treatment of complicated grief: A randomized controlled trial. *JAMA, 293*, 2601–2608.

Shear, K., Monk, T., Houck, P., Melhem, N., Frank, E., Reynolds, C. III, & Sillowash, R. (2007). An attachment-based model of complicated grief including the role of avoidance. *European Archives of Psychiatry and Clinical Neuroscience, 257*, 453–461.

Shear, K., & Shair, H. (2005). Attachment, loss, and complicated grief. *Developmental Psychobiology, 47*, 253–267.

Sireling, L., Cohen, D., & Marks, I. (1988). Guided mourning for morbid grief: A controlled replication. *Behavior Therapy, 19*, 121–132.

Teasdale, J. D. (1999). Multi-level theories of cognition–emotion relations. In Dalgleish, T., & Power, M. J. (Eds.), *Handbook of cognition and emotion* (pp. 665–682). Chichester, UK: Wiley.

Wagner, B., Knaevelsrud, C., & Maercker, A. (2006). Internet-based cognitive–behavioral therapy for complicated grief: A randomized controlled trial. *Death Studies, 30*, 429–453.

Wijngaards-de Meij, L., Stroebe, M., Schut, H., Stroebe, W., van den Bout, J., van der Heijden, P., & Dijkstra, I. C. (2007). Neuroticism and attachment insecurity as predictors of bereavement outcome. *Journal of Research in Personality, 41*, 498–505.

17 Internet-based bereavement interventions and support

An overview

Birgit Wagner

Introduction

Interpersonal communication and relationships have changed dramatically with the growing influence of the Internet. The new platforms offered by the Internet have not only transformed social and professional life, but also opened up new channels of communication for those experiencing bereavement. Specifically, the Internet allows bereaved individuals to seek social support without physical interaction. In recent years, numerous Internet-based discussion forums have been established for bereaved populations (e.g., forums for bereaved parents, widowers and widows, and suicide survivors). These Internet discussion groups are usually self-help groups; many are developed and moderated by bereaved individuals. Online memorial sites on which people who have lost family members or friends grieve and mourn publicly are another expression of grief. In this often very personal form of public grieving, bereaved individuals or communities create memorial websites including photographs to describe the deceased person's life and dying.

Parallel to the development of the social media of the Internet, new forms of psychotherapeutic interventions – therapist-supported or self-help – have been developed for a variety of patient groups. Accumulating research has shown that Internet-based interventions – particularly cognitive–behavioral interventions – can be beneficial for psychological health, with treatment effects comparable to those of face-to-face treatments (Barak, Hen, & Boniel-Nissim, 2008). Specifically, Internet-based interventions for depression have been delivered in different forms, from self-help treatments delivered without therapist guidance to mainly text-based interventions with high therapist involvement (Andersson, 2006; Ruwaard et al., 2009; Spek et al., 2006). Computerized interventions for depression with therapist support showed a mean effect size comparable to face-to-face treatment for depression, whereas interventions with little or no therapist contact had a significantly smaller treatment effect size (Spek et al., 2007). Further, interventions aimed at patients with posttraumatic stress disorder (Lange et al., 2003) and anxiety have proved most effective, whereas interventions targeting patients with somatic problems (e.g., weight loss) have turned out to be less effective (Barak et al., 2008).

A number of Internet-based bereavement interventions have been developed in recent years. The interventions are delivered in various forms, from text-based approaches with therapist feedback (Kersting, Kroker, Schlicht, & Wagner, 2010; Wagner, Knaevelsrud, & Maercker, 2006) to self-help treatments delivered without therapist feedback (van der Houwen, Schut, van den Bout, Stroebe, & Stroebe, 2010). This chapter describes these different treatment approaches, beginning with low-threshold online bereavement support groups, efficacy of bereavement interventions, continuing with Internet-based interventions that include therapist support, and finally discussing self-help bereavement interventions. The chapter presents the procedures and key components of therapist-supported Internet-based grief interventions, and discusses important indications and contraindications for Internet-based therapies.

Online bereavement support groups

The advent of Internet social networking sites has led to a dramatic increase in the numbers of online support groups in recent years. There are Internet support groups for practically every interest group (e.g., breast cancer support groups, survivors of suicide), operating through various Internet applications (e.g., chat rooms, forums, bulletin boards). These groups can be especially beneficial for individuals who feel socially stigmatized or have difficulty linking up with others facing the same challenges in the offline world. The opportunity for social exchange with others in the same situation is one of the main advantages of online support groups (Davison, Pennebaker, & Dickerson, 2000). These groups can provide a sense of belonging (McKenna & Bargh, 2000) and help users to learn to cope with their bereavement. Moreover, the lack of geographic boundaries enables even individuals living in remote areas to participate in highly specific groups. In face-to-face groups, aspects of physical appearance such as attractiveness and ethnicity play a key role in determining participants' interactions and the development of friendships. Whereas these first impressions are difficult to overcome in face-to-face settings (McKenna & Seidman, 2005), in online settings, first impressions are based on the kind of opinions expressed and the kind of information users reveal about themselves, rather than on physical features.

Mourning and loss support groups account for some 10% of the electronic support groups in the health and wellness section of Yahoo! Groups (van der Houwen, Stroebe, Schut, Stroebe, & van den Bout, 2010), making bereavement the third most popular topic. However, there has been little research into these groups and their effects on the mental health of users. One of the first empirical studies in the field compared parent suicide survivors using online support groups with those participating in face-to-face support groups (Feigelman, Gorman, Beal, & Jordan, 2008). The study revealed that the Internet group experienced greater social stigmatization and less social support and showed higher symptom levels of depression, grief, and suicide ideation. These results are in line with the findings of the cross-sectional Swiss Bereaved Parents Study, which reported that 36% of respondents were active in Internet discussion groups for bereaved parents. This group showed significantly higher incidence of symptoms of depression, posttraumatic stress, and complicated grief (Kelly, 2008). However it is unclear whether these symptoms were caused by the frequent use of online groups, in which grief-related feelings were regularly actualized and re-experienced, or if bereaved individuals with higher symptom levels were more likely to seek out and participate in online support groups. Furthermore, the two groups were not randomly allocated to the Internet versus the non-discussion group, and therefore conclusions regarding the effect should be drawn carefully. Of the bereaved parents participating in Internet discussion groups, 15% spent more than 2 hours per day in these forums, 22% used them for less than 1 hour per day, and 33% logged on at least once per week. In addition, 45% of participants in online discussion groups felt better accepted in their online relationships than in their face-to-face ones.

Van der Houwen and colleagues (van der Houwen, Stroebe, et al., 2010) recruited participants for their study exclusively over the Internet. Of their respondents, 62% used online mutual bereavement support groups, spending an average of 7.4 hours per week in these forums. This group was compared with bereaved individuals who had never used online bereavement support groups. The online support group members were significantly younger, more likely to have lost a child, and less likely to belong to a religious community. They showed poorer mental health, higher emotional loneliness, and lower levels of social support. Vicary and Fraley (2010) evaluated students' reactions to the shootings at Virginia Tech in 2007 and their use of social media networks on the Internet. Only a few hours after the shooting, students had created online support groups on Facebook. Students were interviewed 2 weeks and 2 months after the shootings, and their depression and posttraumatic stress were assessed. The results showed that depression and symptoms of posttraumatic stress disorder (PTSD) 2 months after the shooting were not related to the number of Facebook groups the student had joined, the number of messages the student had posted, or the frequency of using the Facebook wall to discuss the shootings. Overall, Internet use was not related to depression or PTSD-related symptoms 2 months after the shootings. However, most students indicated that they perceived the use of the Internet as beneficial.

Effectiveness of bereavement interventions

A number of meta-analyses and reviews of bereavement treatments (Allumbaugh & Hoyt, 1999; Currier, Neimeyer, & Berman, 2008; Kato & Mann, 1999; Rowa-Dewar, 2002; Schut, Stroebe, van den Bout, & Terheggen, 2001; Wittouck, Van Autreve, De Jaegere, Portzky, & van Heeringen, 2011) describe the results of preventive interventions, interventions for complicated grievers and for high-risk groups, individual and group therapies, and cognitive–behavioral related treatments. However, studies of the effectiveness of bereavement interventions yield inconclusive results, and some reviewers claim that there is no strong empirical evidence that these interventions are effective (Currier et al., 2008; Schut & Stroebe, 2005). A number of methodological limitations have been addressed: Interventions are largely methodologically flawed, and inclusion criteria are incoherent because of a lack of commonly agreed DSM-IV criteria (Kato & Mann, 1999). Only a small number of studies fulfill the inclusion criteria of a randomized controlled trial. The results of these various reviews and meta-analyses show that the overall benefits of bereavement interventions are small (Schut et al., 2001). Interventions appeared most effective if they were aimed at high-risk groups or if the grief process was already complicated (Allumbaugh & Hoyt, 1999; Currier et al., 2008; Schut et al., 2001).

Schut and colleagues (2001) critically query meta-analyses of bereavement interventions because of the enormous theoretical and conceptional differences of these studies. In their review of efficacy studies they showed the difference of effects of primary preventive interventions, preventive interventions of high-risk groups, and the treatment of individuals who suffer from symptoms of complicated grieving. The secondary preventive interventions for high-risk groups (e.g., high levels of distress, traumatic loss, loss of a child) showed modest effects, and improvements were either temporary or non-existent. The tertiary preventive intervention for individuals suffering higher levels of distorted and prolonged grieving symptoms seemed to show more beneficial effects. Wittouck and colleagues (2011) have published the newest meta-analysis of prevention and treatment of complicated grief. In this meta-analysis, a stringent inclusion criterion was used, and therefore only randomized controlled trials in which the outcome variable was complicated grief measures were included. In this meta-analysis 14 studies met the inclusion criteria. Of these studies, nine were studies on preventive grief interventions and five examined the treatment of grief interventions. The preventive grief interventions in this meta-analysis showed inconsistent support. Altogether four studies in this meta-analysis reported positive results with respect to complicated grief measures. All four of these studies were based on cognitive–behavioral techniques. The results of this meta-analysis revealed that treatment interventions aimed at patients suffering from complicated grief seemed to be efficacious in the reduction of complicated grief symptoms.

Internet-based intervention for complicated grief

First studies of treatments involving cognitive–behavioral components in bereavement interventions have shown treatment efficacy (Boelen, de Keijser, van den Hout, & van den Bout, 2007; Shear, Frank, Houck, & Reynolds, 2005; Wagner et al., 2006; Wittouck et al., 2011). Parallel with this, the effectiveness of cognitive–behavioral therapy for PTSD has been well documented in a series of meta-analyses (Bradley, Greene, Russ, Dutra, & Westen, 2005). Confrontation with intrusive memories of the traumatic event has proven to be a key element of effective psychotherapy for PTSD. Exposure to traumatic stimuli (e.g., memories, pictures, or fear-provoking situations) has been found to significantly reduce avoidance behavior. Given the similarity of some symptoms of complicated grief disorder to those of PTSD, it is conceivable that cognitive–behavioral treatments designed for PTSD (Foa & Jaycox, 1999) might trigger similar healing mechanisms among individuals with complicated grief.

An Internet-based therapy for complicated grief (Wagner et al., 2006) has been developed on the basis of the Interapy treatment approach for PTSD (Lange et al., 2003). Lange, van de Ven, Schrieken, and Emmelkamp (2001) developed an online intervention for PTSD, in which communication between therapist and patient is exclusively text-based and asynchronous. The intervention consists of structured writing assignments based on the cognitive–behavioral therapy approach and the written disclosure procedure developed by Pennebaker and colleagues (Berry & Pennebaker, 1993). Lange and colleagues' first studies of their online intervention (Lange et al., 2001) showed a large reduction in PTSD symptoms and high treatment efficacy, comparable to that reported for face-to-face cognitive–behavioral interventions.

The Internet-based intervention for complicated grief consists of three modules: (1) self-confrontation, (2) cognitive reappraisal, and (3) social sharing. As the therapy is conducted exclusively over the Internet, a detailed online diagnostic procedure is needed to ensure that this form of therapy is appropriate for the patient. Because there is no possibility for therapists to respond immediately in crisis situations, some patient groups are not ideally suited to Internet-based psychotherapy. The current consensus is that the Internet offers insufficient support for people who are severely depressed or suicidal, or have dissociative and/or psychotic symptoms. The same applies to people who have a history of alcohol or substance abuse. All measures were self-reports administered through an online diagnostic assessment. Newer studies conducted in the field of online interventions use telephone interviews for structured clinical interviews. Patients are set ten 45-minute writing assignments over a 5-week period. The instructions are based on a treatment protocol, but individually tailored to patients' needs. The treatment is delivered by psychologists trained in cognitive–behavioral psychotherapy and with special training in the use of writing assignments to treat complicated grief. At the beginning of each phase, the patient receives detailed psychoeducation on the principles of the treatment module and sets a date and time to complete the writing assignment. After every two assignments, the patient receives feedback and instructions for the next two assignments (for a case study, see Wagner, Knaevelsrud, & Maercker, 2005). The treatment begins with a self-confrontation phase. Imaginative confrontation is a technique that encourages the patient to revisit feelings, emotions, and images surrounding the death of a significant person that are repressed or trigger fear. This first phase of the therapy focuses on confronting painful memories, thoughts, and feelings concerning the circumstances of the death. The patient is asked to describe the most painful moment in as much detail as possible, focusing on the most difficult aspects. In the second phase, cognitive reappraisal, the patients are instructed to write a supportive and encouraging letter to a hypothetical friend. They are asked to imagine that this friend has also experienced the loss of a significant other and is now facing the same difficulties. The letter should reflect on guilt feelings, challenge dysfunctional automatic thinking and behavior patterns, and correct unrealistic assumptions. The patients are encouraged to think about rituals to remember the deceased by, to re-access positive memories of the deceased, and to identify ways of activating resources such as social contacts, positive competences, and experiences. In the final phase, patients take symbolic leave of the traumatic event by writing a letter to a significant person, to someone who witnessed the traumatic event, or to themselves. The letter can be sent after finishing the therapy, but this is not obligatory.

Results of a randomized controlled trial showed that, relative to a waiting list group, the treatment group experienced statistically and clinically significant reductions in the main symptoms of complicated grief and in general psychopathology at posttreatment and at 3-month follow-up (Wagner et al., 2006). These beneficial treatment effects were maintained at 1.5-year follow-up (Wagner & Maercker, 2007). However, there was no control group against which the outcomes of the treated sample could be compared. Of the participants who began the treatment, only 8% did not complete the intervention. The impact of the intervention on posttraumatic growth and optimism was also evaluated (Wagner, Knaevelsrud, & Maercker, 2007). In the cognitive restructuring module, participants were to address questions such as the following in their letter to the hypothetical friend: "Is it possible that your friend learnt something from the death of her daughter or from what happened after this loss? Has he or she discovered something about life that she would otherwise not have known – or found out only much later?" The results indicated that posttraumatic growth increased significantly in the treatment group, while optimism remained unchanged (Wagner et al., 2007). An explanation for this finding could be that optimism is a relatively stable aspect of personality (Scheier & Carver, 1985) and that the treatment was too short to affect it.

Based on the outcomes of the intervention for patients with complicated grief, an Internet-based prevention program was developed for high-risk complicated grief groups (Wagner & Maercker, 2008). This intervention is shorter than the intervention for complicated grief, consisting of two 45-minute sessions per week over 3 weeks. The intervention consists of the following modules, each involving one writing assignment: (1) describing the circumstances of the death, (2) using the life-imprint method to explore the biography and life imprint of the deceased, (3) keeping a daily diary of social activities and sleep hygiene, (4) cognitive restructuring of dysfunctional thoughts, such as responsibility for the death and feelings of guilt, (5) communication within the family, (6) gender-specific coping with bereavement, and (7) bond with the deceased. Findings from a pilot study showed that this intervention resulted in significantly reduced symptoms of grief and depression (Wagner & Maercker, 2008).

Internet-based treatment for parents after prenatal loss

Pregnancy loss occurs in up to 20% of recognized pregnancies (Savitz, Hertz-Picciotto, Poole, & Olshan, 2002). The loss of a child during pregnancy causes significant psychological distress for many women, and may lead to long-lasting bereavement difficulties and psychological illnesses (Kersting, Dorsch, Kreulich, & Baez, 2004; Kersting et al., 2005, 2009; Mann, McKeown, Bacon, Vesselinov, & Bush, 2008). Women with a history of pregnancy loss are at particular risk of disturbances in their psychological adaptation in a new pregnancy (Bergner, Beyer, Klapp, & Rauchfuss, 2008). A number of interventions have been developed for women in the aftermath of pregnancy loss; however, few patients are actually offered this specific treatment after prenatal loss. Currently, the efficacy of an Internet-based therapy for complicated grief (Wagner et al., 2006) in this specific patient group is being evaluated. To date, the outcomes of the 5-week intervention replicate previous findings (Kersting et al., 2011; Kersting, Kroker, Schlicht, & Wagner, 2011), with the intervention group showing significantly reduced symptoms of grief, PTSD, and depression at posttreatment relative to the waiting list group. This symptom reduction was maintained at 3-month follow-up. An Internet-based therapy has a number of specific advantages for parents who have lost a child during pregnancy. Members of this subgroup of bereaved patients are proficient users of online technologies; young women, in particular, regularly use the Internet to obtain information about health-related topics. The temporal independence of this form of therapy is especially useful for these patients, who are often unable to participate in face-to-face treatment as many who have children would need to organize childcare.

Self-help interventions for bereaved individuals

Internet-based interventions can be delivered in different forms, with various levels of therapist involvement or as self-help treatments without therapist contact. Based on the research of Lange et al. (2003), Wagner et al. (2006), and the principles of the Pennebaker paradigm, van der Houwen, Schut, and colleagues (2010) have developed and evaluated a self-help intervention for bereaved individuals. The treatment involves no personalized therapist feedback and consists of just five structured writing assignments. These five assignments cover the three treatment modules outlined by Lange et al. (2003): (1) exposure; (2) cognitive restructuring; (3) integration and restoration. This self-help approach has been found to lead to decreased feelings of emotional loneliness and increased positive mood. However, no significant change was found in grief-related symptoms or depression. The attrition rate in this study was 46% (59% in the intervention and 27% in the control condition) over the course of the study.

These results are similar to findings about self-help interventions reported in a meta-analysis of Internet-based depression interventions (Andersson, Carlbring, Berger, Almlov, & Cuijpers, 2009), which found that therapist support had a strong influence on treatment outcomes. Computerized interventions with therapist support showed an average between-group effect size of $d = 0.61$, which is comparable with the effects reported for face-to-face treatments for depression. However, interventions without or with very little therapist contact had a significantly smaller treatment effect of $d = 0.25$. Further, studies on self-guided programs have shown not only reduced treatment effects, but also substantial attrition rates (Christensen, Griffiths, Mackinnon, & Brittliffe, 2006; Clarke et al., 2002, 2005; Kaltenthaler et al., 2008). Analyses of the relationship between the amount of therapist time in minutes and treatment outcomes have revealed a significant correlation between therapist time per participant and the between-group effect sizes of Internet-based interventions (Palmqvist, Carlbring, & Andersson, 2007). Based on the findings of their Swedish studies, Andersson and colleagues (2009) have suggested that about 100 minutes per patient spent by the therapist giving comments on homework and providing feedback can be sufficient for a 10-week program. Overall, these studies suggest that a minimal level of therapist contact is needed to decrease attrition rates and to reduce symptoms.

However, the influence of therapist contact on treatment efficacy in bereavement interventions is still unclear and further research is needed to show if the findings for Internet-based interventions for depression can be generalized to bereaved people. The differences across Internet-based bereavement interventions might be also attributable to symptom severity. As Schut et al. (2001) noted, tertiary interventions for individuals suffering higher levels of distorted and prolonged grieving symptoms show better alleviation of complicated grief symptoms than interventions aimed at all bereaved people or high-risk groups. The self-help intervention for the bereaved (van der Houwen, Schut, et al., 2010) was aimed as primary intervention, whereas the Internet-based intervention with therapist support (Wagner et al., 2006) was aimed at patients who were highly distressed. Therefore, future research is needed to evaluate the relationship of therapist support in Internet-based interventions.

Advantages and disadvantages of Internet-based therapeutic interventions

Internet-based interventions for bereaved individuals are still a relatively new research topic, and future studies need to focus on who benefits and who does not. Research on Internet-based therapy for related mental disorders, such as PTSD or depression, has identified a number of advantages and disadvantages of this form of treatment (Andersson et al., 2009; Wagner & Maercker, 2010). One major advantage of Internet-based therapeutic interventions is their anonymity and the lack of geographic boundaries. The anonymity of the Internet helps patients overcome their initial shame and encourages them to confront themes such as guilt and social difficulties and to disclose painful feelings. The lack of the physical presence of the therapist during the online intervention facilitates intimacy and increased self-disclosure (Cook & Doyle, 2002). Therefore, structured writing assignments provide a promising alternative to imaginary confrontations during face-to-face therapy. Another important advantage is the transparency of the therapy process. The texts produced can be archived, which not only gives patients the opportunity to follow up on their therapy at a later time, but also provides new options for the therapist. The asynchronous, time-delayed nature of the patient–therapist communication gives the therapist time to reflect on his or her responses rather than being pressured to give the patient a quick reply.

However, online therapies also have limitations that require further research and call for caution to be exercised in their implementation. First, Internet-based treatment may not suit all patients; it is important to screen patients carefully and to work only with those who are likely to benefit from this form of therapy (Suler, 2004). One potential challenge of Internet-based treatment is the potential for misunderstandings in the absence of spontaneous clarification. On the one hand, important information might be withheld from the therapist, potentially leading to incorrect conclusions being drawn. On the other hand, the patient might misinterpret the therapist's feedback. For this reason, it is especially important to establish maximum transparency with the patient (e.g., providing the name and telephone contact details of the organization or clinic providing the therapy).

Another concern relates to how the therapist can respond if a patient becomes suicidal or homicidal and expresses such thoughts in an assignment (Wagner, Schulz, & Knaevelsrud, 2012). It is practically impossible to respond to the patient's crisis in a reliable and timely way within the Internet-based approach. It therefore seems advisable to obtain the contact numbers of a personal medical doctor for cases of emergency. Moreover, a careful online or telephone-based diagnosis procedure is essential before the treatment, and clearly defined exclusion criteria must be established to avoid treating patients with suicidal, dissociative, or psychotic tendencies over the Internet.

General conclusions

The Internet has become an integral part of everyday work, family, and local community life. It is thus no surprise that bereaved individuals also turn to the Internet as a coping mechanism. Internet-based communication offers new possibilities for social networking and support beyond those available in a face-to-face context. It facilitates relatively anonymous, asynchronous, and text-based communication beyond geographical and temporal boundaries. However, although the body of research on online bereavement behavior is growing, little is yet known about the characteristics of those who seek mutual or psychotherapeutic bereavement support online. Specifically, research is needed into the widely used Internet bereavement support groups and their effects on users' well-being. Although users describe these online support groups as beneficial (Vicary & Fraley, 2010) and participation in these groups does not seem to influence mental health negatively over a 2- or 3-month period, long-term follow-ups are needed to provide clearer insights into the consequences of online bereavement support for users' mental and physical health.

Other forms of Internet-based bereavement support are interventions involving various levels of therapist guidance and self-help interventions. Cognitive–behavioral interventions aimed at patients suffering from complicated grief have shown high treatment efficacy (Wagner, Knaevelsrud, & Maercker, 2006, 2007; Wagner & Maercker, 2008), with symptom reduction being maintained at long-term follow-up (Wagner & Maercker, 2007). In fact, the effect sizes were comparable to those reported for traditional psychological treatment. Self-help interventions aimed at all bereaved individuals (primary and secondary interventions) have shown lower or no effects on grief-related symptoms. However, these interventions resulted in significantly decreased feelings of emotional loneliness and increased positive mood (van der Houwen, Schut, et al., 2010). All interventions reviewed in this paper are based on a cognitive–behavioral framework and share components (e.g., psychoeducation, cognitive restructuring, exposure) that have proved effective in face-to-face settings. However, little is yet known about the mechanisms through which structured writing or written disclosure leads to change in bereaved individuals. Whereas some studies have reported positive treatment effects for grief-related symptoms, others have not. The crucial difference may lie in the level of grief complications of the participants and the therapist feedback.

To conclude, the development of Internet-based bereavement interventions is still at an early stage and research in this field is scarce. Further empirical studies on Internet-based interventions and online bereavement support groups are essential.

References

Allumbaugh, D. L., & Hoyt, W. T. (1999). Effectiveness of grief therapy: A meta-analysis. *Journal of Counseling Psychology, 46*, 370–380.

Andersson, G. (2006). Internet-based cognitive–behavioral self help for depression. *Expert Review of Neurotherapeutics, 6*, 1637–1642.

Andersson, G., Carlbring, P., Berger, T., Almlov, J., & Cuijpers, P. (2009). What makes Internet therapy work? *Cognitive Behaviour Therapy, 38*, 55–60.

Barak, A., Hen, L., & Boniel-Nissim, M. (2008). A comprehensive review and a meta-analysis of the effectiveness of Internet-based psychotherapeutic interventions. *Journal of Technology in Human Services, 26*, 109–159.

Bergner, A., Beyer, R., Klapp, B. F., & Rauchfuss, M. (2008). Pregnancy after early pregnancy loss: A prospective study of anxiety, depressive symptomatology and coping. *Journal of Psychosomatic Obstetric Gynaecology, 29*, 105–113.

Berry, D. S., & Pennebaker, J. W. (1993). Nonverbal and verbal emotional expression and health. *Psychotherapy and Psychosomatics, 59*, 11–19.

Boelen, P. A., de Keijser, J., van den Hout, M. A., & van den Bout, J. (2007). Treatment of complicated grief: A comparison between cognitive–behavioral therapy and supportive counseling. *Journal of Consulting and Clinical Psychology, 75*, 277–284.

Bradley, R., Greene, J., Russ, E., Dutra, L., & Westen, D. (2005). A multidimensional meta-analysis of psychotherapy for PTSD. *American Journal of Psychiatry, 162*, 214–227.

Christensen, H., Griffiths, K. M., Mackinnon, A. J., & Brittliffe, K. (2006). Online randomized controlled trial of brief and full cognitive behaviour therapy for depression. *Psychological Medicine, 36*, 1737–1746.

Clarke, G., Eubanks, D., Reid, E., Kelleher, C., O'Connor, E., DeBar, L. L., et al. (2005). Overcoming depression on the Internet (ODIN) (2): A randomized trial of a self-help depression skills program with reminders. *Journal of Medical Internet Research, 7*, e16.

Clarke, G., Reid, E., Eubanks, D., O'Connor, E., DeBar, L. L., Kelleher, C., et al. (2002). Overcoming depression on the Internet (ODIN): A randomized controlled trial of an Internet depression skills intervention program. *Journal of Medical Internet Research, 4*, e14.

Cook, J. E., & Doyle, C. (2002). Working alliance in online therapy as compared to face-to-face therapy: Preliminary results. *CyberPsychology & Behavior, 5*, 95–105.

Currier, J. M., Neimeyer, R. A., & Berman, J. S. (2008). The effectiveness of psychotherapeutic interventions for bereaved persons: A comprehensive quantitative review. *Psychological Bulletin, 134*, 648–661.

Davison, K. P., Pennebaker, J. W., & Dickerson, S. S. (2000). Who talks? The social psychology of illness support groups. *American Psychologist, 55*, 205–217.

Feigelman, W., Gorman, B. S., Beal, K. C., & Jordan, J. R. (2008). Internet support groups for suicide survivors: A new mode for gaining bereavement assistance. *Omega (Westport), 57*, 217–243.

Foa, E. B., & Jaycox, L. H. (1999). Cognitive–behavioral theory and treatment of posttraumatic stress disorder. In Spiegel, D. (Ed.), *Psychotherapeutic frontiers: New principles and practices* (pp. 23–61). Washington, DC: American Psychiatric Press.

van der Houwen, K., Schut, H., van den Bout, J., Stroebe, M., & Stroebe, W. (2010a). The efficacy of a brief internet-based self-help intervention for the bereaved. *Behaviour Research and Therapy, 48*, 359–367.

van der Houwen, K., Stroebe, M., Schut, H., Stroebe, W., & van den Bout, J. (2010b). Online mutual support in bereavement: An empirical examination. *Computers in Human Behavior, 26*, 1519–1525.

Kaltenthaler, E., Sutcliffe, P., Parry, G., Beverley, C., Rees, A., & Ferriter, M. (2008). The acceptability to patients of computerized cognitive behaviour therapy for depression: A systematic review. *Psychological Medicine, 38*, 1521–1530.

Kato, P. M., & Mann, T. (1999). A synthesis of psychological interventions for the bereaved. *Clinical Psychology Review, 19*, 275–296.

Kelly, L. (2008). *Psychische Gesundheit und Internetdiskussionsforen für Eltern nach dem Tod ihres Kindes*. Unpublished dissertation, Zürich University, Switzerland.

Kersting, A., Dorsch, M., Kreulich, C., & Baez, E. (2004). Psychological stress response after miscarriage and induced abortion. *Psychosomatic Medicine, 66*, 795–796; author reply 796.

Kersting, A., Dorsch, M., Kreulich, C., Reutemann, M., Ohrmann, P., Baez, E., et al. (2005). Trauma and grief 2–7 years after termination of pregnancy because of fetal anomalies: A pilot study. *Journal of Psychosomatic Obstetric Gynaecology, 26*, 9–14.

Kersting, A., Kroker, K., Schlicht, S., Baust, K., & Wagner, B. (2011). Efficacy of cognitive behavioral internet-based therapy in parents after the loss of a child during pregnancy: Pilot data from a randomized controlled trial. *Archives of Women's Mental Health, 14*, 465–477.

Kersting, A., Kroker, K., Schlicht, S., & Wagner, B. (2011). Internet-based treatment after pregnancy loss: Concept and case study. *Journal of Psychosomatic Obstetric Gynaecology, 32*, 72–78.

Kersting, A., Kroker, K., Steinhard, J., Hoernig-Franz, I., Wesselmann, U., Luedorff, K., et al. (2009). Psychological impact on women after second and third trimester termination of pregnancy due to fetal anomalies versus women after birth: A 14-month follow up study. *Archives of Women's Mental Health, 12*, 193–201.

Lange, A., Rietdijk, D., Hudcovicova, M., van de Ven, J. P., Schrieken, B., & Emmelkamp, P. M. G. (2003). Interapy: A controlled randomized trial of the standardized treatment of posttraumatic stress through the internet. *Journal of Consulting and Clinical Psychology, 71*, 901–909.

Lange, A., van de Ven, J. P., Schrieken, B., & Emmelkamp, P. M. G. (2001). Interapy. Treatment of posttraumatic stress through the Internet: A controlled trial. *Journal of Behavior Therapy and Experimental Psychiatry, 32*, 73–90.

McKenna, K., & Bargh, J. (2000). Plan 9 from cyberspace: The implications of the Internet for personality and social psychology. *Personality and Social Psychology Review, 4*, 57–75.

McKenna, K., & Seidman, G. (2005). You, me, and we: Interpersonal processes in electronic groups. In Amichai-Hamburger, Y. (Ed.), *The social net: Understanding human behavior in cyberspace* (pp. 191–217). New York: Oxford University Press.

Mann, J. R., McKeown, R. E., Bacon, J., Vesselinov, R., & Bush, F. (2008). Predicting depressive symptoms and grief after pregnancy loss. *Journal of Psychosomatic Obstetric Gynaecology, 29*, 274–279.

Palmqvist, B., Carlbring, P., & Andersson, G. (2007). Internet-delivered treatments with or without therapist input: Does the therapist factor have implications for efficacy and cost? *Expert Review of Pharmacoeconomics & Outcomes Research, 7*, 291–297.

Rowa-Dewar, N. (2002). Do interventions make a difference to bereaved parents? A systematic review of controlled studies. *International Journal of Palliative Nursing, 8*, 452–457.

Ruwaard, J., Schrieken, B., Schrijver, M., Broeksteeg, J., Dekker, J., Vermeulen, H., et al. (2009). Standardized web-based cognitive behavioural therapy of mild to moderate depression: A randomized controlled trial with a long-term follow-up. *Cognitive Behaviour Therapy, 38*, 206–221.

Savitz, D. A., Hertz-Picciotto, I., Poole, C., & Olshan, A. F. (2002). Epidemiologic measures of the course and outcome of pregnancy. *Epidemiological Review, 24*, 91–101.

Scheier, M. F., & Carver, C. S. (1985). Optimism, coping, and health: Assessment and implications of generalized outcome expectancies. *Health Psychology, 4*, 219–247.

Schut, H., & Stroebe, M. S. (2005). Interventions to enhance adaptation to bereavement. *Journal of Palliative Medicine, 8*, 140–147.

Schut, H., Stroebe, M. S., van den Bout, J., & Terheggen, M. (2001). The efficacy of bereavement interventions: Determining who benefits. In Stroebe M. S., Hansson, R. O., Stroebe, W., & Schut, H. (Eds.), *Handbook of bereavement research: Consequences, coping, and care* (pp. 705–738). Washington, DC: American Psychological Association.

Shear, K., Frank, E., Houck, P. R., & Reynolds, C. F. (2005). Treatment of complicated grief: A randomized controlled trial. *JAMA, 293*, 2601–2608.

Spek, V., Cuijpers, P., Nyklicek, I., Riper, H., Keyzer, J., & Pop, V. (2007). Internet-based cognitive behaviour therapy for symptoms of depression and anxiety: A meta-analysis. *Psychological Medicine, 37*, 319–328.

Suler, J. (2004). The online disinhibition effect. *CyberPsychology & Behavior, 7*, 321–326.

Vicary, A. M., & Fraley, R. C. (2010). Student reactions to the shootings at Virginia Tech and Northern Illinois University: Does sharing grief and support over the Internet affect recovery? *Personal and Social Psychology Bulletin, 36*, 1555–1563.

Wagner, B., Knaevelsrud, C., & Maercker, A. (2005). Internet-based treatment for complicated grief: Concepts and case study. *Journal of Loss and Trauma, 10*, 409–432.

Wagner, B., Knaevelsrud, C., & Maercker, A. (2006). Internet-based cognitive–behavioral therapy for complicated grief: A randomized controlled trial. *Death Studies, 30*, 429–453.

Wagner, B., Knaevelsrud, C., & Maercker, A. (2007). Post-traumatic growth and optimism as outcomes of an internet-based intervention for complicated grief. *Cognitive Behaviour Therapy, 36*, 156–161.

Wagner, B., & Maercker, A. (2007). A 1.5-year follow-up of an Internet-based intervention for complicated grief. *Journal of Traumatic Stress, 20*, 625–629.

Wagner, B., & Maercker, A. (2008). An Internet-based cognitive–behavioral preventive intervention for complicated grief: A pilot study. *Giornale Italiano di Medicina del Lavoro ed Ergonomia, 30*, 47–53.

Wagner, B., & Maercker, A. (2010). Internet-based intervention for posttraumatic stress disorder. In Brunet, A., Ashbaugh, R. A., & Herbert, F. C. (Eds.), *Internet use in the aftermath of trauma* (pp. 255–267). Amsterdam: IOS Press.

Wagner, B., Schulz, W., & Knaevelsrud, C. (2012). Efficacy of an Internet-based intervention for posttraumatic stress disorder in Iraq: A pilot study. *Psychiatry Research, 195*, 85–88.

Wittouck, C., Van Autreve, S., De Jaegere, E., Portzky, G., & van Heeringen, K. (2011). The prevention and treatment of complicated grief: A meta-analysis. *Clinical Psychology Review, 31*, 69–78.

18 Family therapy for complicated grief

David W. Kissane, Talia I. Zaider, Yuelin Li, and Francesca Del Gaudio

Introduction

Loss never occurs in a vacuum but rather is shared by variously interconnected people, whose most common constellation is the family (Kissane & Bloch, 1994). The quality of relationships involved therein proves determinative of the pattern of adaptation to loss (Kissane, Bloch, Dowe, et al., 1996; Kissane, Bloch, Onghena, et al., 1996), whether through mutual support and shared grief that steadily heals, or through distortion and perpetuation of that relational functioning, which, in turn, exacerbates the intensity and length of mourning. Family therapy has usefully complemented individual and group approaches to bereavement care (Kissane, McKenzie, Bloch, Moskowitz, McKenzie, & O'Neill, 2006). Might we entertain boldly the hope that family therapy initiated during palliative care could prevent the development of complicated grief? Such a prophylactic approach through a model of family-centered care is exactly what we have been studying, and we explore it in this chapter located within the section on therapeutic approaches to complicated grief.

Let us set the stage for this exploration by locating our work within the literature of family interventions in bereavement care, review our conceptualization of which families cope well and which do more poorly when bereaved, and provide an overview of our model of therapy. We share preliminary results from our current National Institutes of Health (NIH)-funded randomized trial of different doses of family therapy delivered to at-risk families, whose therapy is commenced during anti-cancer treatment and continued into bereavement, once the ill patient has been lost.

Why family therapy?

There is a long history of family therapists writing about their work with the bereaved, but few trials conducted to show empirically the benefits of this approach (Goldstein, Alter, & Axelrod, 1996; Kissane et al., 2006). Lieberman first reported cases in which family work was necessary to overcome chronic and complicated grief, for which treatment had been first attempted individually and failed (Lieberman, 1978). Subsequently working with children and adolescents, Rosenthal reported beneficial results from family involvement (Rosenthal, 1980).

In contrast to these two early successes, Williams and Polak intruded prematurely in having the therapist visit relatives with the coroner's assistant following motor vehicle deaths (Williams & Polak, 1979), whereas pediatric family therapy produced improved child behaviors at 1 year following a parent's death, though differences waned by the 2-year follow-up (Black & Urbanowicz, 1987). The latter study did not select at-risk families and struggled with both engagement and compliance. Goldstein, Alter, and Axelrod (1996) conducted an eight-session open trial of a psychoeducational family intervention in an outpatient cancer center, which helped participants adjust.

By the turn of the century, the promise hoped for by Paul and Grosser (1965) had unfortunately not materialized into a strong body of evidence in support of family interventions with the bereaved. Our Melbourne-based Family-Focused Grief Therapy (FFGT) randomized controlled trial showed promise by ameliorating distress and depression post-death through its preventive family intervention (Kissane, Lichtenthal, & Zaider, 2007–2008; Kissane, Bloch, McKenzie, McDowall, & Nitzan, 1998). Since then, a randomized intervention with adolescents and parents with HIV failed to find differences between adolescents who lost a parent and the non-bereaved at 2-year follow-up (Rotheram-Borus, Stein, & Lin, 2001; Rotheram-Borus, Weiss, Alber, & Lester, 2005). Other sterling efforts have been family bereavement programs for parentally bereaved children and adolescents (Rauch & Muriel, 2004; Sandler et al., 2003). Some promise does emerge from research across the past decade suggesting that family intervention has much to offer as a model of bereavement care.

Which theoretical models guide this family therapy?

Let us turn now to theoretical models that inform family processes in mourning to consider further why family intervention for complicated grief has intuitive appeal. Four theories form the backbone of such conceptualization: attachment theory (Bowlby, 1969), cognitive processing theory in adaptation to trauma (Creamer, Burgess, & Pattison, 1992), group adaptation (Whitaker & Lieberman, 1964), and pre-existing resilience (Bonanno, Wortman, & Nesse, 2004). We will briefly consider the relevance of each.

Attachment theory

When considering loss from a relational perspective, attachment theory comes quickly to the fore. The most important relationships are generally found in families, whether nuclear, family-of-origin, or extended family (Shaver & Tancredy, 2001). The nature of the bonds of attachment strongly influence the experience of grief (Ainsworth & Eichberg, 1991). When the emotional impact of a loss is shared among family members, restorative coping responses can be activated as relatives comfort and support one another. Family therapy facilitates both elements of the dual-process model (Stroebe & Schut, 2001) through inviting sharing of grief alongside improved family functioning, in which communication, cooperation, and mutual support are enhanced. Patterns of relationship transmitted across generations through the family exhibit styles of attachment that either facilitate or hinder adaptive mourning.

Cognitive processing and meaning construction

Information about the death and integration of an understanding of what this means follows successful cognitive processing (Janoff-Bulman, 1989), including making sense of events in accordance with one's previously established belief system, as well as modification of the person's assumptive world (Parkes, 1972, 1998), a schema of ideas, values, attitudes, and beliefs that each person organizes about his or her life in the world, to accommodate the new events. Like any trauma, illness and death disrupt the assumptive world schema. At a family level, disclosure of thoughts and feelings helps shape the assumptive worldviews of the family as a whole (Janoff-Bulman, 1989; Janoff-Bulman & Berg, 1998), leading to cognitive reappraisal as either confrontation or avoidance strategies unfold within the family.

How each family communicates and resolves differences of opinion impacts dynamically on each individual's cognitions. Families can challenge negative conclusions and guide the integration of positive meaning (Folkman & Moskowitz, 2000). Family traditions influence the regulation of grieving, recognizing when some degree of avoidance is healthy, but too much is detrimental. Families pursue cognitive reframing iteratively, using the diverse views of members to test out options, solve problems, and mutually support each other in finding new meaning and coping adaptively. In this sense, the meaning attributed to role change within families (Neimeyer, 2011) is a key determinant of adaptive outcome.

Group adaptation

Group discussions shift dynamically between enabling and restrictive solutions, as some members offer a constructive suggestion to resolve an issue, while others urge caution derived from a more fearful viewpoint (Whitaker & Lieberman, 1964). The group, in this case the family, grapples with these options. As debate unfolds, the family seeks consensus, with adaptive choices generally resulting from constructive views. Alas, sometimes a dominant person may impose a deleterious point of view; alternatively, more indecisive individuals can be convinced by the majority. Any difference of opinion can generate ongoing conflict, these disagreements splitting the family and reducing its teamwork. Just as the cohesiveness of a psychotherapy group is the hallmark of its effectiveness in promoting the development and maturity of its membership (McKenzie, 1995), so too with families.

Harnessing family resilience

Robustness and character strength are key ingredients when families are confronted with the loss of a loved one (Bonanno et al., 2004; Boss, 2006; Shapiro,

2008). Use of evident strengths is both cogent and strategic, for it avoids criticism of the family and, indeed, affirms one potential pathway through which it can heal its pain (Zaider & Kissane, 2007). The family provides its own natural support network, through which its constituents can be sustained by its inherent resiliency (Boss, 2006). We broaden the conception of *family* to that of the *fictive kin*, those available persons who prove to be supportive, concerned, and willing to help (Landau, 2007). Close friends, neighbors, or members of the extended family can all bring their generosity, compassion, love, insight, and support to enrich the circle of care.

Thus, affirming any apparent strengths of a family becomes a key dimension of therapy. No matter how dysfunctional they might appear, some strength can be identified in every family! This is endorsed as a dimension of their resilience.

Can we recognize those families in greater need of help during palliative care?

In the palliative care setting, before a patient with life-threatening illness dies, family members can be invited to complete a Family Relationships Index (FRI) (Moos & Moos, 1981), a 12-item true–false scale, which gives information about family cohesiveness, expressiveness of thoughts and feelings, and conflict resolution, and has good sensitivity to identify families at risk of psychosocial morbidity during bereavement (Edwards & Lavery, 2005; Kissane et al., 2003). Those families considered at risk are invited to attend a family meeting, where their issues and concerns about caring for the dying family member can be appraised and continuing family therapy contracted with those present (Kissane, 2000). Therapy readily continues into bereavement once a therapeutic alliance is established.

Repeated studies have confirmed a typology of families based on their relational functioning as defined by the FRI (Kissane et al., 1996, 2003). Two types of families are well functioning. The first is termed *supportive,* and these families are highly cohesive, communicate readily, comfort and support one another, are free of conflict, and have a resilience that protects their membership from psychiatric disorders and complicated grief. The second well-functioning type is termed *conflict resolving,* because their open communication and high cohesion protect their members from difficulties, despite prominent differences of opinion. They are also free of psychiatric disorder during bereavement. Neither *supportive* nor *conflict-resolving* families are in need of preventive family therapy.

Three types of families have reduced cohesiveness and communication, and are troubled by conflict. *Intermediate* families have mild reductions in communication and teamwork, carry some members in need of psychological help, and are readily amenable to being engaged in therapy. Generally six to eight sessions of therapy over as many months will help intermediate families share their grief and protect members from morbid psychiatric outcomes (Kissane et al., 2006).

Of the more dysfunctional family types, *sullen* families have poor communication and cohesion, but muted anger; they carry the highest rates of depression (anger turned in) and accept help, generally needing 8–12 sessions of therapy over 12–18 months to prevent complicated grief (Kissane et al., 2007–2008). In contrast, *hostile* families are fractured by conflict, use distance as their means of survival, and may not be willing to come together for therapy. If they can be engaged, therapists are wise to set achievable goals, but can expect 10–16 sessions of therapy over 18 months to be needed to prevent morbid outcomes for those families engaged in treatment (Kissane et al., 2006). An acceptable compromise is to work with an accessible part of such a family and help those open to this assistance.

This empirical typology helps conceptually to recognize families where attachment processes are more disturbed and accurately predicts rates of psychiatric disorder (Kissane & Bloch, 2002). However, we avoid classifying families by these names clinically, lest harm be done by pejorative labeling. It is sufficient to say to families that experience teaches us the value of meeting with the family as a whole to help patients and their caregivers manage the illness and care provision.

Engaging bereaved families

When a bereaved person presents for individual therapy, it is possible to ask them to bring along a relative to help extend the family story and deepen understanding about what has happened (Kissane & Hooghe, 2011). This approach is consistent with family therapy theory, in which one member serves as the "symptom bearer" or apparent focus of concern and becomes the rationale for inviting other relatives to assemble. Therapists may need to reach out actively to others to ask for their help. A wise therapist works with whoever is available and later invites outliers to attend, telling them something of the dynamics discovered and emphasizing the role they could take up to the benefit of the family or ill family member.

Similarly, family therapy can be conducted as a mode of bereavement care after unexpected deaths, including traumatic or violent deaths, in pediatric loss, and whether the death was that of a child, sibling, or parent. Although our research program has been focused on the cancer setting, its extension into other clinical settings becomes an important feature of its future dissemination.

Ethical aspects of family-centered care

Whereas cancer patients are the primary focus of care in oncology, their family members become second-order patients in the palliative and terminal care setting. Indeed, the philosophy of palliative care includes caring for the bereaved. Practical issues present ethical dilemmas when family care is pursued, including the competing needs of individuals or subsystems within the family, maintaining confidences, family secrets, and the boundaries of therapy. A fuller discussion of these many issues is found in our book on FFGT (Kissane & Bloch, 2002).

Conducting therapy in the home

Arranging therapy in the home of the primary caregiver is common in the hospice setting. This practice increases the ability of the ill patient to take part in early sessions despite his or her frailty and thus become known to the therapist before death intervenes. Families are very appreciative of this and the therapist is later able to bring the deceased back figuratively into the therapy, given personal knowledge of the person. The wishes and hopes of the lost relative can be powerfully used to motivate the family to sustain efforts at mutual support. When high conflict is recognized in families, therapists are wise to conduct the initial assessment sessions on neutral territory rather than the home, until confidence develops about its safety in the home.

Goals of family therapy

Therapists work to facilitate a constructive dialogue that tells the family's story of illness and coping with loss. The following specific goals are pursued:

1 to understand the impact that the illness or loss has on family life and coping, not only for individuals but also for the family as a whole;
2 to examine relationship patterns between family members, contrasting close alliances with distant relationships, and considering their contributions to mutual support or the development of conflict;
3 to clarify any transgenerational patterns in family lifestyle, recognizing those that continue to be adopted and those left behind, in the process naming family strengths and reaching agreement about any perceived vulnerabilities; and
4 to foster their mutual support of each other as they mourn and invite their overt choice about adaptive relational styles that will enhance coping.

Approach to family assessment and therapy

Therapists join initially with each individual through a linear dialogue that learns who each person is, their place and role in the family, their contribution to caregiving, and their hopes, expectations, and concerns about the family. Engaging the family as a whole, however, is dependent on circular rather than linear questions; the former style of questioning invites each individual, in turn, to step into the shoes of others and share perceptions about their coping, strengths, vulnerabilities, and understanding of the illness and prognosis, including their acceptance of what the future holds (Dumont & Kissane, 2009). As understanding is developed, this initial focus on the status of the illness is shifted to a focus on how the family communicates about this, works as a team, and resolves differences in opinions and values. Through the use of integrative summary comments and reflexive questions, the therapist searches to understand how each family is emotionally supportive of one another, what challenges it grapples with, what hopes and aspirations they have, and what fears, issues, or concerns are worthy of continued focus. This agenda setting builds consensus about what might be accomplished through continued family meetings.

Patterns of family relationship and styles of coping can be made explicit through examination of these across the generations, thus recognizing traditions, values, and ways of coping with stress, change, and death (Kissane & Bloch, 2002). Families will sometimes draw confidence from this; at other times, they will elect to choose alternative styles of relating and coping. Therapist skill is needed to recognize and name these patterns, which facilitate the family's development of insight and resultant opportunity to make choices. This technique proves non-critical as families recognize how easily the ways of prior generations can be repeated.

Hypothetical consideration of what is sought in the future (in 1, 6, or 12 months) invites consideration of the family's priorities during the patient's remaining life, discussion of death, and how the family will cope. Patients can poignantly express their wishes and concerns for their loved ones, expressing gratitude, aspirations, and bequests alongside special requests for family cohesion, mutual support, and care in the years ahead. These comments in the final months or weeks of a dying person's life can be powerfully recalled during bereavement work.

Grief work then continues in bereavement with sustained focus on the family's relational goals, mutual support, and coping with the loss. Progress is affirmed, with the emphasis on active sharing of grief countering any tendencies toward avoidance and social withdrawal. The time between sessions is gradually extended from monthly, to sessions every 2 and then 3 months, until termination of therapy becomes appropriate.

Family therapy and complicated grief

In this chapter, we have adopted the definition of complicated grief as prolonged grief whose intensity persists rather than beginning to wane by 6 months of bereavement (Prigerson et al., 2009). Consensus seems to be emerging that some form of separation distress is expressed as continued longing for or yearning for the deceased, which disrupts the functionality of daily life and persists beyond 6 months of bereavement. Using a DSM-style format, accompanying symptoms have varied between counts of four present out of eight, or five out of nine additional symptoms. As discussed further below, we used the 11-item Consensus Criteria for Complicated Grief scale provided by Prigerson in 2005, which required four out of eight additional symptoms reflecting chronic grief.

We closed recruitment at 170 families in our current trial of FFGT, comprising some 616 consenting subjects at baseline. Table 18.1 provides an illustration of their sociodemographic features, including mean age, gender, race and ethnicity, and marital status. Our recruitment rate was 27% of eligible families.

Improvement in family communication

As family therapy proceeds, we have studied each member's perception of their family's communication as a process measure of therapy to see how this changes session by session. The dominant patterns are improvement in communication or maintenance of a high level of communication, where this was present from the beginning. Linear mixed-effects modeling, accounting for clustered family data, was used to determine whether family members' perceptions of communication

Table 18.1 Demographics of participants from 170 families in our current randomized controlled trial of family-focused grief therapy (FFGT)

Sample characteristics (n = 616)	Patients (n = 130)	Other family members (n = 486)
Mean age (range) in years	55.6 (21–92)	42.9 (12–85)
Gender		
Male	54 (42%)	192 (40%)
Female	76 (58%)	294 (60%)
Race[a]		
White (non-Hispanic)	96 (73%)	360 (74%)
Hispanic	20 (15%)	49 (10%)
Black (African American)	11 (8%)	50 (10%)
Asian	4 (3%)	16 (3%)
Other/unknown	2 (1%)	11 (2%)
Marital status		
Married/living with partner	99 (76%)	267 (55%)
Single	17 (13%)	184 (38%)
Divorced/separated	10 (8%)	22 (4%)
Widowed	4 (3%)	13 (3%)

Notes
Not all patients participated in therapy.
a   Three subjects identified as both Hispanic and Black.

changed across sessions. Results suggested that, overall, family members perceived a significant increase in communication across FFGT sessions ($\beta = 1.26$, standard error $= 0.18$, $t = 7.07$, $p < 0.001$).

Promise in ameliorating and preventing depression

Table 18.2 shows the comparison for individual subjects of mean scores at baseline and after 6 months of bereavement on the Beck Depression Inventory-II (BDI) questionnaire (Steer, Ball, Ranieri, & Beck, 1999; Steer, Brown, Beck, & Sanderson, 2001), with these scores further broken out by family subtype. Clearly scores for depression reduce with time, but mean scores for therapy arms reduce to a greater degree. Selecting the 15% of subjects most distressed at baseline on the Brief Symptom Inventory-global scale as a selection criterion for distress, significant reductions in their BDI depression occurred, with reduction of 5.3 points on the BDI with six sessions of family therapy ($p = 0.024$ compared with usual care) and 8.6 points with 10 sessions ($p = 0.010$) in a linear mixed-effects model comparing the change scores across intervention conditions, adjusting for baseline BDI scores.

Table 18.2 Mean and standard deviation scores on the Beck Depression Inventory (BDI) for 220 subjects after 6 months' bereavement displayed by both intervention arm and family type

Family type	Randomization arm	Number completed, mean (SD) BDI scores at baseline	Number completed, mean (SD) BDI scores at 6 months of bereavement[a]
All family members combined	Standard care	$n=158, 13.5 (8.9)$	$n=54, 11.2 (10.2)$
	FFGT 6 sessions	$n=184, 14.6 (9.1)$	$n=89, 9.4 (7.6)$
	FFGT 10 sessions	$n=194, 12.2 (9.2)$	$n=77, 9.8 (8.7)$
Intermediate families	Standard care	11.6 (8.1)	10.9 (10.7)
	FFGT 6 sessions	12.4 (8.9)	8.1 (6.8)
	FFGT 10 sessions	15.3 (9.4)	12.4 (10.1)
Sullen families	Standard care	14.1 (9.0)	13.0 (11.6)
	FFGT 6 sessions	14.4 (8.1)	9.8 (8.1)
	FFGT 10 sessions	9.4 (8.0)	7.8 (6.7)
Hostile families	Standard care	16.8 (9.5)	13.7 (9.5)
	FFGT 6 sessions	18.4 (11.7)	10.4 (6.1)
	FFGT 10 sessions	11.8 (8.8)	7.9 (8.4)

a   Data available for only those subjects completing this phase of study by May 2011.

Potential to prevent complicated grief disorder

Using the 11-item measure Complicated Grief Consensus Criteria (copyright Prigerson & Maciejewski, 2005, personal communication), complicated grief was diagnosed when (A) beyond 6 months of bereavement, (B) a distressing or disrupting sense of longing or yearning for the deceased persisted, (C) with an additional four out of eight symptoms of (1) difficulty accepting the loss, (2) difficulty moving on, (3) numbness or difficulty connecting with others, (4) loss of trust, (5) bitterness, (6) meaninglessness/emptiness, (7) future without purpose, (8) feeling on edge and easily startled, and (D) this state caused functional impairment in social, occupational, or domestic life.

For the first 174 subjects reaching 6 months of bereavement, we found a rate of complicated grief of 25% among individuals receiving standard care compared with 16% for those receiving family therapy. These data raise the possibility that family therapy will reduce rates of development of complicated grief preventively.

Therapy processes

How do therapists achieve these results? Close examination of family therapy sessions, along with feedback elicited from the therapists, has confirmed the strategies that therapists follow. Fidelity coding of the first three sessions ($n = 144$) of recorded therapy delivered to 74 families (299 individuals) by 32 therapists made use of the FFGT fidelity coding measure (Chan, O'Neill, McKenzie, Love, & Kissane, 2004). Inter-rater reliability was satisfactory at 88%.

The therapist behaviors that were rated could be broadly classified as:

1 engaging/joining with the family (e.g., "The therapist elicited expectations for the therapy from family members");
2 conducting a relational assessment of family functioning (e.g., "The therapist asked about family communication");
3 reviewing multigenerational influences (e.g., "The therapist attempted to link family patterns across the generations");
4 exploring family identity and values (e.g., "The therapist attempted to elicit information on an overall family motto or tradition"); and
5 maintaining a realistic focus of therapy (e.g., "The family and therapist identified shared goals and concerns to become the focus of family meetings").

The proportion of family sessions featuring these five processes ranged from 78% (engaging the family successfully) to 59% (creating goals for therapy). Some 98% of assessments elicited the story of the illness, 97% elicited family concerns, 91% identified patterns of relating, 74% a comprehensive discussion about family communication, 75% the family's capacity for teamwork, 72% reinforced family strengths, 66% clarified family roles and values, and 60% beliefs. Less use was made of summaries (42%), family mottos (32%), exploration of family conflict in the assessment phase (32%), and the formalization of a comprehensive family treatment plan (20%). The last may be partly understood as therapists waiting until supervision to fully formulate their treatment plan.

Challenges identified by the therapists

As part of our peer supervision process after every session, therapists completed structured process notes in which they were asked to identify challenging moments during the session. The three most common types of challenges identified by therapists were:

1 establishing and maintaining boundaries in the home setting (e.g., "Family members come and go here, adding to the chaos and stress");
2 attending to grief and open discussion of death and dying (e.g., "Discussing spiritual beliefs and death and dying was challenging"); and
3 determining a useful focus of therapy when there are longstanding familial issues (e.g., "There was too much to talk about and not enough time. We had a marathon session").

The following selected statements from therapists poignantly capture some of the challenging aspects of this work:

From a personal perspective, realizing the degree of Robert's illness had a significant impact. At different moments during the session, Robert felt sick, rested his head between his hands, down to his knees, and closed his eyes.

I felt uncomfortable asking them to pierce their veil of optimism by concretely contemplating a future hypothetical where she is dead if this isn't something her doctors are talking to her about (though I did it anyway!).

Working with the reality that this is such a nice, loving family, where the children are going to lose their father to a terrible illness, is very hard.

When Ellen asked, "How will I know when it is time? I don't feel ready yet," my initial reaction was panic. What could I possibly say? As I looked into her eyes, it became clear why we were all here. It was hard to sit through their pain.

Despite these challenges, the therapist accompanies the family through the multiple losses associated with advanced disease and ultimately death, often getting to know their ill relative rather intimately at the end of his or her life. Almost without exception, therapists were able to attend the funeral, which furthers their involvement with the family. This continuity of care from palliative care into bereavement is invaluable to the family and empowers the therapist to join the family's experience of loss and "put in circulation" (White, 1988, p. 24) the memory of the deceased family member.

Discussion

The data from our trial of FFGT delivered preventively to at-risk families enrolled during palliative care and continued into bereavement show promise for the capacity of family care to prevent complicated grief and depression arising in bereavement. Most families show profiles of increased or sustained family communication over therapy sessions. Our data are in keeping with the literature that suggests that family therapy is an important adjunct to individual and group therapy models of bereavement care (Lieberman, 1978).

FFGT is distinguishable from other approaches to the treatment of complicated grief (e.g., Kavanagh, 1990; Shear, Frank, Houck, & Reynolds, 2005) in two ways: (1) FFGT focuses on prevention, and therefore targets at-risk families *prior* to the death of a loved one, and (2) FFGT privileges the family, rather than the supportive relationship with an individual therapist, as the preferred context in which grief is processed. The cohesive and well-attuned family will mobilize effectively around its vulnerable members in the setting of bereavement. This might include recognizing when one party requires individual professional attention and facilitating such support-seeking behavior (e.g., when a pre-existing psychiatric condition is exacerbated in the setting of bereavement). The fractured, conflict-ridden, or non-communicative family deprives its individual members of a key resource for processing shared grief, and increases the risk of avoidance, isolation, and prolonged distress. The hypothesized mechanism of change in FFGT is therefore the strengthening of family bonds. The therapist specifically looks to improve three areas: constructive communication, capacity to tolerate and negotiate differences, and collaborative problem solving. Both arms of the dual process model of mourning are effectively attended to by the family as a whole.

Because of the therapist's involvement with the family through a time made difficult by one of their number dying, regular peer supervision proves helpful to discuss clinical challenges and process personal grief reactions (Zaider & Kissane, 2009). Contact and exchange of information with the medical team is also encouraged to keep the therapist aware of disease-related developments, the prognosis, hospital admissions, or test results. Our model of family therapy has been taught to many social workers, psychologists, and psychiatrists. We believe that competent clinicians find little difficulty in understanding and applying the model to bereaved families. By improving communication about illness and death together with the resultant grieving and coping, mutual support and teamwork are fostered. Families are helped to tolerate differences of opinion, optimize their functioning as a whole, and share their grief together.

Our model has drawn considerable interest from countries where family traditions are strong and decision making is family centered. It has a natural fit with Japanese, Chinese, South Asian, and Mediterranean families. It is sensitive to the cultural needs of families, yet helps blended families to make sense of their past and respect the strengths of both families of origin. Exploration of religious traditions and the family's use of ritual are grist to the mill. Families are especially appreciative of therapy in the home, beginning during palliative care, so that the therapist gets to know the dying patient and can later recall their comments to the bereaved. This continuity of care has merit, but does not prohibit the recruitment of family members when therapy begins after death. Thus FFGT has utility as a model of family-centered care not only during hospice care, but also in bereavement.

Conclusion

In this chapter, we have shown evidence of the promise for family therapy to both ameliorate and prevent complicated grief. We recognize that individual or group therapy for the bereaved may be all that is possible in some geographic settings. Nevertheless, family therapy can be extraordinarily complementary and, for many, it could be the primary mode of therapeutic intervention.

Acknowledgements

This research has been supported by the National Research Council of Australia, the Bethlehem Griffiths Research Foundation, and the National Institutes of Health (R01 CA 115329 DW Kissane, Principal Investigator; and R03 CA138131 TI Zaider, Principal Investigator). We thank the many clinicians, therapists, research collaborators, and colleagues who have supported this work across two decades.

References

Ainsworth, M. D. S., & Eichberg, C. G. (1991). Effects on infant–mother attachment of mother's experience related to loss of attachment figure. In Stevenson-Hinde, J., & Marris, P. (Eds.), *Attachment across the life cycle* (pp. 160–183). New York: Routledge.

Black, D., & Urbanowicz, M. A. (1987). Family intervention with bereaved children. *Journal of Child Psychology and Psychiatry, 28*(3), 467–476.

Bonanno, G. A., Wortman, C. B., & Nesse, R. M. (2004). Prospective patterns of resilience and maladjustment during widowhood. *Psychology and Aging, 19*(2), 260–271.

Boss, P. (2006). *Loss, trauma and resilience: Therapeutic work with ambiguous loss.* New York: Norton.

Bowlby, J. (1969). *Attachment and loss, vol. 1: Attachment.* New York: Basic Books.

Chan, E. K., O'Neill, I., McKenzie, M., Love, A. & Kissane, D. (2004). What works for therapists conducting family meetings: Treatment integrity in family focused grief therapy during palliative care and bereavement. *Journal of Pain and Symptom Management, 27*(6), 502–512.

Creamer, M., Burgess, P., & Pattison, P. (1992). Reaction to trauma: A cognitive processing model. *Journal of Abnormal Psychology, 101*(3), 452–459.

Dumont, I., & Kissane, D. W. (2009). Techniques for framing questions in conducting family meetings in palliative care. *Palliative Supportive Care, 7*(2), 163–170.

Edwards, B., & Lavery, V. (2005). Validity of the Family Relationships Index as a screening tool. *Psychooncology, 14*, 546–554.

Folkman, S., & Moskowitz, J. T. (2000). Positive affect and the other side of coping. *American Psychologist, 55*(6), 647–654.

Goldstein, J., Alter, C. L., & Axelrod, R. (1996). A psychoeducational bereavement-support group for families provided in an outpatient cancer center. *Journal of Cancer Education, 11*(4), 233–237.

Janoff-Bulman, R. (1989). Assumptive worlds and the stress of traumatic events: Applications of the scheme construct. *Social Cognition, 7*, 113–136.

Janoff-Bulman, R., & Berg, M. (1998). Disillusionment and the creation of value: From traumatic losses to existential gains. In Harvey, J. (Ed.), *Perspectives on loss: A sourcebook* (pp. 35–47). Philadelphia, PA: Brunner Mazel.

Kavanagh, D. J. (1990). Towards a cognitive–behavioural intervention for adult grief reactions. *British Journal of Psychiatry, 157*, 373–383.

Kissane, D. (2000). Family grief therapy: A model for working with families during palliative care and bereavement. In Baider, L., Cooper, C., & De-Nour, A. (Eds.), *Cancer and the family* (pp. 175–197). Chichester: Wiley.

Kissane, D., & Bloch, S. (1994). Family grief. *British Journal of Psychiatry, 164*, 728–740.

Kissane, D., & Bloch, S. (2002). *Family focused grief therapy: A model of family-centred care during palliative care and bereavement.* Buckingham: Open University Press.

Kissane, D., Bloch, S., Dowe, D., Snyder, R., Onghena, P., McKenzie, D., & Wallace, C. (1996). The Melbourne family grief study I: Perceptions of family functioning in bereavement. *American Journal of Psychiatry, 153*, 650–658.

Kissane, D. W., Bloch, S., McKenzie, M., McDowall, A. C., & Nitzan, R. (1998). Family grief therapy: A preliminary account of a new model to promote healthy family functioning during palliative care and bereavement. *Psychooncology, 7*(1), 14–25.

Kissane, D., Bloch, S., Onghena, P., McKenzie, D., Snyder, R., & Dowe, D. (1996). The Melbourne family grief study II: Psychosocial morbidity and grief in bereaved families. *American Journal of Psychiatry, 153*, 659–666.

Kissane, D. W., & Hooghe, A. (2011) Family therapy for the bereaved. In Neimeyer, R. A., Harris, D. L., Winokuer, H. R., & Thornton, G. F. (Eds.), *Grief and bereavement in contemporary society: Bridging research and practice* (pp. 287–302). New York: Routledge.

Kissane, D., Lichtenthal, W., & Zaider, T. (2007–2008). Family care before and after bereavement. *Omega, 56*, 21–32.

Kissane, D. W., McKenzie, M., Bloch, S., Moskowitz, C., McKenzie, D. P., & O'Neill, I. (2006). Family focused grief therapy: A randomized, controlled trial in palliative care and bereavement. *American Journal of Psychiatry, 163*(7), 1208–1218.

Kissane, D. W., McKenzie, M., McKenzie, D. P., Forbes, A., O'Neill, I., & Bloch, S. (2003). Psychosocial morbidity associated with patterns of family functioning in palliative care: Baseline data from the Family Focused Grief Therapy controlled trial. *Palliative Medicine, 17*(6), 527–537.

Landau, J. (2007). Enhancing resilience: Families and communities as agents for change. *Family Process, 46*(3), 351–365.

Lieberman, S. (1978). Nineteen cases of morbid grief. *British Journal of Psychiatry, 132*, 159–163.

McKenzie, K. R. (1995). Rationale for group psychotherapy in managed care. In McKenzie, K. R. (Ed.), *Effective use of group therapy in managed care* (pp. 1–25). Washington, DC: American Psychiatric Press.

Moos, R. H., & Moos, B. S. (1981). *Family environment scale manual*. Stanford, CA: Consulting Psychologists Press.

Neimeyer, R. (2011). Reconstructing meaning in bereavement. In Watson, M., & Kissane, D. (Eds.), *Handbook of psychotherapy in cancer* (pp. 247–257). Chichester: Wiley-Blackwell.

Parkes, C. (1972). *Bereavement: Studies of grief in adult life*. London: Tavistock.

Parkes, C. (1998). *Bereavement studies of grief in adult life* (3rd edn.). Madison, CT: International University Press.

Paul, N., & Grosser, G. (1965). Operational mourning and its role in conjoint family therapy. *Community Health Journal, 1*, 339–345.

Prigerson, H. G., Horowitz, M. J., Jacobs, S. C., Parkes, C. M., Aslan, M., Goodkin, K., et al. (2009). Prolonged grief disorder: Psychometric validation of criteria proposed for DSM-V and ICD-11. *PLoS Med, 6*(8), e1000121.

Rauch, P. K., & Muriel, A. C. (2004). The importance of parenting concerns among patients with cancer. *Critical Reviews in Oncology/Hematology, 49*(1), 37–42.

Rosenthal, P. A. (1980). Short-term family therapy and pathological grief resolution with children and adolescents. *Family Process, 19*(2), 151–159.

Rotheram-Borus, M. J., Stein, J. A., & Lin, Y. Y. (2001). Impact of parent death and an intervention on the adjustment of adolescents whose parents have HIV/AIDS. *Journal of Consulting and Clinical Psychology, 69*(5), 763–773.

Rotheram-Borus, M. J., Weiss, R., Alber, S., & Lester, P. (2005). Adolescent adjustment before and after HIV-related parental death. *Journal of Consulting and Clinical Psychology, 73*(2), 221–228.

Sandler, I. N., Ayers, T. S., Wolchik, S. A., Tein, J. Y., Kwok, O. M., Haine, R. A., et al. (2003). The family bereavement program: Efficacy evaluation of a theory-based prevention program for parentally bereaved children and adolescents. *Journal of Consulting and Clinical Psychology, 71*(3), 587–600.

Shapiro, E. R. (2008). Whose recovery, of what? Relationships and environments promoting grief and growth. *Death Studies, 32*(1), 40–58.

Shaver, P., & Tancredy, C. (2001). Emotion, attachment and bereavement: A conceptual commentary. In Stroebe, M., Hansson, R., Stroebe, W., & Schut, H. (Eds.), *Handbook of bereavement research: Consequences, coping and care* (pp. 63–68). Washington, DC: American Psychological Association.

Shear, K., Frank, E., Houck, P. R., & Reynolds, C. F. III. (2005). Treatment of complicated grief: A randomized controlled trial. *JAMA, 293*(21), 2601–2608.

Steer, R., Ball, R., Ranieri, W., & Beck, A. (1999). Dimensions of the Beck Depression Inventory-II in clinically depressed outpatients. *Journal of Clinical Psychology, 55*(1), 117–128.

Steer, R., Brown, G., Beck, A., & Sanderson, W. (2001). Mean Beck Depression Inventory-II scores by severity of major depressive episode. *Psychological Reports, 88*(3), 1075–1076.

Stroebe, M., & Schut, H. (2001). Models of coping with bereavement: A review. In Stroebe, M., Hansson, R., Stroebe, W., & Schut, H. (Eds.), *Handbook of bereavement research: Consequences, coping and care* (pp. 375–403). Washington, DC: APA Books.

Whitaker, D. S., & Lieberman, M. A. (1964). *Psychotherapy through the group process.* Chicago: Adline.

White, M. (1988). Saying hello again. The incorporation of the lost relationship in the resolution of grief. *Dulwich Centre Newsletter*, Spring (p. 24). South Australia.

Williams, W. V., & Polak, P. R. (1979). Follow-up research in primary prevention: A model of adjustment in acute grief. *Journal of Clinical Psychology, 35*(1), 35–45.

Zaider, T., & Kissane, D. (2007). Resilient families. In Monroe, B., & Oliviere, D. (Eds.), *Resilience in palliative care.* Oxford: Oxford University Press.

Zaider, T., & Kissane, D. (2009). The assessment and management of family distress during palliative care. *Current Opinion in Supportive and Palliative Care, 3*(1), 67–71.

19 Brief group therapies for complicated grief

Interpretive and supportive approaches

William E. Piper and John Ogrodniczuk

In 1986, several members of our team of researchers and clinicians (W. Piper, M. McCallum, and H. Azim) worked together in the outpatient Walk-in Clinic of the Department of Psychiatry, at the University of Alberta Hospital in Edmonton, Alberta, Canada. Because of the high volume of patients seen in our Walk-in Clinic, approximately 2,000 new referrals each year, most patients were treated with group therapy rather than individual therapy. To obtain a more accurate account of the utilization of group therapy, we decided to conduct an informal in-house review of the objectives and apparent achievements of several therapy groups provided in the clinic, particularly the time-limited short-term therapy groups, given their cost-effective potential.

Our review revealed that the short-term therapy groups appeared to be experiencing *task overload*. That is, the groups seemed to be trying to achieve too many things: crisis intervention; support for day-to-day problem solving; assessment of suitability for long-term group therapy; training for new therapists who were inexperienced with group therapy; and treatment for symptom reduction, insight, and development of interpersonal skills and personality change. Thus, in our feedback to the clinic, we concluded that the short-term therapy groups would probably benefit from having a narrower focus with a more limited but more realistic set of objectives. Because the topic of death loss was very prevalent among the patients who were participating in the short-term therapy groups, we decided to conduct a pilot therapy group to determine how well a short-term therapy group that focused on death losses and that had more limited objectives would work. As it turned out, the group worked very well. After discussions with the therapists and clinic administrators, we began providing loss groups for patients who met criteria for complicated grief (CG).

In general, the current chapter focuses on the treatment of CG by means of short-term group therapies. In particular, the chapter focuses on our program of providing one of two models of brief group therapies for CG (Piper, Ogrodniczuk, Joyce, & Weideman, 2011). Unfortunately, although CG is a familiar condition, it lacks a standard definition or a standard set of diagnostic criteria. Typical symptoms of CG include shock, denial, sadness, irritability, preoccupation with the lost person, yearning for the lost person, and searching for the lost person. In addition, dysfunctional behavior with family, friends, and work associates, as well as health-compromising behaviors such as excessive drinking and excessive smoking, is common. Also common is comorbidity with disorders such as depression. The presence of symptoms and dysfunctional behavior as described above, particularly if expressed in high intensity and long duration, is what most clinicians regard as CG; and that is how we regarded it in our initial work with the concept.

During the 20 years in which we conducted the three clinical trials, definitions and criteria for some concepts changed. Fortunately, however, other key concepts remained virtually constant. Such was the case with Horowitz's Impact of Event Scale. The two subscales of this measure (intrusion and avoidance) provided us with two indicators of CG. *Intrusion* refers to the degree to which thoughts, feelings, and memories about the lost person intrude upon the day-to-day functioning of the patient. *Avoidance* refers to the patient's active resistance to thoughts, feelings, and memories about the lost person. Thus, CG, as defined by Horowitz, served as both a cut-off criterion for CG (operational definition) and an outcome variable. For example, in our prevalence study a patient had to attain a score of 10 or above on either the intrusion or avoidance subscale and a score of 2 or above in one of the six areas of the Social Adjustment Scale – Self-report. In addition, the death loss had to have occurred at least 3 months prior to the assessment of the patient.

It has been our impression that losses, the effects of losses on survivors, and the presence of CG criteria usually do not receive adequate attention in intake interviews. In part, this is because assessors are required to obtain a large and diverse amount of information in a limited amount of time. This involves conducting a thorough mental status examination, an inquiry about relevant diagnostic criteria, and a review of possible causes and precipitants of the patient's current problems. Not much time remains available for assessing loss information. To circumvent this problem, we attempted to identify a few items from various loss questionnaires that could successfully detect the presence or absence of CG (Piper, Ogrodniczuk, & Weideman, 2005). Two such items/questions were found. They were: "During the past 7 days, pictures about the loss popped into my mind" and "During the past 7 days, I have tried not to think about the loss." If the patient tested positive on either item, the probability that the patient had CG was 0.90. The assessor could then follow up with a more detailed set of questions to confirm or disconfirm the initial impression. The fact that CG is not in the *Diagnostic and statistical manual of mental disorders* (DSM) probably contributes to the neglect of the recognition of CG.

Prevalence of CG

Large-scale prevalence studies for CG, that is, those with several hundred subjects, are quite rare. Nevertheless, from the few large-scale studies that have been conducted it has been estimated that approximately 20% of all bereaved individuals meet criteria for CG (Zisook & Lyons, 1989–1990). The percentage of psychiatric outpatients who meet the criteria for CG may be even higher.

Studies have reported estimates ranging from 15% to 33%. The findings from our own prevalence study (Piper, Ogrodniczuk, Azim, & Weideman, 2001), which involved 729 patients, were at the high end of this range, 33%. This suggested that approximately one third of the outpatients who walked through the doors of our clinics met criteria for CG.

Differences between our two grief therapies and other therapies in the field

Taken together, the characteristics of our approach to treatment differ from other approaches to treatment in the literature. First, it was a psychosocial form of treatment, in contrast to a biological form such as medication. Second, it was psychodynamic in orientation with a conceptual emphasis on conflictual components such as wishes, anxiety, and defenses, and a technical emphasis on clarification, confrontation, and interpretation. Third, it was a group form of treatment, thereby involving an entire set of patients in interaction with a therapist and one another, as opposed to a more private, one-to-one relationship between patient and therapist. Fourth, it was a time-limited form of treatment with a predefined beginning and ending, as opposed to a form of therapy with an open-ended contract. Fifth, patients were expected to decide what to talk about at the beginning of each session and throughout treatment, rather than being directed by the therapist as in the case of some cognitive–behavioral approaches. Given these characteristics, we could have named the treatment Time-Limited, Short-Term, Dynamically-Oriented Group Therapy. However, for the sake of parsimony, we settled on the simple labels *supportive therapy* and *interpretive therapy*.

Differences between our interpretive and supportive therapies

The overall objective for interpretive therapy is to enhance patient insight about repetitive conflicts and trauma associated with their loss. The conflict may be intrapsychic or external in nature. The overall objective for supportive therapy is to improve the patient's immediate adaptation to his or her life situation. In interpretive therapy, among other techniques, the therapist maintains pressure on the patients to talk, encourages the patients to explore uncomfortable emotions, and provides the patients with interpretations. (Interpretations are statements that make reference to dynamic components such as wishes, fears, and defenses.) In supportive therapy, among other techniques, the therapist gratifies the patients, provides guidance, and provides non-interpretive interventions. (Non-interpretive interventions include brief questions, clarifications, and empathic comments.)

Technical manuals and feedback

It is important to keep in mind that what we have designated as interpretive and supportive forms of dynamically oriented group therapy represent part of only a few reports in the literature about using group therapy with CG patients. To help therapists adhere to the intended forms of therapy, we constructed a technical manual for each of the two forms of therapy. We also provided feedback to each therapist regarding how successful he or she had been in carrying out the two forms of treatment as planned. This feedback was presented to the therapists after every other session in the form of ratings completed by independent raters.

An example of a group therapy being used to treat patients with CG is interpersonal psychotherapy (IPT; Wilfley, MacKenzie, Welch, Ayers, & Weissman, 2000). Although this approach is well described by Wilfley et al. in their book, they report no efficacy studies for this form of therapy. Another example of a group therapy being used to treat patients with CG is described in a study conducted by Horowitz, Marmar, Weiss, DeWitt, and Rosenbaum (1984). Unfortunately, the study did not make clear how much time had elapsed between the deaths and treatment. Most of the variables that were analyzed were process variables and not outcome variables.

The following material from typical therapy sessions illustrates how a therapist can respond to the group either interpretively or supportively.

Illustration of therapist's interpretive statements

(Lengthy silence followed by therapist's interpretive statements.)

Therapist: I think the group is resisting putting what you are feeling into words. I wonder if you can put it into words.

Ed: Yes, I'm trying but I can't find the words.

Therapist: But this is everybody's difficulty, not just Ed's. What about others?

Brenda: Well, I feel that our problems are hopeless.

Therapist: That is definitely the feeling, along with feeling sad. You seem to be on the verge of tears. All of you are in the same boat – feeling hopeless and sad as it sinks in a sea of tears.

Brenda: Well, our therapist is trying his best but we are just hopeless.

Therapist: You don't know what to do with liking me and hating me at the same time. Liking me because I helped you recognize your feelings and hating me because our group is almost finished and you are losing me.

This interaction illustrated how the therapist can use interpretive technical features to maintain pressure on the patients to talk, encourage the patients to explore uncomfortable emotions, and provide the patients with interpretations of conflict.

Illustration of therapist's supportive statements

(Lengthy silence followed by therapist's supportive statements.)

Therapist: Despite the silence, I think that members of the group are working hard.

Ed: Yes, I'm trying hard and I'm almost able to put things into words.

Therapist: Why don't you take a stab at it? Sometimes if one person is able to
                start others are able to start too.
Brenda: Well, I've been feeling hopeless and sad but, in a funny way, I've also
                felt good about what I've learned in the group.
Therapist: Yes, this has been happening in spite of the fact that our group will
                end next week. I suspect that in some ways we will all miss parts of
                each other.

This interaction illustrated how the therapist can use supportive technical features to gratify the patients, provide guidance, and provide non-interpretive interventions.

Clinical trials

Since 1986, we have conducted over 90 short-term loss groups. Over one half of these groups participated in one of three clinical trials conducted by our research team. We refer to the three as the control, comparative, and composition studies. Two forms of dynamically oriented short-term therapy (interpretive and supportive models) were studied. They were similar to each other in structure (e.g., one 90-minute therapy session per week for 12 weeks), but differed from each other in style of therapy (e.g., the therapist's focus on transference in the interpretive model).

The overall objective of treatment was to enhance patient insight about repetitive conflicts and trauma associated with the losses that are assumed to serve as impediments to a normal mourning process. A related objective was to help the patients develop tolerance for ambivalence toward the people whom they have lost. In the sessions, the therapist attempted to create a climate of tolerable tension and deprivation. In the interpretive therapy, the therapist attempted to (a) maintain pressure on the patients to talk, (b) encourage them to explore uncomfortable emotions, (c) make interpretations about conflicts, (d) direct attention to subjective impressions of the therapist, (e) make links between the patients' relationships with the therapist or each other and the patients' relationships with others in their lives, (f) focus on the patients and therapist in the here-and-now treatment situation, and (g) direct attention to the patients' subjective impressions of others outside the treatment situation.

In contrast, in supportive therapy the therapist attempted to (a) gratify the patients, (b) make non-interpretive interventions such as reflections, questions, and provision of information, (c) provide guidance similar to the role of a kindly family doctor, (d) engage in problem-solving strategies with the patients, (e) offer explanations that locate the responsibility for the patients' difficulties outside the patient, (f) praise the patients, and (g) display personal information, opinions, and core values.

We believed that a useful way to conceptualize each of the main features of interpretive group therapy was to regard each of its features as a dimension. For some dimensions (e.g., focusing on transference), the higher their level, the more the therapy was regarded as interpretive. For other dimensions (e.g., gratifying the patients), the lower the level, the more the therapy is regarded as interpretive. Supportive therapy can be conceptualized in a similar way, that is, for some dimensions (e.g., making clarifications) the higher their level, the more the therapy is regarded as supportive and for other dimensions (e.g., making interpretations) the lower the level, the more the therapy is regarded as supportive.

Control trial

The control clinical trial involved only interpretive therapy (Piper, McCallum, & Azim, 1992). We had not yet begun to offer a supportive form of group therapy for loss patients. An immediate treatment condition was compared with a waiting-list control condition.

On the basis of 94 patients from 16 therapy groups, who had been randomly assigned to the conditions, the findings clearly indicated superior outcomes for patients in the immediate treatment (control) condition. Examination of the technical features of treatment confirmed its interpretive nature.

Comparative trial

Although the results for interpretive group therapy were clearly favorable, not all patients benefited. Stemming from work carried out by Rockland (1989) and Werman (1984) in individual therapy and following work that we had been pursuing in the case of short-term individual therapy for a wide range of outpatients in our clinic (Piper, Joyce, McCallum, & Azim, 1998), we suspected that patient personality variables may influence the outcome of therapy. We developed and labeled one such personality variable, the patient's Quality of Object Relations (QOR). We defined QOR as a person's internal enduring tendency to establish certain kinds of relationships that range along an overall dimension from 1 (primitive) to 9 (mature). An assessor conducts a 1-hour interview that focuses on the nature of the patient's relationships during three stages of life (childhood, adolescence, and adulthood). The assessor uses a scoring manual to determine the overall score. In the individual therapy studies we found a matching effect. Patients with higher QOR scores tended to improve more in interpretive individual therapy, and patients with lower QOR scores tended to improve more in supportive individual therapy. We decided to check for the presence of this type of effect in the comparative trial. On the basis of 139 patients in 16 therapy groups, strong evidence for the matching effect was found (Piper, Debbane, Bienvenu, & Garant, 1984). High-QOR patients benefited more from interpretive group therapy, and low-QOR patients benefited more from supportive group therapy.

Composition trial

In the comparative trial, the composition of each therapy group was mixed (heterogeneous) in terms of the patients' QOR scores. We wondered if the matching effect would be even more pronounced in groups composed of all high-QOR patients who received interpretive therapy and groups composed of all low-QOR patients who received supportive therapy. This led to our decision to conduct the composition trial (Piper, Ogrodniczuk, Joyce, Weideman, & Rosie, 2007). Like other terms in the literature such as *complicated grief*, the literature is replete with references to the term *composition* and yet seems to lack a common definition. For the purposes of this study, composition was defined as the proportion of patients in a group with high QOR scores.

Four conditions were created experimentally in the composition trial: (1) homogeneous, high-QOR interpretive groups; (2) homogeneous, low-QOR supportive groups; (3) heterogeneous, mixed-QOR interpretive groups; and (4) heterogeneous, mixed-QOR supportive groups. Our primary hypothesis was that patients in the two homogeneous conditions would experience greater benefit than the patients in the two heterogeneous conditions.

On the basis of 135 patients in 18 therapy groups, we found that the best outcomes were achieved by the homogeneous high-QOR patients who received interpretive group therapy and the poorest outcomes were achieved by the homogeneous low-QOR patients who received supportive therapy. Outcome for the mixed-QOR groups fell in between. Even though our primary hypothesis did not receive support, we nevertheless found evidence for an important composition effect. Using a QOR cut-off score of 4.2, the score that we found to be a useful differentiator in previous studies, we found that the greater was the proportion of high-QOR patients in the group, the better was the outcome. This was true regardless of the patient's own QOR score or the form of therapy (interpretive or supportive) that the patient had received. It is possible that the high-QOR patients beneficially provided peer support and served as models of useful problem-solving behavior. In their absence, the primitive behaviors of low-QOR patients may have led to a group culture in which the provision of support and engagement in problem solving was regarded as intrusive and was met with suspicion and resistance. These, of course, are speculative ideas, which require future research testing and confirmation.

Follow-up

Once the efficacy of a form of therapy has been demonstrated, usually through randomized controlled trials, the question that follows naturally is: Will the effects last? To address the question concerning lasting effects, follow-up data are typically examined. However, for many disorders, follow-up data either are not available or contain significant flaws. Typically, the nature of the follow-up sample is problematic. Inevitably, some patients do not return for their follow-up assessments. Thus, the sample will have decreased in size, which will compromise the statistical power of the analyses. The representativeness of the follow-up sample can also be questioned. Although missing data always create ambiguities, if the number of missing data is relatively small and there is evidence that the sample of missing data is similar to the sample of non-missing data, the findings are usually considered worthy of consideration. We believe that this is the case concerning the follow-up data from our composition trial.

Achieving lasting benefits from brief psychotherapies for certain disorders has proven to be difficult. Such has been the case for the treatment of depression. This is relevant to the treatment of patients with CG because of the overlap of symptoms with depression (e.g., sadness). Overall, the findings concerning the long-term benefits of brief therapies for depression have been disappointing. In the National Institute of Mental Health treatment of depression collaborative study (Elkin et al., 1989), patients received an average of 16 sessions of treatment. Only 33% of the patients who began therapy met recovery criteria, and nearly 40% of those relapsed within 18 months. The investigators concluded that "16 weeks of these specific forms of treatment are insufficient for most patients to achieve full recovery and lasting remission" (p. 782). Similar negative conclusions have been made regarding remission rates in the STAR*D clinical trial (Trivedi et al., 2006) by Fava and colleagues (2004) and in a recent meta-analytic review conducted by de Maat, Dekker, Schoevers, and de Jonghe (2006). In their review, the remission rate for cognitive therapy was 38%, and the relapse rate was 27%. Although these findings have been viewed as promising for advocates of psychosocial therapies, the relapse rates unfortunately have remained high at approximately 30%.

In the follow-up data from our composition trial, of the 110 completers in the study, 84 (77%) provided follow-up data. In addition, we compared patients who provided follow-up data with those who did not on 22 initial status variables. Only 1 of 22 variables was significant. Patients who did not provide follow-up data had higher posttherapy Beck Depression Inventory scores (Beck & Steer, 1987) (mean = 33, SD = 12) than patients who provided follow-up data (mean = 25, SD = 12), $t(106) = 2.99$, $p = 0.003$. However, given the number of analyses conducted, this could easily be a result of error. Thus, there was little evidence of differences between patients who did and patients who did not provide follow-up data. Before examining the findings from our composition trial, several distinctions among types of follow-up and patient outcome need to be clear:

- *Maintenance* refers to recovery during treatment followed by maintenance of recovery during follow-up.
- *Relapse* refers to recovery during treatment followed by relapse during follow-up.
- *Delayed* refers to non-recovery during treatment followed by recovery during follow-up.
- *Non-recovery* refers to non-recovery during treatment followed by non-recovery during follow-up.

These distinctions were used with the data from the 18 therapy groups of our composition trial. Outcome was represented by the achievement of clinical significance for two well-known grief outcome variables in the research literature: intrusion and avoidance. They were the two subscales from the Impact of Event Scale (Horowitz, Wilner, & Alvarez, 1979). Clinical significance was determined by the procedure of Jacobson and colleagues (Jacobson, Follette, & Revenstorf, 1984; Jacobson & Revenstorf, 1988). Recovery was defined as dropping below the clinical significance cut-off score and relapse as rising above the cut-off score. Next, we checked whether the overall proportion of patients who achieved clinical significance at posttherapy was different from the proportion of patients who achieved clinical significance at follow-up. Using the test for a difference between two dependent proportions, there was a significant increase from post therapy (30/59=0.51) to follow-up (42/59=0.71) in the proportion of patients who achieved clinical significance for intrusion, $z(N=59)=2.83, p=0.004$. There was also a significant increase from posttherapy (34/64=0.53) to follow-up (46/64=0.72) for avoidance, $z(N=64)=2.88, p=0.004$. Following this, we determined the percentages of patients for the four types of outcome described previously. For intrusion, there were 46% (27/59) maintenance patients, 5% (3/59) relapse patients, 25% (15/59) delayed-recovery patients, and 24% (14/59) non-recovery patients. The results for avoidance were very similar with 48% (31/64) maintenance patients, 5% (3/64) relapse patients, 23% (15/64) delayed-recovery patients, and 23% (15/64) non-recovery patients. Thus, a substantial percentage of the sample, nearly 75%, achieved clinically significant improvement on grief outcomes (intrusion, avoidance) by the end of follow-up, and a smaller proportion failed to maintain their recovered status or failed to recover at all.

If we focus on intrusion, a total of 71% of the patients achieved maintenance or delayed recovery, which is almost 75% of the sample. If one considered only the outcome from pre- to posttherapy, only 46%, which is a little below half of the sample, would have been regarded as improved. Use of the follow-up data creates quite a different impression regarding the degree of improvement.

Meta-analytical reviews and their critiques

In the field of psychotherapy, effectiveness is often expressed in terms of effect size. It is a statistic that expresses the amount of change in a single sample (e.g., from pretreatment to posttreatment) or the difference in the amount of change between two samples (e.g., treated and control group). Because it is expressed in terms of standard deviation units, comparisons can be made across different outcomes, treatments, and studies. In the studies cited in this chapter, effect size is generally defined as the mean of the pretreatment outcome score minus the mean of the posttreatment outcome score divided by the standard deviation of the pretreatment score. It is commonly symbolized as d. This approach to reviewing the literature is commonly referred to as meta-analytic.

During the past decade only a small number of meta-analytic reviews of the efficacy of treatments for CG have been conducted. This reflects the fact that only a small number of clinical trials and other outcome studies have been conducted. In the literature, there are many descriptions of group therapy treatments of CG including some books on cognitive–behavioral therapy (CBT; Rose, 1989) and IPT (Wilfley et al., 2000). It would have been desirable if the reviews had provided a consensus concerning the efficacy of loss interventions. However, this has not been the case. Even less desirable is the fact that reviewers more often than not have been negatively critical about the methodology and conclusions of other reviewers. At times, the criticism has been sharp and accusatory.

For example, Larson and Hoyt (2007) have suggested that Fortner (1999) and Neimeyer (2000) damaged the reputation of grief counseling by misrepresenting empirical findings.

Allumbaugh and Hoyt (1999) presented an overall effect size of 0.43 in their review, which is somewhat smaller than effect sizes commonly reported in psychotherapy outcome studies. Kato and Mann (1999) provided an overview of four major theories of bereavement with their quantitative analysis. Methodological flaws in all of the studies made the results hard to interpret. They reported an overall effect size of 0.11. They were left with the question whether the interventions were powerful enough or the sample was too small to detect differences. Larson and Hoyt (2007) criticized Kato and Mann regarding their method of selecting studies for their review. In addition, they criticized them for constructing an effect size for each measure in their studies.

Neimeyer (2000) produced a meta-analytical review that included 23 studies. The overall effect size was 0.15. Neimeyer's review generated controversy because it relied heavily on an unpublished dissertation completed by Fortner in 1999. He used an idiosyncratic statistic called Treatment Induced Deterioration Effect (TIDE), which had not been subjective to a peer review. Schut, Stroebe, van den Bout, and Terheggen (2001) provided a review of bereavement intervention research. They concluded that the length of time between the loss and the onset of treatment was directly related to better outcome. Similarly to Kato and Mann (1999) they also concluded that most of the studies in their review had methodological problems.

Currier, Neimeyer, and Berman (2008) provided one of the most comprehensive reviews of the field to date. They included 61 studies in their review. They concluded that the interventions reviewed had small effect sizes from pretherapy to posttherapy. In the case of our three clinical trials, Table 19.1 presents the effect sizes from pretherapy to posttherapy for our two primary outcome variables, intrusion and avoidance. Thus, our effect sizes tended to be larger than most of those reported in literature.

Setting aside the rather unpleasant and at times acrimonious tone of many of the reviews, the critiques have been useful in identifying variables to explore in future studies involving the treatment of CG. Such moderating variables include time since the loss, level of CG distress, individual versus group therapy, random assignment to conditions, and therapist training differences.

Table 19.1 Effect sizes for the two primary outcome variables

Outcome variable (and measure)	Controlled trial	Comparative trial	Composition trial
Intrusion (intrusion subscale of the Impact of Event Scale; Horowitz et al., 1979)	0.56	1.09	0.56
Avoidance (avoidance subscale of the Impact of Event Scale; Horowitz et al., 1979)	0.70	1.05	0.85

Most of these variables seemed to be cited in the literature as afterthoughts rather than being chosen a priori as potential moderator variables. Given the finding that the effect sizes associated with our two models of group therapy were larger than most effect sizes reported in the reviews, one reason for this may be the fact that many of the events in the therapies provided here-and-now opportunities to be addressed immediately rather than impediments to the process of therapy. For example, patient lateness or absenteeism may raise concerns about whether the patient will return. Dropping out may trigger feelings associated with witnessing a death. These events are usually regarded as troublesome events in a therapy group. However, in loss groups these are naturally occurring phenomena that are reminiscent of events related to patients' losses. Discussion of such events is often avoided, and such reticence only contributes to similar behaviors of other patients in the group. Finally, the patients came to the Walk-in Clinic because they were suffering from symptoms and dysfunction related to CG. They did not come in response to advertisements about a study in which they could participate and at the same time receive treatment. No advertisements were used in our studies. Instead, patients were usually referred by their family physician.

Evidence-based treatment

From time to time, researchers have afforded special importance and status to aspects of their work if carried out in a particular manner. Currently, it appears to be very important, if not essential, to be able to refer to one's work or findings as evidence based. Two recently published books, *Evidence-Based Treatment for Personality Dysfunction* edited by Magnavita (2010) and *Evidence-Based Psychotherapy* edited by Goodheart, Kazdin, and Sternberg (2006), thoroughly reviewed the terminology associated with evidence-based treatments. Early terminology advocated by a task force of the American Psychological Association initially favored the term *validated* as in *empirically validated treatment*. The criteria required for this designation were stringent (e.g., randomized control trial design, manualized treatment, and replication). However, because the word *validated* conveyed to many people the impression that further research with the treatment would probably be unnecessary and the stringent criteria created artificial conditions, it was replaced with the term *supported*. Later an even broader category of *evidence-based practice* was recommended. This again emphasizes the policy of offering only treatments that are evidence based. The questions that obviously followed were: What criteria define evidence based and what criteria do not? A debate has ensued over this issue. Some therapists restrict *evidence* to mean the findings of randomized clinical trials. Other therapists accept correlational (naturalistic) and case studies as well as randomized clinical trials.

Over 55 years ago, Cronbach and Meehl (1955) published their classic paper on the topic of construct validity. They argued that the criteria for a construct consisted of the entire set of relationships with other constructs. They referred to this pattern of relationships as a nomological network. In a similar way, the criteria for evidence-based treatment consist of the entire set of relationships with other relevant concepts and outcomes. In defining the criteria for evidence-based treatment, however, we would argue that one should similarly avoid a narrow conception and allow criteria to evolve from the main findings concerning treatment and outcome. In regard to our research, this would mean including the entirety of information about prevalence, control findings, comparative findings, compositional findings, and processes.

Anyone who has ever carried out a psychotherapy clinical trial can understand and appreciate the difficulties and challenges that one must confront. One may experience a sense of satisfaction even when just one significant finding results. However, one should not stop at this point. For example in our research, clarifying aspects of prevalence, control, comparison, and compositional findings goes far beyond the value and usefulness of only the control trial findings.

The achievement of evidence-based treatment in and of itself should not be regarded as a kind of academic trophy that signals the place to stop. In the United States there is a National Registry for evidence-based treatments. There are three levels of programs (or treatments). In ascending order of strength, they are labeled *promising*, *effective*, and *model*. Although they are helpful in providing criteria that can be applied to programs, they should not encourage investigators to stop at the lowest level of the Registry. If they do, there is a clear danger that the term *evidence based* will become just another catch-word to overcrowd rather than clarify our language. In regard to our evidence-based group treatments for CG, the evidence should be regarded as a beginning, not an end.

Publications concerning the effectiveness of short-term group therapy inevitably address the topics of cost and cost-effectiveness. In a recent review of 36 studies that compared individual and group forms of CBT, Tucker and Oei (2007) concluded that the evidence was not strong enough to favor one form of treatment over the other. Another worthwhile study would be to investigate the main effects of length of therapy and form of therapy (individual vs. group), as well as the interaction of the two variables. Our research team used this design in a study that investigated the main effects of length of treatment (6 months vs. 24 months) and form of treatment (individual vs. group) in Montreal in the early 1980s (Piper et al., 1984). The patients who received group therapy did better in long-term therapy than in short-term therapy. Also, patients who received individual therapy did better in short-term therapy than in long-term therapy. Thus, in the case of complicated grief and form of therapy, the more interesting findings involve interaction effects rather than main effects.

Future activities

In regard to our future activities, although we believe that we have identified some interesting and clinically useful findings concerning the matching of forms of therapy and patients' personality characteristics, as well as the entire composition of the group, we know very little about the specific mechanisms that follow from these features to bring about favorable outcome. Consequently, we are currently embarking on an exploration and, we hope, an explanation of the therapy process of the 18 groups from our composition trial as revealed by audiotapes and transcripts of therapy sessions. We would like to discover what mediated the composition–outcome relationship. On theoretical grounds we hypothesize that the greater the percentage of high-QOR patients in a group: (1) the more the content of the group will reflect constructive, mutually productive, and hostility-free interactions; (2) the greater the focus will be on other patients rather on oneself when a patient speaks; and (3) the more the group will engage in dynamic work. The identification of mediating mechanisms may suggest how they can be activated by means other than restrictive group composition (e.g., by excluding low-QOR patients). Instead, patient preparation or therapist's technique could be used. That would facilitate including greater numbers of psychiatric patients with low-QOR in short-term therapy groups for CG.

References

Allumbaugh, D., & Hoyt, W. (1999). Effectiveness of grief counseling: A meta-analysis. *Journal of Counseling Psychology, 46*, 370–380.

Beck, A. T., & Steer, R. A. (1987). *Beck Depression Inventory manual.* New York: Harcourt Brace Jovanovich.

Cronbach, L., J., & Meehl, P., E. (1955). Construct validity in psychological tests. *Psychological Bulletin, 52*, 281–302.

Currier, J. M., Neimeyer, R. A., & Berman, J. S. (2008). The effectiveness of psychotherapeutic interventions for bereaved persons: A comprehensive quantitative review. *Psychological Bulletin, 134*, 648–661.

Elkin, I., Shea, T, Watkins, J. T, Imber, S. D., Sotsky, S. M., Collins, J. E., et al. (1989). National Institute of Mental Health treatment of depression collaborative research program. *Archives of General Psychiatry, 46*, 971–982.

Fava, G. A., Ruini, C., Rafanelli, C., Finos, L., Conti, S., & Grandi, S. (2004). Six-year outcome of cognitive behaviour therapy for prevention of recurrent depression. *American Journal of Psychiatry, 161*, 1872–1876.

Fortner, B. V. (1999). *The effectiveness of grief counselling and theory: A quantitative review.* Unpublished manuscript.

Goodheart, C. D., Kazdin, A. E., & Strenberg, R. J. (Eds.). (2006). *Evidence-based psychotherapy: Where practice and research meet.* Washington, DC: American Psychological Association.

Horowitz, M. J., Marmar, C. R., Weiss, D., DeWitt, K. N., & Rosenbaum, R. (1984). Brief psychotherapy of bereavement reactions: The relationship of process to outcome. *Archives of General Psychiatry, 41*, 438–448.

Horowitz, M. J., Wilner, N., & Alvarez, W. (1979). Impact of Event Scale: A measure of subjective stress. *Psychosomatic Medicine, 41*, 209–218.

Jacobson, N. S., Follette, W. C., & Revenstorf, D. (1984). Psychotherapy outcome research: Methods for reporting variability and evaluating clinical significance. *Behavior Therapy, 15*, 336–352.

Jacobson, N. S., & Revenstorf, D. (1988). Statistics for assessing the clinical significance of psychotherapy techniques: Issues, problems, and new developments. *Behavior Assessment, 10*, 133–145.

Kato, P. M., & Mann, T. (1999). A synthesis of psychological interventions for the bereaved. *Clinical Psychology Review, 19*, 275–296.

Larson, D. G., & Hoyt, W. T. (2007). What has become of grief therapy? An evaluation of the empirical foundations of the new pessimism. *Professional Psychology: Research and Practice, 38*, 347–355.

de Maat, S., Dekker, J., Schoevers, R., & de Jonghe, F. (2006). Relative efficacy of psychotherapy and pharmacotherapy in the treatment of depression: A meta-analysis. *Psychotherapy Research, 16*, 562–572.

Magnavita, J. J. (Ed.). (2010). *Evidence-based treatment for personality dysfunction: Principles, methods, and processes.* Washington, DC: American Psychological Association.

Neimeyer, R. (2000). Searching for the meaning: Grief therapy and the process of reconstruction. *Death Studies, 24*, 541–558.

Piper, W. E., Debbane, E. G., Bienvenu, J. P., & Garant, J. (1984). A comparative study of four forms of psychotherapy. *Journal of Consulting and Clinical Psychology, 52*, 268–279.

Piper, W. E., Joyce, A. S., McCallum, M., & Azim, H., F. (1998). Interpretive and supportive forms of psychotherapy and patient personality variables. *Journal of Consulting and Clinical Psychology, 66*, 558–567,

Piper, W. E., McCallum, M., & Azim, H. F. A. (1992). *Adaptation to loss through short-term group psychotherapy.* New York: Guilford Press.

Piper, W. E., Ogrodniczuk, J. S., Azim, H. F., & Weideman, R. (2001). Prevalence of loss and complicated grief among psychiatric outpatients. *Psychiatric Services, 53*, 1069–1074.

Piper, W. E., Ogrodniczuk, J. S., Joyce, A. S., & Weideman, R. (2011). *Short-term group therapies for complicated grief: Two research-based models.* Washington, DC: American Psychological Association.

Piper, W. E., Ogrodniczuk, J. S., & Weideman, R. (2005). Screening for complicated grief: When less may provide more. *Canadian Journal of Psychiatry, 50*, 680–683.

Piper, W. E., Ogrodniczuk, J. S., Joyce, A. S., Weideman, R., & Rosie, J. S. (2007). Group composition and group therapy for complicated grief. *Journal of Consulting and Clinical Psychology, 75*, 116–125.

Rockland, L. H. (1989). *Supportive, therapy: A psychodynamic approach.* New York: Basic Books.

Rose, S. D. (1989). *Working with adults in groups: Integrating cognitive–behavioral and small group strategies.* San Francisco: Jossey-Bass.

Schut, H., Stroebe, M. S., van den Bout, J., & Terheggen, M. (2001). The efficacy of bereavement interventions: Determining who benefits. In Stroebe, M. S., Hansson, R. O., Stroebe, W., & Schut, H. (Eds.), *Handbook of bereavement research: Consequences, coping, and care* (pp. 705–738). Washington, DC: American Psychological Association.

Trivedi, M. H., Rush, A. J., Wisniewski, S. R., Nierenberg, A. A., Warden, D., Ritz, L., et al. (2006). Evaluation of outcomes with citalopram for depression using measurement-based care in STAR*D: Implications for clinical practice. *American Journal of Psychiatry, 163*, 28–40.

Tucker, M., & Oei, T. P. S. (2007). Is group more cost effective than individual cognitive behaviour therapy? The evidence is not solid yet. *Behavioural and Cognitive Psychotherapy, 35*, 77–91.

Werman, D. S. (1984). *The practice of supportive psychotherapy.* New York: Brunner/ Mazel.

Wilfley, D. E., MacKenzie, K. R., Welch, R. R., Ayres, V. E., & Weissman, M. M. (2000). *Interpersonal psychotherapy for group.* New York: Basic Books.

Zisook, S., & Lyons, L. (1989–1990). Bereavement and unresolved grief in psychiatric outpatients. *Omega, 20,* 307–322.

20 Complicated grief after violent death

Identification and intervention

*E. K. Rynearson, Henk Schut, and
Margaret Stroebe*

Introduction

In periods of peace especially, violent deaths account for only a small percentage of total deaths, with, for example, 7% of annual deaths in the United States falling within the category of murder, suicide, and accidents (National Centers for Disease Control, 2009). However, there is considerable clinical evidence to support the premise that violent dying has specific and enduring effects on bereavement and grief (Rando, 1993; Rynearson, 2001). The violent death of a loved one is a traumatizing experience. In research on family members of murder victims, researchers have drawn attention to the likelihood of strongly intrusive and avoidant thoughts combined with hyperarousal, suggesting the presence of posttraumatic stress reactions (Parkes, 1993; Rynearson, 1994). Because of the often unexpected suddenness of violent death, combined with violation, and often intentionality or culpability associated with the death, those attached to the victim are not only vulnerable to levels of distress that are characteristic of reactions to non-violent deaths, but particularly prone to thoughts of remorse, retaliation, and fears of recurrence related to the act of violent dying. Furthermore, following the work of Janoff-Bulman, it has become widely accepted that fundamental assumptions people hold about themselves, the world, and the relation between these two may be shattered following traumatic loss (Janoff-Bulman, 1992; Matthews & Marwit, 2003), although recent evidence suggests that these effects may not be as strong as has been claimed (Mancini, Prati, & Bonanno, 2011).

In addition, complicating features can include having to deal with legal/crime-related matters and the media. The clinical effects of violent dying are, then, substantive and dynamically divergent from those of natural dying and may be associated with prolonged dysfunction, including complicated grief. These patterns of reactions lead to important questions in the context of this book: Do those who experience the loss of a loved one through violent death have a higher likelihood of suffering from complicated forms of grief? If so, what is the nature of difficulties associated with the grieving process among survivors of violent death? Who among this subgroup are the ones most vulnerable to complications? Can intervention help these persons to come to terms with their loss?

Although the clinical effects of violent dying appear indisputable, they are difficult to quantify and are rarely included in standardized measures of grief or noted in empirical studies. However, given the compelling clinical indications, there is good reason to address the above questions scientifically and to evaluate the body of relevant research, particularly to give directions for future investigation. Unfortunately for current purposes, but not surprisingly given the nature and manifestations associated with violent death, the limited literature on bereavement following this type of death has focused largely on posttraumatic stress symptoms and disorder rather than complicated grief (e.g., Kaltman & Bonanno, 2003; Mancini, Prati, & Black, 2011; Murphy, 2008). However, violent death has typically been understood to trigger two concurrent but distinct syndromes: (1) separation distress as a response to the lost relationship (with feelings of longing, etc.), and (2) traumatic distress in reaction to the manner of dying (with re-enactment thoughts, etc.) (Rynearson & Sinnema, 1999). Following this distinction, the former can be understood as relating to (complicated) grief, the latter to posttraumatic stress (disorder), suggesting the need for scientific understanding of both types of reactions.

Given the focus of the whole book, in this chapter we examine the phenomena and manifestations of *complicated grief* following violent death. We follow the definition of complicated grief provided by Stroebe, Hansson, Schut, and Stroebe, (2008):

> a deviation from the (cultural) norm (i.e., that could be expected to pertain – importantly – according to the extremity of the particular bereavement event) in either (a) the time course or intensity of specific or general symptoms of grief and/or (b) the level of impairment in social, occupational, or other important areas of functioning. (p. 7)

Different forms of complicated grief have been identified in the scientific literature with various labels frequently being attached to them, the main ones being prolonged or chronic, delayed/inhibited, and absent grief (see, for example, Chapter 5 in this volume). It becomes evident that we are talking then of "complicated grief" in terms of a *clinically relevant syndrome*.

Consideration is first given to the concept of violent death in the context of bereavement. Then, in the main part of the chapter, empirical literature on complicated grief following violent death is critically assessed. The focus is on well-designed, quantitative studies.[1] The review covers bereavement following different types of violent death, including studies of homicide, suicide, accident, and natural death. It assesses what we know about complicated grief across these violent and non-violent types of loss in terms of its prevalence and distinctive features, risk factors, models/techniques for assessment, and intervention efficacy. More general concerns about the state of research knowledge are also addressed. Finally, we draw general conclusions and set a research agenda for the future.

On the definition of violent death

In the scientific literature, violent deaths have been defined as those resulting from accidents, suicide, or homicide (e.g., Cleiren, 1991; Mancini, Prati, & Bonanno, 2011), and in many international classification systems these three alternative causes are listed alongside a fourth category, "natural death," featuring illnesses. The category of "fatal accident" includes vehicle crash, drowning, and natural disaster (Currier, Holland, & Neimeyer, 2006). Grouping deaths due to these three causes into the violent death category is usual in the trauma literature (e.g., Kaltman & Bonanno, 2003; Norris, 1992), although it must be noted that some deaths in these categories may not be violent in the sense that they may not be an expression of physical force against other persons (e.g., death from suicide through overdose of sleeping pills, hospital accidents with anesthetics). Traumatic loss is defined mainly in objective terms as a sudden and violent mode of death, characterized by one of the above-mentioned three causes. Violent death is thus more specific than another frequently used categorization including sudden, unexpected, and traumatic death (e.g., Fujisawa et al., 2010). Further to the former categorization, Rynearson's "3 V's" – violent, violation (transgression), and volition (intentional or freely chosen on part of perpetrator or victim) – may pinpoint useful defining properties of these types of death. Not all of the 3 V features may be equally applicable to the different types of violent deaths (e.g., volition does not seem to fit accidents as much as homicide).

Does such a definition into the above three types of violent death suffice? In contemporary society one might consider further specification of the violent categories in terms of military attack, including genocide, and terrorism. However, these massive types of loss are beyond the scope of this chapter, although from a certain perspective these would fall under homicide.[2] Furthermore, euthanasia may merit separate consideration in the context of impact on bereavement, for this too is a non-natural cause of death (though related to natural causes such as cancer), associated with unique bereavement reactions. Like suicide deaths, those following euthanasia take place with the agreement of the "victim." However, regardless of one's opinion on euthanasia, such a death is difficult to include under violent deaths.

A further note of caution is in order when drawing a simple distinction between violent and non-violent (or "natural") deaths. The words of Barry, Kasl, and Prigerson (2002) express the point in relationship to bereavement:

> Researchers commonly classify deaths as violent or non-violent according to how the death occurred. Importantly, deaths perceived to be violent by bereaved individuals may not be classified as violent according to the manner in which earlier studies have defined violent deaths. Such may be the case for a natural death that is accompanied by much pain and physical illness. A death such as this may be perceived as violent by the surviving family member. (p. 454)

Categorization may thus be inaccurate not only because of a failure to specify subcategories of violent death, as mentioned above, but also because deaths may be perceived differently from the formal cause by bereaved survivors. We need to keep this in mind but at the same time we need to be aware of the risk that what are generally regarded as rather clear concepts – such as violent and non-violent causes of death – run the risk of becoming fuzzy, following such reasoning.

Violent death and complicated grief: assessment of the scientific literature

Although there are promising directions in research on this topic, there are also limitations in availability of sound empirical research on bereavement following violent death. It will become evident in our review of the literature, which follows, that there are even fewer studies that stringently examine complicated grief following violent death. Nevertheless, in our view, it is important to assess what is known so far, so that future research can build on the available empirical literature. Furthermore, with this interest in mind too, and in contrast with some other reviewers and researchers conducting empirical research (e.g., Currier, Holland, Coleman, & Neimeyer, 2008; Vessier-Batchem & Douglas, 2006) we made the decision to follow very stringent criteria for complicated grief, in line with the scope of this volume.

Prevalence of complicated grief

With considerable consistency, studies have shown higher intensities of grief following violent than non-violent causes (e.g., Currier et al., 2008; Dyregrov, Nordanger, & Dyregrov, 2003; Mancini, Prati, & Black, 2011), but these do not inform us about *complicated* grief (as a clinically relevant condition). As Hardison, Neimeyer, and Lichstein (2005) commented: "Higher scores [on their complicated grief scale] represent greater impairment ... [providing] a continuous measure of intensity of grief-related symptomatology *rather than a classificatory diagnosis of complicated grief disorder*" (pp. 103–4; italics added).

When cut-off points on questionnaires have been used as indicators of complicated grief (i.e., also not diagnostic categorization), those bereaved from violent causes seem to have excessive rates compared with norms for the bereaved in general. Although one must be cautious about inferring prevalences of complicated grief from such sources (further application of diagnostic criteria and professional clinical assessment is needed), some indication may be derived. For example, Ghaffari-Nejad, Ahmadi-Mousavi, Gandomkar, and Reihani-Kermani (2006) examined the prevalence of complicated grief (intensity) following the Bam earthquake in Iran, which killed thousands. Scores over the established cut-off point for complicated grief were present among 76% of their large sample of respondents. Dyregrov et al. (2003) reported that 78% of parents following the violent loss of their child (suicide or accident) scored above the cut-off levels for complicated grief reactions 1.5 years post loss. The above prevalences are in excess of rates found for complicated grief irrespective of mode of death (which is typically within the range of 5–33%; see Forstmeier & Maercker, 2006). However, the data are not totally conclusive, since some studies do not find higher prevalence of complicated grief after violent death, although this may be because population samples include only small numbers of people bereaved by violent death (e.g., Kersting, Brähler, Glaesmer & Wagner, 2011).

Some researchers have drawn conclusions about the comparative impact of the different modes of violent death (e.g., Cleiren, 1991; Currier et al., 2008;

Dyregrov et al., 2003). For example, in terms of highest ICG scores, Currier et al. (2008) reported homicide to be the most perturbing cause of death, followed by suicide, accidents, natural sudden, and natural anticipated deaths. Dyregrov et al. (2003) found similar differences in high levels of grief among bereaved parents following the death of their child as a result of suicide or accident. Some studies have focused on intensity of symptoms following loss from specific types of violent death compared with non-violent death, for example for suicide (Bailley, Kral, & Dunham, 1999), providing insights into differential types of reactions, but so far not comparing prevalences of complicated grief across types of death.

Distinctive features of complicated grief

Just as there are no scientifically stringent studies comparing the prevalence of complicated grief reactions following violent as compared with non-violent causes of death, so is there little sound investigation of distinctive features across these modes of death. The literature on bereavement following homicide is a case in point. There is frequent reference to the excruciating, long-lasting, and extremely complex reactions following this type of loss (e.g., Horne, 2003; Pynoos & Nader, 1990). Causal statements (e.g., about mechanisms contributing to resilience) are often made on the basis of small-scale qualitative studies of the homicide bereaved (e.g., Burke, Neimeyer, & McDevitt-Murphy, 2010; Johnson, 2010). Although these studies provide fine-grained descriptive accounts of what these persons are encountering, it remains unclear to what extent the identified reactions are characteristic of bereavement in general, or specific to homicide bereavement in particular. Clearly, for this purpose, one needs to compare homicide bereaved with other bereaved groups.

Are there any studies of complicated grief that have included control groups of bereaved from non-violent death causes, to take us a step further toward discerning unique bereavement reactions following the different types of loss? To our knowledge, only one study comes near to reaching the necessary criteria. McClatchey, Vonk, and Palardy (2009) investigated the prevalence of "childhood traumatic grief" (CTG) among bereaved children, using a cut-off score indicating "clinically-significant frequency" (p. 312). Children who had lost a parent through violent/sudden or through expected death were compared. Rather in contrast to what one would expect from studies reviewed so far, the incidence of CTG did not differ between these groups. However, it must be noted that this study did not completely follow our definition for violent death: This category included sudden non-violent deaths (heart attacks). This may partly explain why no differences were found between the groups.

Risk factors

Not surprisingly, given the state of knowledge described above, no information is available about risk (or protective) factors that may make some individuals more (or less) vulnerable to complicated grief following a death through murder, suicide, or accident. Future research needs to cover a broad range of risk/protective factors. So far, leads have been provided by researchers examining the relationship between intensity of grief and sense making or meaning making and found these factors to be particularly problematic following violent (compared with non-violent) death circumstances (e.g., Currier et al., 2006, 2008). Likewise, based on previous research (e.g., Wickie & Marwit, 2000), there are good reasons to assume that the shattering of world assumptions should be systematically and differentially related to mode of death. Furthermore, in a recent study by Mancini, Prati, and Black (2011) self-worth was found to mediate the effects of violent loss on posttraumatic stress symptoms and depression, but not on levels of grief. However, extension beyond meaning making and world assumptions to other intra- and interpersonal risk and protective factors is essential.

Conclusions

Our review of the empirical literature has revealed that there is remarkably little sound empirical research on complicated grief following violent compared with non-violent death. Such comparisons are essential to establish the unique consequences of violent types of death. Quite consistently, studies have shown higher intensities of grief following violent than non-violent causes, but these do not inform us about *complicated* grief. Likewise, those bereaved from violent causes seem to have highly excessive rates compared with norms for the bereaved in general, but evidence is weak: We could not find a single well-controlled study that compared complicated grief rates following violent versus non-violent death. A research design to overcome these gaps in the literature would comprise a (preferably) longitudinal comparison across violent and non-violent modes of death of the prevalence and manifestations of complicated grief assessed by means of clinical interviews. The ideal study would be large-scale, use a prospective design, assess violence incrementally, not use cause of death and violence interchangeably, and consider the circumstances of the bereaved. A research agenda for the future should include examination of risk/protective factors, map different patterns of complications following different causes of violent death, and go beyond diagnosis based on total symptom score, to consider complicated grief due to some particular, idiosyncratic feature. Furthermore, we need to test the models and strategies of psychotherapeutic intervention; examining the effectiveness of these programs is critically important.

Even with such guidelines, the challenge remains for researchers and clinicians to decide who among the bereaved should be included in the complicated grief category in future investigation of bereavement following violent death. As stated earlier, our interest is in complicated grief as a clinically relevant syndrome. Simply using a continuous measure of intensity of grief symptoms that indicates increasing impairment is not – in this context – informative (it simply shows the intensity of grief-related symptomatology). Using a validated cut-off point to ascertain the likelihood of complicated grief is at least a first step toward establishing the presence of complicated grief. However, this by itself is not sufficient when we are striving to investigate complicated grief as a clinically relevant syndrome. Thus, as indicated above, in our view, it is necessary for trained professionals to conduct clinical interviews to establish "complicated grief." The criteria they use for determining this are also not set in stone, but are currently likely to include use of a cut-off point on a validated grief questionnaire for initial screening, making use of criteria proposed for the future DSM category system, and further information from the bereaved person in the clinical interview(s).

Violent death and complicated grief: conceptual issues

We have already considered the definition of *complicated grief* in some detail. However, other conceptual issues arise from our review. In particular, when suggesting new directions for research, it is important to step back and consider whether extension of current directions is sufficient, or whether we should be extending the scope of our investigation. Although far from comprehensive, the following two issues illustrate the sorts of extensions that we think deserve attention.

Different causes, different complications?

Finer-grained quantitative examinations of comparative *patterns* of complication associated with the different types of violent death are completely lacking. Studies that have provided qualitative or descriptive accounts of bereavement following the different modes of death can be drawn on for identification of variables for inclusion in future studies (see, for example, Armour, 2006, for comparison of experiences among those bereaved following accidents, suicide, and homicide). It is noteworthy that there are more qualitative studies focusing on homicide (e.g., Asaro, 2001a, 2001b; Burke et al., 2010; Clements & Burgess, 2002; Goodrum, 2005) and suicide (e.g., for reviews, see Jordan, 2008; Jordan & McIntosh, 2010; Sveen & Walby, 2007) than on accidents. A notable exception is the study of traffic accident survivors by Lehman, Wortman, and Williams (1987), although, again, the focus is not on complicated grief but on other consequences such as depression and general psychiatric symptoms. Thus, more studies specifically on (complicated) grief reactions following accidental death circumstances are needed too.

A few studies have looked in general (i.e., not cause of death specifically) at the comorbidity of complicated grief with posttraumatic stress disorder, depression, or anxiety disorders (e.g., Morina, Rudari, Bleichhardt, & Prigerson, 2010) but, to our knowledge, none have compared patterns of comorbidity following violent versus non-violent causes.

Accumulation of symptoms versus idiosyncratic complications?

Complicated grief may be overlooked if the focus is limited to high accumulated levels of symptoms or even diagnostic assessment, rather than identifying essential and unique bereavement reactions relating to a particular mode of death (violent and non-violent). In other words, assessment of complicated grief following a violent death which is based on an initial score above a prescribed cut-off point on a questionnaire and/or confirmed by diagnostic investigation may still exclude persons who do suffer complications. Following violent death, complications in the grieving process may have more to do with a specific aspect than elevation of symptoms, or accumulation of symptoms, to reach diagnosis. For example, following suicide, a specific difficulty may have to do with the overwhelming feeling that one should have prevented the death, or with the extreme strain of feeling one has to keep the actual cause of death a secret. These types of thoughts are reported more frequently following suicide than following other types of death (Bailley et al., 1999). In this context, it is important to note that assessment of the level of grief may vary according to whether general grief instruments or mode-of-death-specific instruments are used (see Sveen & Walby, 2007, for suicide bereavement).

Psychotherapeutic intervention following violent death

The review of empirical evidence presented above identifies limited, yet valuable, knowledge about complicated grief following violent death and areas for research in the future. However, as will have become evident from the preceding review, although such lines of investigation are potentially informative, they are unlikely to provide a comprehensive picture, and certainly not one that is sufficient for clinical purposes. They can usefully be complemented – and enriched – through examination of principles of psychotherapeutic intervention and assessment. In our view, there are good reasons to bring research and practice together to address these topics, to provide further insight into complicated grief following violent death, which will also contribute to the forthcoming research agenda.

Effects of psychotherapeutic interventions

Given that few studies have specifically isolated complicated grief reactions following violent deaths, it is not surprising that there is little information available about the efficacy of intervention programs specifically on complicated grief following violent loss. Very few studies have even focused on other consequences of intervention (e.g., on lowering posttraumatic stress symptom levels) for bereaved persons after violent death. Most of the studies that have done so also include people who have encountered other impactful events without lethal consequences (e.g., Brom, Kleber, & Defares, 1989; Layne et al., 2008). These studies do find positive results of the interventions put to the test, but results are not presented for bereaved and other victims of these events separately, and no attention is paid specifically to recovery from complicated grief.

A study conducted by Murphy (Murphy et al., 1998; for a recent overview, see Murphy, 2008), however, specifically focused on parents who have lost a child through suicide, homicide, or accident. In this study, the parents were randomly assigned to a mixed problem- and emotion-focused intervention condition or a non-intervention control group. Results show that mothers with high initial levels of distress improved more in the intervention condition than did similar mothers in the control condition. By contrast, mothers with relatively low levels of distress at baseline were worse after intervention than the control group. The number of fathers participating in the study was small, but results did not indicate an effect of the intervention for fathers. The impact specifically on complicated grief, however, was not investigated in this study (the grief measure was an unvalidated scale developed by the investigators for this particular study).

A recent review by Szumalis and Kutcher (2011; for a further review, see McDaid, Trowman, Golder, Hawton, & Sowden, 2008) summarized results for the effectiveness specifically for postsuicide intervention programs, including their impact on grief symptoms (though again not specifically on complicated grief). Improvements in grief experiences, both short and long term, were reported.

These results are promising in that they suggest that intervention programs may be effective in reducing distress, but it is evident that more research into the effects of intervention after (specific types of) violent bereavement is needed too, and for subgroups undergoing complications in their grieving.

Turning to specific techniques of assessment: At this time, to the best of our knowledge, there are five manualized, time-limited, focused interventions specifically designed for non-natural dying. Three of these (Cohen et al., 2006; Layne et al., 2008; Salloum, 2008) have been designed for children and adolescent outpatients and two (Rynearson et al., 2006; Murphy, 2008) for adults. Although evidence so far seems to suggest decrease of grief symptoms and trauma distress, further methodologically sound investigations are needed to establish efficacy (only the Murphy study met the necessary criteria for current purposes). Four of the interventions applied combined techniques from CBT and narrative therapy. CBT principles included structured, time-limited agendas (10–12 individual or group sessions), relationship-based collaboration, clarification of connections between thoughts, feelings, and behaviors, affirmative guidance, relaxation exercises, modeling, and teaching techniques of imaginative exposure. We illustrate this by describing next the two adult approaches developed by Murphy and Rynearson.

The support groups designed by Murphy and colleagues (e.g., Murphy, 1996; Murphy, Baugher, Lohan, Schneidermann, & Herrwagen, 1996; Murphy et al., 1998) included problem-focused and emotion-focused support. This program was professionally led, and designed specifically for parents who had lost a child to violent death. Twelve sessions of 2 hours were held, one each week. The first hour in each session (apart from the first and last, which were data-collecting sessions) was dedicated to the problem-focused support dimension of providing information and building coping skills, addressing areas such as managing cognitive and emotional responses; health issues; parental role loss; legal concerns; partner and family relationship concerns; feelings toward others; and expectations for the future. The second hour, of more direct emotion-focused support, assisted parents to share their experiences; obtain feedback to help reframing of aspects to do with the death and its consequences; and receive emotional support.

Narrative therapy (Rynearson, 2010; see also Currier & Neimeyer, 2006, and Currier et al., 2008, for their related meaning making approach) contrasts in some respects with the problem- and emotion-oriented support program of Murphy and colleagues. Strategies based on the narrative approach encourage the retelling of the living and dying story of the deceased with a restorative goal of creating a more plausible and coherent retelling of the narrative imagery, of re-enactment, promoting alternative outcomes and a transcendent perspective. Rynearson (2010) recently described his narrative therapy approach in some detail. According to this perspective, in the case of violent death, storytelling is distorted, focusing intensely, even obsessively, on a re-enactment of the dying (further complicated by the public and legal processes surrounding this type of death). Fundamental to this approach is the understanding that established clinical assessment principles (based on narrative analysis) and associated constructs for guiding therapeutic interventions give insight into complicated grief following violent death. It is understood that, in order to assess the impact of the death on the bereaved person, the clinician needs to listen to and help the client to revise his or her personal account of the loss and its aftermath. This is likely to be necessary for bereavement in general, but it may be even more important after violent death. Characteristic of narratives of bereavement after violent death are themes of horror and helplessness and topics such as remorse, re-enactment, retaliation, and retribution that distort the dying story structure (Currier & Neimeyer, 2006).

The procedures of Murphy and Rynearson may overlap, insofar as participants presumably shared their narratives of the living and dying of the deceased spontaneously during the support group of Murphy and colleagues. There are also apparent differences between the Murphy and Rynearson (and other) approaches (the Murphy program has no sessions of direct exposure and retelling of the traumatic dying re-enactment, whereas the Rynearson one does). However, none of the manualized interventions cites a specific corrective mechanism, and that is presumably because the explanation of treatment effects is non-specific. It seems plausible that the various interventions are successful because they are based upon the common principles of stress moderation, reconstructive exposure, and meaningful re-engagement, which are basic to time-limited trauma or grief treatments. Three main goals of such interventions are (see also Rynearson, Correa, Favell, Saindon, & Prigerson, 2006):

1 The moderation of distress (through a confiding relationship, a safe setting, psychoeducation and stress reduction strategies) that fosters mastery of personal safety and autonomy.

2 Exposure and reconstructive processing of the dying and grieving narrative through an active procedure of reliving the narrative fixation (through imaginary verbal and non-verbal retelling). This would foster coherence and motivation for re-engagement by revising the teller's role (identity) within the narrative.

3   Meaningful re-engagement with valued, vital activities and relationships within the family and community in an altered identity that honors the transformation.

Apart from the Murphy investigation (which included examination of grief reduction but not of clinically assessed complicated grief), we know of no studies that have put such approaches to strict scientific test. Nor do we know of any that have compared these assessment techniques in relationship to the effectiveness of an intervention based on their protocol. Specific investigation of their impact on complicated grief for bereaved persons following violent loss is also lacking. These are all matters for future investigation. A useful strategy would be to follow the example of Shear, Frank, Houck, and Reynolds (2005), who conducted a study of the efficacy of intervention for bereaved persons with complications in their grieving, comparing the efficacy of two different scientifically based programs. They assigned their clients either to traditional interpersonal psychotherapy or to a treatment program that followed the principles of a specially derived protocol, based on the dual-process model (see Stroebe & Schut, 1999), called complicated grief treatment, and examined the course of their grief over time (the latter treatment program was associated with faster and better adjustment). Naturally, inclusion of a non-intervention control group to compare the treatment conditions with natural recovery trajectories would be advisable; this was not feasible in the Shear et al. (2005) study. For our current interests, it would be useful to extend such intervention efficacy examination of its impact on those bereaved following the violent death of a loved one, specifically. It is useful to note in this context that Asukai, Tsuruta, and Saito (2011) recently conducted a pilot study using a modified version of Shear and colleagues' complicated grief treatment for a small sample of Japanese women bereaved by violent death. The results were promising, with reporting of a significant reduction of grief symptoms but, as for the Shear et al. study, a non-intervention control condition was not included.

General conclusions

To convince governments and funding agencies of the importance of supporting those dealing with the violent death of a relative, one needs, first, to demonstrate that these survivors encounter greater and/or different extreme difficulties than do other bereaved persons and, second, to show how professional intervention can actually help reduce suffering associated with this type of death. However, our review of scientific evidence on complicated grief following violent death revealed remarkably little sound knowledge to date in terms of recovery from complicated grief through intervention. However, research is moving toward addressing issues surrounding the prevalence of complicated grief and comparing violent and non-violent causes. Although more fine-grained research is needed, results do suggest violent death to be a risk factor for complicated grief. We highlighted new research directions, ranging from prevalence (e.g., good comparative studies of impact, focusing on symptomatology and complicated grief "caseness") to intervention efficacy studies (to elucidate what works best for whom, following specific types of violent death). As illustrated above, promising research along these lines is already being conducted (e.g., Fujisawa et al., 2010; Kersting et al., 2011). We outlined how different approaches, including the narrative approach to clinical assessment and intervention, can fuel future research, and how such approaches provide guidelines for the treatment of complicated grief experienced by some bereaved persons following the violent death of a loved one. We hope that researchers and practitioners can work together toward building a solid knowledge base, thereby improving the evidence base of care for these bereaved persons.

Notes

1 It is beyond the scope of this chapter to cover qualitative investigations of complicated grief following violent death. In fact, most qualitative studies also highlight posttraumatic stress rather than complicated grief reactions.
2 For an example of empirical research in this category, see Schaal, Jacob, Dusingizemungu, and Elbert (2010). For a review of the consequences of disasters on individuals, families and communities, see Bonanno, Brewin, Kaniasty, and La Greca (2010).

References

Armour, M. (2006). Violent death: Understanding the context of traumatic and stigmatized grief. *Journal of Human Behavior in the Social Environment, 14*, 53–90.

Asaro, M. (2001a). Working with adult homicide survivors, Part I: Impact and sequelae of murder. *Perspectives in Psychiatric Care, 37*, 95–101.

Asaro, M. (2001b). Working with adult homicide survivors, Part II: Helping family members cope with murder. *Perspectives in Psychiatric Care, 37*, 115–136.

Asukai, N., Tsuruta, N., & Saito, A. (2011). Pilot study on traumatic grief treatment program for Japanese women bereaved by violent death. *Journal of Traumatic Stress, 24*, 470–473.

Bailley, S., Kral, M., & Dunham, K. (1999). Survivors of suicide do grieve differently: Empirical support for a common-sense proposition. *Suicide and Life-Threatening Behavior, 29*, 256–271.

Barry, L., Kasl, S., & Prigerson, H. (2002). Psychiatric disorders among bereaved persons: The role of perceived circumstances of death and preparedness for death. *American Journal of Geriatric Psychiatry, 10*, 447–457.

Bonanno, G., Brewin, C., Kaniasty, K., & La Greca, A. (2010). Weighing the costs of disaster: Consequences, risks, and resilience in individuals, families, and communities. *Psychological Science, 11*, 1–49.

Brom, D., Kleber, R., & Defares, P. (1989). Brief psychotherapy for posttraumatic stress disorders. *Journal of Consulting and Clinical Psychology, 57*, 607–612.

Burke, L., Neimeyer, R., & McDevitt-Murphy, M. (2010). African American homicide bereavement: aspects of social support that predict complicated grief, PTSD, and depression. *Omega, 61*, 1–24.

Cleiren, M. (1991). *Adaptation to bereavement*. Leiden: DSWO Press.

Clements, P., & Burgess, A. (2002). Children's responses to family member homicide. *Family Community Health, 25*, 32–42.

Cohen, J. A., Mannarino, A. P., & Staron, V. (2006). A pilot study for modified cognitive–behavioral therapy for childhood traumatic grief. *Journal of the Academy of Child and Adolescent Psychiatry, 45*, 1465–1473.

Currier, J., Holland, J., & Neimeyer, R. (2006). Sense-making, grief, and the experience of violent loss: Toward a mediational model. *Death Studies, 30*, 403–428.

Currier, J., Holland, J., Coleman, R., & Neimeyer, R. (2008). Bereavement following violent death: An assault on life and meaning. In Stevenson, R., & Cox, G. (Eds.) *Perspectives on violence and violent death* (pp. 175–200). Amityville, NY: Baywood.

Currier, J. M., & Neimeyer, R. A. (2006). Fragmented stories: The narrative integration of violent loss. In Rynearson, E. K. (Ed.), *Violent death: Resilience and intervention beyond the crisis* (pp. 85–100). New York: Taylor & Francis.

Dyregrov, K., Nordanger, D., & Dyregrov, A. (2003). Predictors of psychosocial distress after suicide, SIDS, and accidents. *Death Studies, 27*, 143–165.

Forstmeier, S., & Maercker, A. (2006). Comparison of two diagnostic system for complicated grief. *Journal of Affective Disorders, 99*, 203–211.

Fujisawa, D., Miyashita, M., Nakajima, S., Ito, M., Kato, M., & Kim, Y. (2010). Prevalence and determinants of complicated grief in general population. *Journal of Affective Disorders, 127*, 352–358.

Ghaffari-Nejad, A., Ahmadi-Mousavi, M., Gandomkar, M., & Reihani-Kermani, H. (2006). The prevalence of complicated grief among Bam earthquake survivors in Iran. *Archives of Iranian Medicine, 10*, 525–528.

Goodrum, S. (2005). The interaction between thoughts and emotions following the news of a loved one's murder. *Omega, 51*, 143–160.

Hardison, H., Neimeyer, R., & Lichstein, K. (2005). Insomnia and complicated grief symptoms in bereaved college students. *Behavioral Sleep Medicine, 3*, 99–111.

Horne, C. (2003). Families of homicide victims: Service utilization patterns of extra- and intrafamilial homicide survivors. *Journal of Family Violence, 18*, 75–82.

Janoff-Bulman, R. (1992). *Shattered assumptions: Towards a new psychology of trauma.* New York: Free Press.

Johnson, C. (2010). When African American teen girls' friends are murdered: A qualitative study of bereavement, coping, and psychological consequences. *Families in Society, 91*, 364–370.

Jordan, J. (2008). Bereavement after suicide. *Psychiatric Annals, 38*, 1–6.

Jordan, J., & McIntosh, J. (2010). *Grief after suicide: Understanding the consequences and caring for the survivors.* New York: Routledge.

Kaltman, S., & Bonanno, G. (2003). Trauma and bereavement: Examining the impact of sudden and violent deaths. *Anxiety Disorders, 17*, 131–147.

Kersting, A., Brähler, E., Glaesmer, H., & Wagner, B. (2011). Prevalence of complicated grief in a representative population-based sample. *Journal of Affective Disorders, 131*, 339–343.

Layne, C. M., Saltzman, W. R., Poppleton, L., Burlingame, Pasalic, A., Durakovic, E., et al. (2008). Effectiveness of a school-based psychotherapy for war-exposed adolescents: A randomized controlled trial. *Journal of the Academy of Child and Adolescent Psychiatry, 47*, 1048–1062.

Lehman, D., Wortman, C., & Williams, A. (1987). Long-term effects of losing a spouse or child in a motor vehicle crash. *Journal of Personality and Social Psychology, 52*, 218–231.

Mancini, A. D., Prati, G., & Black, S. (2011). Self-worth mediates the effects of violent loss on PTSD symptoms. *Journal of Traumatic Stress, 24*, 116–120.

Mancini, A. D., Prati, G., & Bonanno, G. A. (2011). Do shattered worldviews lead to complicated grief? Prospective and longitudinal analyses. *Journal of Social and Clinical Psychology, 30*, 184–215.

Matthews, L. T., & Marwit, S. J. (2003). Examining the assumptive world views of parents bereaved by accident, murder, and illness. *Omega, 48*, 115–136.

McClatchey, I., Vonk, M., & Palardy, G. (2009). The prevalence of childhood traumatic grief: A comparison of violent/sudden and expected loss. *Omega, 59*, 305–323.

McDaid, C., Trowman, R., Golder, S., Hawton, K., & Sowden, A. (2008). Interventions for people bereaved though suicide: Systematic review. *British Journal of Psychiatry, 193*, 438–443.

Morina, N., Rudari, V., Bleichhardt, G., & Prigerson, H. (2010). Prolonged grief disorder, depression, and PTSD among bereaved Kosovar civilian war survivors: A preliminary investigation. *International Journal of Social Psychiatry, 56*, 288–297.

Murphy, S. (1996). Parent bereavement stress and preventive intervention following the violent deaths of adolescent or young adult children. *Death Studies, 2*, 441–452.

Murphy, S. (2008). The loss of a child: Sudden death and extended illness perspectives. In Stroebe, M., Hansson, R. O., Schut, H., & Stroebe, W. (Eds.). *Handbook of bereavement research and practice: Advances in theory and intervention* (pp. 375–395). Washington, DC: APA.

Murphy, S., Baugher, R., Lohan, J., Schneidermann, J., & Herrwagen, J. (1996). Parents' evaluation of a preventive intervention following the sudden violent deaths of their children. *Death Studies, 20*, 435–468.

Murphy, S., Johnson, C., Cain, K., Das Gupta, A., Dimond, M., & Lohan, J. (1998). Broad-spectrum group treatment or parents bereaved b the violent deaths of their 12- to 28-year-old children: A randomized, controlled trial. *Death Studies, 22*, 209–235.

National Centers for Disease Control. (2009, April 17). *Vital Statistics Report, 57*, 14.

Norris, F. (1992). Epidemiology of trauma: Frequency and impact of different potentially traumatic events on different demographic groups. *Journal of Consulting and Clinical Psychology, 60*, 409-418.

Parkes, C. M. (1993). Psychiatric problems following bereavement by murder or manslaughter. *British Journal of Psychiatry, 162*, 49–54.

Pynoos, R. S., & Nader, K. (1990). Children's exposure to violence and traumatic death. *Psychiatric Annals, 20*, 334–344.

Rando, T. (1993). *Treatment of complicated mourning.* Champaign, IL: Research Press.

Rynearson, E. K. (1994). Psychotherapy of bereavement after homicide. *Journal of Psychotherapy Practice and Research, 3*, 341–347.

Rynearson, E. K. (2001). *Retelling violent death.* New York: Brunner-Routledge.

Rynearson, E. K. (2010). The clergy, the clinician, and the narrative of violent death. *Pastoral Psychology, 59*, 179–189.

Rynearson, E. K., Correa, F., Favell, J., Saindon, C., & Prigerson, H. (2006). Restorative retelling after violent dying. In Rynearson, E. K. (Ed.), *Violent dying: Resilience and intervention beyond the crisis* (pp. 195–216), New York: Taylor & Francis.

Rynearson, E. K., & Sinnema, C. S. (1999). Supportive group therapy for bereavement after homicide. In Blake, D., & Young, B. H. (Eds.), *Group treatment for post traumatic stress disorder* (pp. 137–147). New York: Taylor & Francis.

Salloum, A. (2008). Group therapy for children experiencing grief and trauma due to homicide and violence: A pilot study. *Research and Social Work Practice, 18*, 198–211.

Schaal, S., Jacob, N., Dusingizemungu, J.-P., & Elbert, T. (2010). Rates and risks for prolonged grief disorder in a sample of orphaned and widowed genocide survivors. *BMC Psychiatry, 10*. doi: 10.1186/1471-244X-10-55.

Shear, K., Frank, E., Houck, P., & Reynolds, C. (2005). Treatment of complicated grief: A randomized controlled trial. *Journal of the American Medical Association, 293,* 2601–2608.

Stroebe, M. S., Hansson, R. O., Schut, H., & Stroebe, W. (2008). *Handbook of bereavement research and practice: Advances in theory and intervention.* Washington, DC: APA.

Stroebe, M., & Schut, H. (1999). The dual process model of coping with bereavement: Rationale and description. *Death Studies, 23,* 197–224.

Sveen, C. A., & Walby, F. (2007). Suicide survivors' mental health and grief reactions: A systematic review of controlled studies. *Suicide and Life-Threatening Behavior, 38,* 13–30.

Szumalis, M., & Kutcher, S. (2011). Post-suicide intervention programs: A systematic review. *Canadian Journal of Public Health, 102,* 18–29.

Vessier-Batchem, M., & Douglas, D. (2006). Coping and complicated grief in survivors of homicide and suicide decedents. *Journal of Forensic Nursing, 2,* 25–32.

Wickie, S., & Marwit, S. (2000). Assumptive world views and the grief reactions of parents of murdered children. *Omega, 42,* 101–113.

Part VI
Conclusions

21 Complicated grief

Assessment of scientific knowledge and implications for research and practice

Margaret Stroebe, Henk Schut, and Jan van den Bout

Our objective in compiling this edited volume has been to provide an up-to-date, state-of-the-art account of scientific research on complicated grief (CG), one that is hoped to be useful for researchers, practitioners, and policy makers alike. We have included diverse contributions, representing contemporary research and thinking from a variety of disciplines and perspectives. Scientific and societal issues have been addressed throughout, and it will have become evident that our authors have at times come to different conclusions on fundamental issues. In this concluding chapter, we reflect on the research presented in this volume, to summarize developments, highlight implications, and indicate current understanding – as well as gaps in our knowledge – regarding CG. We try to draw together the different lines of argument, so that readers can form their own conclusions about scientific knowledge on CG and associated implications for research, practice, and policy.

We order discussion mainly according to the themes of each part of the volume, given that these reflect our chosen scope. We cover a range of general issues suggested by the contributions, and we highlight topics which merit further scientific attention.

The nature of complicated grief

A fundamental question that we wanted to explore in compiling this volume was: *What is CG?* Is it a specific disorder or an overarching term for several different disorders? Can we describe its defining features/symptoms? Although there appears to be quite some similarity between authors' conceptualizations, what has emerged is that there is still a lack of a well-accepted, standard definition for CG or agreement on a set of diagnostic criteria (if it is to be considered a mental disorder). There does seem to be considerable – at least implicit – agreement that CG denotes a *syndrome*, that is, a pathological condition, one that merits the attention of health care professionals. In this section, we focus on the concept of CG per se; in the next, we discuss the related issue of CG as a mental disorder.

CG definition

Some authors have basically followed the lead of Prigerson and her colleagues, conceptualizing CG as one specific disorder, prolonged grief disorder (PGD), using the scale of assessment and criteria derived from her extensive body of research, both of which have evolved over time. Others have criticized this approach as being too narrow, potentially leaving out subtypes of CG (we return to this below). Boelen, van den Hout, and van den Bout, following PGD, define CG as:

> a clinical condition that encompasses specific grief reactions (including separation distress, difficulties accepting the loss, and moving on without the lost person) that cause significant distress and disability at least 6 months after the death occurred. Symptoms of PGD are distinct from normal grief, bereavement-related depression, posttraumatic stress disorder (PTSD), and other anxiety symptoms and syndromes, and, if left untreated, associated with significant impairments in health and quality of life. (Chapter 16)

Others adopt definitions along the lines of the definition set out in Chapter 1:

> a clinically-significant deviation from the (cultural) norm (i.e., that could be expected to pertain, according to the extremity of the particular bereavement event) in either (a) the time course or intensity of specific or general symptoms of grief and/or (b) the level of impairment in social, occupational, or other important areas of functioning. (Stroebe, Hansson, Schut, & Stroebe, 2008, p. 7)

Boerner and colleagues add further specifications to this latter definition, incorporating avoidance processes, self-redefinition problems, and difficulties forming new relationships. Rando has perhaps the broadest definition, covering four types of CG presentations: symptoms, syndromes, diagnosable mental or physical disorders, and death.

Hopefully, as researchers continue to work toward further conceptual clarity, a robust definition (and operationalization) and possibly typologies/subtypes of CG will emerge.

Normal versus CG

To increase understanding of CG, it has sometimes been considered in relation to normal grief (NG; some prefer to label this uncomplicated grief). For example, Dyregrov and Dyregrov discuss patterns of NG and CG in children (noting that this distinction is actually much more difficult to make for children). Three defined features that were mentioned above to characterize CG are deviations/differences (from NG) (1) in intensity, (2) in quality, and (3) in duration. These have been subject to critical scrutiny in this volume; we consider each of the three next.

Questions about intensity relate to whether CG is simply a higher (or even lower) level of symptoms or a distinct syndrome with different symptoms. Wakefield notes that some bereaved people have to deal with greater and deeper challenges than others, and that this does not make an intense response automatically into CG. Along similar lines, Rynearson, Schut, and Stroebe argue that, even if higher scores on a CG scale represent greater impairment (indicated on a continuous measure of intensity of grief symptoms), this does not constitute a classificatory diagnosis of CG. The question then is: What is classificatory CG? Again, different aspects have been considered, relating to intensity. O'Connor, from a physiological perspective, writes that it is still unknown whether CG represents merely acute grief in a bereaved person whose process of adaptation has been interrupted, or a wholly other process than non-complicated adaptation. She mentions in conclusion that most affective disorders are better described on a continuum than as discrete categories and that CG may well turn out to be similar in this regard. The physiological perspective may have potential to answer this question, but O'Connor cautions that we should not expect a one-to-one correspondence between any particular physiological or neurobiological marker and CG. However, "by measuring these markers, we may see what contributes to poor adaptation or what the physiological predictors of CG are" (Chapter 15).

If CG phenomena/symptoms are qualitatively different from NG this would lend plausibility to the claim that CG symptoms are "pathognomonic for a disorder with a distinct etiology" (Chapter 8). Wakefield points to statements of other researchers that support this view but argues that most have failed to find distinct symptomatology. So Wakefield, although not denying that some grief disorders might exist, queries whether CG has distinctive, pathognomonic symptoms separating it from normal grief; there is according to him little support for a categorical conceptualization of NG and PGD. According to Burke and Neimeyer, contemporary research suggests that grief can be evaluated on a continuum ranging from low-level normative grief to a severe grief disorder, but these authors cautioned that lack of a genuine cut-off point, at which grief responses are considered in need of treatment, necessitates the use of personal or consensual judgments about a given griever's level of impairment and distress. Equally, viewing NG and CG as symptomatically different is associated with difficulties too. For example, Burke and Neimeyer argue that, if some individuals grieve in a diagnosably disordered manner (i.e., with different symptomatology from NG), there is potential for them to be socially and personally stigmatized.

Is CG distinguished from NG by incorporating a longer duration of basically normal symptoms? Wakefield argues that interminability (at 6 or 12 months) is not a valid criterion for CG, describing it as a scientific myth. He cites Bowlby, making the point that NG is of much longer duration than is generally acknowledged and arguing that to forget this warning pathologizes normal grief. By contrast, Boerner and colleagues identify two trajectories indicative of CG, namely their so-called chronic post-loss distress and chronic pre- and post-loss distress trajectories, which they contrasted with uncomplicated patterns described as resilient and improved trajectories.

It becomes clear from our chapters that understanding of the role of intensity, quality, and duration of symptoms in CG can (and needs to) be deepened in future research and that different disciplines, from philosophers to neurophysiologists to (cultural) psychologists, have a part to play in this endeavor.

Subtypes/variety of CG patterns

A lot of discussion has surrounded the issue of whether there are subtypes of CG, and what form(s) these might take. We noted that the PGD/CG approach of Prigerson and colleagues has sometimes been considered too narrow (e.g., by some clinicians, as noted by Rando). In the context of considering subtypes of CG, Boelen and Prigerson's statement deserves consideration: "criteria . . . should cover the many different forms the clinical picture of PGD/CG may take" (Chapter 7). Thus it becomes evident that this team of researchers acknowledges variety, if not explicitly subtypes. CG can comprise different combinations of symptoms, leaving room for the identification of subtypes (although it is more difficult to see how absent grief could be included within the PGD framework).

Furthermore, many researchers have identified subtypes of NG and CG. For example, attachment theory describes insecurities of attachment that mirror onto subtypes of CG. Interestingly, these subtypes were described long before attachment theory came to have such an influence on the bereavement research field. Mikulincer and Shaver describe how attachment insecurities are involved in complicated patterns of grief. Dyregrov and Dyregrov mention subtypes of CG among children, based on Bowlby's classification, but note the lack of recognition of trauma, a subtype that they add. Likewise for adults, Raphael, Jacobs, and Looi identify traumatic grief as the coexistence of grief and trauma phenomena, and the different reactive phenomena that may follow these different stressor experiences. Bonanno and colleagues built up a research program to investigate types of grieving in a fine-grained manner, and distinguish chronic grief from chronic depression. In addition to describing different CG trajectories, Boerner and colleagues take understanding beyond the one pattern of NG (previously understood as moving from a period of distress to recovery). Exceptions to that pattern used to be considered CG, but these investigators showed how other patterns can also be uncomplicated, notably a pattern that resembled resilience.

One of the most debated issues in subtypes concerns absent/delayed/inhibited grief. Most consider it to be a CG phenomenon, but others have emphasized that such absence need not always represent CG. Some research teams have reported little empirical confirmation of this subtype of CG, particularly the team of Boerner and colleagues – who actually nevertheless acknowledge the existence of a subtype of delayed/absent grief (they also stress that exhibiting hardly any grief reactions can be a form of NG). Mikulincer and Shaver make a strong theoretically based case for two subtypes of CG, including absent grief, based on Bowlby's attachment theory analysis: Whereas attachment anxiety is said to underlie chronic mourning, attachment-related avoidance contributes to the absence of grief. There is acknowledgement that apparent absence of grief may reflect a real absence of distress. This used to be difficult to distinguish from CG but Mikulincer and Shaver report their sophisticated experiments, which have supported this distinction well. Furthermore, they provide empirical evidence linking attachment insecurities to CG. Their conclusion was unequivocal: "Overall, these findings emphasize that researchers should take seriously Bowlby's (1980) cautions about assessing grief responses among avoidant people, because 'in all studies except those using the most sophisticated of methods, it is easy to overlook such people and to group them with those whose mourning is progressing in a genuinely favorable way'" (Chapter 14, quoting Bowlby, 1980, p. 211). Dyregrov and Dyregrov discuss the phenomenon of postponed grief in children, an aspect that may be rather special among children, being related to the fact that they lack emotional tolerance. These authors suggest that children attempt to regulate their grief in tolerable doses and use more avoidance than adults.

In sum, there is a need for scientists to come to agreement on the existence of various subtypes of CG and to develop methods of assessment that could better identify and map these (particularly, absent grief).

Subgroup differences in CG

Clearly, one size does not fit all. Throughout the book it has become evident that there are variations in manifestations and phenomenology, and in appropriate assessment for and treatment of CG across different groups of bereaved people. Perhaps most strikingly, this is true for different cultures, as Rosenblatt's chapter has made amply clear, as in the opening sentence of Chapter 3: "Psychiatric diag- nostic categories and psychiatric standards for what is normal and healthy and what is not are saturated with the standards of Western culture." Rosenblatt has raised questions about the possibility of a universal definition of CG. Although separation distress is recognized by many as a universal emotional response, fol- lowing Rosenblatt's line of reasoning, since there are no universal manifestations of grief, there cannot be a universal definition of CG. So should CG usage/explo- ration be restricted to Euro-American cultures? This would seem a deplorable state of affairs, not least because of the pluralistic nature of society in the twenty- first century. Scientific investigation should strive for culturally appropriate understanding of CG; extension is needed to incorporate a worldwide perspective. This point extends to treatment issues. For example, as Kissane points out, the application of family therapy will require different approaches in countries where family traditions are strong and decision making family centered. Finally and importantly, Rosenblatt's cultural perspective makes one aware that we cannot consider scientific research on CG in a vacuum. For example, we need to be aware that psychological treatment sometimes takes place in the context of economic, political, or environmental turmoils.

The chapters selected to cover two within-culture subgroups, bereavement of children and adolescents and that following violent death, serve to illustrate the uniqueness of CG in different subgroups. For example, children form more misinterpretations than adults, as they lack life experience and direct access to information about what happened. It seems highly plausible, especially in the light of the research on adults by Boelen and colleagues, that misinterpretations would be closely linked with high risk of CG. This needs further investigation in children. It remains of concern too that children are not mentioned in the proposals for a new grief disorder.

Evidently, there is considerable room for expansion of research with regard to understanding CG within specific subgroups of bereaved people.

Prevalence of CG

Given the difficulties in defining CG, distinguishing it from NG, demarking different subtypes and establishing patterns of similarities across subgroups, it is understandably difficult to talk about prevalence of CG in any simple terms. Yet, with some consistency, it has been reported that CG occurs in only a significant minority of individuals. Reported prevalences vary considerably (because of differences in types of loss, sample characteristics, criteria for assessment, etc.). Not surprisingly perhaps, the percentage of psychiatric outpatients who meet criteria for CG is higher than for the bereaved in general (Chapter 19). Indications are that those bereaved following a violent death have still higher prevalences of CG (Chapter 20), but more studies are needed (much more research following this type of death has been on PTSD). Unresolved is the issue whether these higher prevalences are to be conceptualized as reflecting intense, lengthy NG or really indicating CG (and detailing still unspecified forms of CG). Suggestions are that, for other specific subgroups too, prevalence is likely to be much higher, but in general there is reasonable consistency between the research on the prevalence of CG and that on resilience. Boerner and colleagues report that most bereaved persons are resilient. Most suffer from normal grief and some have consistent minimal distress.

In our view, one must be extremely cautious in making statements about the prevalence of CG, or in generalizing from any one set of prevalence figures – which are frequently presented in terms of simple percentages – to other samples or populations, particularly in view of the lack of agreement on precisely how to define and/or operationalize CG.

Different conceptual/theoretical approaches

Different theories and models have been employed in this volume to understand the phenomena and manifestations of grief and grieving, and to guide clinical treatment and various sorts of intervention.

One of the most frequently cited theories for understanding phenomena and for guiding intervention for CG is attachment theory. It figures prominently in diverse chapters, not surprisingly, given that it is a theory of interpersonal relationships and that bereavement involves the loss of a close relationship. Mikulincer and Shaver describe the relevance of this theory's basic postulates, relating it specifically to CG. In particular, they demonstrate how theory can be embedded in empirical research, making use of all kinds of methodologies and paradigms.

This theory is also drawn on by Dyregrov and Dyregrov for understanding CG in children. Raphael and colleagues link CG to disruption of the attachment to the deceased, suggesting an ongoing, complicated attachment of the bereaved to the deceased person. The stressor is regarded as being the disruption of the attachment, its loss. O'Connor draws on attachment theory too, emphasizing the role of the attachment figure in physiological as well as psychological regulation. She describes the attachment-specific stress response involving physiological systems when separated from the attachment figure, relating these reactions specifically to CG. Kissane and colleagues draw on this theory to frame their family therapy perspective.

Cognitive (stress) approaches of various sorts also figure prominently. These range from more general ones such as Boelen and colleagues' theoretical basis and specific model following CBT principles for CG (treatment), to identification of specific cognitive processes, such as Watkins and Moulds's focus on repetitive thought (RT). Other approaches within this category that have provided frameworks for understanding CG include meaning construction (e.g., Kissane et al.) and the narrative (e.g., Rynearson et al.) perspective. Stress theories have been employed at different levels and for various purposes, including traumatic stress theory (Raphael et al.) and general stress response theory (O'Connor).

Contrasting with the cultural perspective of Rosenblatt are psychiatric/medical model approaches (e.g., Raphael et al.) and physiological/neurological/biological/genetic ones (e.g., O'Connor; Cooper). To illustrate, in the latter category, O'Connor points out that underlying aspects of the body's stress response show promise in distinguishing CG from non-CG or CG from PTSD. Her work demonstrates that CG is a physiological as well as psychological reaction (and that different theories can be called on at the same time). She argues that this stress response may specifically include CG symptoms. If these symptoms are mediated by attachment, she reasons, then understanding the physiology and neurobiology of attachment will assist in treating the CG response to bereavement. Such lines of research are still in their infancy; much needs further exploration, including answers to questions such as: What genetic vulnerabilities constitute a risk of CG after bereavement (see O'Connor)? Is CG a biological dysfunction (see Cooper)?

It will have become evident that some investigators employ more than one theoretical approach and that the CG field in general is characterized by diversity in theoretical approaches. Indeed, a continuation of theoretical pluralism may be helpful or even essential in the coming years, given the complexity of the nature of CG, as already indicated.

CG as a disorder and diagnostic categorization

Another fundamental question in this volume has been whether or not CG should become a formal mental disorder in the DSM. What are the arguments for and against this? Many disciplines, from philosophical to psychiatric ones, contribute to this debate. The issue is particularly topical now, given that – as we go to press – CG is a candidate for inclusion in the new edition of the *Diagnostic and Statistical Manual of the American Psychiatric Association* (DSM-5).

Definition of CG as a mental disorder

Some authors have reflected on the concept of mental disorder in general, in their efforts to consider CG as such a category. Providing a general perspective, Cooper raises issues from her philosophical perspective: What is a (mental) disorder? What is a dysfunction? She presents different viewpoints: on the one hand the key question is not whether CG is a mental disorder, but whether it can helpfully be treated by health care professionals; on the other hand, she also maintains that CG could plausibly be considered a disorder, which was in line with her general conclusion.

Psychiatric accounts are naturally linked with the DSM system. DSM-IV defines a mental disorder as a

> clinically significant behavioral or psychological syndrome or pattern that occurs in an individual and that is associated with present distress (e.g., a painful symptom) or disability (i.e., impairment in one or more important areas of functioning) or with a significantly increased risk of suffering death, pain, disability, or an important loss of freedom. (APA, 1994, p. xxi)

Boelen and Prigerson basically follow the DSM definition of diagnostic disorder, basing their conclusions (that empirically based PGD can be defined as a formal disorder) on five taxonomic principles for establishing the validity of a mental disorder; they argue that these criteria are met and that it should therefore go into DSM. Wakefield, however, basing his arguments on the same taxonomic principles, presents other lines of reasoning (e.g., that DSM presents impairment as a necessary condition for disorder, not one that is sufficient by itself) and concludes that PGD cannot be seen as a mental disorder in terms of DSM. However, he argues that some form(s) of complicated grief exists, remarking that, since any biological response can malfunction, it is plausible that some grief disorders exist. However, in his view, these other potential grief disorders have not yet been detected.

We return to the above debate in the following section, but here we would like to stress that, although our authors are in substantial agreement about the existence of CG as a mental disorder, it must be kept in mind that most bereaved people do not suffer from it. Even though acute grief is extremely painful and debilitating, it usually does not need clinical intervention.

Current DSM status: criteria and problems

Currently, there is lack of agreement on criteria for CG inclusion in the DSM-5 system. Boelen and Prigerson include the three different sets of criteria that have been proposed, namely, for PGD, CG, and bereavement related disorder, in their Table 7.1. A lot of discussion continues, as reflected in the pages of our volume.

Empirical validation of the different systems is a major concern, with Boelen and Prigerson pointing to the extensive research basis for PGD/CG, but also recognizing the need for further study (e.g., search for diagnostic algorithms that best distinguish those who are at risk from those who are not; examination across heterogeneous groups of bereaved). Strong voices of dissent about PGD are also heard. For example, Rando rejects a category based on PGD alone, regarding it as a subtype in an overarching category.

A major issue is still whether or not CG should go into DSM at all. Boelen and Prigerson argue that PGD meets the definition of a mental/psychiatric disorder and should therefore be included in DSM system. Others support this position, arguing along the lines that, if other disorders such as PTSD are in the DSM system, why should CG not be (see van den Bout & Kleber)? Cooper's conclusion is not so unequivocal (there are arguments on both sides about considering it a diagnostic category). Wakefield's title makes his position clear: The proposal to add a category of CG to DSM is conceptually and empirically unsound, despite the fact that he regards it as being one of the most thoroughly studied proposals in DSM history. In his view, the proposed diagnostic criteria identify conditions that are not due to psychiatric dysfunctions, but are instances of lengthy, intense normal grieving. Nevertheless, he is respectful of the research efforts of the Prigerson group (and others), which he acknowledges as having added substantially to understanding symptoms and trajectories of grief and grieving.

Other issues concern specific, highly important details, for example the three sets of criteria cover different durations of bereavement (the APA DSM-5 workgroup suggests 12 months; others 6 months' duration at least). PGD/CG criteria have also changed over the past couple of decades (e.g., differing symptoms) as investigators have striven to standardize these (making comparison of results of studies across time difficult). Some problems about CG as a potential new category of mental disorder apply to other established psychiatric disorders too (see Boelen & Prigerson), and others point to unique difficulties. For example, Wakefield criticizes the DSM-5 workgroup's label *bereavement related disorder* on the grounds that it is insufficiently specific (many disorders other than disordered grief itself can be related to bereavement), arguing for the use of the label CG (but he still points to difficulties distinguishing it from normal grief). Wakefield also argues for "far more stringent diagnostic criteria than those proposed, if massive false positive diagnoses are to be avoided" (Chapter 8).

Again, subgroup differences are an issue in the context of DSM inclusion. For example, Dyregrov and Dyregrov point out that DSM would need to reflect the uniqueness of children's grief and that an adult diagnosis should not be used inappropriately for children. In particular, this relates to the fact that children have immature systems for emotional and cognitive regulation, and that they are dependent on adults who may also be grieving (p. 13). Likewise, cultural background needs to be taken into consideration when reflecting whether the (mental health) language of DSM and the proposed criteria are applicable (see Rosenblatt). As Rosenblatt illustrates, assumptions across cultures differ. What we consider deviant may not be so in a different culture; CG as we see it may not even be considered a complication. Boelen and Prigerson argue for testing in heterogeneous groups, supporting a global grounding for PGD/CG, but is DSM (and are the proposed criteria) sensitive enough to the full range of cultural differences?

As this volume goes to press, it remains uncertain whether – or, if so, according to what criteria – CG (or another label) will go into DSM-5. On the one hand, there are convincing arguments that this should take place; on the other hand, there are equally good reasons for caution, which leads us to our next point.

(Dis)advantages of the diagnostic category of CG

What are the (dis)advantages of including CG as a category of mental disorder in the DSM system? Again, there has been much debate but a short overview must suffice here. Boelen and Prigerson consider benefits and harms, and van den Bout and Kleber look to the lessons to be derived from the inclusion of PTSD in DSM. Advantages include the facilitation of empirical research and recognition of suffering of a significant minority of bereaved having difficulties in their process of recovery. Boelen and Prigerson argue that it would imply not medicalization of something normal but a normalization of something that mostly is not but sometimes is indeed pathological. Clients with CG would receive needed treatment more easily (see van den Bout & Kleber). On the negative side, Wakefield warns against pathologizing normal grief, using a case study to argue that diagnosis and treatment may not be the best option in every case and could even "'derail' such individuals from the hard work they need to do to change their circumstances and themselves to create a new life" (Chapter 8). However, others have noted that a DSM disorder provides the possibility, but not the requirement, to start treatment.

There is need for careful weighing up of the pros and cons of CG entering DSM-5 as a category of mental disorder. Proponents should not sweep disadvantages under the carpet; opponents need to realize the consequences of exclusion of such a category for bereaved persons who suffer from CG symptomatology.

CG and other disorders

Various issues relating to CG in the context of other disorders have been raised. First, is CG a distinct disorder or variant of some other condition? Many perspectives have contributed to our understanding of this issue (e.g., Rando from a clinical orientation, as a major issue in her chapter; Cooper from a philosophical one). Cooper argued that multiple answers to this question might be justified: For some purposes it is helpful to consider complicated grief alongside other conditions; for others it might best be considered separately. Empirical studies have added much to this debate; for example, Raphael and colleagues point out that recent research has confirmed that CG, depression, and PTSD are separate syndromes. Again, O'Connor points to the potential of including neurobiological and physiological markers in study designs, as these markers can sometimes be used to discriminate between disorders such as depression and CG, or PTSD and CG, "even when a clinical gestalt may be murky" (Chapter 15). Rather differently, an important distinction Boerner and colleagues make is between chronic grief (post-loss onset) and chronic depression (pre-loss onset), raising the questions: Should there be two distinct categories of disorder, or is bereavement only an exacerbating factor for the chronic depressive group?

A related matter concerns CG in the context of (i.e., parallel to) other conditions/disorders. Our authors confirm what has become well established in the scientific literature: that there is a range of health consequences associated with bereavement, of which, in most researchers' minds, CG is one (with the exception of Rando, who considers other consequences such as physical illness and mortality as types of presentation of CG). Authors attest to a range of consequences including but not limited to mental and physical health debilities/disorders and social dysfunctions. Among children and adolescents, for example, as reviewed by Dyregrov and Dyregrov, there are both short- and long-term consequences, ranging from increasing mental health problems, decline in school performance, social withdrawal, and behavioral problems to somatic complaints. A minority experience more severe problems, even mortality and increased risk of depression in adulthood. Finally, adding to the already complex picture, some investigators, including Burke and Neimeyer, view CG as a risk factor for other psychological and physical health problems (cardiovascular illness, substance abuse, depression, anxiety, and overall life disruption).

Not surprisingly, given the range of consequences of bereavement, there is also comorbidity. For example, Raphael and colleagues focus on CG and PTSD in adults; Dyregrov and Dyregrov do so among children. Raphael and colleagues detail the reactions to the different stressors of loss and trauma, with different etiologies and different implications for management (among adults and children). They clearly separate the two, including a demarcation of the differing triggering events (see Tables 10.1 and 10.2: phenomena of posttraumatic reactions and bereavement, and other signs of each reactive process). They also provide empirical evidence to back up their analyses.

Taken together, these lines of research indicate that bereavement can exacerbate other mental disorders and that comorbidity with CG can pertain. One ongoing concern in this context is when and how to treat coexisting disorders. Another is the role of pharmacology in therapeutic management. For example, Raphael and colleagues note that, for CG and PTSD comorbidity, this remains to be established.

Risk factors, processes, and mechanisms

We have stressed that most people adjust to bereavement in the course of time, but that a minority experience CG. Research on risk factors, processes, and mechanisms underlying CG all help us understand differential vulnerabilities to CG between bereaved persons.

Risk factor research

Research on risk factors has much to offer in terms of scientific understanding of CG and its application. For one thing, it would seem important for health care professionals to know the characteristics and circumstances that may increase the likelihood of CG. Identification of some of these (not all) may enable health care professionals to address some of the issues in the time prior to bereavement, as Boerner and colleagues point out, for example, to help find additional support when caregiving begins to be overwhelming; to guide severely distressed bereaved toward appropriate care services; and to make referrals to clinicians who can diagnose CG and provide intervention tailored to the individual's specific needs.

However, this is a difficult area of research, one that is "rife with complexity," in Burke and Neimeyer's words (Chapter 11). Rather than reviewing the full range of risk factors here (indeed, Burke and Neimeyer have done that extensively), it is perhaps useful to highlight these difficulties. These relate to many different aspects. There are multiple factors covering different types of risk, and there are also *protective* factors (e.g., Dyregrov and Dyregrov) and *resilient* characteristics (Boerner et al.). Just to illustrate the range: On the one hand, as Dyregrov and Dyregrov write about bereaved children, a good family climate will be protective whereas a negative family climate is associated with risks. Post-loss factors emerge as critical: If death leads to massive changes in the child's daily environment, the possibility of negative consequences increases; good parental or primary care capacity and discipline are protective. They point to the need to strengthen parental capacity (for intervention too). On the other hand, Kissane and colleagues describe a different type of risk factor: They identify families at risk versus those that are well functioning using a Family Relationships Index. So-called sullen and hostile families were found to be at high risk of complications.

Some variables are poorly defined. Moreover, variables frequently interact with each other to further increase risk. There are control group problems and issues to do with causality. Added to these are the facts that some factors are changeable/modifiable (and therefore psychotherapeutically relevant) whereas others are not; that there is a huge range within the general risk category, from mechanisms to protective variables; that some variables are not at all static (e.g., belief in an afterlife; bereavement is possibly a crisis time for that); or that there may be third factors operating, ones that have not been taken into account. Also, as Burke and Neimeyer point out, some factors may equally predict CG and other disorders and symptoms (depression, suicidality). Are there universal risk factors, or to what extent are they impacted by different cultural, economic, and political contexts (see Burke & Neimeyer; Rosenblatt)? Also, cross-sectional studies frequently form the basis for statements about risk factors for CG (no causality statements are then possible). Burke and Neimeyer point to the need to distinguish between correlates or consequences of CG and genuinely prospective predictors per se, and they identify potential and confirmed risk factors in their review.

An important issue touched on above concerns whether the risk factors are grief-specific or generic. To what extent are the risk factors identified by Burke and Neimeyer, such as social support, insecure attachment styles, or neuroticism, reflective of the general associations between these variables and ill-health, which they are known to have, or to what extent are they unique predictors among the bereaved, predicting pathology over and above the level of association found in general? To unravel this, one needs to compare patterns of risk for bereaved with non-bereaved controls. Obviously grief is non-existent in non-bereaved groups, but proximal measures (e.g., depression) make comparisons with non-bereaved people possible. One can, for example, compare depression for (non-)bereaved men and women and establish the relative excesses between men and women.

What is the way forward in this complex area of research, to establish who is susceptible to CG? One step that Burke and Neimeyer suggest is a meta-analytical review of risk factor effect sizes, one that would include other relevant bereavement outcomes (PTSD etc.), different study designs, and diverse samples. Clearly, this is no easy task, but there may now be sufficient empirical basis to attempt it.

Processes and mechanisms

Scientific investigation in recent years has witnessed a move toward more micro-level examination of cognitive processes (on CG), as illustrated by Watkins and Moulds's focus on repetitive thinking (RT) and Golden's on autobiographical memory (AM) and overgeneral memory bias (OGM) processes in CG. These processes are examples of transdiagnostic processes, which are becoming more and more familiar in the field of CBT. Repetitive thought (Watkins & Moulds) encompasses processes that are relevant to normal and complicated grief, the consequences of RT varying according to whether its content is positive or negative, concrete or abstract. So there are subtypes with distinct functional consequences (negative and abstract with maladaptive/pathological functioning). Watkins and Moulds examined RT's specific role in integrating the loss into existing mental structures and detailing earlier unspecified operationalizations such as "working through." Golden examined AM and OGM specifically in relation to CG, showing that OGM bias is present in individuals with CG. Such processes have attracted considerable attention in recent years and undoubtedly represent an important line of future research as scientists use newly available techniques and apply lab methods, particularly to unravel more about underlying mechanisms associated with or underlying CG.

A range of additional processes and mechanisms have come under investigation in relationship to CG. O'Connor noted that self-regulation at the psychological as well as physiological level may be important in coping with pangs of grief and assist in acceptance of the death of an attachment figure. Avoidance (symptoms) has been examined not only in absent grief but in chronic grief (PGD) too (see Mikulincer & Shaver; O'Connor). Some knowledge about processes and mechanisms of CG has emerged from research inspired by CBT theorizing. In the work of Boelen and colleagues, three interrelated processes are identified: (a) insufficient elaboration and integration of the loss within autobiographical memory; (b) negative thinking; and (c) anxious and depressive avoidance behaviors. These authors reason that these three processes interact and play a mediating role in CG. Wagner's Internet intervention for CG contrasts with that of Boelen and colleagues but is also based on a CB framework. Three modules were included: self-confrontation, cognitive reappraisal, and social sharing. Quite different processes emerge from other treatment perspectives, such as the use of resilience as a family strength and group processes, in the family and psychotherapy group (Kissane et al.). Rynearson and colleagues' treatment included processes furthering mastery of personal safety, confronting the death through "reliving," and developing an altered identity through re-engagement with activities and relationships.

Physiological processes/mechanisms are a growing focus of research. O'Connor provides evidence for a physiological co-regulation basis of CG. She reviews empirical work supporting the role of physiology and neurobiology in CG, drawing on her conceptual analysis of two types of physiological stress: (a) the general stress response (fight-or-flight), similar to CG criteria, including efforts to avoid thoughts of the deceased, associated with failure to integrate the reality of the death, leading to continuously realized acute grief; and (b) the attachment-specific stress response driven by loss of rewarding aspects of attachment, analogous to CG criteria including yearning for the deceased.

Investigators of processes underlying CG in this volume all point to the need for further empirical testing of their hypotheses. They recommend the use of multiple methods and extension beyond self-report questionnaires (social cognition techniques; diary-keeping methods), and incorporating experimental research to test the proposed directions of causality between variables. Research needs to establish whether these are the crucial pathways or central mechanisms in influencing clients' emotional problems, or only epiphenomena.

Treatment of complicated grief

Two topics strike us as particularly noteworthy in the context of professional treatment for CG. First, details to do with the conceptual basis of the programs themselves need consideration. Second, efficacy of intervention needs to be addressed.

Principles, paradigms, and procedures

Psychotherapeutic treatments for CG have been described in this book. How have they gone about treatment? What changes do the treatment programs aim to bring about? Just as investigators have identified different processes and mechanisms (described above), so are there differences in the principles, paradigms, and procedures adopted in interventions.

Not surprisingly, Watkins and Moulds suggest training individuals with CG to be more concrete or shift to more adaptive forms of RT, whereas Golden argues that OGM bias should be targeted in therapy, presenting evidence to support this conclusion. The treatment program of Boelen and colleagues includes different CBT interventions to achieve various aims: (a) to integrate the loss with existing knowledge, (b) to identify and alter unhelpful thinking patterns, and (c) to replace unhelpful avoidance strategies with more helpful ones. Wagner reviews Internet research on treating CG, covering various forms, from text-based approaches with therapist feedback to self-help treatments without guidance. Her own intervention follows a treatment program originally developed for PTSD, using structured writing assignments. Advantages of Internet over traditional methods have been discussed, including the possibility to interact with others any time one wants; anonymity and no geographic boundaries; a lower threshold (perhaps for men, who are less inclined to accept psychotherapy?); the availability of social support without physical interaction and costs; and time for the therapist to reflect. However, it may not suit all clients; the potential for misunderstandings is possibly greater; dealing with a crisis such as suicidality may be more difficult; and there is a need for careful diagnostic procedures before participation (see Wagner).

Although most therapy for CG has been directed toward individuals, we included two very different group perspectives. First, over a number of decades, Kissane and his colleagues have developed a program of family therapy, following the understanding that loss does not occur in a social vacuum but is shared by people, commonly the family. It is also different from other treatments in that it is initiated during anti-cancer treatment before (and continuing through) bereavement, adding the possibility of *preventing* the development of CG, by identifying problem families, and also (as in other approaches) of *ameliorating* it. Kissane and colleagues do not take the stand that family therapy should replace individual modes but argue that it may be an important adjunct to them. These investigators explain that the hypothesized mechanism of change is the strengthening of family bonds. Second, Piper and Ogrodniczuk describe cost-effective time-limited short-term therapy groups, two different models, specifically for patients who meet CG criteria. They describe two types of group therapy, interpretive (to enhance patient insight about repetitive conflicts and traumas associated with their losses) and supportive (the therapist gratifies the patient, provides guidance, and provides non-interpretive interventions), and describe their ongoing research on the effectiveness of these.

Different treatment paradigms seem appropriate for different subgroups. Raphael and colleagues describe assessment and management of CG with trauma syndromes as comorbidity, giving examples of programs for treating such comorbidity, for adults and children. Dyregrov and Dyregrov mention the need to strengthen parental capacity for children, indicating that there may be unique elements at stake in the case of children with CG.

Other approaches reflect theoretical analyses (and their related empirical findings). For example, Mikulincer and Shaver provide an attachment theory perspective on grief resolution and counseling, proceeding on the assumption that, if attachment insecurities are risk factors for CG, then regaining a sense of attachment security (e.g., security priming or provision of a secure base) should ameliorate CG.

The concluding comments on the previous section apply here too. In the context of therapy, we need to establish the specific processes or mechanisms that bring about favorable outcomes of intervention programs (e.g., Boelen and colleagues ask "whether or not CBT indeed produces alleviation of distress because it lessens negative cognitions and avoidance"; Chapter 16).

Efficacy of intervention for CG

There has been pressure for evidence-based treatment (including RCTs) in recent decades, and some of the main players in this domain have contributed to this book. The results of the effectiveness of psychotherapeutic treatment for CG have been quite positive. Piper and Ogrodniczuk and Wagner reviewed studies (the latter including recent meta-analysis) of efficacy of intervention programs in general, concluding that they are effective for CG. Similar conclusions were drawn by Wagner for Internet studies, and she gave evidence for effectiveness of her own program for CG. Nevertheless, limitations were pointed out: Little is as yet known about the mechanisms through which the structured writing or written disclosure in these programs leads to improvement in CG, a feature that others identified too (e.g., Piper & Ogrodniczuk). Kissane and colleagues have been examining the efficacy of family intervention in improving family communication and report some indication that family therapy reduced the rate of development of CG preventively. This is an ongoing program of research in which efficacy is being further investigated. Boelen and colleagues were able to provide some evidence for the postulated underlying processes as well as the effectiveness of CT treatment for CG. Piper and Ogrodniczuk performed different trials and compared the two models of group treatment, documenting patterns of benefits for some groups. Rynearson and colleagues drew attention to the paucity of research on efficacy of intervention following the extreme case of bereavement following a violent death, in which professional treatment may be more needed than following non-violent, timely deaths.

There are considerable difficulties in conducting such research, as Piper and Ogrudniczuk describe. For example, follow-up investigation of the efficacy of an intervention program at later points in time is essential (e.g., symptoms may increase, before any benefits of the treatment become evident), but this not always done. There are different models and ways to evaluate efficacy for reducing CG. Usually this includes treatment and a waiting-list control condition, whereas an attention-placebo control condition would be better but is not always feasible.

In our view, it is essential that high-quality studies be conducted to establish the efficacy of clinical intervention for CG. Providing sound evidence that our therapeutic techniques are effective – even economically advantageous – can help convince governments and funding agencies of the importance of supporting bereaved people who need help.

Conclusions

In this closing chapter, we have highlighted both the advancements in science as well as limitations in knowledge about CG that have emerged from the foregoing chapters of this book. We have indicated directions for future research in this area. So what about the future perspective in general? In our view, this can build on the multidisciplinary approach to CG, as represented in the pages of our volume. There would be advantages to extending this multidisciplinary approach to make it a truly interdisciplinary one, whereby researchers would collaborate and share their particular vantage points, working toward a common knowledge base to acquire deeper understanding of CG. Indeed, some chapters already show evidence of following such interdisciplinary lines, as exemplified in their integration of different types of theoretical perspectives and multi-method approaches.

This interdisciplinary effort should, we think, not only take effect on a purely scientific level, but also involve practice (and at times even other societal stakeholders such as policy makers). In most publications on CG (ours is for the most part no exception to this) the central idea has been that scientists can provide knowledge that can be subsequently applied in practice (and in society more generally). However, the channel of scientific communication and inspiration in the CG field needs to go both ways: Research needs to look toward practice (and societal concerns more generally) for much of its impetus too. To illustrate this from the therapy area: Some clinicians may consider a particular technique to be effective, but it may not be evident precisely why this intervention works. Researchers can take note of the therapeutic principles adopted in the therapeutic approach, and probe further to discover underlying processes that may explain why the approach or technique is actually effective. So, it is necessary not only to listen to researchers in order to build on our CG knowledge base, but to listen to clinicians as well, and to try to understand what they are in fact doing and then unravel what it is that makes their techniques effective.

Following an interdisciplinary approach and such dual-direction strategies as that described above will, in our view, lead to greater wisdom concerning the phenomena and manifestations of complicated grief, and help to provide health care professionals with a scientifically grounded foundation for conducting their work with bereaved persons.

References

APA. (1994). *Diagnostic and statistical manual of mental disorders* (4th edn.). Washington, DC: American Psychiatric Association.

Bowlby, J. (1980). *Attachment and loss, vol. 3. Sadness and depression*. New York: Basic Books.

Stroebe, M. S., Hansson, R. O., Schut, H., & Stroebe, W. (2008). *Handbook of bereavement research and practice: Advances in theory and intervention*. Washington, DC: American Psychological Association.

Author index

Subject index